From Landscape to Literature

From Landscape to Literature

The River and the Myth of Geography

Wyman H. Herendeen

Duquesne University Press
Pittsburgh

Published in the United States of America
by Duquesne University Press
600 Forbes Avenue, Pittsburgh, PA 15282

Distributed by
Humanities Press International, Inc.
Atlantic Highlands, NJ 07716

First Edition

Library of Congress Cataloging-in-Publication Data

Herendeen, Wyman H., 1948–
    From Landscape to literature.

    Bibliography: p.
    Includes index.
    1. English poetry—Early modern, 1500–1700—History
and criticism.   2. Rivers in literature.   3. Landscape
in literature.   4. English poetry—Classical influences.
5. Classical literature—History and criticism.
I. Title.
PR545.R57H47   1986   821'.009'36   85–27410
ISBN 0–8207–0182–3

For Mary

—————

flumina senserunt ipsa

Contents

Preface

This attempt to provide a fairly thorough survey of the river in our cultural geography, myth, and literature has been a labor of love, one no less difficult than pleasing. I have been travelling the rivers for over a decade now; they have taken me far from my initial interests in Spenser and Drayton and back again. I have tried to spare my readers some of the redundancies inevitable in such a work and to achieve a balance between scholarly thoroughness and critical incisiveness. Some will argue that when you have seen one river, you have seen them all. This book is not for them, but for those who can see unity and coherence in a many-faceted idea or object, as the river is. An author can only ask the reader to allow himself or herself to be drawn into the current, to be led through varied landscapes by rivers which are not one's own. I hope that this book will bring readers of different interests to these waters for different reasons, and that each will find some refreshment. I would like to think that this work might provoke further, more specialized studies of the river and landscape literature.

I leave these waters with a sense of humility, aware that this work, long in its gestation and delivery, is a strange thing, a rather unorthodox approach to a critical, intellectual, and literary subject which is itself a little peculiar. Whatever my progress on these waters has been, I am very sensible of the assistance that I have received all along, and which enabled me to keep going in white water and in shallows. I am especially grateful to the Canada Council and the trustees of the estate of Dorothy J. Killam at Dalhousie University for grants which kept my bark afloat, and otherwise outfitted me with the needs of my journey. The librarians and assistants at various ports of call, particularly at the North Library and Student Room of the British Library, at the Bodleian Library, the Warburg Institute, the Public Records Office, the

Society of Antiquaries, and the Centre for Reformation and Renaissance Studies, Victoria College, University of Toronto have been my ship's chandlers in my journey from river to river, and in matters of bibliographic supplies, they have kept me well victualled and have made me at home in their ports.

To fellow scholars who have shared my fascination with the rivers over these years, and who have diverted the currents of their learning into my own channels, I am greatly appreciative. With their counsel and curiosity they have shown me new rivers and reminded me of the interest that the topic can inspire. To William F. Blissett and Millar MacLure I am most indebted. They have read my work over the years, and over long hours as the light changed outside, they were attentive while I, Marlow-like, told my tales of the river, and they, like Marlow's patient hearers, with their sound judgment, urged me to make my narrative clearer. If I have only outlined the shape of the map and have shed no light on the interior, the fault is mine and my gratitude is no less.

My debt to my wife, to whom this book is dedicated, is greatest. Her deep waters have run smooth through these years of exploration. A scholar could ask no more of his helpmate in the way of assistance and support, and in being a perennial help and not a torrent, than she has given willingly — without her, we would have foundered.

Toronto, 1984

List of Illustrations

In addition to the debts of gratitude to the institutions cited above, I would like to express particular thanks to: the Society of Antiquaries for kind permission to reprint the photograph of the coronation of Edward VI (fig. 10); the Founders Society, Detroit Institute of Arts, for allowing me to reproduce photographs of the Bruegel etchings (figs. 14 & 15; ACC. 0915185, 40.23); the Trustees of the British Library, for the photographs printed in figures 6, 8, 9, and 21–23; the Trustees of the British Museum, for photographs of coins reproduced in figure 5; to the National Portrait Gallery, for permission to reproduce the Ditchley Portrait and the portrait of Sir Henry Unton (figs. 17 & 19); to the Thomas Fisher Rare Book Library, University of Toronto, for the photographs reproduced in figures 11–3, 16, 18, and 20; and to Fratelli Alinari for photographs reproduced in figures 1–3, and the Albertina Graphics Collection, for figure 24.

If narration. . . be made of those things which are performed, without the observation of the places wherein they were done, or if histories be read without topographical knowledge, all things will appear so intricate and confused, as we shall thereby understand nothing but obscurely, nor draw thence any knowledge but with greatest difficulty.

(Arias Montanus, *History of the Holy Land*)

Aristotle. . . plainly affirmeth the Region of Egypt (which we esteem the ancientest Nation in the world) was a meer gained ground, and that by setling of mud and limous matter brought down by the River Nilus, that which was at first a continued Sea, was raised at last into a firm and habitable Country.

(Francis Bacon, *Enquiries into Vulgar and Common Errours*)

[It is] both on earth and in heaven. . . . Eridanus, which is here and is there, which is within and is without, and which is high and is low, and which has the nature of the celestial . . . and the terrestrial . . . is fit to be named, called upon, and revered.

(Giordano Bruno, *The Expulsion of the Triumphant Beast*)

Introduction

IT IS NO EASY MATTER, describing a river. It is more difficult than describing a stone, a tree, or a mountain, for example. While these, too, exist both in space and time (the multiple dimensions that make the task so difficult), at least their relation to them is fairly stable and simple. However, the river itself seems to be continually changing — between historical, linear time, and future, cyclical time; between a definite spatial context, and one which is continuous. The more one meditates on the river, the more completely the subject erodes the distinctions between and definitions of time and space, until finally these basic concepts by which we set the world in order are flooded by a chaotic sea of confusion in which all things seem one, and in which there is no time and there are no spaces, only space unfolding.

The river challenges our epistemological concepts, our language and understanding. It forces us to work toward ordering concepts, and yet it defies them; it tends toward unity while we require the separation of waters: as Carlos Fuentes says, "The nature of waters is always to communicate with one another and to reach a common level. And this is their mystery."[1] Paradoxically, these elusive, indefinable qualities have made the river one of the most popular metaphors for life, time, and consciousness, and for death, timelessness, and dissolution.

Rivers seem to force us to ask certain basic questions, such as: What is a river? Where does one point when locating it? What is it materially? Is it identified by its mountain source, or by its outlet in the sea — its head or its mouth, the one of which often remains unlocated while the other keeps moving? Is it the water between its banks, or the banks which embrace that protean element? If the water, is it not also the springs and streams that feed it, and all that circulates in the hydrologic cycle as one water as it was for Thales

3

and Plato? If the banks, created by the furrowing water, is it not also the meadows, fields, and forests which are no less the product of their movement, as it is in *Upon Appleton House*? And if so, then is it not also the cities and communities, the churches and palaces and varied architecture that also grow organically on its banks, fed, as trees and meadows are by its waters as it is in Virgil, Ovid, and Spenser? Is it not also each individual and private life constituting these communities, each child raised alongside it, as it is for Hesiod, as well as Wordsworth, and Coleridge? If it is defined by its banks, is it not then, paradoxically, all the terrestrial globe that forms the topography channelling the flowing water—the world itself—just as it is all water if we define it in terms of that element?

And when is a river? How does one locate it in time, as one must, since it is in constant movement, and since it has a history, just as any other object involving human beings has? The question takes us back to the problem of arresting it in space. Can we speak of the Rhine between Mainz and Strasbourg, thus stopping its flow through time and space? Obviously not, if we are concerned with the river in any comprehensive sense. To do so would annihilate the river, turning it into a still life, leaving us with a segment of the river as it never existed in nature. This would also remove it from the realm of time, for a river is in the eternal present, constantly moving in time and space from source, to outlet, to source—unceasing, it has no time. To section the river in this way, like in a worm in a biology laboratory, is to kill it to make time.

Of course all efforts at definition are reflexive, anthropocentric. Thus we can fabricate a temporal scheme for a river in terms of its relation to human affairs. Time is by necessity measured in terms of something external to the object whose age is being calculated. In this way all our cognitive principles are the arbitrary creations of the intellect. Rivers can be located in time in terms of their human history, or their appearance on that vaguer frontier of myth. We can speak of the Roman Thames from the channel to London, and the early medieval Rhine from Basel fo Strasbourg, for example. In this sense, the Tiber is older than both of these: it feeds the Rhine, the Rhône, and the Thames, and is itself fed by the Acheloüs and the ancient Nile. As we go further back, we pass from literature and history to myth. For Western culture, the Jordan is historical, the Tigris and Euphrates mythical; the Nile hovers in an uncertain realm between the two, as archetype. The Orinoco is—or seems to be—a younger river, as Spenser suggests.

But these historical constructions say more about the human mind than about the river; they obviously tell us nothing about the intrinsic temporal span of a river, what geologists, speaking of distant prehistoric phenomena, speculate on. These historical terms virtually identify the river with history, and therefore are of little use as definitions or descriptions. The river is coextensive with history, unfolding as history itself does, and sharing the cultural consciousness of each successive age. It is not only the present, but also the past and the future. William James's use of it as an image of the subjective consciousness and of psychological experience suggests a useful link between individual and cultural perceptions of time: "Every definite image of the mind is steeped . . . in the free water that flows round it. . . . Consciousness does not appear to itself chopped up in bits. . . . It is nothing jointed; it flows. . . . Let us call it the stream of consciousness, or of subjective life."[2] In many ways his image is an ancient one, as we will see, but in other respects it is the product of the era in which James is writing and reflects trends in modern philosophical thought. Yet James's paradoxical use of the river's undefinability to define the subjective nature of our consciousness says much about the richness of the subject.

The river, in geography and as an image, takes on the characteristics of the culture of which it is a part. Although it would be no mean achievement to be able to identify the river as Braudel does the Mediterranean, in terms of complex interrelations between the physical world and human history, this is not quite possible. He is dealing with one sea, one name, with a comparatively finite (albeit vast) and ultimately homogeneous set of physical and social conditions, and this is rather different from the diversity which attaches to the rivers of Europe. The Mediterranean is coherent as the river is not. There are countless rivers, each embracing a wide range of geographical and social variety, and defying and sharing in the art by which we shape nature. The Mediterranean is an environment with which society has managed to work in harmony. Rivers are a natural condition with which we are always contending—crossing, damming, fleeing, or flocking to, and generally trying to tame in one way or another. One suggests the harmony between our arts and nature, the other the limitations and frustrations of that ideal.

And yet there is a great deal of coherence in society's experience of rivers. We frequently speak of time and the river (to adapt the title of Thomas Wolfe's novel), yet historically this is only part of the river's complex network of associations. While it has always

been linked with time (historical, cultural, mythical), this obscures
the range of specific meanings that have been confluent in the river
for millennia. In fact, no single aphorism captures the complicated
significance of the river in Western society, and in attempting to
understand the origins of the motif and the nature of its place in the
classical tradition, I have tried to avoid oversimplification.

Although to identify it with time is not sufficient, the creation of a
historical context for it is certainly one of the principal problems
when talking about the river; paradoxically it seems to exist outside
of time, while also highlighting the times. What it most resembles is
protean nature itself: mutable yet constant, gaining meaning by
virtue of human ability to make something of it. Thus its specific
significance will vary from age to age. It is the world's potential (and
thus time), and therefore has meaning only insofar as we are able to
give it meaning. It is, in effect, the world, and its image changes with
our response to the world, as we can see in a river metaphor taken
from Augustine: "This [world] like a confluence of waters, is the
fuller of dangers as it is the larger."[3] For the twentieth century the
river is a vaguer entity—symbolically and naturally—than it had
been, and perhaps this is because nature for us is so thoroughly
disguised or hidden. We seldom see unfettered rivers; they are
subdued by hydroelectric plants, paved over with roads, or made
unapproachable by embankments. Their force is still there, if unseen, and their power is still something to be contended with, as
Florentines and Londoners know only too well. However, we are
now so unsure of our own and nature's potential, and so doubtful of
our ability to redeem the fallen world through our intellect, that the
river's symbolic significance is perforce unclear. In ancient times,
though, this was not the case: to tame a river was to improve upon
nature and to vie with the gods—a risky but challenging and necessary business. Believing that we were bettering ourselves, we have
always been wrestling our gods to their knees; now they labor
enchained in servitude, and nature's potential seems spent.

The river in geography and in intellectual history manages to defy
absolute boundaries, and attempts to chart it have always raised
questions about our ability to know anything about the world and
ourselves. This correlation between the river and human cognition
originates in the primitive response to nature and the foundation of
riparian society. We see it in the early myths and histories recording
human attempts to understand the world and to comprehend it
within social and linguistic arts. In the earliest records of our

struggle with the physical world and in our ancient artistic and literary expression the river has focused the importance of the relation between art and nature, and emphasized the way in which our perception of the landscape represents the desire not only to tame nature, but to remake it and bring it into the compass of our powers of expression and creation.

In defying the limits of time and space, the river seems to participate in the infinite, and in so doing, it suggests not only that the world is ultimately incomprehensible to humanity but also that whatever we do know of it, we know through the diviner, intellectual qualities of our imaginative faculties. This is one of the most important, though often implicit aspects of the river: in a literal and figurative way it keeps us in touch with our first experience and reasserts the relation between the cognitive arts and the world of mutability. The river, and all the physical world, is inseparable from the shaping art of language. Its moving waters are reminders that mankind have never known the natural world free from the imprint of art. Biblically, the world is the creation of the word—language, or *logos*, immediately transformed to reality as the waters of heaven and earth are separated: word and deed are one. The creation is reenacted by Adam as he names and thus knows the natural world (*Genesis* 2:19–20). His experience of reality is mediated by language, and all cosmogonic and geographical literature, indeed all literature, shares in this recreative process by which the world is remade by the word, and by which we try to reaffirm that unity between *logos* and *numen*: nature separate from art and the organizing perceptions is inconceivable. According to our cultural myths, our world is a garden, an artistic construct whose order and names were first impressed upon original man. The reestablishment of the orderly relation between these verbal labels and the physical world is the goal of the poet whose myths, cosmographies, and visionary descriptions of the world are expressions of his divine role as "maker." Thus, while, as E. R. Curtius says, "nature seeks to realize in matter a life which attains to consciousness,"[4] so too the intellect strives to realize itself in nature through words and language: to embody the *logos* in physical reality.

The river has an inordinately important place in the literature which represents and interprets the creation and the first human experiences—more important than any other aspect of nature, and that is at least partly because the earliest communities were all attached to rivers. They were literally a link with society's oldest communal memories and seemed to lead the way back to those first beginnings, and even to share in the creative process by which the world evolved. Bringing together the element that both descends from above and rises from beneath, the river's cyclical forces seemed to embody the essential patterns of nature, as well as the relation between the intellectual and physical worlds. For this reason the river had a natural affinity with the two basic impulses behind the creative and mythic process, what in Christian terminology are called incarnation and transubstantiation, although the ideas are fundamental to secular conceptions of the artist and of individual's place in the universe. Thus, as we will see, in ancient cultures the waters are identified with the divine element in nature; as the principal manifestation of the word in the world, they are expressive of the divinity of nature. At the same time the river represents nature's ability to transcend itself, to return to a purer dimension free of the mutability of the fallen world: to be resurrected. Within the terms of each particular culture, the river was a sign of the world's order and perfectability. It figured on the one hand the ability to realize our higher powers in nature, and on the other, the capacity to transcend nature itself.

These are the two extremes reconciled in the river motif, and by concentrating our attention primarily on the geographical rivers of the world, we can see how they emerge as an image of the humanist's endeavors to perfect himself by simultaneously realizing his divine powers and elevating nature. This is not to deny important differences in the rivers of individual cultures and periods. On the contrary, by taking on the distinctive characteristics of their particular society, the rivers accentuate the differences in cultures' self-images, in their sense of *humanitas* and of the goals and objectives of society. But whatever the period and whatever the culture, the river retains its fundamental identification with the material world and its more divine potential: it is the thread joining the body and mind. It is in such beginnings, where history and myth, geography and cosmography, science and magic are all but indistinguishable, that one must first look for the river, and it is there that our cultured responses to landscape are formed.

As the rivers spread throughout the world after its cosmogonic beginnings, society followed them and settled on their banks. The evolving complexity of our culture mirrors the dispersion of the rivers, so that to follow them is to follow the course of our social development. These literal and figurative dimensions of the river are always close together. In one sense, the serpent of the Garden of Eden is the river that leads the first couple from Paradise, away from the one source, or Godhead, and through the world. Their descendants settle in increasingly complex societies along the banks of the four rivers emanating from that one source (*Genesis* 2:10), never wholly cut off from their access to that first beginning, but always further removed from it. For the Jews and the early exegetes, as well as for the Middle Ages and the Renaissance, the rivers of the world mark not only the distance from the first waters of creation but also the link with them, and thus the way back to them through the world. In this sense, then, for such diverse figures as Ralegh (in the *History of the World*) and Bosch (in the *Garden of Delight*), for example, the river is the key to their perception of the course of history. This is just one way in which the geographical rivers serve as the embodiment of the myth of history.

As the river participates in the spread of civilization and the establishment of the social arts over the forces of nature, it becomes part of our cultural self-consciousness. Thus, it continues to reflect the power of our arts to subsume nature within their order. For example, the Nile was the matrix of inexplicable forces of creation and decay, life and death, of a vitalistic polytheism, but it was also the origin of a social order and unity having its basis in nature. The conception of the world as a work of art rather than an accident persists in the image of mythic figures grappling with the rivers and shaping the landscape—Bacchus, Dionysus, and Hercules, for example. In time the vitalistic Nile is brought within the ordering vision of Hellenic rationalism, which spreads over the ancient world, working its way back along the rivers to the seat of civilization in the valley of the Tigris and Euphrates. Alexander's campaign against the Persians is a progress from river to river, a process of bridging the destructive element and of spreading reason and Greek traditions and customs through a world of disorder. As Alexander advances, the river gods and other nature deities begin to lose their sacrosanct qualities, to be replaced in the religious iconography by the image of rational and godlike human beings.[5] In its movement downstream society, becoming more and more civilized, also attempts to return to its source, to affirm its link with the past, and to measure, as it were, its progress.

The rivers continue to serve in this way as agents in the world's metamorphosis and the uses to which their waters are put, and the character of the landscapes along their banks change as nature evolves to its new forms. To describe them is, in a small and concentrated way, to describe the world. Thus, the spread of Hellenism prepared the way for Rome's embracing ideal of social order, and the bridges Alexander erected were recrossed by Roman soldiers carrying the image of Caesar. Even more than Greece's, Rome's ideal was to reshape the physical world, to make all its rivers aqueducts leading to Rome, to make its cities extensions of Tiber's banks. Carmentis's prophetic vision, in which that river's wooded banks appear to her as the Augustan Imperial City, is repeated on the Roman Thames, Rhine, and Rhône.[6] These rivers help to transform the Celtic landscape of western Europe, so that all their tributary waters flowed south to the Roman Mediterranean, until a rival river system emerged and, as the historical geographers explain the decline, the Rhine-Danube axis undermined the basis of Roman commercial, economic, and military supremacy.[7] Thus, the rivers participate in a new phase in social and geographical evolution, though it is one that continues to be shaped by the main currents of the classical tradition which developed from primitive antiquity. Both culturally and geographically, Rome defined the limits of the European rivers; the Middle Ages and the Renaissance were the fruits of these ancient classical waters. Indeed, in many ways modern, postclassical Europe relived the experience of landscape that we see in Greece and Rome. Culturally they attempted to realize the vision of the landscape and of humanity reflected in those waters, thus continuing that basic response to the world as it was expressed in the first human experiences recorded in myth and then absorbed into the classical tradition.

With such a place in our intellectual, cultural, and geographical history, the river cannot be viewed merely as an aspect of nature. The river is part of our geography and part of our minds; it is the world and the arts with which we respond to it. An understanding of the motif, then, should also be a reevaluation of our response to topography, and it must involve an awareness of the complex interrelations between our literary, geographical, and historical landscapes. From my experience, no critical work has done this successfully. One of my objectives, then, has been to find new critical approaches to topographical literature, ones that go to the heart of literary creation and touch those instincts which arouse our interest in landscape, and the river is naturally suited to such a task.

Thus what I have done here is to look at the river in terms of the interrelations between geography, history, and literature, allowing

each discipline to take precedence as the topic requires and attempting all the while to keep the three in perspective. While my
original intention was to examine the river motif in classical and
Renaissance literature, it was soon obvious that that was impossible.
The river refuses to be removed from its geographical habitat:
Homer's, Virgil's, Spenser's, Drayton's, and Milton's rivers all send
the reader back to the physical world and further back to the origins
of our conception of the river. There is no such thing as half a river.
It was impossible not to go back to the beginnings of the motif in our
cultural myths and to follow its descent from there, pointing out the
turns in its channel while emphasizing that it is all but one river.
One could not simply pass from Tiber to Thames.

These problems are unique to the river, and there is no precedent
for tracing a primarily literary motif from its origins in geography,
although there are, of course, various interdisciplinary studies
treating points of contact between geography, myth, and literature
from a historical context. Studies of classical nature deities, for
example, are confined by religious and cultural considerations.
Marjorie Hope Nicolson, in *Mountain Gloom and Mountain Glory*,
copes with many of these problems, but her mountain stands still
and is a focal point in our aesthetic (and physical) landscape as the
meandering river is not and cannot be. The river's characteristic flux
denies that degree of stability which enables her to come back to the
same mountain from different points of view. John Seelye, in his
Prophetic Waters: The River in Early American Life and Literature,
avoids many of these problems by confining his travel to one bend in
the river, that which forms on the horizon of the New World, and by
concentrating on specific problems in American history and literature.

In yielding to that instinct to trace the river to its source, we can
observe how the motif evolves from being a mysterious natural
phenomenon that a culture struggles to understand, to being an
image that a poet draws from nature and uses as part of his
rhetorical technique to create the coherent world of his verse. As
society masters the environment, writers acquire greater control over
the literary images that originate in that world, as we see in the rivers
of the creation myths and in Homer and in Virgil, for example. The
poet's skills as "maker" become more formalized, the river tamer.

Thus, as the motif evolves in the Middle Ages, as classical
learning is assimilated into ecclesiastical framework, the river moves
farther out of the realm of nature and into a rarefied celestial

dimension. The rivers reflect the way in which a secular, pagan culture was absorbed into a Christian world view. These are largely cerebral rivers, allegorical or anagogical in character, but they too betray their connection with their beginnings in the physical world, where people first looked for understanding of divine order.

The Renaissance (as it was wont to do) effects a compromise between the transcendent ecclesiastical rivers of the Middle Ages and those of the classical period. Its secular humanism, with its religious and nationalistic foundations and its renewed interest in the world as the place in which to seek human perfection, brings together those divergent intellectual impulses which seek, on the one hand, to embrace the world, or on the other, to be free of it, to abandon it as the mortal shell of an immortal spirit. There is a confluence of what Bacon, in the *Advancement of Learning*, calls the two streams of learning, philosophy and divinity. The potential of the motif is realized in the Renaissance. By using the river to accommodate classical and Christian ideals within a national landscape, authors complete a major cycle in its evolution. The river is so frequently used as a topic locating these ideas in the prose and verse of the period that it emerges as an important literary convention, and the river poem as a genre in itself.

Another of my principal objectives, then, is to demonstrate that the river is a distinct literary convention with certain understood thematic and formal features. Conventions tend to be the discoveries of critics more than the patterns followed conscientiously by writers. That, however, does not mean that they did not (or do not) exist. They are like those lands unseen but nevertheless real which Spenser and Shakespeare write about. But it is for this reason that a long view of the river is necessary: it shows how the river evolves from landscape to myth, and is absorbed into an increasingly formal literature, becoming a topic that authors consistently invoke for the network of associations it carries in its current, and for the shape it imposes on their work. From its mythical role in the creation of the world and in the natural order, the river assumed a signal place in the poet's task of remaking the world. For classical authors, as well as for Catherine of Siena, Spenser, Drayton, and Milton, the river was a place in which to locate ideas about history, time, and the nature of man's relation to the world. And with increasing frequency in the sixteenth and seventeenth centuries, the river dictated the shape of whole works or principal parts of them, so that the literature in which the order of the world is mirrored by the river becomes a popular genre. For Leland, Camden, Spenser, Drayton, Marvell, Milton, and others the river poem resonated with its ancient and classical meanings, and thus enabled them to explore the relation of their world to the humanistic vision of the transformed landscape which they inherited from their classical models, as well as from the Bible and the exegetes. In their work we can see how the world was increasingly perceived in terms of the literary imagination, so that both physical and literary environment grew into the cultural landscape foreshadowed by antiquity. The cultural mythology manifest in this river literature reaches a peak in the Renaissance, after which it yields to the more personal sensibility of later periods. In the seventeenth century the transformation from landscape to literature is complete, and it is there, at that bend in the river, that I have chosen to tie up my bark.

I have tried to approach the convention of river literature circumspectly, letting the evidence speak for itself—there is a great deal of it, and what I have selected for discussion here is but a portion. What becomes unmistakable, though, is that there is a striking continuity in the motif, and in which change and innovation are calculated against convention. Writers in the classical tradition tend to turn to the river when they are most conscious of their art and its relation to their society. A particularly apt modern example of this, one that I have already echoed here, occurs in Curtius, when he speaks of how the historical conception of Europe is the product of nature's evolutionary process. To illustrate his point, he resorts to a descriptive simile (it might be described as a *topos*) which illustrates how the river brings together literal, metaphoric, physical, historical, and literary dimensions. To see modern European literature after 1500 as independent of what went before, he says,

> is as intelligent as if one were to promise a description of the Rhine, but only provided the section from Mainz to Cologne. To be sure, there is a "medieval" literary history too. It begins about 1000—that is, to pursue the metaphor, as far downstream as Strassburg. But where is the period from 400 to 1000? For that one would have to start at Basel. . . . And we must go further back. The literature of "modern" Europe is intermingled with that of the Mediterranean as if the Rhine had received the waters of the Tiber.[8]

In a sense, this is not a simile at all—an analogous pattern drawn from history and geography, but not a similitude based on figurative meaning. The historical development of the river identifies a parallel movement in literary evolution. In offering this example to join the literal and metaphoric dimensions of his idea, he uses an ancient motif in a way that would have been recognizable to Virgil. What I have attempted to do is, first of all, identify the development of this motif which Curtius uses so instinctively, and then examine its literary importance. To do this, I have followed the motif back past the Tiber to look briefly at the primitive waters that fed it. Curtius's own historical map of the European landscape has been invaluable. However, in my own work, I have inverted his Bergsonian emphasis and stressed the way in which the intellect attempts to manifest itself in nature. In seeing nature as art, rather than art as nature, I have married Curtius's idea, that "Nature seeks to realize in matter a life which attains to consciousness," to a somewhat more problematic comment by the humane geographer, E. C. Semple—that "So much is certain: History lies not near but in Nature"[9]—in order to show how the world and our literature are mirroring expressions of our historical consciousness.

In examining the literary history of the river, I occasionally emphasize its use as a *topos*. It is as such that Curtius himself uses it in the above passage, and that it appears most commonly through the Renaissance. In theory and in practice, the word is understood differently by Aristotle, Cicero, Quintilian, Virgil, and Seneca: in the prose and verse of the politicians, orators, and poets, *topoi* assume different forms and functions. But it is not necessary to provide a rhetorical history in order to understand the fundamental nature of *loci communes*, or topics, in prose and verse. Determined by the rules of decorum, they may be topics directing the rhetorician's invention and recitation, and illustrating his ideas, or they may be rhetorical figures locating transitions in his argument. When the river is treated as a *topos*, we can see that (like any other topic) it can dominate an entire work, as it does in Ausonius's *Moselle* or Drayton's *Poly-Olbion*; or it can appear as a topic of succinct importance located in the midst of a larger work, as it does in the *Iliad*, Georgics 4, and in Book 4 of *The Faerie Queene*; or it can provide a kind of rhetorical fulcrum illustrating and advancing an author's ideas, as it does in Seneca's *Naturales Quaestiones*. But what is important is that the river's rhetorical function as the *locus communis* within a work brings it in touch with the most fundamental aspects of the creative process as it was understood by authors throughout the classical tradition.

In this tradition, the poet comes upon—or invents—his poetic world through memory, the most important faculty serving the creative intellect. It is through memory that he reaches back through the recesses of the intellect to the divine wisdom that is accorded the orator and poet. Mentally, he moves from place to place, topic to topic, in the pursuit of understanding. It is often in the *locus communis* that the meaning of the work is concentrated. The essence of rhetorical invention, these *topoi* both draw on and serve the memory. As such, they are, among other things, mnemonic devices, such as those discussed by Frances Yates in her *Art of Memory*. When it retains its geographical identity, the river provides a rhetorical *locus* that the poet explores in his mind's eye, and transforms through the process of description. Like other literary landscapes, the river may be described or created from the imagination (*topographia* or *topothesia*); it may be based in nature or art, but ultimately it represents the union of the two. The discovery of places, or *topoi*, is the process by which a writer strives to realize thought. As the author of the late classical handbook on rhetoric and memory, *Ad Herennium*, says: "thought can embrace any region whatsoever and in it and at will construct the setting of some *locus*."[10] Any "place," whether real or imaginary, becomes the product of the creative mind. This classical conception of topics carries into the Renaissance, and is, for example, implicit in Sidney's Neoplatonic view of poetry in the *Defence of Poetry*, where he speaks of how the poet, with the "vigor of his owne invention, dooth growe . . . . another nature . . . . better then Nature bringeth forth, or, quite a newe."[11]

Thus, the geographical world itself participates in the creative process; the *theatrum orbis* is a symbolic place which both structures and guides our inventive memory. In the Middle Ages meditations on the geography of Paradise, organized around its rivers, were common.[12] Ralegh too uses the rivers of Eden to adumbrate his secular thoughts about the history of the world. Geographical and topographical literature is generally based on this idea of the world as a place that the poet or prose writer can explore and use as a guide to lead his thoughts, and the river consistently appears as a sign fixed on that landscape. This aspect of topographical literature has hardly been touched upon by scholars. However, virtually all the topographical writers working in the classical tradition attempt to recreate the world in this way, and river is just one of the more important physical details having a place in that genre. Without recognizing this aspect of topographical literature, one cannot understand the relation between the poet and the natural world that

he describes. Having these rhetorical, thematic, and generic characteristics, the river can serve as an important critical device, providing interpretive approaches to the heart of certain important works.

In the pages that follow, I have taken the river's natural and
literary qualities and adapted them to a critical approach to some of
the more important but elusive episodes in literature, such as
Homer's treatment of the Scamander in the *theomachia* of the *Iliad*,
Virgil's treatment of the Tiber in the *Aeneid*, the river lore of Ovid's
Metamorphoses, the marriage of the Thames and the Medway in
The Faerie Queene, and the world of Drayton's *Poly-Olbion*. The
very conventiónality of the river makes many works understandable
as they had not been before, and gives them a needed critical
context—Virgil's fourth *Georgic*, Ausonius's *The Moselle*, Camden's *de Connubio Tamae et Isis*, William Browne's *Britannia's
Pastorals*, and the watery work of the Spenserian poets, for example. By coming to them along the river we see them in terms of their
own element and begin to understand something of their authors'
intentions. Thus, I have tried to keep an eye open to the river's
critical potential, and have slowed down from time to time to study
some of the literary monuments that adorn its banks.

In using the motif to look at the relation between landscape and
literature, I have found it necessary to stress the river's persistent
association with language itself. Language is based in nature and in
our response to it. From the early hexameral myths in which the
rivers are "as the voice of God," and the classical literature where
rhetorical eloquence is described as the "flumen orationis," to the
Renaissance, where they represent both the poet's theme and his
style, and even later, when the stream of consciousness describes
the essence of modern narrative art, the topic retains its connection
with the origins of language in our response to nature, and, even
more important, with the model for language in our harmony with
nature. However formal it becomes as a genre, it continues to echo
with the reminder of that past when the world and the word were
one. In this sense, then, the river has its beginnings in human
nature, in our art, our perceptions, and our speech. For this reason
it repeatedly involves themes of the mastery of nature through art;
the briefest river metaphor can serve as a reminder that all human
experience is the product of a creative act, that our perceptions are
organized by language: "the mind cannot conceive or bring forth its
fruit unless it is steeped in the vast flood of literature"; "so shall

thou be fully inspired, and shalt pour out words in swelling torrent from a heart the Muses love."[13]

These admissions of the difficulty of comprehending the river are also, as the reader will have discerned, an acknowledgment of the pleasures and challenge of the task, and I confess to having indulged myself. These methodological considerations serve a larger purpose, for I have also tried to develop an approach to topographical literature which goes nearer to the heart of our response to the physical world than that which currently predominates in English studies. Rather than pick away at the more conventional approaches to the form, I have, starting here in the introduction, begun from scratch and attempted to create a new sense of what topographical writing is by using methods and ideas of various disciplines to explore the significance of one of the most important aspects of the landscape, and the literature that it inspired. In short, I have tried to see somewhat differently the relation between art and nature by focusing on the river. What becomes evident is that art is our response to nature. The poet does not look to the landscape for an extension of himself, but as another way of looking within himself. He does not see the world as external nature distinct from himself, but as another aspect of his and (at the same time) his culture's mental processes. As will become clear in the chapters to follow, we perceive the landscape in terms of perceptual myths which are personal and cultural in their origin and nature. Participating in art and in the natural environment, the river assumes an important place in our cultural self-consciousness and is readily adapted to the expression of our social ideals. At certain times in history these myths are appropriate to the landscape—the landscape, society, and the individual seem to be in harmony, and the perceptual myths seem to embrace all three dimensions. At other times—as the Roman Empire begins to fragment or when Britain enters upon its period of civil strife, for example—this harmony seems absent, and perceptual myths undergo a period of revision; the landscape seems to reject the myth of the individual or society that is imposed upon it, as we see in Ovid, for example, and in the Spenserian poets. The myths are inappropriate because they are no longer vital, no longer drawn from the reality of our experience. In a unique way the river enables us to trace these historical patterns in our response to nature and the perceptual landscape.

My questions about the river were initially centered upon Spen-

ser, Drayton, and Renaissance response to landscape. As I have
tried to demonstrate, the river involves—and envelops—much
besides itself, and for this reason alone it has been necessary to go
back beyond Virgil and Homer to look at more basic questions
about our experience and perception of the world. In looking at
ancient geography and myths I have tried to see old and sometimes
familiar texts and ideas within a new framework—one which, I hope,
will broaden our understanding of how our cultural myths are
contained in our environment.

The thrust of this study, then, is still the English Renaissance and
the river's place in the topographical tradition. However, there is a
cumulative quality to our cultural responses to nature: the landscape
evolves as our intellectual traditions evolve and as we gradually
come to think of landscape differently. I have, then, attempted to
illustrate several major phases in the formation of our response to
geography—to highlight the strata which together give depth and
contour to our interpretation of the world. Thus, the chronological
order of the work is not meant to offer a continuous linear history of
the river motif. Rather, it is meant to emphasize several periods
where we can identify major phases in the development of our
intellectual response to the world, to point out those strata in the
formation of our mental landscape, and to study some examples of
that response which would have been known in the Renaissance.

In this I have also tried to illustrate these phases fairly amply by
letting the river speak for itself—to suggest a vocabulary for the
approach that I attempt to develop. The work, therefore, is also
meant to be bibliographic in scope. In my documentation, in the use
of allusive illustrations and epigraphs, and in my critiques, I have
attempted to locate the river in its multiplicity. I have tried to avoid
any unintentional distortion of the river's importance in certain
works while using it as a critical approach to them. In using the river
as a critical tool, I certainly do not think that it is the only one or
even in most cases the most important one, although it may sometimes seem so. Furthermore, I have used my materials to try to
emphasize continuity in the interest in rivers. Working on the
principle that any idea or work current or known in Renaissance
Britain was probably known everywhere else in Europe long before,
I have chosen to draw heavily on sixteenth- or seventeenth-century
English texts or translations, therefore providing an implicit confir-
mation of the awareness and continuity of that aspect of the river
and its context.

Thus, I have tried to create a cultural landscape for the river literature and lore that I have identified and discussed. But as it has always done, I know that it continues to defy definition, and I am only too aware that it eludes confinement within the limits of this study. The most that I can hope is that I have in some degree managed to show how, reflected in the waters of the river, is a complex and shifting image of the world held in fragile stability.

Halifax, 1979/Toronto, 1984

PART ONE

PRE-RENAISSANCE
CONTEXTS OF THE RIVER

I. *Landscape to God:*

The River in the Ancient World

'Tis reported (most gracious Queene) that Aegypt is watered with the yerely overflowing of Nilus, and Lidia with the golden streame of Pactolus, whyche thing is thought to be the cause of the great fertilitye of these great countries: but upon us, and farther, overall Englande . . . many and maine rivers of Godlynesse, justice, humilitie . . . do most plentifully gushe out, and those not from Tmolus, or other hilles . . . but from that continuall and most aboundaunt welspring of your goodness. (Stephen Lambert to Queen Elizabeth; Norwich, 1578)

THERE ARE THREE MAIN BRANCHES OF THE RIVER which flows forth from antiquity onto the level plain of the Renaissance. They come from Egypt, the Holy Land, and Greece, and in their alluvial deposits are the seeds of the cultures from which they come. It is in Augustan Rome that their waters are confluent, mingle, and with broadened and deeper channel, glide north and west.

But these are three metaphoric rivers which descend from three distinctly different cultures, set in distinctly different geographies that to some indefinable degree determine their characters. We must start, therefore, with the rivers themselves and look generally at their physical characteristics and how they were perceived in the cultures they fostered. As we will see they are of two kinds: the deep-bedded, smooth flowing perennial river—what in Roman law was called a "public" river—and the torrential river, in its season crashing violently like a lion or bull (its usual zoomorphic symbols) down mountainsides, destroying forests, fields, precariously maintained terraces, even entire cities set on the side or at the base of the hills, and annihilating their population, architecture, and artistic

23

and literary achievements. These, in the extreme, are the two kinds of river. Others, of moderate size, the Po or Tiber, for example, partake of both qualities, flooding or damaging city and countryside in the spring, but generally maintaining a swift, often navigable current the year round. But the earliest civilizations settled around the more extreme examples—the Nile, Tigris, Euphrates, Jordan, and the many nameless torrents of Greece.[1]

Whether torrential or perennial, though, these rivers brought their communities necessary gifts. Early Mediterranean societies were all set in arid climates and they depended on the rivers, not local rainfall, for their water supply. Thus they made up the deficiencies of a rainless clime by joining it, through their channels, with moister regions. And if they were deep-bedded perennial rivers, they joined distant lands commercially, bringing in their wake the benefits of human intercourse. These were all holy waters; they supported life and, perhaps more important, they made a life of plenty attainable, and so they were a civilizing force. As societies grew along their banks and observed the regular or irregular patterns of the rivers' descent, they associated them with nature's mysteries and divine order. Violent or calm, the rivers were beneficent, fructifying, and civilizing, and seated precariously on their banks was a wary but grateful humanity. While death and ruin might come unannounced down their channels, so too did life; while they might bring oblivion, they also forced people to establish a pattern to their behavior through legends and records, and so fostered memory. Society, on its rivers, was forced into self-awareness, compelled into a state of cultural self-consciousness from which grew its own characteristic river image.

These ancient societies were fully aware of the basic attributes of their rivers and recognized, often with envy, the distinctions between the torrential and perennial river, while maintaining a patriotic loyalty to their own local *genius*.[2] In characterizing the cultural geography of these rivers we can see the emergence of three kinds of river, each having intellectual and physical attributes in common but each contributing in different ways to the motif as it becomes established in the classical tradition and thus absorbed into newer cultures not necessarily dependent on a river. Through the rivers, then, various cultural myths become embedded in new landscapes. Although the influence of these ancient river cultures on later periods is often indirect, and is far more complex than the emphasis on the river might suggest, the continuity of the river motif is one of the major sources of our modern response to landscape and of the myths and cultural expectations that we bring to it. In the interdependent physical and intellectual growth of these different societies, then, we can perceive the emergence of some of our literary archetypes.

1. Serpent of the Nile

> When he riseth the earth rejoiceth, every man is filled with joy, every bone receiveth sustenance, every tooth sinketh into food. . . . He is the light-giver, appearing from out of darkness. . . . He establisheth the Right. . . . Songs to thee are begun on the Harp. (Hymn of Thanksgiving to the Nile)

> As Egypts draught by Nilus is redrest,
> So thy wise tongue doth comfort the opprest.
> (I. E. Nerembergius, *On Temperance*, tr. Henry Vaughan)

Descending from south to north over some 4,160 miles, unaided by tributaries, is Egypt's river, the Nile, prototype of the perennial river and of rivers generally. While comparatively little of Egyptian culture was transmitted to the West, that which was is almost wholly due to the Nile—its gods, its bounteous nature, the mathematical and astronomical learning that grew out of the Nile's inundation, and the very concept of the river itself, all are nilotic in origin. But then Egypt is inseparable from its river: to the Greeks, who gave us the name for both, Egypt and the Nile signified "the river" and "the stream."[3] Whether we live in the shadow of a torrent, like the Scamander, swathed in the noisome mists of a polluted East River, or in the trickling upper reaches of the Thames, many of our commonplace attitudes about rivers derive from the legendary character of the *fluviorum pater*.

The Nile is a river of mysterious contrasts that make it, among other things, the repository of nature's secrets. For Europeans it flowed in the wrong direction, while for Egyptians Europe's rivers were inverted. The mysteries of its source and annual inundation contrasted with its reliability, and so more readily than other cultures, Egypt could trust in and have faith in the unknown. And the river brought together extremes, most conspicuously those of life and death, for the endlessly long fertile valley, measuring from two to fifteen miles in width, was surrounded by infertile desert. The legendary Nile muds seemed themselves, when warmed by the sun

and moistened by water, to spawn life. In its primitive past it drew
to its waters a vast array of plant and animal life, and as humanity
mastered the cycles of its floods, a life of ease and abundance
poured over its banks, so that later writers from lands less fortunate
in their rivers, wrote with a tourist's envy of the greener waters on
the other side of the Mediterranean:

> Speaking generally, we may say that the Nile surpasses all the rivers
> of the inhabited world in its benefactions to mankind. For, beginning
> to rise at the summer solstice it increases in volume until the autum-
> nal equinox, and, since it is bringing down fresh slime all the time, it
> soaks both the fallow land and the seed land as well as the orchard
> land for so long a time as the farmers may wish. For since the water
> comes with a gentle flow they easily divert the river from the fields by
> small dams of earth, and then by cutting these, as easily let the river
> in again upon the land whenever they think this to be advantageous.
> And in general the Nile contributes so greatly to the lightening of
> labor as well as to the profit of the inhabitants that the majority of the
> farmers as they begin work upon the areas of land which are becom-
> ing dry, merely scatter their seed, turn their herds and flocks in on the
> fields, and after they have used these for trampling the seed in return
> after four or five months to harvest it.[4]

Diodorus's description carries an implicit contrast between Egypt
and the more rugged landscapes of Sicily and Greece, where terraces must be contrived to retain the sparse waters. In Egypt one
has only to scatter the seed and let the cattle trample it into the silt
to sow an abundant crop of wheat, corn, or cotton. In its ease Egypt
seemed to enjoy an uninterrupted Golden Age.

All aspects of ancient Egypt's remarkable culture were the efflux
of its river. As the Nile brought together the extremes of life and
death, abundance and scarcity, it was also a social harmonizer and
unified the kingdoms of Upper and Lower Egypt to create the first
geographically and governmentally centralized society: everything
strove toward the Nile, which fathered not only its society, but also,
according to myth, its godlike pharaohs. Indeed, so centralized was
its ancient society that, like its principal deities, it was virtually
incestuous and had a cultivated self-sufficiency. For various geographic and cultural reasons it eschewed a commercial, maritime
economy. It attracted trade from the East, beyond the Red Sea, but
it did not generally look outward toward the Mediterranean for
other than defensive purposes. Like a vast earthworm it absorbed
the exotic consumables of the East and with a kind of peristalsis
processed them through its central system, finally to eliminate their

wasted residue over the delta and into the Mediterranean. While there was extensive internal trade up and down this main artery, the external trade with other lands was confined to the surplus that filtered downstream and found its way into the sea.[5]

The Nile, then, was a harmonizer of extremes and literally brought unity from diversity. Mastery of the river and the growth of civilization were directly correlated, and their association has persisted. And as the Nile spawned life, it seemed paradoxically to also create land itself. Geographically the Nile is a "land builder," and the Egyptian and Greeks were well aware of the fact that Egypt itself was the creation of the silting process of the Nile.[6] Moreover, not only was Egypt the gift of the deific river, but the holy cities along its banks were as well. Thus the river's abundance extends also to its culture and religion in the form of dependent cities and deities, and these qualities of city founder and principal, creating deity persist as part of the river's set of association:

> For the Egyptians consider Oceanus to be their river Nile, on which also their gods were born; since, they say, Egypt is the only country in the whole inhabited world where there are so many cities which were founded by the first Gods.[7]

Even as late as Plutarch there are objections to Egypt's proprietorial claim to the variety of gods and their sacred cities, and to its rejection of an ecumenism which would make the gods universal property:

> there is nothing to fear, if, in the first place, they preserve for us our gods that are common to both peoples and do not make them belong to the Egyptians only, and do not include under those names the Nile alone and the land which the Nile waters, and do not assert that the marshes and lotus are the only work of God's hand, and if they do not deny the great gods to the rest of mankind that possess no Nile nor Buto nor Memphis.[8]

That the Nile spawned gods as abundantly as it did plant and animal life was a source of irritation for later cultures. The Jews reacted vehemently against its polytheism, while the Greeks and Romans jealously absorbed those gods that they could within their elaborate syncretisms.

It is safe to say that the entire pantheon of Egyptian deities in human and animal form derives ultimately from the primal river whose principal deity, according to Sir E. A. Wallis Budge, is the pre-dynastic god Hapi.[9] He is the essence of the Nile's mysteries, the unanswerable source of its flood and its unknown abode. It is his being that allows all else to exist, and for this reason he was not subject to local cult as other gods were. He is distinctly a local Nile god manifesting the geographical attributes of the river, and this makes him less adaptable to other cultures. Thus it is he who is the unifier of Upper and Lower Egypt and, mythically, of the realms of day and night, life and death. He was represented symbolically by the sequential repetition of a single thronelike hieroglyph suggestive of the procession of life along the ribbon of water, the visual effect of which is not unlike that of more representational art, where the unbroken line of the river makes the visual suggestion of endless continuity. He was the quintessence of life's mysteries as embodied in the Nile—he was the sacrosanct river itself, as well as its indigenous symbol. For later societies, as for the Egyptians, the Nile represented the mysteries of life, of death, the inscrutable creation of all things. Inquiry into the secrets of the Nile was even for the Renaissance synonymous with the quest for knowledge, so that the contemplation of a real topography continued to be an inquiry into the holy mysteries of divine purpose.

Although his local qualities made Hapi unsuitable for export, in his elemental nature he gave birth to other deities who served as ciphers to his mysterious identity and who could shed their native garb and find acceptance and recognizable meanings in other lands, while carrying with them the basic characteristics of Hapi himself. The most important of these surrogate gods were pre-dynastic Isis and Osiris. While they usually retained their specific nilotic identities, they also figured conveniently in Greco-Roman and even mystic Christian cults, such as those of Tyche, Fortuna, Hercules, Bacchus, Dionysus, Christ, and the Virgin Mary. Nevertheless, they retained their links with river myths and, emancipated by the processes of abstraction from strictly local associations with the deep-bedded perennial Nile, their cult extended to all rivers generally. Plutarch, trying to recreate their myth in its original Egyptian form, interprets it in terms of what allegorists described as its "physical allegory". The most "perspicuous" Egyptian mythographers, he argues, "say that Osiris is the Nile consorting with the Earth, which is Isis, and that the sea is Typhon into which the Nile discharges its waters and is lost to view and dissipated, save for that part which the earth takes up and absorbs and thereby becomes fertilized." It has both specific and general application, so that the myth serves to explain natural phenomena in a universal context:

But the wiser of the priests call not only the Nile Osiris and the sea Typhon, but they simply give the name of Osiris to the whole source and faculty creative of moisture, believing this to be the cause of generation and the substance of life-producing seed; and the name Typhon they give to all that is dry, fiery, and arid, in general, and antagonistic to moisture.[10]

The legend was also analyzed in historical and heroic terms in order to explain the origin and character of Egyptian culture. And what have been described as "heurematographic" interpretations of Isis and Osiris explain their myth as an allegory for the technological mastery by which man civilizes nature. Like Dionysus and Bacchus, Osiris and Isis taught the world husbandry, encouraged knowledge and social order, and promoted the arts. Especially in the Greco-Roman world, the technological advances symbolized by Isis and Osiris also carried moral benefits which became inseparable from the river motif: "one of the first acts related of Osiris in his reign was to deliver the Egyptians from their destitute and brutish manner of living. This he did by showing them the fruits of cultivation, by giving them laws, and by teaching them to honour the gods."[11] These lessons of Osiris are also those of the river Nile, and his heroic manifestation in Egypt was the pharaoh. The heroic, elemental, and moral allegories coexist and were embraced by the priests of Egypt, Greece, and Rome.

Osiris, both educator and civilizer, was primarily a public figure drawing his wisdom from his sisterly wife. As the embodiment of the Nile mysteries, she too had a social significance, but she was above all the fount of all learning. In this Osiris was, in a way, her cipher, and as J. G. Griffiths explains, "the Osirian mysteries are means of achieving philosophical truth, and Isis is the repository of wisdom which makes this possible."[12] Isis's learning extended to all of nature's secrets, particularly medicinal matters, fertility, midwifery, and these were attributes later associated with the Greek river nymphs. It also extended to those skills which advance the arts and sciences—the province of Apollo and the muses: "special esteem at the court of Osiris and Isis was also accorded those who should invent any of the arts or devise any useful process."[13] Not only is Isis Osiris's wife and mother, but she is also his mistress-muse and kindles him with divine inspiration. This Egyptian river nymph anticipates virtually all the roles of the Greek river goddesses. She and her brother, as local gods of the Nile, helped to establish those associations that were carried on by Apollo and the muses. They

join the social and educative functions that the Greek deities were
to have, and "for this reason they call the first of the muses at
Hermopolis Isis as well as Justice."[14] From the landscape of Egypt,
then, evolved the river goddess who had the masculine attribute of
justice and feminine qualities of wisdom and mercy. She embodied
the cultural myths that Edmund Spenser would invoke more than
two millennia later when creating an allegorical Isis, who joined
"clemencie" with "that part of justice [which] is equity," and in
whom we see the ideal to which Britomart must aspire (*Faerie
Queene*, 4.7.3 and 22).

Isis and Osiris presided over all human knowledge, by which one
masters and improves the world, and divine revelation, by which
one penetrates the profounder mysteries of nature. Although the
river cult became vague and diversified for the Greeks, in Egypt it
retained its coherence. The two river gods reflect aspects of their
culture's relation to the crucial feature of their environment. The
limits and potential of human understanding, as the Egyptians
perceived them, are projected in their myth, and in this they
embody the extent of that culture's humanistic self-conception.
Apollo and the muses clearly reveal their family resemblance to
their Egyptian forebears, but they have less easily identified relations to one another, to the learning that they each impart, and to
the diversified geography of their culture. The simplified paradig-
matic relation between Isis and Osiris owes much to the simplified
and centralized geography and culture which created them, just as
the multiplicity of the Greek muses owes much to the regionalism
and multiplicity of Greek cults. Indeed, until the fifth century B.C.,
the muses were as numerous as the many trickling mountain springs.
It was Hesiod who put an end to the plurality of the muses by
numbering them at fifty and naming them.[15] Thereafter the relation
between the muses and the river nymphs deteriorated so that
eventually the muses sang to almost any tune, and the nymphs were
little more than bawds for lost or lunatic lovers. But in Isis and
Osiris we can apprehend the harmony that originally brought together Apollo, the river nymphs, and the muses in a single, encompassing cult reflecting humanity's relation to the world.

The paradisiac bounty and the orderly and civilized life nurtured
by the Nile and spread abroad by Isis and Osiris were universal
ideals rather than aspects of local cult. The Nile and the life realized
on its banks formed a model for Greeks and Romans who looked
rather wistfully at their local rills when erecting on their stony banks

the black marble statue of the Nile and poured ablutions of costly imported Nile water into their thin streams to honour Isis and the local gods, hoping to effect a compromise between the two extremes of dearth and excess. There is an implicit logic joining the widely varied material, moral, and social benefits which seemed to flow from the Nile and which were associated with Hapi, Isis, and Osiris. Hapi's mysterious nature finds its comprehensible human form in Osiris's identity as a river engineer, promoter of peaceful cultivation, exemplar of magnanimity, and ambassador of goodwill and hospitality, and in Isis's all-embracing wisdom and oracular powers which find expression in Osiris's actions. Her roles as wife, lover, mother, and sister personify the various nurturing bonds that link Egyptian society with its river. In the three deities we see some of the ways in which a society's relation to a single dominant geographical feature gives rise to a complex social myth dealing with the moral and intellectual basis of its indigenous culture.

2. The Lion of Judea

> Behold, he shall come up like a lion from the swelling of Jordan against the habitation of the strong. (Jeremiah 49:19)

> *There is* a river, the streams whereof shall make glad the city of God, the holy *place* of the tabernacles of the Most High. (Psalm 46:4)

The Nile is the river that rises. Among its mysteries is the inexplicable, invisible increase of its water from below. Contrasting with it are the Jordan, which is the "river that goes down," and the two other major rivers of the Holy Land, the Tigris and the Euphrates. These three rivers lie somewhere between the quiescent regularity of the Nile and the violence and irregularity of the rivers of Greece and the northern Mediterranean. Both the Jordan Valley and Mesopotamia—the "land between the rivers"—rely on their rivers for much-needed water, and for millennia before Christ they had had sophisticated systems of irrigation and water storage. All three rivers flow swiftly to their outlets, and in periods of inundation they frequently leave the surrounding countryside in ruin, buried deep in the rich alluvial soil that they each carry in their waters. Fertility through destruction is an essential paradox for Mesopotamian life, and is a legendary feature of its rivers. Among the most ancient flood myths are those derived from the Euphrates region: early biblical cosmogonic myths—notably Genesis 1:6–10—assimilate earlier Mesopotamian flood stories. The separation of the waters of heaven and earth, and the legendary flood heroes, have their prototypes in this region, and they no doubt originate in the reality of life between the banks of these two dangerous rivers. As do those of Greece, these rivers require every human effort to control nature; unlike the Egyptians' relation to their river, for those on the Jordan or between the Tigris and Euphrates, life was a constant struggle to outguess their rivers and to tame them.[16]

The later civilization that settled after the Exodus on the eastern banks of the Jordan absorbed much of the legendary lore of Mesopotamia. In the Old Testament the archetypal river, often referred to simply as "the River" and figured abstractly as the "waters" in Genesis, is usually the Euphrates.[17] The creation myths and elemental allegories associated with the Jordan were absorbed from the east rather than the south. From the geography of the eastern Mediterranean, then, rises another kind of river suggesting a different relationship between mankind and the world. This branch of the river motif reaches the West in the context of its religious significance in the Old Testament, and it was largely determined by a combination of geographical, religious, political, and historical considerations. Indeed, one of the remarkable features of the Old Testament is the way that it joins revelation and immediacy of time and place in its evocation of the Promised Land beyond the Jordan. The struggle for God and country are one and the same.

The conception of the Jordan, then, is inseparable from the significance of the landscape for its people, but this significance is very different from the Nile's for Egypt. The Jordan too gives life, but a very different life; it too creates cities and civilizes, but of a different kind and of a different order; and most important, it too is the fount of religion, but one very unlike that of ancient Egypt. The Old Testament is a political document as well as a prophetic pronouncement, and it presents the Jewish religion and the Promised Land in terms of a calculated cultural context. Thus there are striking similarities beneath the more conspicuous contrasts between the image of the Jordan and that of the Nile, and this is because the river of the Promised Land is specifically meant to contrast with that of the land of captivity; the monotheistic god of the Jews is meant to supplant the polytheism spawned by the Nile.

> And the land of Egypt shall be desolate and waste; and they shall
> know that I *am* the Lord: because he hath said, The river *is* mine, and
> I have made *it*.

> Behold, therefore, I *am* against thee, and against thy rivers, and I will make the land of Egypt utterly waste *and* desolate, from tower of Sy-ēñē even unto the border of Ethiopia. (Ezekial 29:9–10) [18]

God's voice is like "the noise of many waters," and they are threatening and torrential, worthy of the image of "the lion of Judea"—and their punitive force is aimed squarely at Egypt. Repeatedly, the fluent voice of the angry Jehovah threatens His people's captors with an unnilotic torrent of revenge. Like the Jordan, His geographical counterpart, He is beneficient but threatening, even for His own, stiff-necked race: "And behold, I, even I, do bring a flood of waters upon the earth, to destroy all flesh, wherein *is* the breath of life, from under heaven; *and* every thing that *is* in the earth shall die" (Genesis 6:17). The river is the threat and the promise: "For the Lord thy God bringeth thee into a good land, a land of brooks of water, of fountains, and depths that spring out of valleys and hills" (Deuteronomy 8:7). Its every feature is balanced against the Nile, its culture, its gods:

> For the land, whither thou goest in to possess it, *is* not as the land of Egypt . . . where thou sowedst thy seed, and wateredst *it* with thy foot. . . .But the land whither ye go to . . . drinketh water of the rain of heaven. (Deuteronomy 11: 10–11)

The crossing of rivers traditionally marks a rite of passage, a new beginning. The passage of the Jews over Jordan is the fulfilment of the covenant, and it promises rebirth: "Therefore it shall be when ye be gone over Jordan, *that* ye shall set up these stones. . . . And there shalt thou build an Altar" (Deuteronomy 27:4–5). Here too the river is linked with laws and religion; in the very waters of Jordan reside God and his laws (Joshua 3:13; Psalm 29:3 & 10). Significantly, the first law of the covenant in this new land strikes at the heart—or mainstream—of nilotic polytheism: in this land of hard work and plenty, one does not take fertile life for granted, and therefore "take ye . . . good heed. . . . Lest ye corrupt *yourselves*, and make you a graven image" (Deuteronomy 4:15–16).

The Jordan is as much a mirror of its people's faith and culture as the Nile is to Egypt's, but what is reflected there is as different as the two countries' landscapes. The river serves the same function: in its terrestrial waters are revealed divine order; it dictates the characteristics that the social life will be based upon and promote; it reveals the essence of its indigenous civilization.

But while its general function is the same, through its fusion with

Judaism the river took on a wholly different character, one resembling the geographic reality of the Jordan. Like the river which descends swiftly down a twisting course from the sweet waters of Galilee to the bitter, murky salt depths of the Dead Sea, their God is one of sweet and sour extremes of beneficence and wrath. Here too, then, the river is overtly likened to the voice of God, but its tenor is very different. Egypt's river reflects the public being—humanity striving to form civilization, to understand the basis of its survival and refinement. But one sees more deeply into the mirror of Jordan's waters. The voice of its waters addresses a spiritual self and a moral order. The plenty it promises is a moral richness, and the desolation it threatens mirrors a transcendent order rather than the mysteries of nature. Moses is a spiritual leader rather than a river engineer or magnanimous hero. The river geography, real as it is, is simultaneously the metaphor for a spiritual realm. Thus the Jordan's are not only the political waters of a people and their history; they are also the moral and spiritual waters of the inner person:

> For my people have committed two evils; they have forsaken me, the fountain of living waters, *and* hewed them out cisternes . . . that can hold no water. (Jeremiah 2:13)

> Save me, O God, for the waters are come in unto *my* soul. . . . I am come into deep waters, where the floods overflow me. (Psalm 69:1–2)

The torrential waters of this rugged area contain different lessons about cause and effect in nature's workings. From this landscape, then, another river image flowed West: one which springs from deeper recesses in the lives of its people, and one which reflects a different kind of transcendent order. Ultimately, this gave a new, metaphoric direction to the river, and turned its course inward, to the intellectual realm, freeing it from external nature. These characteristics of the Old Testament river, natural as they are to the geography of the Holy Land, have something universal about them by which they become part of our perception of other landscapes; as in Egypt, the myth is greater than its culture. From roughly the fourth century B.C. onward, the Old Testament influenced perceptions of the world, not only in terms of religious thought, but also in terms of the mythic vision of landscape and geography—a dimension of its intellectual impact which has been all but ignored. The image of the river which emerges from the Holy Land is one aspect of this influence; in it is conveyed the perception of the world as an extension of our inner and moral being:

> I did towards Canaan draw; but now I am
> Brought back to the Red Sea, the sea of shame . . .

> Gods works are wide, and let in future times;
> His ancient justice overflows our crimes.[19]

3. *Erymanthian Boar, Lernian Hydra*

> And all their rivers flow in flood, and many a hillside do the torrents furrow deeply, and down to the dark sea they rush headlong from the mountains with a mighty roar. (*Iliad* 15.390–93)

Around 448 B.C. a ship set forth from the Nile delta, perhaps from the place that 120 years later would become the cosmopolitan port of Alexandria. Its cargo consisted of quantities of wheat and corn, and kraters of water, holy water from the Nile. And so, with the lifting of the trade restrictions between Egypt and Greece, the first fruits of the Nile, its abundant cereals and its gods, sailed off to the Hellenic world.[20]

All the avenues of intercourse with Egypt opened, and the Greeks fully indulged their longstanding curiosity in that ancient land. No nation exerted greater influence on the Greeks, and for various cultural, political and economic reasons, this respect carried over to the Nile, the very symbol of that land. The complex cultural cross-fertilization between these two states was, to a large extent, conducted with the products of the river, and Greece's view of its own rivers was considerably modified by the legendary nature of the Nile. Characteristically, the Greeks adopted the Nile's gods along with its bounteous material benefits, and assimilated them into their view of the intractable torrents of their own jagged realm. And so, Isis's temples throughout Greece, but especially that at Delphi, welcomed travellers from her native land, and served at the same time as repository, not only of her secret wisdom, but also of the grains and the hard currency of her traders. The image of the goddess, bearing a rudder or cornucopia, with the world at her feet and some suggestion of her sixteen-cubit inundation, reflects her nilotic origins and her symbolic attributes, while also acknowledging the importance of her benediction on trade beyond Nile's mouth.[21]

But the Greeks were a maritime, commercial nation as the

Egyptians were not, and they had perfected the art of assimilating their rivals. The culturally insular Egypt found its legends absorbed into those of Greece, and there are numerous obscure river myths testifying to this process of assimilation. Cicero tells us, for example, how Hercules was by some regarded as the son of Nilus, and Diodorus Siculus records one amorphous syncretism that brings Greek heroes to the banks of the Nile, where they rescue the native inhabitants from a flood uncharacteristic of that river:

> While Osiris and his army were thus employed [teaching the Ethiopians how to farm], the Nile . . . at the time of the rising of Sirius, which is the season when the river is usually at flood, breaking out of its banks inundated a large section of Egypt and covered especially that part where Prometheus was governor; and since practically everything in this district was destroyed, Prometheus was so grieved that he was on the point of quitting life wilfully. Because its water sweeps down so swiftly and with such violence the river was given the name Aëtus [eagle]; but Heracles, being ever intent upon great enterprises and eager for the reputation of a manly spirit, speedily stopped the flood at its breach and turned the river back into its former course. Consequently certain of the Greek poets worked the incident into a myth, to the effect that Heracles had killed the eagle which was devouring the liver of Prometheus.

This ambiguous conflation of cults, with its strikingly un-Egyptian details about the river, dates from the second or third century B.C. and may be the product of Apollonius Rhodius, who himself held a kind of dual citizenship. If such myths leave in doubt who is assimilating whom, it should be remembered that it is from Greece that Egypt and the Nile got their internationally accepted names. Hesiod seems to be the one responsible, and he identified the river as among the oldest daughters of Oceanus and Tethys; in recognition of the predictability of its inundation, the name "Nile" had a numerological significance of 365.[22]

The Nile's popularity outside Egypt raises various problems about cultural interdependence. Nevertheless, the Nile became an honorary Greek river, and the Mediterranean seemed to be an extension of the Nile, so that when the river floods, "since the land is a level plain, while the cities and villages as well as the farmhouses are on artificial mounds, the scene comes to resemble the Cyclades Islands."[23] The passage is a good example of how we perceive the world according to cultural predispositions. Notwithstanding their dependence on their own local waters, for social and economic reasons the Greeks gave the Nile a respected place in their local river cults. For example, at the temple of the river Erymanthos, at Psophus, there were statues of all the rivers of the world, carved from white marble, with the sole exception of the Nile which, according to tradition, was done in black.[24]

The Greeks, then, absorbed the Nile into a preexisting cultural response to rivers, and this served to accentuate the obvious distinction between the perennial and torrential waters. No matter how fickle most of their rivers were, with their steep stony banks and precipitous descents and ghastly prospects, such as those that made the Styx and Acheron legendary, they were no less revered than the Nile. And as was the case in Palestine and Egypt, this reverence for the local *genius* took a form suitable to their geographical and cultural milieu. Respectful as they were of the Nile, they had their own archetype of the river in the native Acheloüs: it was the king of rivers and, like the Euphrates and Nile, it was associated with the great river Ocean itself. Together with the Styx it figured a cosmic, creative opposition:

> The Styx and the Acheloüs are regarded as the eldest daughter and eldest son of Ocean: and as the Ocean is . . . regarded as the origin of all things, so Styx represents primeval darkness from which arose the beginnings of life, while Acheloüs is the emblem of organic life itself which spreads over the earth in innumerable streams.[25]

The Acheloüs was also linked with nation founding, and on its banks, in the Pelasgic district of Epirus, was the ancient temple of Zeus and the primitive capital of the Hellenes. The river was long associated with Hercules, the greatest of river engineers, and it was represented in the form of a bull, with a broken horn and cornucopia, figuring both his immense strength and the bounty that resulted from his taming. His was an extremely powerful cult and at the beginning of the Christian era it was still sufficiently vital for Ovid to give it a central place in the *Metamorphoses* (Book 9). Whether or not the myths that grew up around Acheloüs were influenced by those of the Nile, he too is the benevolent spreader of civilization, and he had a distinctly Greek character. In the first century B.C. Strabo thought that the Acheloüs myths represented our struggle to tame nature and make it serve us bountifully:

> Acheloüs, like other rivers, was compared to a bull on account of its noises and the bends in its channel, which are called horns, and to a serpent from its length and its windings . . . and that Hercules, who was usually beneficient, and, besides was going to marry Oeneus' daughter, forcibly confined the irregular current of the river by dams

and dykes, and so drained a great part of the district bordering on the Acheloüs, as a favour to Oeneus; and that is the horn of Amalthea.[26]

This tendency of the river to mirror the human relation to nature becomes a conventional aspect of the motif. But as we can see, nature in Greece is different from that of Egypt, and the river motif reflects that difference. The Greeks too struggle with nature, not just to survive, but to make a highly civilized life of plenty. Their struggle is more difficult, and the river reflects this by everywhere betraying its potential for destruction. The very names of their torrential rivers testify to their violence: "Aracthus" derives from the verb "to smite"; "Thyamis" from "to rush"—the very word for "stream" comes from the Greek verb "to scratch or furrow." Greek etymologies consistently suggest the character, the violence or gentleness of the geography that they identify and name.[27] And if we are attentive to the recurrent use of the river in Greek myth and literature, we get a powerful sense of the precarious nature of their civilization, of the difficulties behind its creation, and of the unique way in which the river torrents epitomize this uneasy relationship with nature.

No mythical figure reveals this cultural self-consciousness more fully than Hercules. The Hellenic Osiris and heroic version of Apollo, he was represented in terms of his technological mastery over nature, and his various tasks repeatedly involved him with rivers. He not only quells Acheloüs, but subdues the Erymanthian boar, the river that periodically destroys the countryside around Mount Erymanthos, and contains the Lernian Hydra by channelling the swamps formed near Argos by the river Lerna and the spring Amymone into nine river beds; the land thus reclaimed was sacred to Demeter and Dionysus.[28] Hercules is also responsible for forming the Peneus river by rending Mount Ossa and Mount Olympus; the result of this heroic feat was the creation of the classical *locus amoenus*, the Vale of Tempe.

Virtually all of the oldest Hercules myths relate to such riverine matters celebrating the culture hero's power to master nature and make life civilized. Hercules's turbulent relations with rivers, however, do not suggest, as some have argued, the conflict of a new cult of Hercules with an older river cult. As we see in the Acheloüs legend, Hercules's violent broils with the rivers are not a matter of animosity, but a basic paradigm for humanity's strenuous but creative relation to the environment and its most protean element, water. The intertwined figures of the hero and the river god present an image of concord being forced from discord.

This ambivalent combination of violence and beneficence is the very nature of Greek perception of landscape and their society, and it enters directly into their art and literature. Their philosophers, geographers, and historians had a sophisticated understanding of the interrelationships between their geography and their society and its history. They saw that their rivers had a literal, not simply metaphoric importance for the founding, maintenance, and also eradication of their communities. Thus, as with the Egyptians, the rivers were associated with memory and the past, and were a means of focusing comparisons between their own and other societies. The *Timaeus*, for example, is a good illustration of this culturally self-conscious literature. Here, introducing the myth of Atlantis, Plato compares the antiquity and learning of Egypt with the discontinuous history of Greece. The comparison is based on geographical differences, and on the relation between a culture, its environment, and its access to the past. We hear of the wisdom of the priests of the Nile, who chided Solon, saying: "you Greeks are always children; there is no Greek that is a greybeard." Solon is told that the reason for this is that

> those who dwell among mountains and highlands and dry places perish more completely than dwellers by rivers or the sea . . . . As for us, the Nile, our universal preserver . . . preserves us from this peril by his rising. On the other side, when the gods cleanse the earth with a flood of waters . . . dwellers in your cities are swept by your rivers into the sea. But on this land of ours, neither then, nor at other times does water descend on the fields from above; its way is even to ascend from beneath. These are the causes and reasons for which the traditions preserved here are reputed the most ancient of any.

Records and history are preserved in the benign terrain of the Nile,

> whereas, with you . . . life has just been furnished with the art of writing and the other requisites of cities, when the torrents come down on you from heaven . . . and leave behind them only the rude and unlettered . . . Your people can recall but one deluge, though there were many before it.[29]

The identification of the river as a link with the past, but set in a natural landscape, becomes one of the most important aspects of its literary treatment.

Clearly, however much the Greeks attempt to endear themselves to the Nile gods, the *genius loci*, the local gods of the region, are the real forces to contend with. Their waters, which, like those of the Holy Land, descend from above with a force of divine judgment, are fundamentally different from those benign Egyptian waters which rise from below. Isis may cooperate with the Greeks to the extent that she can, but her influence is limited, and she has no final influence over the regional powers.

In Greece, then, the customary ways by which rivers serve society are defined, perforce, by local conditions. Theirs was primarily a maritime, commercial society, and while there were gods, like Poseidon, who received honors at each port, their first fealty and affection was for their household gods: the local river deities who were older than the more pretentious members of the pantheon. They were the domestic analogues to the Nile god Hapi, as Prodicus himself seems to have realized: "men of older times considered as gods all things that were useful to them in their lives, such as the sun and the moon, rivers and springs, meadows and fruits, just as the Egyptians regarded the Nile as a god." They were the original *genii locorum*, with incontestable authority; as Percy Gardner explains, "in Greece almost every city had a local nymph, who was mixed up with the legends of its foundation and personified its site. . . . [They were] the most venerable and important members of the tribal pantheon."[30]

The auspice of these river gods and nymphs, who were the offspring of the first elements, was extensive. Isis-like, the local rivers sanctified marriages, guaranteed the participants' purity, ensured fertility and, with their brotherly colleague Apollo, undertook the protection of the young: "Tethys bare to Ocean eddying rivers . . . [and] brought forth a holy company of daughters who with the lord Apollo and the Rivers have youths in their keeping." Leucothea, patroness of childbirth, was herself a river nymph; every child born of woman owed its first vows to the gods of the local rivers, and countless locks of hair were cast dutifully into the mountain creeks of Greece in their honor. Similarly, for the traveller in a strange land, the first source of protection is the sacred place of the local river god, and on safe return home after a perilous journey, one's first expression of gratitude was tendered to the local household gods:

> Glad then was the much-enduring, goodly Odysseus, rejoicing in his own land, and he kissed the earth. . . . And straightway he prayed to the nymphs with upstretched hands:

"Ye Naiad Nymphs, daughters of Zeus, never did I think to behold you again, but now I hail you with loving prayers. Aye, and gifts too will I give, as aforetime, if the daughter of Zeus, she that drives the spool, shall graciously grant me to live, and shall bring to manhood my dear son."[31]

To give a child in name to the local river deities creates for the child a sacred place which is protected by them. The analogue in baptismal and christening rites is clear, although in Christianity the protecting deity, the home or tabernacle, and the *fons vitae* are "catholic" rather than local, transcending time and the river. The association between youth and local rivers is still part of our unconscious. We can see how subtly it enters our literary traditions in Spenser's Marinell, a strapping young man who, at least psychologically, has never left his local river. His emotional limitations are suggested by his inability to be free of his river-nymph mother, Cymodoce. Similarly, in *Comus*, Milton creates a neo-pagan atmosphere in which Lord Bridgewater's children are protected by the river goddess Sabrina; there is a poetic rightness, as well as a conventionality in Sabrina's magical defense of the Lady's chastity.

The nymphs and lord Apollo not only protect youth: they also educate them. For Hesiod, as for Theocritus and others, the nymphs and muses are virtually interchangeable, and their duties are to instruct in both the arts and sciences. At the local waters—most notably, the Heliconian and Castalian springs at Delphi—a three-tiered temple to Apollo, Pan, and the resident nymphs was erected to promote the learning of the village youth.[32] The river muses were a plurality, a cult of no specific number constituting all the *nymphae loci*. Although by the fifth century B.C. the age of specialization had begun for them, the nymphs and muses continued to be loosely linked even through the Renaissance. Along with Apollo they struggle persistently to educate obdurate youth, and even here we can see the characteristic violence behind Greek myths. In the legend of Marsyas, for example, Apollo and the river god, according to some interpretations, compete to prove the superiority of their own musical modes. Marsyas, with his pipes, is not only defeated by Apollo's lyre, but also flayed by his rival for his impudence.[33] The legend is variously explained as the clash of two river cults, the defeat of the primitive by education and science, and the victory of lyric music over the rustic pipe. However we interpret it, we can see that the myth accommodates a number of basic river motifs. From a literary point of view, it is the prototype for the pastoral theme of the contest between two shepherds. It retains its popularity (and its river associations) well into the seventeenth century, in Drayton's contest for the Isle of Lundy in the seventh song of *Poly-Olbion*, for example.

The Greek rivers are unmistakably the product of their own time and place, and their importance is reiterated in their ubiquity in the art, statuary, and literature of the period. Egyptian civilization, influenced by its river, worshipped life; it had a vitalist religion revering life in every form, and believing in its continuation, in all its earthly variety, beyond the river of death. The Jews sought a spiritual life which transcended the corporeal realm; they believed in a moral order based on religious values, and this too was borne in the course of their prophetic rivers. Notwithstanding their indebtedness to their Egyptian counterpart, the Greek rivers have a profounder resemblance to these waters of the Old Testament. Thus, the river cults of Greece have characteristics of both the vitalist Nile and the spiritual Jordan while also reflecting their own landscape and culture. They enshrined intellectual and physical virtues—inner strengths which determine outward behavior and, in turn, irrigate the fields of civilized life. In this, the river mirrors the distinctive quality of their society: it combines the personal and public dimensions of the Jordan and Nile respectively, as we see in the myths of Hercules, for example. His fortitude comes from within and is directed outward, toward ordering his world. However Osirian he is, there is no vestige of the cult of reincarnation; his salvation is his *arête*, not a mystic river bride; his weakness is his own, not part of nature's cycles. Likewise, the rivers, in their destructive and creative capacities, accentuate an ethical rather than a natural order for society and the cult hero.

During the Hellenic age, then, the river begins to take on a more formal symbolic identity, and in the process it becomes useful for the critic as a clue to the way that an author imposes a kind of moral myth on his landscape. The rivers provide keys to the ethical norm of the world described, and thus begin to emerge as *topoi* such as they could not have been in a less literary culture. In its benign form, the river suggests nobility and magnanimity; it welcomes travellers with the worthiest of civic virtues—hospitality. As a destructive torrent it punishes transgressions against moral order and is the voice of a judging god as fierce as Jehovah. Figured in the river is a succinct paradigm of that order or its violation, and most frequently it focuses on the single most important virtue in Hellenic culture, that of hospitality.

Although we might look to Sophocles, Plato, or Theocritus for examples of a literary interest in the river, Homer provides the most sophisticated illustration of accepted conventions for the motif.[34] For example, in the wanderings of Odysseus, we repeatedly see the theme of hospitality and its abuse. Even when battered and desperate, he always performs the rituals of humble petition to the local gods, hoping that his welcome to each new land will be better than his previous ones. Successive strategic episodes in the course of Odysseus's return to Ithaca are introduced by his pious supplication to the nymphs of the local rivers. These are the prayers customarily offered by the weary traveller at the mercy of his host, made in the name of the *genius loci*. Thus, in Book 5, the shipwrecked Odysseus, bruised by a truculent Poseidon and marinated in his briny waters, feels the fresh waters of a "fair-flowing river" as he struggles toward the land of the Phaeacians. The river signals the possibility of shelter, and he invokes the aid of its presiding deity: "as to one greatly longed-for . . . I come . . . seeking to escape . . . Poseidon." This invocation of the sacred privilege of the wanderer is accentuated by the contrast between the refreshing current of the stream and the bitter sea, and his reception among the Phaeacians is foreshadowed by the salubrious welcome that he is accorded by the river god. The rapport between Odysseus and the river god suggests a harmony between man and nature that Virgil will echo in Book 8 of the *Aeneid*: "So he spoke, and the god straight-way stayed his stream, and checked the waves, and made a calm before him and brought him safely to the mouth of the river" (5. 450–453).

This passage (extending from lines 440–453) anticipates the most important and protracted of Odysseus's arrivals, that in Book 13, and his grateful prayers to the "Naiad Nymphs" on his return to Ithaca. His piety toward his household gods reminds us that he is the lord returned to his own home and presages his successful dispatch of the suitors. Homer did not, of course, have to tell his audience what happens to Odysseus—the story was familiar enough. But he is always careful to show *how* things were done, and in these passages, in the rituals that Odysseus dutifully performs, we detect Homer's desire to emphasize the importance of these local river gods and the ethos that they represent. These episodes—Odysseus's prayers and their reception by the gods of the land—serve as the prototype for poets who want to show that their wandering heroes have at last found their natural and destined ports, and that nature itself seems to recognize the homecoming.

Homer uses the river of local cult to serve his literary designs. He draws on its network of associations to establish the context and to delineate the objectives of certain episodes, particularly those which emphasize Odysseus's foreignness or displacement. A more complicated illustration of this occurs in the episode with Eumaeus, in the sixteenth and seventeenth books of the *Odyssey*. A continuation of the homecoming sequence begun in Book 12, here the old retainer's loyalty in the presence of his disguised master contrasts with the arrogant outrage against the local gods and the code of hospitality by Melantheus. The scene is presented with a sentimentality that Dickens himself might have admired. An appropriate setting is created to accentuate the violation of decency: Eumaeus is leading the blind old man, a poor visitor to Ithaca, to the palace, and they come upon a spring with its

> fair-flowing fountain, wherefrom the townsfolk drew water—this Ithacus had made, and Neritus, and Polyctor, and around was a grove of poplars, that grow by the waters, circling it on all sides, and down the cold water flowed from the rock above, and on the top was built an altar to the nymphs where all passers-by made offerings— there Melantheus . . . met them. (17. 204–13)

Homer has savored that passage. Every detail intensifies the nostalgic, holy calm that will be profaned by the goatherd. The presence of the chaste, courteous nymphs is felt, so that we are the more shocked when these two old men are all but mugged by this young hoodlum. The moral tone is established by the goddesses of hospitality, and it is specifically their presence here that defines the poet's objectives. Thus in his helplessness Eumaneus appeals to them in particular: "Nymphs of the fountain, daughters of Zeus, if ever Odysseus burned upon your altars pieces of the thighs of lambs or kids . . . fulfil for me this prayer" (17. 238–43). This homely episode is perfectly composed: it simply cannot be argued that such deliberation is not involved in Homeric literature. The setting by the spring, with the suggestion of the appropriate gods, the act of violation and the petition, all are perfectly balanced to create a melodramatic tableau of the abuse of hospitality. Not only do the nymphs set the ethical norm for the scene, but they also identify it with the nature of the place, and this gives moral and emotional weight to Odysseus's return home.

In the *Odyssey* Homer clearly had one aspect of the river cult in mind as particularly appropriate for reinforcing his account of Odysseus's return to his native land. In the *Iliad* he emphasizes another aspect of the river, one better suited to the epic tale of the wrath of Achilles—that is, the river's torrential force. Although we seem to see two very different rivers in these two works, they are drawn in equal measure from the river cults which had their basis in the cultural geography, and their literary function is virtually the same. Different as they appear to be, they impose the same myth on the landscape. Thus, the torrential rivers of the *Iliad* also provide us with critical insights into that work. Accurate descriptions of torrential destruction are carefully placed to clarify the point of particular episodes, and in this the rivers are used much as they are in the *Odyssey*. In many respects these violent rivers are like the waters of divine judgment in the Bible, but they have a distinctly Greek emphasis on ethical order, rather than on spiritual or moral order. Often the passages have the symmetry of a diptych with details of natural and civic beauty balanced against a scene of destruction by natural and civic disorder, and the contrast serves to urge social harmony and the respect for peace. Such is the context for the setting that prepares us for Patroclus's havoc among the Trojans:

> And even as beneath a tempest the whole black earth is oppressed, on a day in harvest-time, when Zeus poureth forth rain most violently, whenso in anger he waxeth wroth against men that by violence give crooked judgments in the place of gathering, and drive justice out, recking not of the vengeance of the gods; and all their rivers flow in flood, and many a hillside do the torrents furrow deeply, and down to the dark sea they rush headlong from the mountains with a mighty roar, and the tilled fields of men are wasted; even so mighty was the roar of the mares of Troy as they sped on. (16.385–93)

This passage has a striking resemblance to the torrential rivers of Deuteronomy, but its emphasis is essentially different. Here too the rivers are agents of judgment, but the crime is against peace, nature, and justice, not religion. Our perceptions move between vivid details of the ordered life of the city and the country—the rows of tilled fields ripe for harvest, and the agora, the center of communal order—and the black furrows of destruction and the civil violence and discord that mock the "crooked judgments" and iniquities of mankind. The passage brilliantly projects the sense of waste by succinctly showing what is lost, why it is lost, and the agent of destruction. In the turbulence of the deluge we perceive the sodden fragments that remind us of the beauty and peace that have been broken. However, the passage is an extended simile; the glimpse of both human folly and social order is but a shadow of the main event of war and destruction which we can better appraise by this pointed and stylized digression based in landscape description, or *topographia*.

For Homer, as for Hesiod, then, the rivers are "givers of good things" working for human good, and so they are the logical agents in the destruction of an ungrateful people. In a striking scene at the very center of the *Iliad*, during a pause in the action, there is another brief glimpse of time and events beyond the scope of the war. Removed from the turmoil, we can see human impiety and folly and behold the processes of judgment and purification that extend, as Plato also realized, beyond human memory. Again all the details of the setting are contrived to elicit the full range of the river motif:

> But when all the bravest of the Trojans had died and many of the Argives . . . and the city of Priam was sacked in the tenth year, and the Argives had gone back in their ships to their dear native land, then verily did Poseidon and Apollo take counsel to sweep away the wall, bringing against it the might of all the rivers that flow forth from the mountains of Ida to the sea—Rhesus and Heptaporus and Caresus and Rhodius, and Granicus and Aesepus, and goodly Scamander, and Simoïs . . . of all these did Phoebus Apollo turn the mouths together, and for nine days' space he drove their flood against the wall; and Zeus rained ever continually, that the sooner he might whelm the wall in the salt sea. And the Shaker of Earth, bearing his trident in his hands, was himself the leader, and swept forth upon the waves all the foundations of beams and stones, that the Achaeans had laid with toil, and made all smooth along the strong stream of Hellespont, and again covered the great beach with sand, when he had swept away the wall; and the rivers he turned back to flow in the channel, where aforetime they had been wont to pour their fair streams of water. (12.14–34)

The dissolution of the unholy wall, suggestive of a ritual of purification, is performed by the joint forces of Apollo and the rivers. We suddenly see human heroics *sub specie aeternitatis*; the ease and certainty with which the bravest human achievements are effaced emphasize an inscrutable moral order that is realized in nature. The attitude toward the rivers is objective: in their violence is meaning that affirms sanity, decency, and piety in human affairs.

In its repeated use throughout the *Iliad*, the river functions as a touchstone. Its appearances in this formulaic pattern, juxtaposing good, evil, and their judgment, reinforce the strict symmetry of the epic, and enable us to look more comprehendingly at the wrath of Achilles at its height. The most important episode in the *Iliad*, the interlocked sequences of the *aristeia* and the *theomachia*, is a vast magnification of this river motif and, with the accumulated effects of many river passages, it forces us to see the war and the vainglorious values that perpetuate it, from a much larger, more encompassing perspective defined by the river itself.

With the balance characteristic of the *Iliad*, this episode is paired off with the lesser *aristeia* of Achilles's foil, Diomedes, in Book 5.[35] While he seems conspicuous for his nobility, he too is compared to a river torrent in a passage which juxtaposes the beauties of peace with the ugliness of war, even if nobly waged:

> but of Tydeus' son couldst thou not have told with which host of the twain he was joined, whether it was with the Trojans that he had fellowship or with the Achaeans. For he stormed across the plain like unto a winter torrent at the full, that with its swift flood sweeps away the embankments; this the close-fenced embankments hold not back, neither do the walls of the fruitful vineyards stay its sudden coming when the rain of Zeus driveth it on; and before it in multitudes the fair works of men fall in ruin. Even in such wise before Tydeus' son were the thick battalions of the Trojans driven in rout. (5.84–93)

The passage is, typically, a set piece, reminding us at once of the pleasures of fruitful peace, the suffering resulting from natural and unnatural upheavals, and the wrath of the gods. However noble and likable we find Diomedes, the comparison is stark, and ultimately made grotesque through the comic encounter with Aphrodite—a detail that enters inauspiciously into Books 20 and 21. If at this point, in Book 5, we do not realize what Homer means for us to see in the river similes, the successive river passages, particularly those of Books 12 and 16, also set pieces, further accentuate the inevitability of judgment on human folly. Their repetition intensifies our awareness of the effects of war, as does the delicate balance that, for the greater part of the *Iliad*, holds the Greeks and Trojans from total self-destruction. This balance is, of course, broken with Achilles's return to the war, and literally the dykes of restraint are thrown open. The metaphoric havoc of the river similes is now ready to be realized in action. Thus, through Books 20 and 21 there is a systematic intensification of combat that raises the river from its metaphoric dimension directly and dramatically into the action, and finally, in the *theomachia*, into an elemental conflict of the cosmic forces of fire and water.

The sequence begins with Zeus summoning the gods in preparation for war; the first called are the rivers, and "there was no river that came not, save only Oceanus, nor any nymph, of all that haunt the fair copses, the springs that feed the rivers, and the grassy meadows" (20.7–10). The gods take their sides, and here we are reminded of the parallel episode with Diomedes, for the "river Xanthus, and laughter-loving Aphrodite" take the Trojans' behalf. They are not a very awesome couple when we recall the comic result of Aphrodite's previous military efforts. In one last glimpse of the slowly mobilizing gods, we see Hephaestus and Scamander, and are thus prepared for the elemental treatment of the *theomachia* which will conclude the episode.[36]

Achilles then begins his broad sweep of slaughter, destroying in his way a virtual army of river scions. Everywhere throughout this section Homer reiterates the river motif. Achilles himself, however, cannot be compared to a torrent, as his counterpart could be, because he is to act out the metaphor from Book 5 by fighting with a torrential river. Rather, he is compared with the contrasting element: fire (490–493). The conflict of elements, however, remains merely metaphoric at this point.

It comes closer to the dramatic surface, though, as Achilles's fury becomes savage unlike anything else in the *Iliad*. He leaps into the Scamander and flays the fleeing army, preparing his cold-blooded sacrifice in Patroclus's name. As his fury carries into Book 21 (which also opens with an extended river passage), we are told particularly of Xanthus, son of Zeus, and his discomfiture until Achilles encounters Asteropaeus, another son of a river. Achilles taunts his victim with a fiery display of hubris, vaunting that he is a son of Zeus and mightier than the gods: "Wherefore as Zeus is mightier than rivers that murmur seaward, so mightier too is the seed of Zeus than the seed of a river. For lo, hard beside thee is a great River, if so be he can avail thee aught; but it may not be that one should fight with Zeus, the son of Chronos" (21.185–95). Achilles's excesses have weakened his logic, and his false rhetoric betrays the inversion of nature that is manifest in his actions. Achilles has virtually identified himself with Zeus and ignores the Hellenic commonplace that we were carefully informed of at the beginning of Book 21: that Xanthus is among Zeus's firstborn. His diatribe overflows with the kind of false judgment that rivers have been punishing throughout the *Iliad*, and he overlooks the possibility that "his dread thunder whenso it crasheth from heaven" might light on his own head.

Thus, "recking not of the vengeance of the gods," Achilles provokes Xanthus to action, and the river metaphors begin to be acted out. The river god begins to restore nature's hierarchy by invoking Apollo, another "child of Zeus" and, in effect, putting Achilles in his proper place and giving him "the lie direct." What follows is a striking adaptation of the conventional river descriptions:

> the River rushed upon him with surging flood, and roused all his streams tumultuously, and swept along the many dead that lay thick within his bed . . . these he cast forth to the land, bellowing the while like a bull, and the living he saved under his fair streams, hiding them in eddies deep and wide. In terrible wise about Achilles towered the tumultuous wave, and the stream as it beat upon his shield thrust him backward. (21.233–42)

The bull-like river torrent has become part of the action; instead of descriptive digression or a simile illustrating divine judgment, we see Xanthus administering the sentence of the gods on one of false reckoning. We still perceive, in the froth, the river's usual beauty and benevolence, but these have been perverted by Achilles and the need for retribution.

The accretions of river imagery and river action continue as Achilles is inundated by Xanthus—a river torrent described by the simile of a river torrent. Rhetorically, the action and imagery turn back upon themselves like a river in spate:

> he swerved from beneath the flood and fled ever onward, and the River followed after, flowing with a mighty roar. As when a man that guideth its flow leadeth from a dusky spring a stream of water amid his plants and garden-plots, a mattock in his hands, and cleareth away the dams from the channel—and as it floweth all the pebbles beneath are swept along therewith and it glideth swiftly onward with murmuring sound down a sloping place and outstrippeth even him that guideth it;—even thus did the flood of the River ever overtake Achilles for all he was fleet of foot; for the gods are mightier than men. (21.256–65)

The effect here is remarkable. Achilles the city destroyer is compared with the husbandman, and in the shadow of this simile he is reduced to nothing. The river is virtually a primal element that can be compared to nothing other than itself: the world literally becomes a watery realm where creation, destruction, and judgment are one. The river, compared to itself, follows the inevitable course of nature, and Achilles, in the terms of the metaphor, is ejected from the natural realm. Through the devastation we see the possibility of peace—but nothing of Achilles. The significance of the Trojan campaign is obliterated; it is nothing in the face of time and natural order, with which society should be in harmony. The passage allows us to see the heroics of Achilles in a sane perspective—as destructive vainglory contrary to civilized and peaceful nature. His false reckonings have nearly been punished once for all as we watch his almost total defeat. Again, Homer achieves this effect through topographical description.

But the workings of fate extend beyond Achilles, and even beyond the war: the final destruction by the rivers is yet to come, as we have already been told in Book 12. Achilles is preserved because fate transcends him—and because there is one more stage in the intensification of this unnatural combat originating in Achilles's wrath. The final stage is, of course, the *theomachia* itself, where the human conflict is absorbed into that of the elements. Achilles has been defeated by Scamander, we have seen his utter fallibility, but the process of judgment goes beyond him alone, and incorporates all the self-consuming passions of both hosts. Thus, the *theomachia* is the projection of all the human and elemental passions and oppositions which are themselves part of the universal cosmic order. Achilles's heated passion is transferred to Hephaestus who "against the River turned his gleaming flame." The final stage of the holocaust is initiated: Achilles is spared so that the Trojans and Greek can destroy one another. The last bit of restraint which held the world in balance is lifted. Now the full havoc of war, the indiscriminate battle of both gods and men, can be fought out over the passive city—all factions become unimportant.

The Scamander episode is the crisis of the *Iliad*; it marks the extreme of Achilles's fury and strength (Homer's professed subject matter) and allows the final stage in the widening compass of the conflict. But it does something else as well. The river is not a warlike god; he defends the *status quo*, and even the descriptions of his violence reaffirm the beauties of civilization and peace. Without the river we could not apprehend the magnitude of human strength, but we also could not understand the degree of waste, the shortsightedness of human judgment, the danger of unrestrained passion. Against the river landscape we are able to see mankind in perspective. The river motif reflects the potential civilized norm available to society, and in this it sets off the culture that lies behind the war and, ultimately, beneath its rubble. The *genius loci*, Scamander, attempts to preserve the city—even importunes Achilles in restrained and courteous tones. His violation is like the abuse of hospitality in the *Odyssey*. The unmilitant river, withered beneath hot Hephaestus's glare, is mourned by the poet, but its spirit is indomitable, so that, looking ahead in time, we know that "once more in the fair river-bed the flood rushed down" (21.382). Its resilience is like that of Hercules and Acheloüs and the continuing efforts to resist the forces of confusion. Homer could not have made his point more clearly than by having Achilles assault the very river itself.

Homer has made the river a touchstone for understanding the ideas and events of the "heroic" *Iliad*. He has created a cultural myth out of the river and its landscape; in its literary treatment the river is a link between humanity, the realm of nature, and the gods. It is a mirror that remains constant, unchanging in its nature, so that the flux around it becomes comprehensible against its own stability. In both the *Iliad* and the *Odyssey*, then, we see a marriage of myth and geography which amounts to a transformation of nature to art. Later authors, such as Virgil and Spenser, for example, seemed to sense what Homer had done with his river and made similar use of their own.

4. Confluence

Flumina senserunt ipsa (Ovid, *Amores* 3)

It is little wonder that the swollen waters from the East and South should be confluent in the more capacious beds of the Roman rivers. The geopolitical currents naturally tended to harmonize the extremes of the empire from which flowed the cultural, religious, political, and economic lifeblood of Rome, and appropriately, the Roman interest in the river reflects that cultural harmony. If for Moses the west bank of the Jordan was the world beyond, for the Romans all east of the Jordan was "*Perea*," or "the world beyond" Rome. Acheloüs's cult enjoyed an increased popularity and continued to be associated with hospitality, and the quest for a New Troy was also a quest for another Xanthus.

Likewise the Nile continued to figure high civilization in its material manifestation, and threefold syncretisms, such as that of

Isis, Tyche, and Fortuna, continued to reflect the nilotic origins of
the goddess's wisdom and benefits, as we see in the famous mosaic
in her temple at Praeneste.[37] The murals present a panoramic view
of the Nile, foreshortened to give an encompassing perspective of
the full variety of a civilized world fertilized by the river. The
interpretations of the mosaics have been varied, but the most
obvious thing commemorated in them has been overlooked. In that
serene floating world, with noble monuments, peaceful entertainments, the courtly hunt amid the maze of life, is an image of orderly
society—an image of a particular kind of enviable life, overrich with
the physical delights that, any Roman would argue, come from civil
order.

Romans conscientiously cultivated the influence of Greece and
Egypt. In this they were guided by two seemingly contradictory
impulses: on the one hand, a strong patriotic belief in the *Nova
Italia*; and on the other, an affected Hellenism and local pride that
asserted regional identity and fidelity to the Greek tradition. And
throughout Roman literature—in Virgil, Ovid, Horace, even as late
as Ausonius—there is a delicate balance between imperial unity and
local diversity.

The political order has its natural manifestation in the geography,
so that the Italian landscape itself seems to bring together the
different kinds of rivers found throughout the empire. In these
waters we seem to see the unquiet marriage of Nile and Scamander.
Flowing in opposite directions down the mountain spine of peninsu-
lar Italy, the springs, streams, and rivers serve the same essential
needs of a dry land. Many of them flow the year round, but they are
also potentially torrential, having the torrent's chaotic, destructive
violence. As a result the rivers of Rome and Roman art and
literature are conspicious for their unpredictability. We repeatedly
meet with rivers which are "usually" benign but whose "unnatural"
flood waters surprise the local inhabitants with paradoxical regularity:

> Remember to settle with tranquil heart the problem of the hour! All
> else is borne along like some river, now gliding peacefully in mid-
> channel into the Tuscan Sea, now rolling polished stones, uprooted
> trees, and flocks and homes together, with echoing of the woods
> while the wild deluge stirs up the peaceful streams.[38]

The river for Horace is a warning against complacent faith in
fortune, one obviously not well heeded, as anyone knows who has

seen Florence bemired by Arno's silt. Even the larger perennial river systems are a combination of a charging bull of Greece and the reclining peaceful figure of the Nile god. The Po and Tiber provide navigable waterways, but their currents are strong, their floods frequent and, from Virgil to Pliny and Claudian, the tendency was to flatter these fickle deities and to present them as more benign than they in fact were.

In these characteristics the rivers themselves provide an image of the culture that they nourished. Held apart by their mountain rift, they paradoxically unify the realm—keep it together, yet divided. The extremes of their behavior are like the extremes of civil and political unrest that will beset those unmindful of *res publicas*, so that the inundations of Rome by the thundering hordes descending violently from above the Alps is best described in terms of the torrent. More than in Greece, though less than in Egypt, there was a geographical unity which fostered political unity. This unity through diversity, combined with an intense cultural self-awareness, gave the Roman a strong sense of place in which geography was less a part of nature than an extension of his political vision. And so while the rivers from the East and South found their ways onto the plains of Latium and Gallia, they took on still another, more artificial quality characteristic of a more modern society. Thus the rivers of Rome have less of the primitive religious quality, fewer features of magic, myth, or heroic virture, but more of the sense of civic order: we think of Rome in terms of aqueducts rather than rivers whose natural course they alter.

The literature of imperial Rome, especially the epic, was an expression of this cultivated political self-image. Many epics were historical works on popular subjects, with copious geographical digressions which appealed to local allegiance. Such was Naevius's *Bellum Punicum*, a geographical epic of the first century B.C., *Aetna*, and the works of Varro, Rutilius Namatianus, and Coelius. Augustus gave more than casual encouragement to writers using the myths of national origin and Trojan descent, whose works celebrated Italian Rome's identity as the New Troy. In these the rivers repeatedly mirrored this political design. The river thus becomes harnessed in a new way, by a literary technology which had its origins in Homer. This more highly civilized river becomes for the Roman a *topos*, a *locus communis* for his ideas, and as a result it provides a direct critical approach to the literature itself.[39]

This use of the river receives its most imaginative form in the

Aeneid: Virgil's adaptation of the Homeric river motif established the channel that it would follow for centuries thereafter. The complex political objectives of the *Aeneid* find their clearest expression in the relation between Aeneas and Tiber. Throughout the *Aeneid* Virgil uses his consummate art to create an authoritative image of unity—unity of nation and race, of human history and divine destiny, the political unity that enabled Italy to survive the Hannibalic Wars and which would help Rome and the *Nova Italia* retain the civic solidarity necessary to resist the forces of barbaric chaos beyond its frontiers.[40]

Much of the legendary material of the *Aeneid* was outmoded, even rejected outright. But the debates over Aeneas's landing site, the claims of the native opposition, the name of the Tiber itself, indeed even Aeneas's very involvement in their national history were but gnats to Virgil and were swept away by the broad stroke of authority and the consolidating skill of the poet. He revived the Aeneas myth, out of fashion since the third century B.C., relocated the hero's arrival at the mouth of Tiber at the site of Ostia rather than Lavinium, and then displaced the currently popular legend of the founding Alban kings. His objective was to subordinate these details to a unified, coherent view of this nation-founder who brought his household gods from beside the Scamander to the banks of Tiber, built a city, and from whom "came the Latin race, the Lords of Alba, and the walls of Lofty Rome."[41]

Virgil has no greater assistance in consolidating this view of the reconciliation of time and place, and Aeneas has no stronger partisan to help him fulfil his destiny than the Tiber. The entire Italian section of the epic, the culmination of all the action, rests upon the relation between Tiber and Aeneas. The informing idea behind the *Aeneid* derives from the *Iliad*: the Latin hero is Achilles's opposite, and he redeems the destruction wrought by the Greek. In Aeneas's and his household gods' rapport with Tiber we see the restoration of the order that was violated in Achilles's enmity with Scamander. Virgil's creative hero, in harmony with the local genius, is the inversion of Homer's destructive hero at odds with it. Aeneas's quest is for another Xanthus, where his household gods can be installed in their destined home; and this, as he says to Andromache, is the divine purpose behind the dispersion following the fall of Troy:

> Fare ye well, ye whose own destiny is already achieved; we are still summoned from fate to fate. Your rest is won. No ocean plains need

ye plough, no ever-retreating Ausonian fields need ye seek. A copy of Xanthus ye see and a Troy which your own hands have built under happier omens, I pray, and more beyond the range of Greeks. If ever I enter the Tiber and Tiber's neighbouring fields and look on the city-walls granted to my race, hereafter, of our sister cities and allied peoples, in Epirus, in Hesperia . . . of these twain we shall make one Troy in spirit. May that charge await our children's children.[42] (3.493–505)

Throughout the *Aeneid* Virgil emphasizes the concord between the local gods of Italy—the *genii locorum* who are jointly represented by Tiber—and Aeneas's destiny. Like Odysseus, his other literary model, Aeneas is a restless traveller trying to find his way home, and he knows that he is in the right place at the right time only when he arrives at Tiber's outlet. The description of the ordained landing site is contrived to accentuate the rightness of the place—its hospitable appearance, its security, its beauty—and to emphasize this, Virgil has it reverberate with echoes of the arrival of storm-torn Odysseus at Phaeacia, and at Ithaca:

> And now the sea was reddening with the rays of dawn, and from high heaven saffron-hued Aurora shone in roseate car, when the winds fell, and every breath sank suddenly, and the oar blades strive amid the sluggish calm of waters. Then lo! Aeneas, gazing forth from the flood, sees a mighty forest. Through its midst the Tiber with pleasant streams, leaps forth to sea in swirling eddies and yellow with plenteous sand. Around and above, birds of varied plumes, that haunt the banks and river-channel, charmed the sky with song, and flitted amid the forest. He bids his comrades change their course and turn their prows to land, and joyfully enters the shady river. (7.25–36)

Throughout the early sections treating Aeneas's arrival there are such descriptive passages which are clearly meant to show that nature is in harmony with history. In this passage Virgil had to touch up nature to make Aeneas's welcome appear more agreeable. The prevalent view of the landing was that expressed by Fabius Maximus, and it is very different from Virgil's romantic fiction, for he tells us that Aeneas "was not at all pleased to have come to a country so very bare and shingly."[43] But for Virgil the arrival is more like a return home, like Odysseus's in Book 16, and it must be acknowledged with appropriate gratitude: "So speaking, he straightway wreathes his temples with a leafy bough and prays to the genius of the place, and Earth, first of gods; to the nymphs and the streams yet unknown" (7.135–38). Here Aeneas's piety also suggests rightful possession—a homecoming like Odysseus's.

Everywhere in the *Aeneid* Virgil associates Italy with the Tiber and in so doing, transcends contentious issues. The *genius loci* who antecedes all partisan politics ratifies the rightness of Aeneas's claim. It is in the context of the river that the past and the future are to be known and the dynastic theme unveiled, and Aeneas is the central figure in that history. Tiber, in his personified form, thus acts out all the attributes of the invisible river gods of Greek literature, delivering prophecy, assuring the hero's protection, and welcoming him with the courtesy due to a troubled traveller. And in protecting young Ascanius, he also ensures the dynastic continuity by which history is fulfilled.

These central themes of the *Aeneid* are developed early in the Italian section of the poem, when Aeneas, fraught with doubts and plagued by the threats of war, sinks into slumber by the Tiber and is accorded a vision of the "very god of the place, Tiberinus of the pleasant stream." The river reassures the mortal Aeneas that he is acting in harmony with providence in thus relocating Troy:

> "O seed of a race divine, thou who from foemen's hands bringest back to us our Trojan city, and preservest her towers for ever . . . here thy home is sure—draw not back—and sure are thy gods! . . . Not doubtful is my prophecy." (8.31–49)

Virgil has obviously thought about what the ancient river gods were and were meant to do. He is not writing from an implicit belief in the god of Tiber: he has studied their cult and decided that they can best project Aeneas's character as a nation-founder and spreader of civilization, and can best articulate the mysterious design of nature and the prophetic and historical themes, thus consolidating the essence of the epic. When he hears Tiber's prophecy, Aeneas puts himself in the god's hands and embraces his destiny. In accepting the god's claims and his own role in establishing a new Troy, Aeneas accepts his homeland and, no less pious than his Greek prototype, he offers a prayer which effectively ends the Odyssean aspect of the *Aeneid* and prepares for the *Iliad*-like defense of his country.

> "Ye Nymphs, Laurentine Nymphs, from whom rivers have their being, and thou, O father Tiber, thou and thy hallowed streams— receive Aeneas, and at last shield him from perils. In whatsoever springs thy pools contain thee, who pitiest our travails, from what- soever soil thou flowest forth in all thy beauty, ever with my offer- ings, ever with my gifts, shalt thou be graced, thou hornèd stream lord of Hesperian waters. Only be thou with me, and more surely confirm thy will!" (8.71–78)

Solicitous about Aeneas's destiny, Tiber takes him in hand and makes sure that he finds his way to the site of Rome: "I myself will guide thee along the banks straight up the stream, that so, impelled by oars, thou mightest o'ercome the opposing current" (8.57–59). Tiber's promise is, of course, fulfilled shortly after, and we see a conspicuous example of nature's compliance with the demands of destiny as his notoriously swift current abates to facilitate the journey upsteam: "All that night long Tiber calmed his swelling flood, and flowing back with silent wave stood so still . . . that the oars might know no struggle" (8.86–93).

Evolved from his Homeric ancestors, the Tiber acts as the voice of reason and calm wisdom, promoting reconciliation (with Juno in Book 8), moderation, friendship, and faith. It is through Tiber's influence that the warm filial relationship is formed between Aeneas, Evander, and Pallas, and it is specifically in violation of the river's spirit that Lausus vainly and pathetically defies destiny and angrily vows vengeance on Aeneas for the death of his son (10. 833). All the events leading to the fulfillment of destiny occur through the assistance of Tiber, and in the later books, which bear the greatest influence from the *Iliad*, the Tiber's presence, as new-world Scamander, is equally great, particularly in his confutation of the fiery Turnus. When Turnus attempts to fire the fleet in Book 9, Cymodicea turns the ships into river nymphs, and there is splendid irony in Turnus's rather obtuse conclusion that now "one half the world is lost to them, but the earth is in our hands" (9.130–31). And when Ascanius's youthful impetuosity gets him into trouble, these nymphs set out, presumably by river, to warn Aeneas, who is in Etruria gathering allies. Indeed, the roll call of allies echoes with the names of cities and nations whose rivers eventually contribute to Tiber's waters, so that their enumeration accentuates the sense of unity in diversity.[44]

Throughout the *Aeneid*, then, Virgil conflates the myth, history, and geography of the Tiber to lend greater authority to his vision of a dynastic history culminating in Augustus, and to present us with an image of nature enriched by and enriching civilization. In so doing, he develops the central literary metaphor of the *Aeneid*: that the unnatural violation of god and nature which is most vividly presented in Achilles's defiance of Scamander and the destruction of that river's city, is redeemed by Aeneas's concord with Tiber and the establishment of a New Troy in Rome. Thus the alliance of Aeneas and the nation's river results in the defeat of fiery and

Achillian Turnus; Virgil could not better stress the rightness of
Aeneas's claims and the importance of his achievement than by
contrasting him with Achilles and Scamander. What Virgil has done
is extrapolate all that is implicit in the primitive river god of
antiquity, and take the Homeric paradigm in which the river defines
the heroic (and in the case of the *Iliad*, destructive) action, and then
adapt them to his own landscape and his image of the achievement
of civil harmony. For Virgil, then, the river becomes the *genius loci*,
the god of the nation brought fully into the service of a secular,
literary view of history.

Virgil's Tiber is in every respect the naturalizing of the river
motif. The river flows with the national purpose and reflects the
patriotic spirit that thereafter enshrined the three figures Tiber,
Aeneas, and tower-capped Rome for all posterity.[45] The three
components of the river's primary public roles emerge: the river is
the *genius loci*, it is associated with a heroic, moral, or civic *virtu*,
and its banks, remarkable for their beauty and historical significance, provide him with a site for founding a city or nation. These
features, each suggestive of certain secondary ideas, are only implicit in the Homeric treatment of the river, and in the river's place
in primitive cult, but in Virgil they become *topoi* essential to the
poet's art. The river is never quite the same after Virgil.

This literary use of the river in the *Aeneid* was not lost on Virgil's
contemporaries and immediate successors. Consider, for example,
Lucan's *The Civil War*. Virgil, having an artist's sense of form, saw
the relation between the rivers of landscape, religious myth, and the
Homeric epics, and he put them together at the center of his epic.
Lucan had only to look at the *Aeneid* to know how to use the Italian
rivers for his theme of a nation divided and at war with itself. He is
"working," or developing multiple variations on a literary motif
defined by Virgil; we will see the same relation between originality
and invention in the English tradition in the river motif of *The
Faerie Queene* and *Poly-Olbion*. As Drayton would do later, Lucan
takes the motif that he finds in his model and makes it dominate the
entire structure of his work; there is no more important or more
often repeated image in *The Civil War*.[46] His heroine is always
Rome, though the combatants are the twin figures of Pompey and
Caesar. The idea of "two-ness," of opposites paired off, pervades
the work, and the corollary for the political and military division is
developed in terms of the geography of Italy and its rivers, with

their common source and divergent descent. The feud between Caesar and Magnus divides the nation like a great natural rift:

> he [Caesar] resolved to make Capua the base of his chief campaign, and from there to disperse and extend his forces in order to meet the enemy where Apennine raises up the centre of Italy. . . . Midway between the two seas . . . the mountains stretch. . . . From vast springs the mountain engenders mighty rivers and scatters their streams along the water-sheds that lead to two seas. Eastward flow the swift Metaursus and rushing Crustumium . . . and there the Po, as mighty a river as any which earth discharges. . . . But the waters that run down the western slopes of Apennine give birth to the Tiber and the Rubuta . . . and also . . . swift Vulturnus . . . and the Sarnus (2. 392–424)

The irresoluble opposition of the two leaders is just part of the natural primitive bifurcation of the land. In full, the passage, which is generically an epic river catalogue, is a powerful piece of descriptive verse, its solid rhythms conveying a geological strength and evoking primitive disruptions in the very earth's foundation. The self-destructive clash of these two commanders is like the earth's own self-inflicted violence:

> the ridge was once longer than Italy is now, before the pressure of the sea sundered the isthmus and the water drove back the land; but when the earth was crushed out by the two seas, that end of the Apennines was surrendered to Pelorus in Sicily.
>
> Caesar, frantic for war, rejoices to find no passage except by shedding blood; it pleases him that the land of Italy on which he tramples supplies him with a foe, that the fields which he assaults are not undefended. (2.435–442)

The confrontation of Pompey and Caesar is as much the product of the correspondence of time and place as was Aeneas's arrival at Tiber mouth, but the forces which drive nature are far more ominous.

In evoking a primitive awesomeness in their meeting, Lucan also suggests that they represent moral opposites, and here too the river provides the necessary defining imagery, for "the first place that saw the rivals halt and pitch their camps side by side was the land which the swift Genusus and gentler Hapsus encompass with their banks. The Hapsus is made navigable by a lake, which it drains imperceptibly with quiet flow; but the Genusus is driven fast by the snows" (5.461–66). The rivals, "side by side," implicitly share in this contrast of the rivers; after the river description Lucan makes the

comparison explicit, speaking of Magnus's love and gentler qualities, and "frantic" Caesar's compulsive eagerness for war.

Pompey is Lucan's heroic personification of Rome, but the author
is careful to emphasize that Rome herself is always the real victim.
The picture of civil disorder through the violation of law is characteristically Roman, and, from what we have already seen of the river
motif, it is perfectly appropriate that it should become the vehicle
for this aspect of Lucan's theme. Where we see virtues reflected in
Homer's rivers, in Lucan's we see law. Thus Caesar's initial crime
involves the violation of the Rubicon, where civil law is embedded
just as divine law was in the Jordan. In peaceful Rubicon resides the
jurisprudent *genius* of the realm, the very spirit of the Roman
populus, and when Caesar

> reached the little river Rubicon, the general saw a vision of his
> distressed country . . . her face expressed deep sorrow, and from her
> head, crowned with towers, the white hair streamed abroad . . . and
> her speech was broken by sobs: "Whither do ye march further . . . if
> ye come as law-abiding citizens, here must ye stop." (1.186–95)

The humble river, even when swollen by three days of rain, is but a
thin thread forming the border between peace and war, and its
transgression, however perverse it might be, is a simple enough act
for one like Caesar:

> First the cavalry took station slantwise across the stream, to meet its
> flow; thus the current was broken, and the rest of the army forded the
> water with ease. When Caesar had crossed the stream . . . he cried,
> "here I leave peace behind me and legality which has been scorned
> already." (1.215–26)

Again, descriptive detail comes to the service of Lucan's greater
design, as the strategem to break the river's current complements
the unnatural ease with which law, then peace are left behind. The
victory over gentle Rubicon is perversely simple. ·

Lucan is a master of such symbolic landscapes. However symbolic
they are, though, with their moral and mythic encrustations visible,
they are always remarkably real and true to nature. Like Virgil he
apprehends a divine pattern in the landscape, but for him it is an
inauspicious one. When he prepares the setting for the battle of
Pharsalia, his description of the landscape incorporates the heroic
legends which tell of its formation—those of Ossa, Olympus, Pe-
lion, Pindus, Hercules and his rivers, and the heroes who created
Tempe, Pharsalia, and other legendary settings. For Lucan the hero

is inseparable from his landscape, and history is like a system of interconnecting rivers;

> in this way the swamp was parted and broken up into many rivers. From there the Aeas, clear but of little volume, flows westward to the Ionian sea; with no stronger stream glides the father of ravished Isis; and he who came near to marrying the daughter of Oeneus and silts up with his muddy waves the Echinad Islands; and there is Euhenos, stained with the blood of Nessus.

By tracing these rivers Lucan outlines the historical evolution shadowed forth in the landscape of classical myth. But the seeds which result in the slow growth of civilization are also those which lead to war and destruction: "In this land the seeds of cruel war first sprang to life. From her rocks, smitten by the trident of the sea, leaped first the Thessalian charger, to portend dreadful warfare" (6:348–99).

Thus, from the act of rending Ossa and Olympus, and their subsequent physical opposition to one another, flow all the good and evil of civilization, just as the waters of the Peneus flow through the cleft mountains. This basic moral opposition is manifest in the successive events that the landscape nurtures, and it is in this respect that Lucan's rivers are the articulated landscape's moral analogue. Pompey and Caesar are assimilated into a larger pattern that has its very origins in the *genius* of the land and which has spawned the degeneracy within Rome itself. Pompey, his army wasted, must seek the aid of his friend Deiotarus, who vows, Odysseus-like, by the pure rivers of his nation, the Tigris and Euphrates, to assist his friend. The strength of these two rivers which flow beyond the Roman frontier is contrasted with the deceitful cunning of the Nile, which in its way serves Caesar and which finally spreads its slime over the mutilated body of Pompey (9.85). The rivers of the world not only expand the scope of the combat, they continually clarify the moral contrast between Pompey and Caesar and the weakness that resides in the very spirit of Rome. As Pompey's star sinks (after 8.713), and Rome's with it, the imagery is almost wholly usurped by the Nile. The river's fertility here derives from profane and deadly mysteries which Lucan presents as exotic and effeminate; Caesar's obsession with the Nile figures his own infernal compact with evil forces, and Rome's unnatural subjection to Egypt. The long digression on the river, constituting Book 10, suggests Rome's pervasive infection by Nile's inundation. Of Rome's two great men, one is possessed by the mysteries of the Nile and his Roman spirit subjected, and the other, Pompey, is vulnerable to and finally the victim of the internal corruption that Caesar represents. Caesar's obsession with the black heart of the Nile is what destroys Rome: "Give me an assured hope to set eyes on the springs of the river and I will abandon the war" (9.191–92).[47]

Lucan uses the river to create something of a genealogy of the gods of the landscape, to create a myth of history in terms of nature. He achieves this while he is also describing the landscape, and his success shows how the interest in and technique of topographical description have evolved since Homer. In the descriptive epithets on the rivers and their gods, with the emphasis on names, nature, and history, we have a foreshadowing of Spenser's technique in Book 4 of *The Faerie Queene*.

In Lucan we also see the extent to which the rivers have become associated with Roman self-consciousness. Gods of the land have become the products of the society itself, and are adapted to the national literature. It is easy to see how, the more accepted the river becomes as a defining *topos*, the more useful it is as a critical device. What Homer did instinctively Virgil did in the spirit of innovative imitation. Lucan and others get carried away with Virgil's good idea. In literature as in society itself, the river afforded a civilizing influence. Primitive societies which are not formed near rivers tend to be lawless and violent.[48] And just as it was a civilizing factor in society, so too it served as an index to civil or uncivil behavior in art and literature. Clearly Virgil and Lucan sensed this, and Ovid, probably in response to his contemporary, developed it even more fully. For this reason the rivers provide a remarkably useful entry into the shadowy world of the *Metamorphoses*. In them we can perceive the mythic order beneath the shifting styles and ironic tones in which Ovid conceals his dynastic and political themes.

The irony which obscures Ovid's theme is also a manifestation of the decline from the godlike and heroic Golden Age that is chronicled in the *Metamorphoses*. The world of the poem is primarily one of vanities where human passions reduce the gods to subhuman objects, and where vice is unpunished and virtue unrewarded. However, the *Metamorphoses* is also a playful, amoral *carmen perpetuum* that relates the genealogy of the gods that Aeneas brought with him from Troy (15.860–70). This "genealogy" traces the devolution of mores in the empire, and Ovid's irony is the proper tone for describing such a fallen world.

There are, however, exceptions to this pervasive mood which give us a contrast necessary for understanding the poet's objectives. In a manner very like Homer's (and which Drayton will emulate a millennium and a half later), Ovid uses his rivers to provide a kind of tonal relief to the prevailing mood. With remarkable consistency the rivers—Acheloüs, Peneus, Arethusa, Cyane, to name only the most prominent—present dignified, courteous, and unambiguous examples of the virtue which is otherwise repeatedly and egregiously violated by mortals as well as gods. In Book 1, for example, in preparation for the tale of Jove's abduction of Io, the river god Peneus is presented as a figure of the prudent, generous governor. Where Lucan emphasizes the landscape, Ovid emphasizes the god: "There is a vale in Thessaly. . . . Men call it Tempe. Through this the River Peneus flows. . . . Here, seated in a cave of overhanging rock, he was giving laws to his waters, and to his water nymphs." The orderly river, with his thoughtful concern for his troubled brother, Inachus, contrasts markedly with the tale that he introduces: "Inachus only does not come; but hidden away in his deepest cave, he augments his water with his tears, and with utmost wretchedness laments [that] his daughter, Io, was lost" (1.568–85). The rivers have access to noble human feelings present nowhere else in the *Metamorphoses*. As in Homer and Virgil, sanity and common sense are mirrored in their waters. For example, Cyane boldly rebukes Pluto for his impertinent methods of winning a wife: "She stood forth from the midst of her pool as far as her waist, and . . . cried to Dis: 'No further shall you go! Thou canst not be the son-in-law of Ceres against her will. The maiden should have been wooed not ravished'" (5.411–18). And while Ceres raves in her grief, Arethusa shows uncommon delicacy and kindness in her consolation:

> Then did Arethusa . . . lift her head from her clear Elean pool and . . . thus addressed the goddess: 'cease now thy boundless coils and do not be so grievously wroth with the land which has been true to thee. The land is innocent. . . . It is not for my own country that I pray, for I came as a stranger hither. . . . Pisa is my native land'. (5. 487–97)

The legend of Arethusa's disappearing waters has been subordinated to Ovid's concern for character. The language of reason and moderation, spoken by Homer's Scamander and Virgil's Tiber, is also the language of Ovid's rivers. In Roman fashion, he sets out the landscape that is shaped by river myths and gives its local *genius* a message of civil order which at times has a Homeric, or even a

Jehovan wrath, as when Jove, in Book 1, "summons his rivers to council" and urges them on as agents of destruction:

> 'Put forth all your strength . . . open wide your doors, away with all restraining dykes, and give full reign to all your river steeds.' So he commands, and the rivers return, uncurb their fountains' mouths, and in unbridled course go racing to the sea. . . . The rivers overleap all bounds and flood the open plains. And not alone orchards, crops and herds, men and dwellings, but shrines as well . . . do they sweep away. (1.274–90)

The deluge of the Deucalion legend is a river judgment like that which obliterated the unholy Danaan wall and that which was the promised revenge on Egypt. In giving us a glimpse of orderly social life and the beauties of peace before its effacement, Ovid's passage clearly conforms to its Homeric model.

Repeatedly Ovid's rivers reveal feelings and values which belie the general mood of the work. They are usually exemplars, and their actions or the tales they tell express an unambiguous moral order very different from the amorality which characterizes the rest of the action. Although there are numerous examples throughout the work, this treatment of the rivers dominates the central and most extensive narrative episode, which takes place in Acheloüs's cave. The episode is too long to examine in close detail: it begins in the very middle of the *Metamorphoses*, in Book 8, extends into Book 10, and contains within its framing action several other exemplary river tales. It provides the necessary introduction to and commentary on the dynastic theme and the climax of the entire work, the apotheosis of Hercules. Its centrality, length, and narrative importance, as well as its moral and tonal qualities, give the episode an unmistakable prominence. As we will see, in his method of involving river metaphors within the action of the sequence, Ovid seems to be emulating the *aristeia* and *theomachia* of the *Iliad*.

Ovid works the river motif to its full capacity, touching on its distinctive features whenever possible.[49] The principal characters are not only morally uncontroversial, they are also traditional components of river lore: Acheloüs and Hercules's heroic analogue, Theseus, magnanimous city-founder and civilizer. To initiate the action Ovid uses a favorite poetic tactic: he dramatizes his metaphors, in this case, the paradox of the beneficent river torrent. Theseus is waylaid by Acheloüs's torrent, and the river kindly warns him of the dangers of his flood and invites him to his cavernous home to await its abatement: "do not entrust yourself to my greedy waters. The current is wont to sweep down solid trunks and huge boulders" (8.547ff). Here and in other Ovidian river sequences (*Amores*, 7, for example) we enjoy the wit of a poet playing with literary convention.

The paradox of the rude flood's courteous warning, and the subsequent hospitality inform the rest of the episode: good comes from seeming evil, a Roman version of the fortunate fall. Acheloüs provides his guests with unmeasured bounty and good fellowship, and he and his company exchange morally instructive tales. Ovid's intention is to show the revival of the gods in the Greek virtues, and appropriately his emphasis is on hospitality and bounty.

The tales that are told are likewise exemplary. They are about rivers, and Ovid presents them in contrasting pairs. They illustrate the lesson that is being dramatized in Acheloüs's cave itself: the importance of civility and piety. The first tales, told by the river god, are moral etiologies, about the Echinades Islands and one other island, Perimele, washed by the river's waters. In response to Theseus's inquiries, Acheloüs explains that the Echinades were once nymphs who neglected him, their local god, "and so, terrible in wrath, terrible in flood, I tore forests from forests, fields from fields; and with the place they stood on, I swept the nymphs away" (8.584–87). The second story tells of the nymph Perimele, beloved of the Acheloüs, whose angry father cast her from the cliffs into the waters below. Acheloüs however transforms her to an island and catches her in the embrace of his waters, where she still lies.

The two-sided tales of good and evil are meant to be unambiguous. They touched the noble chords of the guests—all but one, the god-scoffing Pirithoüs, son of Ixion, who serves to highlight Ovid's moral distinctions. The worthy Lelex then sets out to defend Acheloüs against his detractor with another tale of piety, humility, and hospitality: that of Baucis and Philemon. Their solitary willingness to shelter the gods is rewarded, while their neighbors, who had refused the gods, are destroyed by flood. Again, there is a clear resonance between the "tale" and the action that frames it.

The next tale, that of Erysichthon, is the perfect pendant to its predecessor: exemplary good rewarded is contrasted with absolute evil punished, here by drought and famine. And that the tale is told to us by Acheloüs himself reminds us that in his floods and droughts he is the agent of judgment. In the course of the entire episode, the narrative and dramatic levels diminish as the metaphoric and literal reflect one another in reiterating images. Thus, the next tale, having two sides to it, is overtly about Acheloüs himself: it is a river god telling a tale centered on the river *topos*, and the *topos* is then reiterated by the actions of the narrating river god.

It is the tale of the defeat of Acheloüs by Hercules and is narrated, with self-effacing humility, at the request of Theseus (9.2–7). The river god confesses his embarrassment at his defeat but concludes that it was an honor to have fought with one so noble. As Acheloüs describes the struggle, he is reclining in the position of the classical river god (8.727). The narrative relates the story behind the Hellenic river image of the charging bull:

> there remained to me my third refuge, the form of a savage bull. And so in bull form I fought him. He threw his arms around my neck on the left . . . dragging upon me; and finally forced down my hard horns and thrust them into the earth . . . holding my tough horn in his pitiless right hand, he broke it off and tore it from my forehead, mutilating me. (9.80–86)

There could hardly be a better example of witty and self-conscious use of the river than this scene of a river god, positioning himself "by the book," and proceeding to narrate the legends behind conventional river metaphors. Two kinds of river god are presented. Acheloüs's access to humility through defeat and mutilation is the transformation from the charging bull to the open-handed reclining host of the land. Ovid is careful to make clear that Acheloüs's defeat also results in bounty and the virtues of humility and hospitality. Acheloüs explains that "the horn the naiads took, filled it with fruit and fragrant flowers, and hallowed it. And now the Goddess of glad Abundance is enriched with my horn" (9.87–89). He "was humbled indeed by the loss of his beauteous horn" but the gain was greater than the loss (9.98–99).

The moral here, of unequivocal material and moral gain coming from seeming loss, is the consummation of all the tales. It explains the paradox inherent in the very geographic reality of rivers. Acheloüs's tale was told in response to the disbelief of Perithoüs. And if the tale itself did not convince the doubter of the god's verity, just as the river humbly concludes the story of the transformation of his horn, "lo, a nymph just like Diane, one of the attendants with locks flowing free, appeared and served them from her courteous horn with all the fruits of Autumn" (9.89–92). The metamorphosis of myth to reality occurs before the disbeliever's very eyes. The reader watches as the levels of the narrative dissolve into one another, as the river motif and the river god realize each other.

The whole of this protracted episode began with Theseus saying to the god Acheloüs that "he would take . . . his advice." We sense that these several tales are that advice—the divine lessons by which Theseus acquires his heroic virtues. In this sequence a dual metamorphosis takes place. There is the embodiment of the tales as their lesson becomes manifest in action, and there is their disembodiment, their literary existence as part of the mythic dimension of the *carmen perpetuum*. The cleverly and clearly designed intricacy of Ovid's narration here stands out. In tone, in moral clarity as well as in its technical virtuosity it is unique, and without it we would be unable to apprehend the intentions and design of the whole. It is from Ovid that Spenser learns some of these intricacies of the narrative art.

What Ovid has done in leading us, with Theseus, to Acheloüs's cavernous source is to expand one other aspect of the river motif which also has its early literary appearance in the *Odyssey* and its mythic beginnings in the realities of primitive life. The river's dwelling, or cavernous "head," is here a place of learning, the source of nature's secrets. Here Theseus learns about the gods and about nature's order: Acheloüs is literally the fount of knowledge. This idea is inherent in the quest for rivers' beginnings, and the quest continues in the solemn exploration of crystal-covered cave interiors where earth, water, fire, and air become one, and all rivers have their subterranean origins. The exotic river habitat is commonly presented as the paragon of nature, where all nature's arts are contained and perfected. This visionary realm of water is like the interior of a crystal ball, and its prescient inhabitant delivers oracular wisdom that the initiate, such as Theseus, seeks above ground. The cave of rivers is an extremely popular river motif, particularly in the Renaissance, and it serves as the *locus communis* for ekphrastic treatment of art and nature, where history and prophecy come together. The narratives which have their dramatic beginnings in the cave present a mythic geography for the world of the *Metamorphoses*, and in so doing, they give an unobtrusive order to the entire work.

Ovid's treatment of the river's source as the source of wisdom is cunning; he camouflages it in a dramatic and casual mood. His intention, however, seems to be the expansion of his literary prototype in Virgil. It is in the fourth book of the *Georgics* that we find the most important illustration of the cave of the rivers, and it is here that the Renaissance river poets—Sannazaro, Leland, Spenser,

Drayton, and Milton—looked for their model. Here the river continues to function much as it has in the *Iliad*, the *Aeneid*, and *The Civil War*, but in the Aristaeus episode the river's varied themes are concentrated in the nymph's cave dwelling. The episode itself is an epyllion and is set off with a conspicuous awkwardness from the rest of the *Georgics*, having a narrative wholeness characteristic of the genre. It also gives us Virgil's last words on his georgic theme, for it is placed at the very conclusion of the last book. With this conspicuous placement, the episode comments on the rest of the *Georgics*, and stands out as a cipher by which we can learn to "read" and understand what has gone before.

The pious and patriotic design of the *Georgics* is meant as didactic advice to the husbandman and as glorification of the nation's peaceful prosperity. The most important nature gods are invoked in these books: those of wood and stream, Pan, Minerva, and Ceres. But nature is as mysterious as the *Georgics* are vague. Nature is often destructive, and its mysteries as impenetrable as Virgil's real intentions behind this sophisticate's guide to field and stream. Throughout the *Georgics*, though, Virgil reiterates enigmatically that nature has never "brought ill to man unwarned" (1.313): that out of seeming ill comes wisdom, even good. Human beings are capable of reading the book of nature and thus, in stoic fashion, of becoming less vulnerable: *"felix, qui potuit rerum cognoscere causas"* (2.490–91), Virgil's speaker pronounces after naively renouncing the world for the pleasures to be had on the banks of Sperchios and Taygetus.

But the sententious knowledge of the *Georgics* always remains superficial and jejune against the more serious themes of Caesar's death, the nation's religion, the destiny of Rome, and the need to restore natural order in the country (1.498–513). The beguiling tale of Aristaeus demonstrates the need to penetrate further into nature's mysteries. Its fable-like quality is obtrusive: Aristaeus, son of Cyrene (nymph of the river Peneus) and Apollo, loses his bees— and here we want to remember Apollo's and the nymphs' concern for the education of youth. Thus, at the end of the *Georgics's* extended lesson on husbandry, we have a fable of its failure: something has gone awry with Aristaeus's husbandry. Like Orpheus, with whom we are meant to compare him, Aristaeus laments his plight instead of attempting to remedy it.[50] He flees to the "sacred font at the stream's head, and with many plaints called to his mother thus: 'O mother, mother Cyrene, that dwellest in this flood's depths, why, from the gods' glorious line . . . if indeed as thou sayest, Thrymbraean Apollo is my father . . . didst thou give me birth, to be hated of the fates?'" (4.320–24). Initially the tale of Aristaeus seems to give the lie to all that has preceded in the *Georgics*.

His resignation is an abdication of his Apollinian parentage. But deep beneath the river's waters his cry has been heard by the fleece-spinning river nymphs, Cyrene's consorts who are exchanging secrets about the gods' private lives. Arethusa notifies Cyrene of her son's plight, and what follows—the lamentations, the son's welcome beneath the waters, and the descriptive setting—is itself a much imitated parody of the wounding of Paris. The river nymph's cave is described as the mysterious and orderly center of the earth, the source of all its hydraulic workings:

> And now, marvelling at his mother's home, a realm of waters, at the lakes locked in caverns, and the echoing groves, he went on his way, and, dazed by the mighty rush of waters, he gazed on all the rivers, as, each in his own place, they glide under the great earth—Phasis and Lycus, the fount whence deep Eneipus first breaks forth, whence Father Tiber, and Mysian Caicus, and Eridanus, on whose bull's brow are twain gilded horns; no other stream of mightier force flows through the rich tilth to join the violet sea. (363–74)

It is from here, the first cause of all things, that Cyrene educates Aristaeus, tells him how to master the mysteries of nature and thus restore his aviary to rights. He must, like Hercules himself, go to no less a figure than Proteus: "To him we nymphs do reverence, and aged Nereus himself, for the seer has knowledge of all things—what is, what hath been, what is in train ere long to happen" (391–93). This diminutive Hercules must quit his passive role and actively wrestle with this mysterious figure, "for without force he will give thee no counsel, nor shalt thou bend him by prayer." Hard work and knowledge in the active assertion of mastery over nature's protean flux are necessary for the learned husbandman.

Aristaeus undergoes his trial successfully and learns that his problems all derive from Orpheus and Eurydice, from his responsibility for her death, and that "the nymphs with whom she was wont to tread the dance in the deep groves, sent this sore havoc on thy bees. Offer thou a suppliant's gifts, craving grace, and do homage to the gentle maidens of the brooks . . . for they will grant pardon to prayers, and relax their wrath" (532–36).[51] Having thus learned "the causes of things," Aristaeus is able to bring order to his aviary.

The epyllion, light in tone and seemingly frivolous, is an interpretative key to the *Georgics*. The humble descendant of Apollo, like numerous other literary and mythic figures, must go to the rivers' source to understand nature, to learn finally how to render nature serviceable through piety, knowledge, strength, and perseverance. Notably, in his mother's cave he does not learn the specific remedy to his problems; this he learns from Proteus. Rather, he learns a profounder wisdom: how to cope with protean nature itself. He learns about knowledge, rather than the particulars of husbandry which have occupied us through the rest of the *Georgics*. Aristaeus's weakness and vulnerability are thus overcome and he has learned a lesson greater than any other single lesson contained in the *Georgics*.[52]

As amorphous Greek myth became absorbed into institutional Roman religion and individual virtue was translated into codes of civic order, the river too was transformed from the realm of nature to that of art. Or, more accurately, it flowed between and joined the two realms. As we have seen in Virgil and Ovid, the river was part of nature, it was the *vox naturae*. But nature was destined to be improved upon by Rome, and so the rivers became part of her vast aqueduct system.

The river became more and more a literary motif identifiably linked to its origins in myth and geography. Because of its primitive origins the river's place in the formalization of literature was remarkably prominent. Classical literature is always culturally self-conscious, and so it naturally looks to a "geomythology" that was the first cause of the culture itself. Virgil exploited this aspect of the river to create Aeneas, for example; but the river is a constant while the particular legends or ideas it conveys may vary. Regardless of these differences, when Romans look at the river, they look with a civilizing eye, and the river reflects in its waters the primitive impulse of that vision. Thus, in the initial book of his mythological calendar cycle, the *Fasti*, Ovid develops a different legend of Roman origins, but the river is, nevertheless, a fixed feature of his version as well. As Carmentis and Evander approach Tiber's mouth, much as Aeneas did, she sees in the river and on its unadorned banks a vision of the future, and she too raises a prayer to the gods of the place:

> "All hail!" she cried, "Gods of the Promised land! And hail! thou country that shalt give new gods to heaven! Hail rivers and fountains, which to this hospitable land pertain! Hail nymphs of the groves and banks of Naiads! May the sight of you be a good omen to my son and me! And happy be the foot that touches yonder bank."[53]

In her vision she decks the banks with the now traditional architectural adornment, and she civilizes them with the distinctly Roman feature of social order: "Am I deceived? or shall you hills by stately walls be hid, and from this spot of earth shall all take law?" (1.515–18).

And in Book 3 the New Year feast of Anna Perenna draws upon the most primitive origins of river worship to celebrate the purification of and redemption from the destructive forces of the past. Ovid modifies traditional aspects of the feast to make greater use of the *topos*, so that the placation of Anna, Dido's tormented sister, is reflected in the very nature of the calm, divinely wise river that takes her soothingly into his embrace.[54]

> The conscious river checked and hushed his stream. Herself appeared to speak: "I am a nymph of the calm Numicius. From a perennial river I hide, and Anna Perenna is my name." Straightway they feast joyfully in the fields over which they had roamed, and feast themselves and their day in deep draughts of wine. (3.650–56)

The perennial river's new calm and Anna's own blessing figure the auspicious New Year's beginning and the placation of distraught Anna's spirit. The Roman past is redeemed and the future is assured. Ovid uses the river motif to create a primitive natural vitality appropriate for a New Year feast. He has altered all aspects of the feast to make greatest use of the *topos*.

As Rome's golden hue turned to silver, the river's remarkable importance persisted; it continued to be the frontier joining and separating art and nature. The Roman view of nature became increasingly artificial, and the river, accordingly, became more stylized while continuing to echo Homer, Virgil, Ovid, and Lucan. It is from this late phase in the evolution of Roman literature that we get the country house poems that are conventionally perceived as the *locus classicus* for later topographical literature. We can see, however, that they are part of a tradition in which the descriptive response to landscape is also a process of mythologizing it. In these poems we see a fundamental human reaction to nature, one in which we impose on the landscape our cultural myths. For these poets the river continues to be the moral mirror for the individuals who are being praised, and we can see that it serves their patrons much as the Tiber served Aeneas: "behold eloquent Vopsicus's cool retreat at Tiber and the double dwelling threaded by Anio's stream . . . see the friendly intercourse of bank with bank."[55] In the *Castle of Pontius Leontius*, Sidonius's description of the rugged landscape reveals his debts to Lucan and Virgil, although the river motif has become a stylized adornment of nearly baroque richness: "There is a place where two rivers, the Garunna, sped whirling down from a dripping mountain-crag, and the mossy Duranius, which rushes with like swoop to the plain . . . . commingle their slowing streams.''[56] This is a weaker version of Lucan's riparian projection of Magnus and Caesar and his realization of primitive essential distinctions in their natures. But it is above all a compulsive view of order which reflects a passion for balance and restraint, and in thus describing the landscape it carries to the extreme the Roman attitude toward human and external nature. The epideictic verse of Sidonius and Claudian adapts the landscape to their political ends, emphasizing the theme of order by developing conventional river motifs. For example, Sidonius, honoring Anthemius, has the *genius Italiae* visit the "glassy blue abode of Tiber" in the search for a leader. From the cavernous river depths he learns who can best govern the nation in her need.[57] However, in their moral and political landscapes these poets differ only in degree, not in kind or genre, from their predecessors.

In countless similar passages these argentine poets refine and polish this image of nature, and the success of their art rests on their ability to join the extremes of artifice and nature. The *topos* becomes more firmly embedded in the poetic vocabulary. Eventually, the myth of Roman order begins to sound rather hollow against the clamor that reaches Tiber's banks from the not-too-distant provinces. And yet when these set pieces of geographical description are most successful, they evoke an immediacy and power which is still impressive and which still captures the sense of place, much as Homer and Plato were able to do:

> He is a savage who delights in punishment and seems to make vengeance of the laws his own. . . . But he whom reason, not anger, animates is a peer of the gods, he . . . weighing the guilt, can with deliberation balance the punishment. . . . Gently flows the Nile, yet it is more beneficent than all rivers for all that no sound reveals its power. More swiftly the broad Danube glides between its quiet banks. Huge Ganges flows down to its mouths with gently moving current. Let torrents roar horribly, threaten weary bridges, and sweep down forests in their foaming whirl, 'tis repose befits the greater; quiet authority accomplishes what violence cannot, and that mandate compels more which comes from commanding calm.[58]

The myths of nature, as they are embodied in the rivers, have not lost all their impact for the silver poets. The powerful, beneficent, seemingly reasonable, potentially punitive river is still a moral example, although its myths seem less suited to the cultural reality addressed by its poets.

By the beginning of the Christian era, then, the river *topos* had long been established and was undergoing the endless process of refinement. The range of its themes was considerable, but obviously they are closely interrelated, and perhaps the poem which best demonstrates the self-consciousness of river conventions is the playful sixth complaint in Book 3 of Ovid's *Amores*. The poem is addressed to an anonymous river, and in it the poet parodies the respect usually accorded his subject. The river is, as usual, unexpectedly in spate, and the lover cannot cross to join his mistress. In his request that the flood abate, the lover obviously expects the river's sympathetic compliance ("Stay, for a little time thy waters"). But this gradually gives way to frustration, fury, and threats that rival the abuse that Achilles hurls at the Scamander. Instead of the long-lasting poetic renown that Horace promises Bandusia's stream, Ovid's lover vows a poetic legacy of his hatred, immortalizing the river's foul nature: "Thine, O torrent, will be hate unbearable, believe, if I perchance am said to have been kept by thee—I a lover."

He cajoles the river, praising the virtues that are traditionally associated with them: "Rivers ought to aid young men in love; what love is, rivers themselves have felt," and he follows up with examples of historical rivers which have loved or promoted love. The river, however, is obdurate, and the lover is provoked to a violent violation of the usual respect shown to rivers: "What have I to do with thee, mad stream? Why dost thou defer the joys I am to share? Why dost thou, churl, break off the journey I have begun?" And so he raves in a passion Theseus was too wise to succumb to when he was crossed by the Acheloüs.

His insults shift to other vulnerable aspects of rivers' reputations— the durability of their names, the maintenance of their channels, the familiarity of their source: "wert thou a river of name, were thine greatest fame o'er all the earth . . . but thou hast no name, thou art but gathered from failing rivulets, and hast neither fountain-source nor fixed abode! In place of a source thou hast only the rain and melted snows, riches that sluggish winter serves to thee." Ovid's profane, god-scoffing figure combines the hubris of Achilles and the agnosticism of Ovid's own Pirithoüs; subject to such indignities, the river has lost its place among the gods.

This Latin lover is fed up with the fickle nature of this small torrential stream, and all the features poets have praised in their hyperbolic river passages, all the flourishes that give the rills their poetic fame, are denied this treacherous creek. Its foul waters comfort no traveller; it is unreliable, but when it does flow it damages fields and flocks. And finally as the speaker's *aristeia* reaches its intensity, this local Achilles repents ever having associated this stream with great and virtuous rivers, such as Acheloüs, Inachus, and the Nile, and he invokes all the elements to war with this lesser Scamander: "Indeed, for thee, as thou deservest, O torrent aught but clear I pray that suns be ever fierce and winter ever dry."

Aside from providing a very tantalizing suggestion about Ovid's reading of the twentieth and twenty-first books of the *Iliad*, this elegy, pointing out the fallibility of the mortal lover, is a very compendium of inverted river themes. Each stage of his persuasion and rebuke, each imprecation and invective draws on and parodies the established conventions of river literature, and is based on the initial association between the river nymphs and the youthful lover. We have here Ovidian levity of the first water. The success of the poem derives from the sense of wicked irreverence and from our recognition of the conventions Ovid is violating. The lover is a comic Hercules, his desire is but to love—a humble way of spreading civilization—but in such a fallen world, the gods' assistance is rather less to be relied upon than myth would have us believe. Lovers are distinctly mortal creatures, always drawn closer to real nature, and here the artificial *topos*, perceived through the angry eyes of self-centered man, is brought down from its deific status and returned, parodically, to its mutable natural form. This ironic inversion of river themes suggests how, even for Ovid, the motif had begun to lose the immediacy that forms the vital link between a myth and its culture. Here we can perceive how the cultural self-consciousness that joined the river with its society has yielded to a literary self-consciousness, and we will see this pattern repeated at the end of the Renaissance.

[FIGURES 1–5]

In antiquity, god and nature are one; the river deities reside in the landscape. To create their image is to separate the inseparable: to identify the essence and physical sense of the landscape, to isolate them and yet bring them together. Ancient iconography of the river joins different kinds of representation to suggest its physical characteristics, even its topography, and its symbolic significance. The Nile and its gods were generally represented in black (figs. 3 & 4) because of the river's dark, fertile waters. Its principal deity, Hapi, was figured in terms of a repetitive series of hieroglyphs suggesting the river's unfolding waters, the numerous sacred cities on its banks, and the succession of rulers, also its progeny. Isis, popular throughout the Mediterranean, retained the identifying symbols of her Egyptian origins and significance—in the pitcher of Nile water, the sistrum associating her with music and the spheres, for example. The Temple of Isis-Fortuna was decorated with mosaics showing a foreshortened view of the Nile delta which combined topographical description with symbolic stylization to present an image of the inundation and the social and material life presided over by Isis and the river (fig. 1).

Like other kinds of iconography, that of the rivers seeks metaphors which signify its secrets and in the process unlock them, thus hastening the demythologizing process which moves from magic to science, mystery to history. Greek coins, themselves of religious significance, often portrayed local river deities through metaphors of strength and violence, such as the charging bull (fig. 5a), lions or driven chariots (fig. 5b). Varying degrees of personification suggest stages in the detachment of the deity from the landscape, of idea from object, as in fig. 5c, showing the nymph of the stream Himera sacrificing at the altar, with signs of abundance above, and the figure of the river and the bull-headed fountain behind.

Similarly overlapping perceptual myths can be seen in the Greek statue of the Nile god (fig. 2). On its base is a representational bas-relief of the river, its flora and fauna; it supports the personified god reclining on one arm and whose position suggests the benign perennial river and is a metaphor for the landscape; he leans on a sphinx and supported cornucopia, and around him crawl sixteen *putti* figuring the sixteen cubit flood— these being abstract symbols of the river's cult. Similar combinations of description and figuration occur in other classical depictions of river gods, such as the "Farnese Cup" (fig. 4), where the various icons of the river evoke a metaphysical landscape.

Throughout antiquity and the classical period, in the movement between the extremes of representation and personification, description and figuration, and in which local details are preserved but often abstracted, we see the basic problems of iconic representation of natural landscape—the paradox of conveying in a figure both idea and image, mystery and nature—and these are the problems that persist in other forms of landscape representation.

Figure 1. Nile mosaics. Temple of Isis-Fortuna, Palestrina. First century B.C. (Alinari). The stylized landscape decorating the temple establishes the identification of the goddess with the geography.

Figure 2. Nile statue. Greco-Roma, first century, B.C. (Alinari). The reclining figure of the river god very early became a convention of monumental and graphic art. The statue was recovered in 1513 and was frequently reproduced and copied; see Michaelangelo's *Palazzo del Campidoglio* in Rome, and G. Franzini, *Icones* (1599).

Figure 3. Isis-Fortuna. Greco-Roman, first century, B.C. (Alinari). The late Greek version of Egyptian images of the goddess shows the syncretic development of her figure.

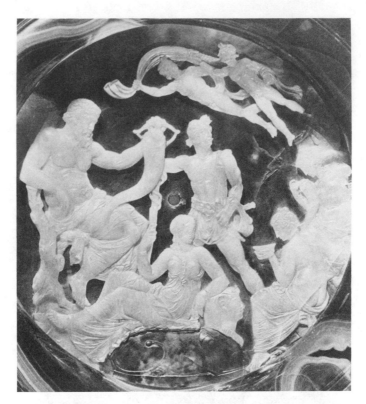

Figure 4. "Farnese Cup". Alexandrian, second century, B.C. Various phases in the iconography of the Nile cult are represented, in the figure of *Nilus* (left), the river itself (lower center), Isis (reclining) and Tyke (above).

Figure 5. Silver coins, Sicily, fourth century, B.C. 1) Acheloüs figured as a charging bull; 2) River goddess Himera driving a chariot; 3) Himera sacrificing at the altar, before a fountain in the figure of the bull. Renaissance medallists imitated river figures of such coins; see G. Symeoni, *Illustratione die gli Epitaffi Antiche* (Lyon, 1558), p. 154.

II. *Landscape to Literature:*
Late Roman and Medieval Contexts of the River

Fontes potius quam rivulos sectari debemus. (Cicero, *De inventione*)

Also though a welle be lytyll in his owne Sprynge, yet for it spryngyth contynuelly it is orygynal cause of many grete Ryvers, for there is noo ryver but he spryngeth oute of some welle knowen or unknowen.
(Bartholomaeus Anglicus, *De proprietatibus rerum*)

What boots it to have shed our blood in Northern lands, where we conquered the Rhone and the Rhine? As a reward for so many campaigns you have given me civil war. (Lucan, *The Civil War*)

1. *Rivers of Empire: The Roman Legacy—Seneca and Ausonius*

To thee, O Tiber, belong this higher praise, that thou dost guard the seat of empire and the homes of Rome. (Ausonius, *The Moselle*)

BETWEEN THE FIRST AND SIXTH CENTURIES A.D., as the weight of the empire became too great to be sustained and the provinces were eventually forced to assume greater autonomy after the fall of Rome in 547, and as Christianity became established, the geographical orientation of Europe shifted away from the Mediterranean. Geographically, Rome outgrew its ideal of imperial unity. Its cultural myth was superseded by political changes in an increasingly fragmented world where geographical and political divisions of the landscape again became a part of the popular consciousness. Long before the actual collapse of Rome the historian can detect the political division of the empire into separate kingdoms, into European provinces whose strength and importance drew attention away

79

from the Roman Mediterranean. The myth of imperial unity naturally evolved in meaning: as the Roman world became consolidated,
forces of expansion and colonization were replaced by managers
and administrators. In the literature of the period we can observe
the greater familiarity with this larger, more orderly world. Authors
collect their learning and lore from the more readily accessible
provinces, and we see this in the various kinds of compilation by
authors such as Pliny, Tacitus, and Diodorus.

Culturally, ideals of unity also nurture ideas of regionalism and
autonomy, and the process of consolidation reveals an awareness of
multiplicity. These dual forces of imperial Roman unity and local
identity and autonomy form a cultural ambivalence that is characteristic of the early modern sensibility. Ultimately, of course, this
balance, superintended by Rome, became unhinged, and the empire fell to pieces. Politically and to some extent physically the
landscape of Roman Europe became a ruin. But the myth of
European order or unity had been planted in the cultural consciousness. The Roman legacy was a geographical myth that endured after
political dissolution, and the perception of the European landscape
would never lose it. Fragmented as Europe was after, say, the fifth
century, its constituent parts had to live with their Roman past—to
restore it, assimilate it, perpetuate its memory or transcend it—but
there was an idea of geographical community and of the Roman past
that could not cease to exist. Physically, politically, and intellectually Europe retained the imprint of Rome and its cultural ideal while
entering a new historical phase in which it seemed to look forward
and backward at the same time. Response to landscape and the
world's geography reflects this ambivalence and changing focus
away from Rome, and it is particularly evident in the culturally
sensitive motif of the river.

This chapter looks at several important illustrations of late
Roman and early medieval river literature to see how they demonstrate the perceptions of landscape characteristic of their period,
how they embody a cultural perspective which is still with us, and how
they show both continuity and change in the motif. By no means a
history of medieval literature, these pages look at works that illustrate particular aspects of our intellectual response to landscape and
the river that can be identified with the period. In them we see the
emergence of a different, more intellectualized way of perceiving
and understanding the European geography. Relatedly we see the
allegorization of rivers of the world and their formalization either as

religious symbols or as secular images of cultural identity. These are two perceptual modes which have remained with us. In each case we can see how authors responded to the Roman legacy while forming cultural myths appropriate to their own milieu. First, I want to look at related geographical and literary contexts of the river in late Roman authors who, in one way or another, bridge the classical and early modern periods.

The intellectual constructs within which authors perceived the world expanded as the Roman world became more consolidated. Efforts to describe its compass imaginatively and scientifically also became more comprehensive. In encyclopedic works such as Tacitus's *Annals* and *Germania*, and Pliny's *Natural History* we see attempts to understand the world's immense variety (and its geography) by describing it. If late Roman literature is not as inspiring as its Augustan antecedents, it is not because the imagination informing it was less capacious. Able to conceive of remoter lands because their reality had developed greater immediacy, authors had stronger rather than weaker needs for supporting myths of geography, as we see in works such as Pliny's and Tacitus's. Plutarch's essay *The Name of Rivers and Mountains*, for example, consisting of the legendary and mythical lore of all the principal rivers of the world, is a virtual *thesaurus fluviorum*, a generic hybrid of Ovid's *Metamorphoses* and Pliny's *Natural History*.

Nevertheless, as the world became larger, it also became more mundane. Although the pagan gods survived in European literature of the Latin Middle Ages, they could not entirely resist the demythologizing forces. Yet, if authors such as Cicero advocated more reasonable explanations of the nature of the gods, the river continued to be *the* protean element, retaining its mythic qualities while the mysteries and knowledge with which it was associated evolved according to the temperament of the age. We have a good example of how the river expresses the philosophical tone of its culture in Seneca's *Naturales Quaestiones*, for example, where he turns natural philosophy to a demonstration of the uncertainties of the world and an argument for stoic self-sufficiency. The rivers of nature conflate with those of rhetoric to form a *topos* in which he can locate the crucial question: "What is important in human existence?" and through which he can arrive at the answer, that it is "to have seen the universe in your mind and to have subdued your vice . . . to raise your mind above the threats and promises of fortune."[1] The study of natural geography will, he says, "free the mind" and help us to understand "the mysteries of nature." And in the important third book, he goes on to focus his argument on the terrestrial waters. Interestingly, when he interprets the river according to the example of Virgil and Ovid and looks back on these classical authors as moral hydrologists who teach us to "study the waters of the earth or investigate . . . the causes that produce them," we can see that he is already at the frontier of the allegorical tradition with its "modern" view of the ancients.

The world's mutability is the foundation of the stoic's thought, and water is both the symbol and agent of change. Its fecund penetration of the earth is the source of life, and more important for Seneca's argument, the torrential deluge is nature's greatest, most awesome act of creative destruction: "there is nothing so violent as the full force of water, nothing so uncontrollable, so unyielding." Seneca's vision of death by water serves as the key to understanding life. In the *Naturales Quaestiones*, then, the river and its hydrological cycle represents the essential paradox of the earthly condition. As such, it functions as a *locus communis* within the work, so that Seneca can say that "when you have come to grasp the true origin of rivers, you will understand that you do not have any further questions."[2]

Seneca's is a very literary, essentially agnostic natural philosophy, and it is very much the product of its age. Imposing his stoic natural philosophy on the scientific and moral view of the river that he adapts from Homer, Thales, Plato, Virgil, and Ovid, his work is largely exegetical in character: he glosses his pseudo-science with a contemporary moral myth. In the *Naturales Quaestiones* we can see how the rivers of landscape and the mind come together. Paradoxically, Seneca is too worldly to confine his thought to local rivers. But it is not enough to say that he is not interested in them. His is a philosophical landscape, not a descriptive one, and it offers us the distillation of the nature of the river. His sophisticated, secular myth of geography, which makes maximum use of the motif's rhetorical potential, replaces the nature cult of the local river, although it also reflects Seneca's interest in the physical world. His abstract moralized river of nature has characteristics that we also see in the allegorical tradition that begins to take shape at this time and will flourish for the next several centuries. We will see a similar evolution—from nature to rhetoric—in the response to the physical world during the Renaissance.

Generalizing on Seneca's example of the intellectual response to landscape, we can say that the cosmopolitan writers of the late Roman and early Christian period show little concern for their local rivers and are more interested in abstracting meaning from a larger environment. Their attraction to and understanding of the river motif is, in part, a curiosity about the physical world. Significantly, they try to interpret it in terms of their cultural predecessors—that is, the writings of the ancients, Plato and Aristotle particularly—and this in itself illustrates the peculiarity of their perspective.[3] The world of nature is one mode of access to the learning of the past. In this, Seneca illustrates an important phase in the development of an intellectualized view of the world. The particulars of the rivers do not interest him: the universals adumbrated by them do, and to understand them, he draws on his intellectual patrimony. As we will see, this process of understanding nature by analyzing the learning of the past becomes entrenched over the next centuries, and it persists in the Renaissance. Thus, in various ways the river helped to provide continuity from the wisdom of the ancients to the revealed knowledge of the moderns. As the moralists of the Middle Ages were to perceive, it contributed to the "two streams of history" by establishing some of the correspondences between paganism and Christianity—"the theme of parallel streams and concords" that was inherent in early modern literature.[4]

The motif, then, like any other aspect of a culture's rhetoric, reflects the cosmopolitan attitude nurtured by the expansion and eventual consolidation of the Roman world, while its cultural headwaters continued to be recognizably in the Roman tradition. The evolution of the motif was the natural result of maturation as well as of changing geographical focus, since the river mythology of Celtic Germany, France, and Britain was not so very different from that of the Greco-Roman cults which worked their way north. Different as the provincial rivers were from their shallower and unpredictable Mediterranean counterparts, they too fostered a cult of household gods and were the *genius loci* figuring at once "strength, the powers of destruction, fertility."[5] As in Greece and Rome the river gods and nymphs, or fays, were protectors of the place and its youth, and they too had their prophetic and magical powers that associated them with the source of sacred wisdom in pagan Celtic religion. Even their iconographic representation resembled that of the classical river gods, so that Roman and Celtic deities were highly compatible, as is suggested by the popularity of the cult of Isis, which in the sixth century was still firmly established on the banks of such distant rivers as the Thames (at London) and the Ouse (at York).[6]

It would be impossible to unravel the tangled skein of cultural, intellectual, and socioeconomic influences that were the result of Rome's colonization of northern Europe, but it is useful to keep these generalizations in mind when thinking of the Roman impact on our perception of landscape. It is possible to see that Rome's expansion brought it into contact with the more capacious and militarily and economically more useful rivers of Europe and that the use of them—of the Seine, the Moselle, the Rhine, the Danube, the Loire, and the Thames— influenced literary perceptions of the landscape much as it influenced political and economic structures. Geographers and historians, for example, have argued that Rome's greatest impact on the cultural life of Europe was the spread of urbanization. The proliferation of Roman cities linked by sophisticated routes of communication by land and water added to the commercial and industrial complexity of Europe. This served to relocate major centers of population, to alter the relative importance of geographical sites, and to encourage forms of agriculture and production where they had not developed before, and these highly artifical systems of social interdependence among Europe's urban centers are largely those that still exist today.[7]

Interestingly, this reshaping of Europe is the result of a concept of the city very different from that which prevailed in Greece, and in part this difference has to do with the nature of the river systems. Unlike Greek cities, whose locations were chosen for their defensibility, Roman settlements were chosen for their accessibility and developed with an eye for potential military and commercial supply and transport systems. Cities were established at commercial crossroads and on crucial waterways rather than in inaccessible valleys safe from piratical incursion. Strabo's description of the rivers of Gaul gives some sense of the interest in navigable rivers even before the Christian era and suggests how the Mediterranean's geographical importance had already begun to diminish:

> Now the whole of this country is watered by rivers which come down from the Alps, the Cevennes and the Pyrenees and discharge into the Ocean and the Mediterranean. Further, the districts through which they flow are plains, for the most part, and hilly lands with navigable water-courses. The river beds are by nature so well situated with reference to one another that there is transportation from either sea into the other; for the cargoes are transported only a short distance by land with easy transit through the plains.[8]

In effect, Rome's approach to colonization opened up the interior of Europe and eventually contributed to a decline in the importance of the Mediterranean as the magnetic center of socioeconomic development.

The evolution of the physical landscape corresponds to changes in the way that the landscape is perceived. Perhaps the relation between the two cannot be defined, but it is safe to say that the gods of commerce are different from those of nature. Turned to the goals of sophisticated social intercourse rather than the mysteries of nature, the river myths reinforce humanity's inclination to idealize itself and its achievements in all its secular glory. Further tamed and valued for its links with "the world beyond" (or "Perea") as much as for its identification with "the place itself," the river's local cults yield to broader social myths which continue to reveal their cultural origins in Rome. Thus, notwithstanding these changes, the traditional aspects of the river are not lost—indeed, they are accentuated. Rivers become more overtly associated with the founding of cities and the spread of civilization. The river, in nature and in myth, harmonizes the opposing strains of local identity and imperial suzerainty, so that displays of Roman wealth on the banks of Celtic rivers serve as reminders that all waters are tributaries of the Tiber.

We can see how these geographical and political influences carry over into late classical and early modern literature in Ausonius's *The Moselle*. Although a comparatively minor work dating from the fifth century, it has been described as the first modern and the last classical poem, and this "transitional" quality is very evident in its handling of the river landscape, which is its theme. Coming to it from the classical literature of Rome, we can sense how differently Ausonius views the local and European geography. The difference is conveyed in his political affiliations, which vacillate between an ideal of Roman hegemony and local identity. The author tactfully suggests that the Celtic Moselle is ultimately tributary to the imperial Tiber and then praises the aesthetic charms of his local river while speaking of the Tiber as guarding the seat of empire:

> But if to thee, O divine Moselle, Smyrna or famed Mantua had given its own poet, then . . . Tiber would not dare to set his glories above thine. Pardon, O pardon me, mighty Rome! Rebuffed—I pray—let Envy withdraw, and Nemesis who knows no Latin name! To thee, O Tiber, belongs this higher praise, that thou dost guard the seat of empire and the homes of Rome.[9]

Like his politically more involved contemporary, Claudian, Ausonius succeeds in embodying political discretion in the details of natural description, but from the tension between local landscape and imperial politics emerge contrasting values that are located in the rivers. With all its beauty, the Moselle is still only a tributary to something greater than itself. The river is no longer of primarily local significance, but is part of a complex system of human relationships and values which are suggested by the landscape and which adumbrate the Roman Empire and Europe. The poem simultaneously emphasizes and reduces the cultural, geographical, and moral distinctions between locales by alluding to the differences between the Moselle's beauty and the Tiber's strength and greatness.

If we see European literature as one continuous stream rather than as several intermittent torrents, then the problem of Ausonius's position as a classical or a modern author disappears. If not compelling verse, *The Moselle* is strikingly original in Eliot's sense of the word—it could not have been written at any other time before, and, if very traditional, it is also radically new in its handling of its material. In its very modesty it belongs inextricably to its own time and place. Ausonius, a native of Bordeaux, *grammaticus* and tutor to the young Gratian and recipient of impressive but largely honorific official titles, was himself as much a product of the age as his poem was. Enjoying the wealth of Rome without the dangers of responsibility and observing the crisis of empire from the privileged perspective of his provincial sinecure, Ausonius in his poem reflects the peculiarities of his historical position. Ausonius was steeped in the literature of the classical tradition and knew how its poets used the local streams in their verse. In particular, he used the river journey in Book 8 of the *Aeneid* to shape the whole of his poem, although in describing the beauties of the Moselle and its banks as though from the perspective of a river barge, he reveals a sensibility radically different from Virgil's. When Tiber turns back upon himself and aids Aeneas in his journey upstream, we know that we are witnessing something miraculous and momentous. Ausonius's voyage is downstream; it is slow and leisurely and has a very un-Roman purposelessness. His indulgence in the beauties of natural observation has an equally un-Roman quality to it. Art and nature go willingly and, if you will, naturally in the same direction: their harmony requires no miracle. Rejecting a contrast between art and nature, he makes the former contribute to the pleasures of the latter. The result is a delight in natural description for its own sake which is uncharacteristic of Roman verse and which is firmly fixed in its indigenous locale:

> the free breath of transparent day withholds not sight of the sun's pure rays and of the aether, dazzling to the eyes. Nay more, the whole gracious prospect made me behold a picture of my own native land, the smiling and well-tended country of Bordeaux—the roofs of country-houses, perched high upon the over-hanging river-banks, the hill-sides green with vines, and the pleasant stream of Moselle gliding below with subdued murmuring. (11.15–22)

The Mediterranean landscapes of Virgil, Ovid, and Lucan, for example, emphasize art, social order, history, and destiny, but Ausonius enjoys a voluptuous *otium*: "I, scorning what wealth and riches have bestowed, will marvel at Nature's handiwork, and not at that wherein ruin wantons . . . delighting in her waste" (11.50–53). The river prospect gives him an aesthetic pleasure; he delights in the *trompe l'oeil* with which nature tricks the observer. Thus, if his description of nature's art owes much to Virgil, his objective is very different and his mirrored landscapes, confusing illusion and reality, might be compared with the curious perspectives of Marvell's *Upon Appleton House* rather than Virgil's *Aeneid*: "Yon is a sight that may be freely enjoyed: when the azure river mirrors the shady hill, the waters of the stream seem to bear leaves and the flood to be all o'ergrown with shoots of vines. . . . The deluded boatman tells o'er the green vines" (11.189–98).

Ausonius presents us with a human landscape which emphasizes pleasure rather than industry or greatness, and in this he makes unique poetical capital of a navigable river. The pleasant scene of leisurely and distinctly serene commercial activity is foreign to the usual Roman view of the river. His perspective is more like that of a feudal lord overseeing with satisfaction the active, harmonious scene of commerce, fishing, and youthful entertainments. *The Moselle*, then, is a river idyll quite removed from the distant thunder of the empire, although his political and poetical dependence on Rome is readily acknowledged. At the same time, though, he reveals a regional affinity that is not entirely assimilated into his Roman self. As a member of the Celtic *haute bourgeoisie* and sometime official in the crumbling Roman Empire, he emerges as a divided man with a complex cultural identity that is evident in his poem, where the river is at once Roman and not Roman. The cultural idea behind his geography, with its civilization, learning, and greatness, is Roman, while his personal voice suggests another myth, of separateness, of a local rather than a unified landscape.

Ausonius's poem has a modernity that we often see in original works. In adapting Virgil to his own response to the natural landscape, he establishes the form of the river poem that will be rediscovered and become extremely popular in the Renaissance. The passage downstream, the descriptive praise of the river's bounty and its natural and artificial beauties, and the fragmentary accounts of its local history, all modulated to create an image of the cultural ideal that flourishes on the river bank, are the literary characteristics and objectives that will be emulated by poets much greater than Ausonius. But in *The Moselle* Ausonius succeeded in influencing the past: he made later poets see Virgil, Ovid, Horace, and even Homer through his own eyes and in a new light, and in so doing he also influenced the future.

2. *Exegetes and the Myth of Landscape: Philo Judaeus and the Holy Land*

> Asia stretches right from the south, through the east to the north. . . . [It is] bounded in the east by the sunrise, on the south by the Ocean, in the west by the Mediterranean, in the north by the river Tanais. It contains many provinces and districts whose names and geographical situations I will briefly describe, beginning from Paradise.
> Paradise is a place lying in the eastern parts, whose name is translated out of the Greek into Latin as *hortus*. It is called in the Hebrew tongue Eden. . . . Uniting the two gives us Garden of Delight. . . . From the middle of the Garden, a spring gushes forth to water the whole grove and, dividing up, it provides the sources of four rivers. (Isidore, *Etymologies*)

From this same late Roman, early modern world there emerged a rather different, far less mundane view of the landscape: an allegorical, sometimes mystical one which interprets geography in a way that we might today call semiotically. Most historians agree that imperial Rome provided the cultural climate suitable for the spread of Christianity: that the universalism of a catholic church is, intellectually, the evolutionary descendant of Roman Europe. Medieval writers forged intellectual and historical syncretisms in an attempt to establish links between the pagan and Christian eras, and modern cultural historians continue this process, although using different kinds of data. The allegorizing of the landscape is one aspect of the effort to find unity and continuity in human history, and is itself a manifestation of a mind which sees the world in terms of universals, as one intellectual as well as political body. The Church Fathers' allegorical interpretations of historical landscapes, and of the Holy Land in particular, reflect a geographical syncretism parallel to that which harmonizes the learning of the Greco-Roman world with the revealed knowledge of the new Church. It too recalls the Roman ideal of cultural unity.

Thus, there is a dual influence at work on the river *topos* at the beginning of the modern era, the one religious and the other secular, and both evolve more or less naturally from the classical tradition. These are two tributaries to the development of the secular Christian treatment of the motif during the Renaissance, and they are at many points confluent, for they both reflect efforts to achieve a broader, more embracing view of the individual's place in the world, and of the course of our intellectual traditions. Nevertheless, there were some, such as Jerome, Ambrose, and Augustine, who in varying degrees persisted in trying to separate the sacred writers from the profane in their efforts to comprehend the wisdom of the ages.[10] The allegorical tradition, our present concern, approaches divine text as a gloss to the *liber naturae*, and it did much to formalize the river motif. These interpretations of the Bible were also interpretations of the world. At the foundation of their allegories is a mode of perceiving the landscape. Indeed, although the fact has been largely ignored, these allegorical descriptions of Paradise and the Holy Land formalize the tradition of the moral geography, and much of the way that we analyze geography for its moral order originates in this tradition. Modern literary critics are too accustomed to viewing these settings as disembodied myths or allegories rather than as physical realities. But for the exegetes, as for John Denham or Andrew Marvell, the landscape embodies its own meaning; there is no "dissociation of sensibility." One early commentator, for example, when defining his descriptive and exegetical method in terms of the rivers of Paradise, warns against this tendency to view allegory as an extended intellectual exercise and to forget about the reality that lies behind it. Speaking specifically about the tradition of allegorizing scriptural landscapes, Epiphanius, bishop of Cyprus, says:

> *Si Paradisus non est sensibilis, non est etiam fons; si non est fons, non est flumen; si non est flumen, non sunt quatuor principia, non* Pison,

non Gehon, *non* Tigris, *nec* Euphrates; *non est ficus, non folia, non comedit* Eva *de Arbore, non est* Adam, *non sunt Homines sed veritas iam fabula est, & omnia ad Allegorias revocantur.*[11]

This attempt to interpret biblical geography suggests how far myth has been removed from the physical world and the way in which the myths of landscape have evolved over the centuries. In the exegetical and allegorical writers of the period we can observe the tension between allegory and landscape—and it often focused on the rivers of the world. This is, of course, only one aspect of medieval literary tradition, but it is an important one in the development of our perception of the world.

The best figure to illustrate the place of the river motif in this tradition is also the earliest and most important: Philo Judaeus. A somewhat older contemporary of Seneca, he too looked to the rivers for knowledge; in particular, he studied the rivers of scriptural geography—the *flumen naturae* and the *flumen verborum*—for lessons in divine wisdom and human virtue. Quite literally, there he sought the moral *fons et origo* of the universe. Quoting and commenting on Genesis 2:10, he says:

> "A river goes forth from Eden to water the garden: thence it is separated in four heads. . . ." By these rivers His purpose is to indicate the particular Virtues. These are four in number, prudence, self-mastery, courage, justice. The largest river, of which the four are effluxes, is generic virtue, which we have called goodness. . . . Generic virtue takes its start from Eden, the wisdom of God which is full of Joy, and brightness, and exultation, glorifying and priding itself only upon God its father.[12]

For Philo the created world and the Word are one. The rivers of Eden provide the paradigm by which we understand how we are created in the image of God: the waters originating in the garden are divine goodness and wisdom, which all the garden partakes of and relies upon for its being. In them is reflected the relation of microcosm to macrocosm, and all the material world is the recreation of divine *sapientia*. The analogy is made explicit as Philo explains how the mind is like the Garden of Eden:

> "And a spring went up out of the earth and watered all the face of the earth." He calls the mind a "spring" of the earth and its senses its "face" . . . and the mind like a spring waters the senses, sending to each of them the streams suitable to it.

The key to the landscape and to the allegory is the rivers of Paradise, and his method of reading them is characteristic of the exegetical mode that he influenced. Other commentators might have somewhat different interpretations or emphasis, but they too saw the geography and its moral or intellectual meaning as inseparable. The river of Eden, with its single source and four branches, consistently figures as the most important feature in the landscape, although it may represent divine wisdom, goodness, or peace. Ambrose, for example, identifies the river with wisdom and the four cardinal virtues through which we gain eternal life. As the cult of rivers yields to allegorization in the hands of the patristic writers, we see its pagan characteristics universalized, made catholic:

> *sicut ergo fons vitae est sapientia, fons gratiae spiritalis, ita fons virtutum est ceterarum, quae nos ad aeternae cursum dirigunt vitae. ex hac igitur anima, quae culta est, non ex ea quae inculta fons iste procedit, ut inriget paradisum, hoc est quaedam diversarum frutecta virtutum, quarum sunt quattuor initia, in quae sapientia ista dividitur. quae sunt quattuor initia virtutum nisi prudentiae, aliud temperantiae, tertium fortitudinis, quartum justitiae?*[13]

Behind this allegorical formula, however, are the rivers of Paradise and the attempt to describe the geography of the Holy Land. Ambrose goes on to describe the nations watered by these rivers, the nature of their waters, and how they came to be associated with their particular virtues.[14] In thus describing the *multitudinam aquarum* and the complexity of the biblical world, Ambrose urges us to see in the rivers' unity with their source and outlet an example of Divine Oneness and the peace that comes from our unity with God.[15] In these exegetical texts, taken at large, we are always aware of the geographical world behind the allegory—the physical analogy that we must struggle to understand. As Ambrose makes perfectly clear, the rivers water both the inner spiritual world and that of the external world of nature. It must be remembered that the exegetes, starting with Philo, were attempting, through explanation and description, to regain a harmony between language and the Spirit, and physical reality. The same objective is present in varying degrees in all modern literature, including, for example, *The Faerie Queene* and *Paradise Lost*. Looking at the rivers of the Bible and the Greek hexameral literature, and those of the exegetes and Church Fathers, we must recognize the difference between the mythic mode which *presents* the waters of the world as wrathful, prophetic, or healing, and those writings (mainly allegorical) which *interpret* mythological texts and use them as an approach to divine knowledge. In the latter case, there is an attempt to bridge the gap between experience and understanding through language; this is the very nature of all exegetical and critical writing. This, after all, is what writers of all periods attempt—to understand what writers of another period seemed to understand better, more clearly, or more immediately. To some extent, Philo is attempting to restore myths of landscape, and in this he is not unique; Hesiod was trying to do the same thing in the *Theogony*; so too was Ovid, though in a more specialized way, in *The Metamorphoses*. What is important, though, is that we see the difference between the *text* of Genesis or Deuteronomy, where the riverscape is the vehicle for certain divine attributes, and the *commentary*, which in trying to understand them invokes new ideas and brings new myths to the landscape through the text itself. Similarly, Hesiod, revitalizing cosmogonic wisdom of an earlier generation effectively creates new myths which reflect his own sensibility. What Philo and the Church Fathers attempt is not exactly original in method, but it is original inasmuch as it reflects their own historical vantage point, and in this it marks important changes in the treatment of landscape and the river. Theirs is a different world from that of Homer and Ovid. It is a larger world, and they experience their biblical landscape vicariously, in more rarified and intellectual terms. Appropriately, their myths, emphasizing a universality characteristic of their Christianity, also reflect the larger world of late Roman and medieval Europe. In this respect, we cannot imagine their commentaries being written at any earlier period.

It is well to remember that the exegetes were not only the fathers of church doctrine, but were also scholiasts commenting on and preserving the entire corpus of pagan learning and absorbing it into a Christian framework. Their perception of the world is syncretistic, and they look at the landscape of the ancient world to reconcile seemingly conflicting or erroneous lore with their own revealed knowledge. As Curtius says, in their hands Homer and Hesiod are the literary descendants of Moses and the Prophets.[16] Writers such as Origen, Lactantius, Jerome, Isidore, and Ambrose—indeed, the vast body of the *Corpus Christianorum*—represent an encyclopedic view of human learning, and their erudition embraces Homer, Hesiod, Plato, Moses and the prophets, Virgil, Ovid, and Lucretius.[17] But their perception of the world is intellectual, at a remove from the landscapes of their sources, and in this they are the religious counterparts to the secular tradition represented by Pliny, Strabo, and Seneca.[18] Thus, the sententious rivers of Dionysius the

Areopagite, for example, are clearly of the same world as those analyzed by Seneca:

> Thus contemplating them, we should reverence a fountain of Life flowing into Itself—viewing It even standing by Itself, and as a kind of single power, simple, self-moved, and self-worked, not abandoning Itself, but a knowledge surpassing every kind of knowledge, and always contemplating Itself, through Itself.[19]

Meditating on the rivers of Divine Oneness, he uses the same river *topos*, based on the same natural phenomenon that Ambrose is referring to when he describes the rivers of Paradise:

> *Hoc itaque majoris miraculi est, quomodo omnes congregationes in unam congregationem defluxerint et una congregatio non adimpleta sit . . . omnes torrentes eunt in mare, et mare non adimpletur. utrumque igitur ex praecepto die, ut et fluat aqua et non superfluat.*[20]

Each of these authors imposes a moral or religious myth on the same natural mystery behind the hydrological cycle that Plato and Aristotle examined: that of the ever-flowing river and the never overflowing sea. For each, the enigma of the river leads to the very brink of divine knowledge, demarks the limits between human understanding and God, and forms a border between the divine and the mundane. The natural mystery that inspires this exegetical trope first finds its expression in Ecclesiastes 1:7: "All the rivers run into the sea; yet the sea *is* not full: unto the place from whence the rivers come, thither they return again." The scientific explanation for this changes little until the nineteenth century, but the myths of moral and spiritual order that were read into it vary from age to age.[21]

The Christian exegetes derive a myth of universal order and oneness discernible in the nature of rivers. This is a religious myth comparable to Seneca's secular stoicism that, at least in the *Naturales Quaestiones*, is located in the rivers of the world. This myth-making process, identifiable as it is with the process of allegorizing the landscape, becomes fundamental to our perception of geography. More particularly, the attempt to find a universal order, whether religious or secular, in rivers also becomes characteristic of the larger world view which is part of the Roman legacy. The rivers are not only local waters with local affiliations. They are part of a world beyond their principal city and they suggest a religious, moral, and cultural order which exceeds the influence of the *genius loci* and flows into a larger concept of human identity.

In certain fairly clear ways, then, these rivers of grace and of the mind are direct descendants of the local rivers and their presiding spirits and household gods. But we can also discern how the exegetical and encyclopedic imagination—Isidore's, for example—is radically different from Virgil's or Ovid's. The mind which attempts to describe a world order, such as Pliny's, Plutarch's, Ambrose's, or Isidore's, may have much intellectual lore in common with Virgil or Ovid, but the world and their response to it is very different. Late Roman and medieval writers show us rivers which are a part of a larger landscape and whose virtues are spiritual and universal rather than local and political.

The exegetical and allegorical traditions are not the only place where we will find this myth of order imposed on world geography. We see a similar conflation of moral order and descriptive geography in many medieval world maps, and those reproduced in this chapter are fairly typical. In their conceptualized image of geography, either Paradise or the Holy Land is usually the point of reference, and emanating from it is the river whose four branches go forth and divide the rest of the world. After separating Asia, Africa, and Europe, they flow back to their source again, completing a geographical and historical cycle by reuniting with the world-embracing river Oceanus. Implicit in the maps is a historical and metaphysical design which is suggested by the rivers. The paradisiac center yields to the politically and geographically divided post-lapsarian world, but the cycle of Christian history is completed by the confluence of the rivers with their unifying circumambient source in the sea, and in which the order of the world is restored. The metaphysics of the map imply a self-perpetuating world order embodying a redemptive historical process, and there is a similar religious and historical order in the less representational T-O maps of the same period. We can see that the world charted in this way is analogous to that described in the historical allegories of the exegetes. In using the rivers to understand the moral shape of the world, these authors and cartographers impose upon it an ideal of unity and community that has grown out of its Roman past but has been transformed by its Christian present. It is a myth without a geographical center, unless it is in Jerusalem or Paradise itself. However, it *is* a cultural myth in that it reflects a culture's consciousness of its own role as the repository of an intellectual tradition and a historical growth to be directed by their more enlightened Christian perspective.

3. *Rivers of Grace: Allegory and the Disembodied River—*
Catherine of Siena

> Scogan, that knelest at the stremes heed
> Of grace, of alle honour and worthinesse,
> In th'ende of which streme I am dul as deed,
> Forgete in solitarie wildernesse.   (Chaucer, *Lenvoy . . . a Scogan*)

> Time, who cannot stay, but always goes without returning, like water
> which is always descending, never returning a drop backward . . . for
> Time destroys and devours everything; Time, who changes every-
> thing, who makes all grow and nourishes all.
>> (Guillaume de Lorris, *The Romance of the Rose*)

> We should doubtless understand, in his promise to the good, the
> "river of peace" as the abundance of his peace. . . . This is the river
> which he says he will send down upon those to whom he promises
> blessedness so great that we may understand that all things in that
> heavenly region of felicity have all they want of this river.
>> (Augustine, *De Civitate Dei*)

> The nearest thing to it [the soul] that one will be able to find will be a
> spring, which is so truly the beginning of water that . . . it is not said
> to be born of anything, for if it were it would not be the
> beginning. . . . Just as the sources are not easy to discover from
> which pour forth the Nile, the Po, the Danube, and the Don . . . let
> your mind run back to the soul as a source, the motion of which . . .
> is evidenced by our thoughts, joys, hopes, and fears. Its motion is the
> discernment of good and evil, love of the virtues, yearning for the
> vices, from which flows all the streams of action that arise in use.
>> (Macrobius, *Commentary on the Dream of Scipio*)

In the encyclopedic and exegetical traditions we see how the Roman
legacy helps to free the river from the landscape while preserving its
associations with nature. The highly metaphoric language of the
river which we see in the classical rhetoricians, the *flumen orationis*,
is carried to further extremes in those authors for whom the distinction between description and symbol, between the *flumen naturae*
and the *flumen verborum*, becomes less clear. As perceptions of
nature become increasingly intellectualized, the river gains more of
its meaning from the dimension of language, rhetoric, and extended
metaphor: from the imagination rather than from nature. The
allegorists insist on the analogy between the word and the world,
but in the hands of still other authors, the world of nature is lost
sight of altogether. Their concern is not with exegesis and preservation of ancient learning or revelation, but with the ideas and

application of doctrine and Scripture, and so their language is naturally at a further remove from the material world from which so many of their *exempla* derive. In them we see another, significantly different aspect of the treatment of the river motif. Some of the descriptions which were used by the exegetes when locating the rivers of Paradise are adapted as rhetorical *topoi*, abstracted from the biblical geography.

The extent to which the idea of the river supplants the river itself, and to which the channels of rhetoric direct its description, can be see in Bernard of Clairvaux's meditation on the motif at the beginning of Sermon 13:

> Just as the sea is the ultimate source of wells and rivers, so Christ the Lord is the ultimate source of all virtue and knowledge. For who has power to endow us with virtues if not he who is the King of Glory? And what are we told in the canticle of Anna but that God himself is the Lord of all knowledge? Hence from him as from a well-head comes the power to be pure in body, diligent in affection and upright in will. Nor is this all. From him too come subtlety of intellect, splendor of eloquence, urbanity of bearing; from him, knowledge and words of wisdom. Indeed in him are hidden all the treasures of wisdom and knowledge. Shall I add still more? Chaste thoughts, just judgments, holy desires—are they not all streams from that one spring? If the waters that surround us inevitably return to the sea by hidden underground channels, only to gush forth again without fail and without weariness for the refreshing of our sight and the relief of our needs, why should not those spiritual streams return unerringly and without interruption to irrigate our souls? Let the rivers of grace circle back to their Fountain-Head that they may run their course anew. Let the torrent that springs in heaven be channelled back to its starting point, and be poured on the earth against with fertilizing power.[22]

Bernard's river, very much a *topos* here, derives from the same natural phenomenon that we have seen elsewhere, but Plato and his hydrology are left behind and the sententious rhetoric of rivers has thrown the world into eclipse. There is no landscape behind the descriptive elements of Bernard's meditation, and in this he differs much from the patristics. Nevertheless, the myth of unity that they found manifest in the material world is preserved in the rhetoric. The point of contact between the river and God's grace in this extended simile is in rhetoric and the imagination, and serves to turn our thoughts away from the material world. Not really interested in the river, nor even in the idea of the river (and Philo was interested in both), Bernard uses it as an effective Ciceronian device, the language of which just happens to continue to reflect its origins in nature. Paradoxically, then, the image of nature works against nature itself as it is tamed and turned to the service of rhetorical artifice. What is remarkable, though (and this is the peculiar feature of the motif), is that Bernard's river reveals its ancestry in ancient myth and landscape. Its association with virtue, knowledge, chastity, and eloquence, all deriving from a divine source, reminds us of less urbane rituals enacted on more secluded banks of primitive rivers.

In the metaphoric, highly cerebral rivers of Bernard, and the descriptive, scholastic style of the encyclopedists (such as Isidore) we see two rhetorical modes that also suggest two extreme views of nature and human nature which take shape at this time: one, infused with Christian doctrine, tries to transcend the physical world to save the soul; the other, humanistic and secular in its emphasis, embraces created nature in its quest for knowledge and human perfection, although it too might be reinforced by doctrinal arguments. The opposition itself is a commonplace in medieval literature. Indeed, all Western thought could be seen in terms of this polarity, but the dialectic is all the sharper when put into the context of Christian epistemology and the questions that arise from it about the extent and nature of human knowledge in a fallen world. We can see that Christian asceticism, with its spirit of *contemptus mundi*, and Christian humanism, with its impulse to seize the day and receive the world as a bountiful and good gift from God, are both part of the Roman legacy and represent two aspects of its myth of community, which sees the individual and his local environment absorbed into a larger more catholic order. The river, associated with nature and with divinity, assumes an ambivalent place in this dialectic, one like our own, and it flows between these two steep ideological banks. In a unique way, then, it demonstrates a basic duality in medieval literature—a duality which is largely resolved in the Renaissance. In this and the next section I want to illustrate briefly how the river, as an image with well defined associations, was used by medieval writers to locate their thoughts about nature's divinity or its potential for redemption. A few brief examples will show how the use of the motif suggests an author's place within these two extreme intellectual and literary impulses.

Catherine of Siena (d. 1380), for example, uses the river for its identification with mutable nature, but she turns the motif back upon itself to develop her metaphysic of *contemptus mundi*. In the

Orcherd of Syon she meditates on the redemption and transcendence of the soul through Christ. Not only does her Christian asceticism resemble Seneca's stoicism, but her use of the river motif is also very close to his. She creates an allegorical topography in which the soul's access to heaven from a fallen world is over a bridge, which figures Christ: "God made a brigge of his sone whanne þe wey of goynge to hevene was broke by inobedience of Adam, by þe which brigge alle trewe cristen men mowen overepasse . . . it recheþ fro þe erþe upe into hevene."[23] The image of the bridge by which we transcend the river of nature is all the more resonant if we think of the traditional associations against which Catherine is working. Vividly conceived as having stone foundations and three ladders of ascent and a vaulted roof, it is an architectural image that the humanist might use to suggest civic achievement and human ability to perfect nature. And, crossing from the realm of death in life to that of eternal life after death, it is also reminiscent of sacred crossings into the other world of pagan times over the Nile or the Styx: it "streccheþ fro þe heigt of hevene down to þe erþe," and so is of both worlds, one end being fixed in immutable heaven, and the other being firmly set in the transient world.[24]

The river that this structure crosses also has its origins in antiquity: it is the Christian analogue to the vague chaotic limbo of pre-Christian escatology. For Catherine it is protean *mundus* itself, the world in all its alluring but fickle variety, and to trust oneself to its waters is to be lured by the "likyngis of þe world." Thus, beneath the bridge flows all that is mutable, worldly, vain, and without "sustentacioun," and to reject the bridge is to be cast into the river of death in life: "Þerfor so as the watir renneþ, so renneþ sich a man þat so setteþ his love, albeit þoru his blyndnes siche þinges seemen to hym good and not veyn." Catherine's warning that the "blynd wrechche [who] . . . putteþ hersilf to the flood . . . taketh noon heed how sliper and how swift þe watir is, and abideþ nobody"[25] is the Christian aescetic's rejection of the lesson Virgil offers in the second book of the *Georgics*, where he urges man, knowledgeable of nature's warnings, to ford dark rivers boldly.

In her contempt for the world, Catherine denounces this "flood [as] a fervent see of this wreechid liif," full of "many grevances." Her bridge resembles the Roman *pervius*, a causeway over the sacred rivers, the crossing of which requires a special blessing, an "*auspice peremnia*," and vows at the Temple of Janus, the god who looks upon both this world and the next.[26] But for Catherine, the bridge which assures passage is Christ. It is made of the stones of Christian virtue and mounted by three ladders: the desire of the soul, virtuous love, and sweet peace. As in pagan lore, no evil can pass over it, and once the other side has been reached, one comes upon the heavenly analogue of the earthly river, the "liifly waters of grace."[27] Catherine's allegory of the soul is a sophisticated literary work in which we can see the instinctive adaptation of what had been religious rituals of pre-Christian Roman life. This process of adaptation is part of a culture's evolving response to the world. Not just an accident of the allegorical language of her meditation, it reflects also a world view at once Christian and Roman. Indeed, the dominant metaphors in her Christian allegory were entrenched in the cultural self-consciousness of Rome, as we see in the survival of the ancient title of "Pontifex Maximus," which was assumed by the Holy Roman Emperor.[28]

Whether by accident, design, or inspiration, Catherine has worked out certain essential features of mythological lore by concentrating her meditation on the river and the bridge. She seems to have apprehended the way that, particularly for the Christian, the river captures the troublesome anomalies which arise when one tries to reconcile life and religious belief: the conflict between incarnation (or immanence) and the transcendent or supernatural. In the most primitive myths the rivers of the world have their divine models in celestial order. As Marcia Eliade says of Mesopotamian myths, "Tigris had its model in the star Anunit and the Euphrates in the Star of the swallow."[29] Perfection in the world, when the earthly coincides with the heavenly, is achieved only when something realizes or repeats its archetype, and the river is one of the most natural if not the only image of this potential in nature. The recognition of the vanity of the world that Catherine describes, and the transcendence through mystic meditation to the celestial analogue in the perennial waters of grace, figure a similar correspondence "by knyttinge togydere dyvine nature with the pure nature of the manheed," and the result is a strikingly thorough Christian treatment of the river along the basic patterns of primitive myth.[30]

In the allegory of *The Orcherd of Syon* we see distinct rhetorical links with the patristic writing of the tradition represented by Philo Judaeus, although generically it is very different from the Bible commentary. Moreover, in exploiting the river's rich associations to urge us to renounce nature and the material world, Catherine moves further away from Philo in both style and thought. Hers, however, is just one extreme position in the scholastic and polemical literature of the Middle Ages, and others use the motif in rhetorically similar ways to pose quite different arguments. Brief mention of two such authors who make casual but interesting use of the motif will serve to illustrate its intellectual range.

In the renaissance of the twelfth century, for example, Bernard Silvestris, in his *De universitate mundi*, develops a similar entelechy between the terrestrial and celestial realms: the Uranian sphere, where the etherial rivers flow pure fire and water, is mirrored in the lower world by an idealized classical culture. Trying to revive the humane arts of antiquity, Bernard suggests that the transcendent realm of perfected nature had its corresponding social order in the classical world, the revival of which would restore that harmonious ideal that he figures forth in images of the four elements. Thus, in his allegory, the pure elemental nature in the celestial sphere is the ideal that we emulate through an ethical and intellectual ideal of secular humanism. Bernard, avoiding questions of Church doctrine and morality, presents us with a view of nature which is antithetical to that which we have seen in Catherine of Siena: it is secular and humane rather than mystical and transcendent. Their literary objectives are wholly different, but they both draw on classical motifs and use similar allegorical methods to universalize them.

The tension between transcendence and incarnation that we see in Catherine and Bernard is mediated by Alan of Lille (fl. 1150). For him, the opposition between Theology and Nature is reconciled by the secular virtues, Concordia and Phronesis (or Wisdom), which serve to join the earthly and heavenly realms. As a rhetorical motif and an aspect of the natural world, the river figures anagogically in the *Anticlaudianus*, where his principal concern is to understand the place of nature in a cosmos interpreted in the light of Christian Platonism. Rejecting neither the world nor the spirit, he sees the two as interpenetrating, and the river is, if you will, something of a bridge between them.

In these three authors, though, in Bernard Silvestris, Alan of Lille, and Catherine of Siena, we see a similar process of abstraction by which the river moves further from its specific geographical contexts and becomes associated with Nature itself. The treatment of the river—and hence its symbolic importance—may vary radically according to the intellectual and religious views of the author. In part what we are speaking of is the development of Christian and Platonic allegory, but it can also be seen as the result of literary, cultural, and geographical changes as the classical world is transformed from within. While it must be emphasized that these are but three examples and that the river is not a dominant image in Bernard, or Alan of Lille, each of them uses the river as a way of temporarily focusing his ideas about the place of nature in the universal order, and in this sense, they are useful illustrations of how the classical motif was used in the Middle Ages. And more important, the tradition that they represent defines the fundamental ambivalence in attitudes toward secular learning in a world in which an evolving Christianity is still adjusting to its classical inheritance, and these are the questions that are absorbed into the largely secular world of the Renaissance.

Certainly there are many other instances of very different treatments of the river in medieval literature—in the saints' lives, the ballads, in the work of Deschamps and Guillaume de Lorris, and even in Chaucer. Nevertheless, in looking at these examples from the medieval allegorical tradition in the light of some of the cultural, geographical, and literary changes from the classical period, we can see that the mind and imagination have become more, rather than less far-reaching: just as the *topos*, never wholly divorced from its worldly confines, has a clearer channel through the realm of the intellect, so too the medieval imagination embraces a far wider, more complex intellectual, moral, and psychological, indeed even physical dimension, and more examples would only reinforce this conclusion. It is true that medieval authors were never quite free from either the fetters of orthodoxy, which were secured by the Church Fathers, or those of classical learning, and the very nature of the river motif reflects how firm but knotted these bonds were. But the river also helps mark the emergence—for good or ill—of the individual imagination, and the greater freedom with which the mind can range over this world and comprehend realms unseen. In this, the river, in all its formalism, helped these medieval explorers in their discovery of the mind; its rhetorical qualities, instead of being an insurmountable obstacle, were an avenue of discovery and exploration in the imperfectly know world of the imagination, not of the physical world.

4. *Rivers of the World: The European Landscape and the Myth of Geography*

> But because this peace of incorruption and immortality is to flow thence upon earthly bodies as well, he said that he will send down this river, so that it may somehow flow from the upper regions even to the

lower and may make men equal to the angels. (Augustine, *De Civitate Dei*)

Above all ryvers thy Ryver hath renowne,
  Whose beryall stremys, pleasaunt and preclare,
Under thy lusty wallys renneth down,
  Where many a swanne doth swymme with wyngis fare;
Where many a barge doth saile, and row with are,
  Where many a ship doth rest with toppe-royall.
O! Towne of townes, patrone and not compare:
  London, thou art the floure of Cities all. (Dunbar, *On London*)

Watering the neighbouring fields was the Simois, which has come from another part of the world to see Troy. It hoped by its long wandering past so many realms and cities to have earned the right to disembogue as a Trojan into the rolling sea; and while with unwearied gaze it looked in wonder at Pergamum, it checked its declining course, braked its flow still slower, and determined to embrace all the city that it loved. (Joseph of Exeter, *De Bello Troiano*)

The changes of the Middle Ages also helped to identify the second cultural impulse that I want to illustrate, and it is perhaps more obviously related to the geopolitical transformations of the period. This is the secular impulse which embraces the world and sees in it the potential for human perfection and nature's redemption. With its preoccupation with images of society, it also represents an interest in the political geography which finds clearer expression than it had received in antiquity, and in this we also witness imperial Rome's evolution into the Holy Roman Empire and the establishment of a universal church in a European rather than Mediterranean political setting.

In identifying this redefined interest in social, political, and geographical subjects, I want to call attention to that large body of literature in which the individuated landscape is described, and the city or nation is its ostensible concern. It is here that the modern European political geography is presented as it had not been presented before and perceived in terms of the distinctive historical landscapes that are still associated with it. In forms such as the *laus patriae* and the *encomium urbis*, in the travelogues, chorographies, and chronicles, we can see clear links with the classical forms on which they were modelled, but we also see the fragmentation of the European political world, the emphasis on cultural and political separateness, and the emergence of national identity; in short, in the old forms we recognize a new world. This is a literature of regional identity different from that of the classical world; in it we see a society of wide rivers, good roads, and large and powerful cities having Europe, not the *mare nostrum*, as its defining idea, and as such, it is animated with the spirit of growth rather than recovery. Although it exhibits the separateness of regional literature, behind it there is also an impulse toward unity—an ideal of community that is never quite articulated until the Renaissance.

It too has that element of humanistic self-awareness which is present in the religious writing of the Middle Ages, but there is, perforce, a difference which perhaps accounts for its increasing popularity through succeeding centuries, and that is that literature which is primarily topographical in interest is never written *de contemptu mundi*. It embraces the world's variety and regards society and its manifold forms of self-expression as essentially good. As Plato, Aristotle, and Augustine had before, it sees the city as an image of human prefectability, as an artistic creation mirroring an ideal celestial city. Such an earthbound vision apprehends an image of the world in which human redemption is a real possibility, so that this shaping view of cultural geography combines the moral ideal of the Church Fathers and the social ideal of the Greeks with the utilitarianism of the Romans.

Topographical literature, with its image-making rather than purely descriptive objectives, generally has an interesting combination of highly artificial rhetorical ornament and immediacy of discovery and observation which is appropriate for its theme of human ability to perfect nature by marrying it to the diviner arts; together, these make fertile territory for the irrigating waters of the river *topos*. Forms such as the *laus patriae* and *descriptio urbis* are part of an eclectic tradition that reveals an understanding of how the ancients thought of their rivers as reflecting the struggle to tame nature. Antiquity (including the Bible), as the matrix of humanism, provided medieval writers with generic models on which to graft their own moral and social vision, as we see in Joseph of Exeter's idealization of Pergamum, which, in presenting the city in terms of the harmony of art and nature, stands as a model of the *encomium urbis* (see the epigraph to this chapter). The generic and thematic characteristics that appear in these early modern forms, with their classical and contemporary elements, become essential ingredients for all topographical literature.

This regional self-awareness conveyed in primarily topographical contexts manifests itself in many different forms and genres. We see it, for example, in Dante and Petrarch, as well as in the literature of the Crusades. But the purest (if not the most compelling) illustrations of this civic impulse to look to the landscape are to be found in the encomiastic descriptive literature of which Dunbar's poem (the second epigraph for this chapter) is a late example. Since the influence of this form on the more ambitious topographical literature of the Renaissance is both great and direct, and since it poses comparatively few literary problems, it will be useful to look at how the river is used in two or three of these works.

The immensely popular *encomium urbis* had its specific models in the epideictic verse of Sidonius, Statius, and Claudian, although the ideal of urban self-sufficiency, with interdependent parts contributing to the life of the whole, came from Plato.[31] To his secular city Augustine added the element of Christian purposefulness. The form was, above all, the product of the increasing civic spirit which strove to establish a distinct historical and cultural self-image, and in this it is an extreme example of that culturally self-conscious literature designed to fabricate an urban, even a national identity. With its pagan and Christian prototypes, it draws widely upon literary and historical sources to create for itself a pattern which the civic history must thereafter strive to emulate, and this proud but contrived sense of local identity is an essential factor in the development of modern Europe.

The city descriptions, then, were generally compounded of Christian and secular features. The cities were described as naturally suited to their geographical setting, which was praised for its salubrity, beauty, natural defensibility, and economic potential; the river figured as the common element harmonizing each of these natural assets. It frequently insulates the town, either naturally or through the assistance of human ingenuity in the form of canals, thus realizing in the geography the urban ideal of a microcosm, such as the world is and the individual is—alone and sufficient, but also embraced by the divine element that makes it a part of the rest of the world. Thus the river provides ready means of defense, food, recreation, refreshing breezes, as well as commercial and social opportunities beyond the precincts of the town itself. In addition to these natural advantages, authors also praised its cultural attributes: its fortifications and other architectural wonders, its commercial vitality, its heroic past (particularly the founders and heroic leaders), and its ecclesiastical history (the beauties of its cathedral, its

relics, and the life of its patron saint), and these cultural achievements, too, customarily involve the river.

In the twelfth century the city was no longer regarded merely as a
figure of secular and ecclesiastical strength, as some have suggested.[32] Rather, it represented a cosmopolitan ideal, an urban *locus
amoenus*, beautiful yet secure, rich with pleasing variety, whose
populus can vary public life with the refreshing *otia* of learning,
leisure, or holy meditation. William Fitz-Stephen's *Description . . .
of London* (c. 1174) is fairly typical of the form. It is organized by
his circumambulation of the city along the Thames and the other
bordering streams. The landscape thus gives the city its shape—
defines its natural dimensions. For Fitz-Stephen, London is by no
means merely a military stronghold; he speaks of the seven gates
and the walls of the city as having "in a long tract of time [been]
totally subverted and carried away" by the Thames.[33] Instead of
rude military strength, he emphasizes cultural attractions: London's
antiquity (which, he stresses, is greater than Rome's), the measure-
less variety of its provisions, its cosmopolitan population and their
activities—all seemingly provided in abundance by the navigability
of the tidal Thames.

There is something wholly appropriate about the fact that the
Description . . . of London is inserted in Fitz-Stephen's life of
Becket, and this appropriateness is all the greater because his real
delight in London is in worldly things: not merely material wealth,
but diversity of experience. He particularly emphasizes that in the
midst of the urban clamor there is also the opportunity for quiet
retirement along the riverside, and for the tranquil atmosphere
needed for learning:

> Round the city again towards the North, arise certain springs at a
> small distance, whose waters are sweet, salubrious, clear, and whose
> runnels murmur o'er the shining stones. Amongst these, Holywell,
> Clerkenwell, and St Clement's Well, may be esteemed the principal,
> as being much the best frequented, both by scholars from the schools,
> and the youth of the city, when in a summer's evening they are
> disposed to take an airing.

For Fitz-Stephen, then, whose acknowledged model is Plato's *Re-
public*, the city also incorporates the pastoral world; it is a concord
of secular and religious activities where people's spiritual, intellectual, and physical potential is amply nurtured as if by the god-given
bounty of the river. If the description is not a literary marvel, which

it is not, its very vitality does, nevertheless, engage us. Fitz-Stephen is animated by a social ideal that he clearly sees alive in the city: an ideal which incorporates natural and artistic growth, richness of material, intellectual, and spiritual, social, and private experience. And the city, given shape by its network of rivers and enriched by the resources of the Thames, is a microcosm in which vital energies thrive and in which the relation between the present and the past is a creative one.

The *laus patriae* and related topographical descriptive forms (such as the chorography) have similar literary and cultural objectives, and the rivers often have a similarly important function. In them, and in the *encomium urbis*, we can see quite clearly how the literary tradition reflects the altered perceptions of the political geography of Europe. The classical encomiastic forms shape and are shaped by their new geographical contexts, and in this process we can observe the evolution of the topographical literature that we associate with the Renaissance.

One of the earliest and most influential of such works to reveal Europe's geographical and political shift from its Mediterranean center is Gildas's *De excidio et conquestu Britanniae* (c. 550), a work that echoes with the cultural interdependence between Rome and the provinces. Gildas frequently uses conventional river motifs to focus the theme of Rome's defeat of Britain and the advent of Christianity. If his rhetorical amplification seems classical in style, it also has local color, which adds a degree of naturalness and immediacy to offset its artificiality. As a result, his landscapes are both Roman and British, and in this they reflect an implicit social ideal.

Gildas delights in his river descriptions, and indeed, he seems to have been the one to initiate the convention of viewing Britain in terms of rivers in whose waters antiquity and modernity mingle. For him, Britain is a land whose potential is figured in its rivers. As though realizing how the tamed river of antiquity was a symbol of human ability to bring civilized order from protean chaos, he too describes how the torrents of the land have been made tractable. Although ostensibly local description, many of his passages, for all their immediacy, have suspiciously literary and Mediterranean (or biblical) qualities to them: "Nor will I call out upon the mountains, fountains, or hills, or upon the rivers which are now subservient to the use of man, but once were an abomination and destructive to them and to which the blind people paid divine honour." Gildas has a cunning ability to combine vague literary echoes within his descriptions in order to make the landscape embody his cultural and religious ideals. The undeveloped, wild landscape is analogous to the unenlightened, spiritual blindness of its inhabitants. For Gildas, the river torrent of pagan antiquity has been tamed by a kind of Christian technology in which one's spiritual self-mastery corresponds to the control of the world, and the result is an ecclesiastical and secular bounty which is further enhanced by the union of an ornate rhetoric and the natural landscape.

Gildas too has an unmistakable love of the world, and throughout his *descriptio de situ Britanniae* natural wealth is eyed for its commercial potential. He often resorts to an imagery which is not only exotic, but also resonant with Christian meanings. Admiring the castles and towers that adorn the rivers, he quite literally describes the landscape in terms of the marriage of art and nature:

> it is decked, like a man's chosen bride, with diverse jewels, with lucid fountains and abundant brooks, wandering over the snow white sands; with transparent rivers, flowing in gentle murmurs, and offering a sweet pledge of slumber to those who recline upon their banks, whilst it is irrigated by abundant lakes, which pour forth cool torrents of refreshing water.

Having tamed his metaphoric mistress, man is ready to wed and bed her. The conjugal landscape, sanctified with a hint of the *Song of Songs*, has in its sensuous beauty the suggestion of the civilized pleasures that (five hundred years later) Fitz-Stephen was to enjoy in his London, as the torrent, once directed against the pagans, is eventually transformed to a flood of refreshment. Here, too, the highly ornate style is also remarkable for its fusion of classical *copia* and topographical description, so that this exotic *locus amoenus* combines the atmosphere of romance, suggestions of classical and Christian humanism, and firsthand observation.

To complete his image of Britain, Gildas even adapts the classical river motifs to British settings and history. The Mediterranean mountain torrent is introduced through a digressive simile into his description of Rome's help in ridding the island of its invaders. Rome's trained forces

> mow them down like leaves which fall at the destined period; and as a mountain-torrent swelled with numerous streams, and bursting its banks with roaring noise, with foaming crest and yeasty wave rising to the stars, by whose eddying currents our eyes are as it were dazzled, does with one of its billows overwhelm every obstacle in its way, so did our illustrious defenders vigorously drive our enemies' band beyond the sea, if any could escape them.

There is a rather satisfying decorum to the image here: the Homeric reference to Jove's judgment is modified to a vague suggestion of the "destined" order to human events, and the image of the torrent is brought naturally into the context of British history, thus giving it a dignity and importance appropriate to its subject matter.

Gildas also uses biblical analogues to define further his image of Britain as the successor to antiquity and spiritual descendant of Israel. As the British are led by their protomartyr Saint Alban across the spiritual waters from paganism to Christianity, the land-scape itself provides the implicit parallel to the Jews' passage over the Jordan:

> Like the Israelites of old, who trod dry-foot on unfrequented path whilst the ark of the covenant stood sometime in the sands in the midst of Jordan; also the martyr, with 1,000 others, opened a path across the noble river Thames, whose waters stood abrupt like precipices on either side.[34]

Gilda's technique can be described as one of topographical (rather than literary) allusion, for it is based on his perception of the native landscape. His method of interpreting his settings is to impose on them the ideals he extracts from analogous real or fictional settings from the Bible or the classics.

It is plain that one often-used technique of image-making for Gildas is to identify the national landscape in terms of literary analogues, many of which involved rivers. Distinctly "modern" description conflates with the impulse to find suitable rhetorical figures to embody the meaning of his historical vision, and the result is an interesting imbalance of simplicity and ornateness. The land-scape echoes with resonances both antique and modern, exotic and plain, and the sounds are carried along like a silvery mist through the river valleys.

This process of image-making in which classical and nonclassical settings seem to merge becomes increasingly subtle over the centuries as authors writing in different forms set out to define the ancient origins of their nations. Because of the greater scope of most of these works, the river is not always as conspicuous as it is in the *encomium urbis*, for example. Nevertheless, it continues to be important, so that, particularly in Britain, the naturalized river motif provided a way of temporarily focusing the national image. Geoffrey of Monmouth (d. 1154), the most audacious of these national mythologizers, repeatedly uses the rivers of Britain to underscore his heroic version of the history of the kings of Britain, and to give the native landscape a literary respectability, so that his history has at once its elements of Celtic romance and classical epic. Thus, when Brutus, nation-founder and grandson of Aeneas, arrives at the site of London, the landing and the naming of Troia Nova contain echoes of Virgil and Ovid. Travelling up "the River Thames [he] walked up and down its banks, and so chose a site suited for his purpose. There and then he built his city and called it Troia Nova." Indeed, the congenial setting of the isle itself has a natural suitability comparable to that of Tiber's mouth for his displaced grandfather, Aeneas.[35] Likewise, later in the Roman history of Britain, Dunvallo Mulmutius, when establishing the first code of Roman law in Britain, in good Roman fashion builds a sanctuary on the river Thames, next to the Temple of Concord, thus romanizing the British landscape.

But the Roman presence always seems grafted onto a distinctly un-Roman setting. The rivers are also those of Celtic legend and so remain very much the *genii loci*. The river lore which provides countless place-names, such as the tale of Locrinus and Humber, or that of Estrilda and Hebren, is indigenous. The rivers, however romanized or Christianized, are also protective deities, with youth in their charge, and remain as vestiges of local cult as we see in the oracular rivers of Merlin's prophecy, "The Seven Seas shall flow forth through seven mouths and the River Usk shall be boiling hot for seven months . . . three springs shall burst forth in the town of Winchester and the streams which run from them will divide into three parts."[36] Whether in Arcadia, Latium, or Britain, the river never completely loses its local identity; it absorbs foreign influences but never finally succumbs to them; it always flows with the thick blood of its people's history. As in the river marriage in Book 4 of *The Faerie Queene*, the rivers here seem at once familiar and yet distinctly novel, and that is because their traditional literary functions are subordinated to the primacy of place and local myth; they have been adapted to a native place and the context which has itself been created with cunning literary design.

Geoffrey's rivers, and those of other medieval chroniclers and topographers, are very much the product of their desire to create a literary image of the realm at once analogous to those of ancient cultures and yet adequate to their own conception of their place in history. Thus, their work reveals un-Roman features, such as the strong interest in nature and landscape for their own sake. Giraldus

Cambrensis (d. 1223), for example, has an irrepressible desire to see and describe as well as to propagandize. He repeatedly invokes Homer, Virgil, and Ovid as his models, and yet in his *Description of Wales*, he describes himself as a painter who will "describe and . . . adorn, with all the graces of composition, such remote corners of the earth as . . . Wales"; his *Itinerary Through Wales*, written in "the scholastic style," seems to have been inspired by Pliny and Tacitus in its attempt to chronicle the "names of springs and torrents . . . and the natural history and description of the country"; delight in his native land and its lore combines with encyclopedic erudition.[37] In his use of classical models and forms we can see how the medieval writer continues to look at his native landscape with foreign eyes. Throughout his vivid and perceptive topographies he interweaves his political and ecclesiastical designs much as Geoffrey of Monmouth uses history and topography to achieve his unique literary objectives.

All of these writers perceive the presence of antiquity in their local settings; there is a protean adaptability like that of the river itself in their ability to embrace all influences, pagan and Christian, Greek and Roman, and to make them seem like the natural alluvia of history poured forth on the rich plains of Britain. Theirs is not a neoclassical kind of imitation, but a modernizing of those less adequate rhetorical rills, for their objective is to proclaim national identity, not to efface it. In their rivers the imagination betrays a cultural ideal based on classical antiquity which provides the vocabulary for their individual response to the real landscape. From their work we get a sense of the distance of Rome and Athens from Britain and modern Europe. Like history and geography, the rivers are an extension of their humanity, their culture, and themselves, and so, they are the natural vehicles for thought, expression, and self-realization. It is not surprising that these descriptions reveal more about the authors' intellectual inheritance than about the landscape itself. As humanity becomes more at home in the world, its images of the river reflect the tendency to look on all things with a proprietorial eye. Modern Europe, made smaller by its large, deep-flowing rivers, assumes the appearance of an artificial landscape. Although such familiarity does not necessarily breed contempt, it certainly does dull the respect formerly paid to the sacred rivers, so that these reverend household gods become rather like beloved but familiar objects in the crowded parlor of the European imagination. And yet, if Europe has become smaller, the cultural, political, and national distances (and differences) between cities and regions has, paradoxically, increased, and both culturally and geographically, the river serves to traverse this distance.

[FIGURES 6–10]

Medieval and early Renaissance images of the river reflect a cultivated, highly ordered, even schematic sense of the landscape in which symmetries of knowledge and faith frame the unknown or less orderly. The world itself was perceived in terms of a Christian historical context which shaped, for example, the medieval maps, where the globe is supported by Christ, Paradise is the point of orientation (top center) for the rest of the world, and Jerusalem is at the center (figs. 6 & 8). The rivers of Paradise divide a historical world into its continental landmasses and often rejoin the circumambient ocean, so that the rudimentary geography presents a metaphysical and historical geography, conceived in terms of its spiritual and historical origins and ultimate end.

Maps, like other arts, are based on what is known or presumed about reality, and the rest of the world takes shape around this. In the T. O. maps (fig. 10), the rivers provide order rather than information; in the local and world maps, such as Ranulphus Hidgen's (fig. 8) the rivers are the expression of what is known, and the arteries extending into and embracing the unknown, like arms of civilization or revelation. In this, they are both the literal and symbolic, imaginative and descriptive manifestations of the river's role in the pursuit of knowledge.

The same intellect that orders as it describes the world is evident in other arts — such as the books of hours and illuminated manuscripts, where symbolic or allegorical settings transform historical events and places (fig. 9). In figure 9, the symmetry which literally channels the force of nature also makes the White Tower, the city, and the commemorated events rise like symbols of the celestial city from the banks of an ideally ordered nature. As in the mosaics at Praeneste, we have here and in the copy of the commemorative painting of Edward VI's coronation (fig. 10), scenes of heightened reality. In the coronation painting, the river traces a natural order that finds its ceremonious parallel in the Royal procession, so that history, ceremony, and topography move, as it were, in the same direction.

Figure 6. Psalter *mappa mundi*. Fourteenth century.
The form conventionally incorporates geography
within the framework of history and theology.

Figure 7. T. O. Map. Sallust
manuscript, fourteenth century.

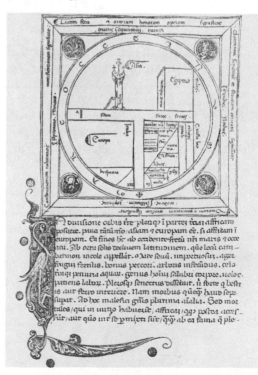

Figure 8. Ranulphus Hidgen. *Mappa Mundi*, fourteenth century.

Figure 9. Charles D'Orleans in the White Tower. Illuminated manuscript, fifteenth century. The use of local geographical details in religious and secular illuminated manuscripts was a common practice.

Figure 10. Coronation of Edward VI. Eighteenth-century copy of a contemporary painting.

PART TWO

LANDSCAPE AND LITERATURE: RENAISSANCE RIVERS AND THE EMERGENCE OF THE RIVER POEM

It is as difficult a task to finde out the Original of some Nations and Cities, as it is to finde out the Spring of the mysterious River of Nile which impregnates the womb of Egypt. (James Howell, *Londinopolis*)

But in Albion the wonder of Islands lovely Thamesis, fairest of fair Nereides, loves sea-borne Queene adoring, vaunts the glory of her maiden streames, happy harbourer of so many Swans, Apollos musical birds . . . . The faire Nymphs keeping tyme with the billowing of her Chrystall waves, carrying to the Ocean with her ebbe, doth there echo them to her astonisht sisters which assemble in those vast flouds by timely confluence. (John Dickenson, *Arisbas, Euphues amidst his slumbers*)

III. _Renaissance Contexts_

I think it is in Macedon where Alexander is porn. I tell you, captain,
if you look in the maps of the 'orld, I warrant you sall find, in the
comparisons between Macedon and Monmouth, that the situations,
look you, is both alike. There is a river in Macedon, and there is also
moreover a river at Monmouth: it is called Wye at Monmouth; but it
is out of my prains what is the name of the other river; but 'tis all one,
'tis alike as my fingers is to my fingers, and there is salmons in both.
(Shakespeare, _Henry V_)

It was a happy revolution of the heavens, and worthy to be chronicled
in an English Livy, when Tiberis flowed into Thames, Athens removed to London, pure Italy and fine Greece planted themselves in
rich England: Apollo, with his delicate troupe of Muses, forsoke his
old mountains and rivers, and frequented a new Parnassus and
another Helicon, nothinge inferior to the olde when they were most
solemnly haunted of divine wittes. (G. Harvey, _Pierce's Supererogation_)

LITERARY TRADITIONS, like history itself, indeed, like personal
and cultural self-images, resemble rivers, not only in that they are
constantly evolving, but also because they are cumulative, always
comprising what has gone before, inconceivable without the self-
renewing link with their source in a process of self-realization
through "in-fluence." Cultural achievements—our literature, the
events of history, our built and rebuilt cities—just as the regenerat-
ive process of our bodies and the reversals and successes of our
emotional lives, all consist of moments of self-realization strung
together like beads, when past and present exist in a lucid harmony:
the decay of the old body and its regeneration through a new one
seem to be mirrors of one another: when the body is conscious of
assimilation and growth, dissolution and uniqueness all at once. Past
and future intersect in a moment of recognition. Such moments, or

117

periods in history have a quality of self-awareness by which the currents of continuity turn for a time back upon themselves so that forward movement is performed with a backward glance, the past is recognized as being a realization of the present.

Historically, the Renaissance, particularly the English Renaissance, is such a period, and the two epigraphs above suggest something of what I am trying to say: not just in *what* Fluellen and Harvey say in their efforts to compare the present with a classical past, but in the cultural self-consciousness and the ahistorical quality of the prose itself, where "then" and "now" stand together in indeterminate self-reflection. They reveal a sense of historical immediacy, of the uniqueness of the present, but paradoxically, this is communicated in terms of vivid recognition of the past: nothing very specific of the present (or future) is said, but there is a genuine self-recognition formulated wholly in terms of the past. The two passages are familiar examples of Renaissance "sensibility," but they *say* nothing about the past, the present, or the future. They consist of names, geographical and mythical labels or tags, verbs of movement, all of which lack real movement or meaning, and all that is conveyed is a sense of "presentness" or self-awareness outlined by allusive labels charged with vague historical associations.

The passages also suggest how this cultural self-consciousness is manifested in Renaissance perceptions of landscape, and how the river is one, if not the only detail that brings together geographical and literary past and present. They show a strong sense of the interrelationship of time and place, while saying little about either. Culturally, though, they adumbrate much for the reader, though they do so through a process of literary gesture. What we see in much of the literature of the Renaissance is this sort of geographical and intellectual reflexiveness in which authors analyze their cultural identity self-referentially. The process of self-definition (or self-recognition) is like a child's, performed in terms of its own limited self-knowledge and self-centeredness, but through a fragmentary conception of the past which, half-knowingly and half unaware, it emulates and tries to recapitulate. Looking with another's eyes, understanding with imperfectly comprehended secondhand ideals, and feeling with the vital intensity of youth, Renaissance authors, like a child, create a strange discrepancy between past and present—they borrow their ancestors' intellectual wardrobe to examine their own cultural identity. In the passages from Harvey and Shakespeare (and many other examples might be cited from Petrarch, Sannazaro,

Sidney, or Spenser), we see the authors trying on the clothes they have found in their ancestral cupboard, studying their own images in the glass. This is a process of exploration, a search for the self through the past, and as such it is also a process of cultural introspection. The exploration is not the superficial kind, of unknown lands before unseen, but of the familiar but imperfectly known that lies within their own borders. As in personal development, historically, European nations perceive themselves with an acute self-consciousness.

Geographically, we see Europe living into its inherited landscape and its geopolitical structures. We observe the coordination of its various physical parts as the old avenues of commercial, political, and social intercourse become more sophisticated, are used more capably, more "gracefully"; the European world runs more smoothly (if not more harmoniously) and becomes more unified. In terms of landscape description and the many literary forms which involve the rivers, we see that the world is observed and described according to commonplaces and ideals which are part of the cultural inheritance, even if they have little to do with the landscape itself. This is not simply a process of idealizing the landscape, although that does take place too. Rather, the physical world, including the rivers, is understood through intellectual constructs and labels learned, like all else, from the past. The language of landscape, and of the rivers which dominate it, is replete with the ideas and ideals which authors naturally—and methodically—used to comprehend and describe their own world. Thus, the distinction literary critics usually make between topographical description and *topothesia*—between the description of real landscapes and of imaginary ones shaped by rhetorical modes and literary genres—is not a genuine one; both are rhetorical modes that can complement one another.[1] "Imaginary" and "real" overlap; the real setting is perceived often in terms of the fictional, and fiction is often adapted to a real, physical world, as in Book 4 of *The Faerie Queene*. Description is subordinated to the author's literary objective: *topographia* and *topothesia* are rhetorical tools used to serve larger literary or intellectual ends. As we will see in the chapters that follow, mental and physical landscapes are closely interrelated and distinctions between them are not always easy to make.

When Renaissance authors write about the landscape, prominent in their thoughts is always how previous periods (classical and medieval) thought about their world.[2] The rivers are often the dominant feature in the physical world, but predictably, we see comparatively little of their geography when they are described; rather, they are presented in terms of ideas embodied in the cultural past. The rivers were one of the literary and geographical features by which authors were able to give meaning to or find meaning in their own world. In the next two chapters I want to prepare for fuller examination of this culturally self-conscious aspect of Renaissance topographical literature by demonstrating first how pervasive the interest in the geographical river is, and secondly, how fully and carefully authors culled earlier literary materials for their understanding of it. What I hope to show is how keenly interested Renaissance writers were in its physical geography, how they attempted to understand it in the context of some of the myths of landscape that they adapted from the past and made to serve their own perceptions of the world. As we will see, the result of this sensibility is a blurring of the distinctions between "topographical" and "topothesical" landscapes. The first three sections will suggest how Renaissance writers thought of the rivers of the physical geography; the last one will look at two extreme forms of literary representation of topography and will therefore be less concerned with the geography itself. Together, they establish some of the contexts for studying the poetry of rivers in the next chapter.

1.   Old Waters in New Rivers

> Some demi-god or nymph not only the ancient Britons, but most nations and poets, have ascribed to each river. (Thomas Westcote, *View of Devonshire*)

> If you shall but examine your owne knowledges, you shall find that in the whole dominion of *England*, there is not any one Town or City which hath a Navigable River at it, that is poor, nor scarce any that are rich, which want a River with the benefits of Boats. (John Taylor, *A Discovery by Sea*)

The river appears ubiquitously in Renaissance literature, and it retains the manifold associations and protean forms of its past, while evolving naturally from its medieval contexts. Moreover, it is clear that when authors turned to it as a literary topic or discussed the river of geography, they did so with a full awareness of its literary and cultural history. Renaissance geographers, historians and political scientists, theologians and philosophers, poets and writers of prose romances, instinctively worked their forms according to precedent, and this is no less true of their use of the river motif, so that all the rivers of Europe, even the Mulla and Bregog, are at once the literary and geographical progeny of the classical waters.

Authors were not only aware of the metaphoric significance of the river, but also of the geographical differences between their "modern" rivers and those less useful waters of the classical world, and they compared their own geographical knowledge with that of the ancients. Thomas Browne, for example, repeatedly attacks his contemporaries' inaccurate reading of the geographical lore of the ancients, and scoffs at those who accept their reports unquestioningly. For him, and for numerous others, the river in geography becomes associated with knowledge itself, and this is an important aspect of the *topos* in the Renaissance.[3]

But he is also aware of the historical implications of geographical development, and of the cultural significance of the navigable rivers of northern Europe and the limitations of those to the south, and he observes that the "advantages of these ["sea rivers," as he calls them] . . . were not neglected by the old Gauls and Romans in the conveyance of their commodities which as Strabo delivers they sent up the Atax & so overland unto the Garumna, & likewise up the Rhosne, & so overland to the Seine & so into the Ocean."[4] Browne is aware of the importance of the river systems for inland trade, but he is also interested in the historical development of the rivers, and relatedly, in the implications of Roman expansion in the provinces. His observations are the germ of a historical geography and reflect the difference between classical, medieval, and secular Renaissance perceptions of the European landscape.

Browne's clear understanding of the evolution of historical geography is not unique in the Renaissance. For example, the importance of the basic distinction between torrential and perennial rivers for the development of cities and for the general character of their societies is analyzed by the sixteenth-century Italian political scientist, Giovanni Botero. Comparing the landscapes of France and Italy, he says that

> as for Rivers, Nature hath shewed her selfe most benigne to France. . . .
> For in France, the Rivers for the most part, quietly and calmly glide. . . . They also runne not amongst Mountaines . . . but many hundred miles, by open distended Champaines . . . they enrich divers Cities and Territories, with the tribute of their waters.

Italy's rivers, on the other hand, are violent and unnavigable, and are confined by mountains into a "short course, wherein they

deserve rather the titles of Torrents, than names of Rivers," and
they "becommeth not only formidable to Country villages, but to
the most strongly fortified Cities."[5]

Renaissance writers are continually exploring the relation between geography and cultural history, studying the ancient, humanized landscape for clues to the course of human events. For them, as
for the modern, geography is the search for first causes, and the
pursuit of rivers' sources and courses is symbolic of the objectives of
the discipline itself, and of the pursuit of knowledge generally.
Knowledge of landscape enables one to correct the errors of the
ancients, and to read more wisely the meaning of myth and history,
as Abraham Ortelius emphasizes when he tolerantly corrects the
inaccuracies of Virgil's account of Aeneas's arrival at Italy:

> Aeneas did not stay at Tibris, but at Laurentum . . . and landed not
> with above sixe hundred men, as Solinus reporteth . . . for that both
> by ancient histories and moderne experience, we finde that Tibris,
> the river which runneth by Rome, is not capable of a fleet or navy of
> any bignesse.

The book of nature corrects the book of history, and leads Ortelius
to the conclusion that Virgil's principal concern was not with *topographia*, but rather with *topothesia*: "it is to be thought that the Poet
fained this of his own head, or els spake it in love and commendation of this river."[6] Ortelius realizes that the poet creates a metaphoric geography which assimilates and improves upon that which is
interleaved in the book of nature.

The Renaissance recognized and imitated all aspects of the classical interest in physical and metaphoric rivers. Thus their objective
was not to define scientifically what the rivers—modern or ancient—
tell us about nature, although that interested them too, but to
identify what they can teach us about human cognition. The many
accounts of miraculous rivers did not generally inspire scientific
inquiry into the natural causes of the phenomena—at least not until
the seventeenth century. More often they inspired *sententiae* about
nature's inscrutable variety, and perhaps the identification of a
similar wonder in classical literature. Occasionally, a writer might
produce a scheme for the practical application of the phenomenon.
It is true that authors continued to search for (or more precisely, to
talk about) the source of the Nile and of other important rivers; the
British especially were compulsive in their search for river sources.
But as with Lucan's treatment of Caesar's obsession with the Nile in

The Civil War, the rivers represented the mysteries of nature, and the search for their wellsprings figured the powers and limitations of the intellect. The quest usually took them to libraries rather than into the field. Scholars studying the known world beheld it in terms of acquired intellectual contexts, and they formed their questions not from experience, but from a literary training that constantly drew from the past to understand the present, and in which the mythical and the physical worlds overlap. Thus their world presented them with a wide variety of ideas as well as with experiences, and it is this quality, for example, that makes Montaigne's travels so cerebral. Likewise, when a person contemplates the essential mysteries of the created world, as Lambert Daneau does in *The Wonderful Woorkmanship of the World*, and reflects, "what felicite shall I attain unto, if I knowe where Nilus riseth, or whatsoever the naturall Philosophers do write concerning heaven? Yea, moreover, there is no certain knowledge of those things, but only opinion," he is thinking less about the river Nile than about Lactantius and his treatment of the nature and origin of wisdom as they are submerged among the mysteries of that river.[7]

Such questions surrounding the ancient rivers also determine the response to the local landscape of modern Europe. William Harrison, for example, complains that people "make as much adoo" of the first beginnings of the Thames "as in times past of the true head of Nilus, which . . . was never found . . . nor shall be."[8] Just as European nations regarded themselves as successors to Troy and Rome, so they regarded their landscapes as the modern analogues to those of antiquity. Their minds were as crowded with fragments of geographical history as their landscapes were with vestiges of Roman presence, so that the mental traveller was quite in his element in Renaissance Europe. Appropriately, as classical humanism yielded to Renaissance nationalism, the pursuit of river sources became associated with inquiry into national origins, thus retaining its link with nation-founding. So, when speaking of his intellectual methods and objectives in his *Britannia*, William Camden offers a striking insight into the historical geography of rivers. He argues that he is "convinced that the origin of the nations of remote antiquity are necessarily obscure, like places rendered scarce visible by distance . . . as the courses, windings, confluences, and mouths of great rivers are well known, while their sources are for the most part undiscovered"—his journey through time in search of the ancient divisions of Britain is analogous to a physical journey.[9] The river is likened to time here, but rhetorically, vehicle and tenor converge, so that the river is also seen to have a shaping influence on history itself. Modern cultural geographers make a similar point, that the historical importance of a river increases toward its outlet, while its unknown, prehistoric significance lies farther upstream.[10]

To know the rivers, then, is to know the world, not only its physical form, but its history and its philosophical and intellectual traditions. To understand geography, according to the Renaissance scholar, one must understand the myths and literature that interact with the physical world. Such a point of view is more complex than that of the Middle Ages, for it embraces all the ambiguities of human history. All that we can know derives ultimately from our understanding of the environment; as William Cuningham says in his *The Cosmographical Glasse* (1559), this knowledge is "so requisite and neadfull, that you shall not understand any boke, either of th'old law or Prophets . . . being in this Art ignoraunt." Furthermore, those who would penetrate the conceits of poetry "cannot fullye understande the pleasaunt invention & perfite sense of the witty Poetes, but by Cosmographies aide."[11] Fabulous as it may be, literary geography, that of *The Aeneid*, *The Faerie Queene*, or the *Arcadia* for example, has its beginnings in that very real, if misty realm where the mind is at work transforming and being transformed by the historical landscape, so that Joseph Hall can speak unambiguously of the principal works of Sidney, Spenser, and Camden as all of a kind.[12]

The pursuit of rivers' origins is not restricted to physical topography alone. Another illustration of Renaissance awareness of ancient interest in rivers is the fascination with river names and etymologies, which is just another kind of search for sources. Within its scope, etymology embraces all the complexities of historical thought, and the rivers were recognized as name-givers *par excellence*. The varied names, scattered over a sixteenth-century map like alluvia on a flooded plain, tell a more mysterious tale than any other cartographic symbols and designations of human activity—the enclosures, castles, cathedrals, and other images that humanize the geography. Names such as Verlamchester, Maidstone, Thames, Severn, and Avon cast their own shadows and are more telling evidence of our mutability than are architectural ruins—a defaced monastery, for example—for they tell an older and more complicated history and remind us that we seem to have lost forever our ability to find the right names for things around us. More than any broken column could, the names adumbrate the struggles of human history and the slow effacing effects of time, and thus they expose the futility of our efforts to control nature and establish order.

Names suggest their histories in at least two ways. Their descriptive and prescriptive qualities tell of the identifying human or natural features in the landscape. In naming the landscape, we humanize it and proclaim our knowledge and control, although the process is never the easy victory over nature that the name-giver expects it to be. Thus, for the influential philologist and lawyer William Lambard, Maidstone is "Medway's Town," and Medway itself is (anachronistically) so named for being midway between the two bishoprics which divide the county.[13] There is something of a tug-of-war between man and nature in the claim for etymological origins. For Humphrey Lhuyd, the name "Verlamchester" tells of a church or temple on the banks of the River Ver, and virtually everyone in England was convinced that the name "Thames" (or variously, "Tame-Isis" or "Thamesis") identifies that river's geographical parentage, for it tells contractually (as the Renaissance would have it) of the confluence of Tame and Isis; the word here embodies the geographical phenomenon. More allusively, "Severn" bespeaks the river's local history and eternizes the tale of Sabrina, Estrilda, and Locrine and their story of chastity, infidelity, and death. And more elusively, the name "Avon" defies any imprint of human history: it is self-naming, it is itself, "Avon, the river," and as such it proclaims its essential, elemental quality and the perseverance of nature.[14]

All these names suggest the complicated relation between art and nature, particularly as it pertains to the founding and naming of cities, towns, or bridges, or to our more immediate contact with the element in the identification of falls, fords, and other geographical features. We can sense how the conflict troubled Renaissance scholars when we realize that many of their etymologies are false, derived from their own intellectual preoccupations rather than from accurate scholarship. While in fact "Medway" is a descriptive place-name and derived from the word "mead," Lambard works himself into a conundrum by wondering whether the town names the river or the river the town. Even more problematically, according to his explanation, the river seems to have been nameless until the advent of Christianity and the formation of bishoprics. As did countless of his contemporaries, Lambard approaches his etymologies in terms of preconceptions—about philology, local history, and various ramifications on the theme of art and nature—so that the landscape seems to be the expression of a cultural ideal.

The very nature of names provides a second way in which they epitomize history. As confluent streams vie for the principal role in the naming of the subsequent river—as dark Thame absorbs Isis into his name, and quiet Taw prevails over Torridge, who loses his name in her waters, there is a linguistic give-and-take in the names themselves which reminded poets, such as Spenser and Drayton, as well as topographers of the eclectic nature of British history and so made the rivers the sagest and most articulate local historians. Thus the British river Ver joins peacefully with the Roman town to form Verlamchester, and the name quietly acknowledges the violent conflict that destroyed that ancient cultural center. The historical manifestation of the conflict between the social arts and human nature could obviously be self-destructive, for neither the original town nor the river existed in the sixteenth century; only the vestigal name remained, itself displaced in current usage by a Christian successor, Saint Albans, which reflected neither aspect of the original name. Place-names, with their heterogeneous elements, are at once preservers of the past and reminders of its insignificance. They put human affairs into perspective, and as Spenser realized in *The Ruines of Time*, they embody in a name the warning that half of cultural pride is folly.

There are numerous such place-names which reflect linguistically the British, Roman, Saxon, and Christian phases of British history, the names themselves often being the only enduring evidence of the past. Their importance as name-givers linked the rivers with history while giving them an element of timelessness, and this is especially true in England, where the historic bones and sinews of the language show through so clearly—much more so than in sixteenth-century French, for example, although the interest in philology existed throughout Europe. And it is partly because of the philological phenomenon by which the rivers embody the history of the land that they were associated with the *genius loci* and were regarded in a quasi-mythical way as being descendants of the classical *genii*.[15]

The search for etymologies, then, is also part of the Renaissance awareness of classical treatment of rivers. Here too their response to the national and regional landscape is determined by what they understood to be the process of name-giving that antiquity recommended to them. And, of course, local landscapes were frequently presented in terms of the descriptive place-names of antiquity:

Lambard's Kent and Westcote's Devonshire were thought of as Mesopotamian because of their rivers; Thames's name is formed on the same principle (so it was thought) as Jordan's—that is, the confluence of two rivers' names, the Jor and the Dan; the Isis was named for the ancient river deity who, according to some accounts, was Albion's ancestor and even visited England—anciently, there had been a riparian Temple of Isis on the site of Saint Paul's Cathedral.

The volumes of topography which proliferated during the sixteenth century devoted pages to the examination of the origins of ancient river names as well as to their topography and attendant myths. The process of naming intrigued the Renaissance, and they respected the power and historical importance behind it. Ortelius, in his *Theatre of the World*, for example, traces the evolution of nations' and rivers' names in each of his descriptive chapters; his philology shows how thoroughly he realized that the events of ancient and modern history are echoed in geographical names. The Nile, because it is the greatest of rivers, is "therefore called & knowen by the greatest variety of names." He has done much research into the historical significance of the river and its name:

> Some have called it AEgyptus (from whence the whole country tooke the name); others Oceanus (the sea . . .); Aetos (an eagle, for the swiftness of the streame); Nigir, Melas . . . Triton, Chrysorrhoas (Golden-flood . . .). . . . Arias Montanus affirmeth, that in the Holy Scripture it is named Phison, because . . . his waters do spread themselves, swell, and wax so high, that they flow over . . . the whole land; Sihore, that is black . . . The Africaines . . . commonly call it Nil, that is . . . liquid, thinne, dissolved and apt to runne.[16]

If Ortelius's scholarship is at times imprecise, it is because he strives for inclusiveness. Even the most abstruse myths about the Nile are recorded here, and he has perused nearly all that had been written about the river. Similarly inclusive surveys of the lore of lesser rivers were compiled by other authors having more regional concerns.

River names provided Renaissance writers with the occasion to develop ideas about their language, their culture, and their history. In this too, then, the river touches upon something distinctly human and humane, and as we shall see, its association with language extends naturally to matters of style and rhetoric. But here, in the quest for etymologies, it also figures in small the quest for the *flumen orationis*. For William Lambard, tracing the history of river names is identified with the process of revitalizing the English language, for it is a return to the natural springs which gave rise to language. It is also the abstract of the historian's art, for it goes to the very source of all learning. Similarly, Camden, defending his own frequent exploration of etymologies, explains that if "all [such] conjectures are to be excluded, I fear a very considerable part of . . . literature, and I may add of human knowledge, must of course follow."[17]

2. Secular Exegesis and the Modern World; Ralegh's History of the World

> Adam dwelt on the banks of the river, or in the land which was watered on eyther side, if we thinke good to take Paradise for that which is compassed about with the rivers. (John Calvin, *A Commentarie . . . Upon . . . Genesis*)

> As from the Ship, men through their swift sayling, trees and Townes seeme as it were to depart; So through the swift course of Time, first childhood departeth, then youth, and so at length old age. (Robert Cawdrey, *A Treasurie . . . of Similies*)

> Methinks it would well please any man to look upon a geographical map, on account of the incredible variety and pleasantness of the subject, and would excite to further steps of knowledge; Chorographical, Topographical, Delineations, to behold . . . all the remote Provinces, Towns, Cities of the World, and never go forth of the limits of his study. . . . A good prospect alone will ease melancholy. . . . What greater pleasure can there now be, than to view those elaborate maps of Ortelius, Mercator, Hondius. . .? To peruse those books of cities put out by Braunus, and Hogenbergius. . . to read those exquisite descriptions of Maginus, Munster . . . Boterus . . . Camden . . . those pleasant Itineraries of Purchas . . . Hentznerus . . . P. Gillius. (Robert Burton, *Anatomy of Melancholy*)

From the previous section we can see that even for writers having primarily topographical interests, the river-scape was an intellectual as well as a physical phenomenon. The river was a source of invention having its basis in landscape and language, and authors explored the topic's potential through methodical investigation and inquiry. When they studied ancient or modern geography they also studied the river myths and their allegorical traditions, which they resolved into syncretistic readings of the world's historical and moral order. For example, nymphs and their friends in landscape, the *genii loci*, are commonplace features in Renaissance literature— they appear frequently and are apostrophized by every sort of writer. They were recognized as being the rivers' attendant spirits: John Selden tells us that this tradition is common not only to the Greeks and Romans, but also to the Hebrews.[18] The Renaissance also knew of the water nymphs' identification with Apollo and the muses, and of their association with poetry and learning. Indeed, they traced the nymphs' historical beginnings—Richard Linch, in *The Fountaine of Ancient Fiction* (1599), for example, identifies their connection with Diana, and her own Egyptian origins in Isis (called, appropriately enough, the "genius of Egypt").[19] William Slayter's *Palae-Albion* (1621) provides one of the most extensive examinations of that musical and civilizing proto-nymph. Missing none of the many associations that she acquired in antiquity, he gives her a prominent place in the founding of Britain and even adapts the legend to incorporate Hercules, whose labors, as we have seen, continually involved him with rivers and nation-founding. Isis was active elsewhere in Europe as well, for Giles Corrozet tells us of her role in the founding of the original, insular *Cité de Paris*; her temple was erected on the banks of the Seine where Notre Dame is, and the city's insignia is a ship afloat in the embrace of its waters. What is important, however, is not any single legend, but the fact that the full range of the river deities' original associations was recognized and traced back even to their Egyptian forms before being naturalized in the modern European legendary landscape.

The river's elemental allegories were also dissected, and their traditions sought in Thales, Hesiod, Ovid, and Isidore.[20] These, in turn, were extended naturally to physical and geographical allegories explaining such well-known etiological river legends as the creation of the Vale of Tempe and the river Peneus by Hercules, the maiming of Acheloüs, and other mythical histories that have their origins in the Mediterranean landscape—those of Alpheus and Arethusa, Inachus and Io, and many others that were drawn from the depths of Ovid. Again, the important thing is that the Renaissance realized that behind these myths, many of which are not in any obvious way topographical, is a response to the geographical world. For example, Thomas Westcote perceives the topography of his beloved Devonshire in terms of the Acheloüs myth and analyzes the story of the cornucopia along the lines of its geographical allegory and its association with the rivers.[21] Although there are numerous other examples—the treatment of Tempe, the legends of Hercules, the rivers of the Holy Land and the Nile, to name only four—further illustration is hardly necessary: according to Renaissance rhetoric, all myths were open to elemental and geographical as well as historical, moral, and divine allegorical interpretations which could, in turn, be imposed on the local landscape.

Thus, landscapes were also read for their euhemeristic allegories. In varying degrees, authors interpreted river legends and their heroes historically, and in this they followed the precedent of the classical historians, particularly Diodorus Siculus. Bacchus, Dionysus, Hercules, Achilles, Odysseus, and other gods and heroes with and without links with the river all dwelled in a nebulous realm of fact and fiction where a higher form of poetic truth existed. And if classical and Christian history threatened to conflict with one another, writers such as Camden and Ralegh reconciled the two through typological interpretations. It was customary for topographers of the period to resort at their convenience to euhemeristic analyses of the nation-founding river heroes, implicating variously Hercules, the Homeric heroes in their quest for a new Troy and a new Scamander, or the descendants of Aeneas in their search for a land offering a welcome as warm as that of Tiber for Aeneas. Indeed, these classical "histories" were even mapped out by cartographers. The highly respected Dutch geographer, Abraham Ortelius, adds a *Parergon* to his *Theatre of the World* which consists of maps and synopses of major events in the classics and the Bible, thus providing his readers with a visual syncretism coordinating the events of mythical and biblical history.

In quite a different vein, but reflecting the same awareness of various dimensions of river myths and their adaptability for local landscape, is Pontus de Tyard's *Douze Fablfs de Fleuves, ou Fontaines, avec la descriptions pour la peinture & les epigrammes* (Paris, 1586). A collection of river legends with interpretive abstracts and hints for their visual representation, this is very much in the tradition of Plutarch's essay, *Of the Names of Rivers and Mountains, and of such things as are to be found therein.* Tyard's objectives are, of course, very different, for his essay was designed as a descriptive guide for the preparation of a series of tapestries on the river theme which was to complement the royal fêtes at Fontainebleau and the Château d'Anet. Such water festivals, arranged around the gods of rivers and seas, were favorites with Catherine de'Medici. The politically important fêtes at Fontainebleau in 1564 and at Bayonne in 1565, whose diplomatic theme was unity, were organized around these aquatic motifs, and masters in all the arts were gathered together to transform the court and parks into *tableaux vivantes* depicting an extravagantly artificial Ovidian antiquity. Through dance, music, poetry, tapestry, sculpture, and painting,[22] this river lore and the cultural ideal that it was meant to represent were grafted onto the local landscape. Such ekphrastic treatment of the river was common throughout Europe and was not confined to the myths of antiquity, but was also adapted to local legends, particularly in England. Elizabeth and James were often welcomed in their progresses by a presiding *genius* or nymph of the place, and the lord mayor's pageants commonly made use of the *genius* of the Thames.[23] It would be superfluous to record here the pageants, entertainments, and other water fêtes that were so popular in Europe from the fifteenth through the seventeenth centuries; in a later chapter we will look at some of them for their political and thematic content. But it is important to realize that they offer a major example of the tendency to see the national landscape in terms of carefully allegorized myths (both classical and indigenous) which depicted or suggested through implicit analogy the realization of a cultural ideal in the marriage of art and nature.

Not just a popular topic, then, the river was assimilated into the local landscape and literature by writers who thoughtfully sought its variants and analyzed its meanings. Moreover, authors did not only adapt the rivers in their classical forms, but they also drew on the allegorical and mystical rivers of the Middle Ages, and it should be remembered that the medieval allegorical readings of classical authors who used the *topos*—of Homer, Ovid, and Virgil in particular— were known in the Renaissance. Thus, the river of grace, the *flumen perennis et indeficiens* in Henry Hawkins's *Parthenia Sacra* (1633), is unmistakably in the medieval allegorical mode, although it is a product of the Counter-Reformation, and Spenser's elfin Sir Guyon owes something to the patristics and their interpretations of the rivers of Paradise. Likewise, the Neoplatonists (and we might include Spenser here), using the river as a *topos* of Divine Love and Concord, are in the medieval tradition of religious allegory that originates with Philo Judaeus.

It is on this allegorical tradition, for example, that Henry Reynolds draws in his *Mythomystes* (1632). His work is something of a beginner's guide to allegorical methods, and he explains how, in any given myth, several levels of meaning coexist simultaneously. Poetic allusions to gods and nymphs, he argues, signify many things at once, but first and most obviously they represent a geographical and, relatedly, elemental allegory which, in turn, adumbrates divine and moral allegory. In the elements which such figures signify we can apprehend "the force of Love or agreement in Naturall things." Such literary devices as the river nymphs and gods, he suggests, are used to shadow both forth "that equality and concord between those warring Elements . . . in Man's body."[24] Nor is Reynolds alone in seeing in geographical myths generally, and in the rivers particularly, an enlargement of the moral forces and universal order which also exist in the individual—the landscapes of Western literature are also maps of the spiritual resources of the inner self. Reynold's "soft" Platonism and the illustrations he offers suggest not only the *theomachia* of the *Iliad*, but also the marriage of the Thames and the Medway in *The Faerie Queene*, the river epyllia of *Colin Clouts come home againe* and the *Cantos of Mutabilitie*, and the presentation of elemental Concord and Harmony in the writings of Marsilio Ficino and Pico della Mirandola;[25] but what is clear is that Reynolds perceives a coherent and continuous allegorical tradition which incorporates the river. Because of its ability to reconcile classical and medieval aspects of the mofif, this Neoplatonic treatment of the river is one of the commonest in the Renaissance.

Notwithstanding the extraordinary variety of the river motif, and the fullness of its literary history, writers had no trouble forming a clear and coherent view of its general thematic significance, and channelling its literary resources into the mainstream of their own principal concerns. Ralegh's *The History of the World* (1614) is a good example of how the various currents of the motif were mastered and brought together as a vehicle for the author's view of the forces which determine the secular history of the individual and society. As such, it underscores some differences between the medieval and Renaissance river.

Ralegh uses the river in the early books of the *History* to develop a syncretistic view of human history; in thus coordinating the Christian and secular literary and geographical dimensions of the motif, he develops its potential as an organizing device. During his long years of imprisonment, Ralegh obviously thought carefully about the organization of his sage, encyclopedic work, and he gathered all he could learn about the intellectual, political, and religious history of the world to create a conspicuously Renaissance, very secular, and even political image of the individual and society. His achievement provides one of the most encompassing and interesting examples of the Renaissance obsession with literary self-images. It is a subtle and thoughtful work, projecting overlapping images of the microcosm and the macrocosm. Ralegh did not fail to notice the river's place in accounts of the creation and later human history, and aware of the classical and medieval models, he uses the river as a topic in which to locate the meaning and design of *The History of the World.*

Ralegh had no problem deciding where to begin his history: being a history of the world (and a very worldly one at that), it must begin with the creation. In that act, and in the juvenescence of the world (not of mankind), Ralegh perceives the course to be followed by all ensuing events, as well as the essential problems of history itself. With the initial creation of the world, spirit and matter were joined, held together by a divine *Logos*; moral and physical order were inseparable and were figured in the rivers of Paradise. In the descent of those four rivers is the dissemination of that order—at once a dispersion throughout the world and a unification of the world through their embrace. At the same time, there is a loss of paradisiac integrity—from one source emanate four branches, none of which embodies all the initial virtues once united at their source. Prefigured in this descent from the source is also the separation of mind and matter; historically, the physical world relies increasingly upon the complement of the *numen*, the link with the source, the intellectual dimension that supplies the moral and spiritual element which is incompletely contained in the physical world. For Ralegh, the direction of human history is clearly projected by the geographical image of the world after the creation; quite literally, it contains the wellspring of human, intellectual, religious, and political development, and so suggests the order of history and embodies its meaning. The same kind of determinism (Ralegh uses the word "necessity") that directs the flow of waters over the earth also influences the course of history. Ralegh the historian is something of a Hercules figure trying to change the face of the world in order to alter human destiny. History is coextensive with the rivers of Paradise: as they disperse, so too does society, and as history becomes more complicated by its complex windings, our cultural memory of the original source of these rivers and of their meaning becomes dimmer. Nevertheless, even if the unifying *Logos* is not perceived, it does not cease to exist. For Ralegh, knowledge of the world and of our inner selves can restore the clarity of our vision and the integrity of our lives.

It is from such a secular exegetical view of Genesis that Ralegh's history unravels, and doubtful legends as well as creditable pagan and Christian history all mark stages in the descent from the original, integral Paradise where knowledge and being were one: they are phases in the obscuring of human judgment. *The History of the World* is most obviously in the patristic tradition. Not only do the early books examine the problems that preoccupied the Church Fathers, weigh the merits of those authors (many of whom were discussed above), and seek out the situation and implications of all the particulars of Eden (placing the customary importance on the four rivers), but, like one branch of the patristic tradition, they also emphasize the importance of accepting the physical (as opposed to purely allegorical) dimension of Paradise and its rivers.

There are, however, important differences which reflect Ralegh's own historical perspective. He places even more emphasis on the world—his is not, as the Church Fathers' writings were, a description *de loco sancto*, but of the world, a divinely created but secular organism which shapes and is shaped by a variegated human history: this important interrelationship is identified by the rivers of Paradise. His objective in the early chapters is to start at the true first beginnings of history, not to deduce Church doctrine. He is able to use the ideas and methods of the patristics to locate his conception of the origins of history in the physical world, and the logic and order of its evolution. His exegesis is philosophical, or more particularly epistemological, rather than theological; within the historical context of Scripture he explores the relation of mind to matter, and the nature of knowledge. This is emphatically the case in the early books, where his method and matter are necessarily prescribed by Scripture, which the Renaissance regarded as the oldest historical document. Scripture provides the only true glimpse into that past when there was greater harmony between the word and the world, and it is in these sections that he concentrates his ideas about his own methods. He often emphasizes how his view of history is also his view of literary technique, and the lines from Epiphanius, which we gave quoted at length above: "*Si Paradisus non est sensibilis, etiam non est fons*" stand out conscpicuously as a conflation of Ralegh's method and manner, and they most clearly define the rigid necessity by which all things decline from that first microcosm of Eden. They in fact are a synthesis of Ralegh's view of history and help to explain the prominence of the rivers in the early stages of his argument. Expanding on the logic of Epiphanius's rebuttal of the allegorists, Ralegh uses the passage to suggest the unifying principle that joins Scripture and the other secular and classical motifs which also figure in the *History*. Thus his Renaissance world view is truly of a macrocosm which involves all the descendants from that first wellspring of history, and it projects in large the nature of the microcosm—of the individual driven by forces no less grand than those of history—and offers a secular view of the rivers of Paradise.

The first chapters are (as convention prescribed) much concerned with the significance of the rivers of Paradise, and Ralegh systematically prepares for his larger argument by introducing the topic through their analogue in the individual. He reminds us that the world's history is human history and that the individual is "the brief story of the universal"; one's body is a little Eden, and one's "blood, which disperseth itself by the branches or veins through all the body, may be resembled to these waters which are carried by brooks and rivers overall the earth." Not only is the circulatory system comparable to the world's hydrology, but history too is as a river following its natural course—but with one difference: "For this tide of man's life, after it once turneth and declineth, ever runneth with a perpetual ebb and falling stream, *but never floweth again*."[26] The difference, that the stream returns to its source and so is ever renewed, while human life flows once from its source to the sea of death, is intentionally spurious, for Ralegh is reminding us, on the one hand, that the world's natural cycles are not eternally self-renewing but also have their destined and final end, and on the other hand, that though we follow an earthly, historical course but once, we too return to our real, heavenly source. The analogy, with a secular emphasis which is characteristic of Ralegh, is the fitting introduction to the examination of the rivers of Paradise, the geographical manifestation of the four cardinal virtues whose descent figures the history of the *humanum genus*.

Ralegh surveys the various theories about the location and character of Paradise with the scholarly thoroughness that Ortelius showed in studying the literature about the Nile. He assesses that tradition which considers the whole world as the original Eden, as well as that propounded by the Nestorian Christians, that Eden was an island afloat in the waters of the Tigris. Although he dismisses the more fantastic allegorical interpretations, always showing the explorer's interest in the physical place of Paradise, his reason for introducing them is unmistakable: our intellectual history (and our capacity for understanding) flows from the springs of Genesis, from the very act of the creation, and subsequently, from our response to the world. By implication, our own response to the world reveals our kinship to the original Adam, and in this we can see the inherent importance of landscape literature. Furthermore, for Ralegh, the springs of thought are as important as the flow of events. Thus, while he is aware that his exegetical inquiry into the "situation" of Paradise may be criticized as "old-fashioned," it is, nevertheless, the key to his methods in the entire work:

> But it may be objected, that it is needless, and a kind of curiosity, to enquire so deligently after this place of *Paradise*, and that the knowledge thereof is of little or no use. To which I answer, that there is nothing written in the Scripture, but for instruction; and if the truth of the story be necessary, then by the place proved, the same is also made more apparent.[27]

Comparison of Scripture and landscape amounts to the collation of two variant texts in the book of the Divine Word; for Ralegh, and for the Renaissance generally, geography provides an irrefutable guide to history.

With utmost precision Ralegh maintains the interchangeability of the history of the microcosm and the macrocosm; the strict order of necessity holds together the world of geography, of the mind, and that of his own *History of the World*. History cannot be understood if its beginnings are not first ascertained. His method is very much that of the patristics, but he uses his biblical geography to support a secular history, and this too is a characteristic of Renaissance topographical writing. The lines he adapts from Arias Montanus's *History of the Holy Land* to describe his own methods are also part of the intellectual tradition that includes William Cuningham: "if histories be read without topographical knowledge, all things will appear so intricate and confused, as we shall thereby understand nothing but obscurely."[28]

Ralegh continues to develop the river motif after he has established the location and reality of Paradise. Sticking close as he does to the motif of the rivers as the founts of human history, he sees ancient cultural landscapes as also being shaped by the rivers. The geography of the Holy Land continues to exert its influence on human affairs, and Ralegh skillfully weaves other of the river's traditional associations into his historical narration. As the pre-lapsarian garden landscape yields to the post-lapsarian urban setting, and the simplicity of natural virtue gives way to sophisticated social arts, we can still apprehend the common source from which these changes flow. For Ralegh, the cities of fallen man are no less the product of the rivers than the garden was. Thus, Nimrod, that complicated example of fallen man—city-founder and promoter of various ambiguous social arts—is influenced in his movements by these waters. He knows their utility and settles on their banks out of a natural sense of cunning: "So Nimrod, who out of wit and strength usurped dominion over the rest, set down in the very confluence of all these rivers which watered Paradise." The four principal virtues of their waters are perhaps less pure than they had been, but they continue to serve society in its need for order, and so, as Nimrod directs "the world's plantation," he urges his people to keep to the banks of the rivers so that "they might at all times resort, and succour one another by river."[29]

Ralegh has very cleverly created a historical geography in the modern sense of the phrase. As history gets more complicated, and as human beings do what they were told and increase, they move further along the original rivers. The grace and virtues infused in humanity and its landscape become less recognizable, but they are, nevertheless, present in the transformed social geography. The river's mythical role as city-founder is perfectly integrated with Ralegh's interpretation of geography and history. For him, as for many others in the Renaissance, the city is our new Eden, our attempt to reclaim our lost state. The early cities were established just downstream from the first Eden:

> Now as Nimrod the youngest, yet strongest, made his choice of Babel . . . which both Tigris and Euphrates cleansed and enriched,. so did Havilah place himself upon Piso-Tigris; Ramaah and his son Sheba further down upon the same river . . . Chus himself upon Gehon, the fairest branch of Euphrates. And when they began to spread themselves further off, yet they always fastened themselves to the rivers' sides: for Nineveh, Charran, Reseph, Canneh, Ur in Chaldea, and the other first peopled cities, were all founded upon these navigable rivers, or their branches, by which the one might give succour and assistance to the other.[30]

Ralegh, one of Nimrod's own kind, gives a characteristically secular and social, rather than moral reading of biblical history, and it is one which combines a geographical sense of the river's importance with an awareness of its place in the literary landscape.

Ralegh's interpretation of early human history is syncretistic, as is his use of the river motif. Rather as Seneca does in his *Naturales Quaestiones*, he too sees the waters as the principal divine agent on earth—in this he resembles others as well, Philo Judaeus and Augustine, for example, but in his pre-Christian history his rivers are closer to those of Plato, Homer, Seneca, and the classical tradition. In his discussion of the flood, the next major event in the transformation of the river-crossed landscape, he coordinates the Old Testament torrents with a wide variety of classical analogues, including the legends of the Nile, Isis and Osiris, and Hercules. For Ralegh the literary tradition of the river torrent consists of variants of the apocalyptic floods of the Old Testament. At the time of the flood, he says, the waters were infused by "the Fountain of all power, strength and faculties supernatural." The rivers—and he seems to be thinking of the original four rivers of Paradise— "poured over the whole face of the earth by a power above nature, and by special commandment of God himself."[31] He alludes to the various torrents of classical literature, and conceives of them as types of the principal flood of Genesis. Interestingly, it is in this context that he says that "it cannot be doubted, but that Homer had read over all the books of Moses, as by places stolen thence almost word for word may appear"[32]—he too has observed the similarities in ancient river literature.

Ralegh's treatment of the story of Noah illustrates how carefully he designed *The History of the World* to project an image of human society and secular history. In Ralegh's view of Old Testament history, Noah is an especially important figure of the *humanum genus*, for he represents those who "lived safely on the waters." This new Adam, responsible for the spread of civilization, is forced to come to terms with the unpredictable waters of the fallen world, and Ralegh explores all of the analogies for this figure. Triton, Dionysus, Bacchus, Osiris, and other heroic figures who bring together the river and the spread of civilization are identified with this "second parent of mankind," the founder of cities in a land "most oppressed with waters of all the world."[33]

Contending with the flood of divine wrath, and attempting to establish his city and to perpetuate his memory by giving his and his children's names to the mountains, rivers, and regions of the earth, Noah is, for Ralegh, the principal archetype for the social being— the choice tells us something about the difference between the Middle Ages and the Renaissance. But it is hardly a surprising one—Ralegh no doubt identified with him. More important, though, Noah is a figure who would naturally appeal to Renaissance ideals of social harmony, to their interest in exploration and the nature and origin of human society, and to their belief in individual fame. In him Ralegh saw a man who imposed his own enlightened cultural vision on the world. And in like manner, through him

Ralegh was able to bring together classical and biblical river motifs, to use them to impose his own, characteristically Renaissance cultural myth on a landscape having meaning for both the private and public person.

As we will see more clearly later on, Renaissance writers thought of their environment in terms of topographical archetypes, particularly the garden and the city—both figures which drew heavily on received ideas about the river. Noah was the Christian image of the city-founder; his ark, afloat on the waters descending from Paradise, was, as Ralegh says, a "figure of the city of God."[34] His plight, like those of his lesser types, is that of all civilizers, and his task, like Dionysus's and Hercules's, is presented in terms of the reconciliation of the extremes of earth and water. The image of his ark embraced by the waters is transformed, with all its Christian and social ideals, to the common Renaissance figure of the city insulated by its rivers. Ralegh's objective in the early books of the *History of the World* and in his concentration on the rivers, has been to show us how our human destiny—a mixture of necessity and self-mastery—is written in the landscape. Ralegh is emphatically concerned with the physical world as a historical text; but he reads it against the numerous collations of ancient and modern authors, in this way deriving from them his own myth of history in geography. Where the rivers of Paradise leave off, his own narrative continues by tracing the course of our intellectual history. Thus, Ralegh completely revises the patristic tradition which is the model for his history of the Holy Land in order to create a thoroughly Renaissance *imago mundi*— one in which people contend, like Hercules, with the physical world, with humanity and themselves; let them master these, Ralegh seems to say, and they need not fear for their souls.

3. Geographical Contexts: The Unified Landscape

I may fittly compare these two Waters to two great Princes of these two great Countries, comming to be maried at this Great City. . . . In which allusion, I make the Rhosne (which in the French toung is of the masculine gender) the Savoyard Prince; and the Soane, which is likewise in this language, the feminine, the Princesses of Burgundy; which conceit is the better warranted, because Le Rhosne is a very swift and furious River, which well agreeth with the nature . . . of the man; and La Soane, a still and sweet water, which rightly symbolizeth with the quality of a woman.

I would our Poet, that made a marriage betweene the Medua and the Thames at Rochester, had the handling of this matter; for it becomes a Poeme better than a Relation. (Richard Dallington, *The View of France*)

Britain, excluded from our warm clime
Is now surrounded with a Roman stream.

(Anonymous, cited in the Britannia)

. . . so the spring,

The well-head, and the streame which they foorth bring,
Are but one selfe-same essence, nor in ought
Doe differ, save in order, and our thought
No chime of time discernes in them to fall,
But three distinctlie bid one essence all.

(Drummond of Hawthornden, An Hymne of the Fairest Faire)

The history, geography, and literature of rivers interested the Renaissance *literati*. The interest, however, tended to be turned culturally inward, so that Europeans studied their own landscape—which is to say their own present and future—in terms of intellectual contexts and ideals that were part of the inherited classical tradition. Geography and the imaginative, or inventive, faculty worked together. Even Ralegh turns history—and the river motif—into a mirror for Stuart England. *The History of the World* is ultimately a creative and imaginative, not an exegetical work. Its is a literary world evolving its own inclusive aesthetic and moral order, rather than adhering to an exclusive doctrine, and in this respect it is in the tradition of other encompassing world fictions having a predominantly national focus, such as Ronsard's *Françiade*, Camões's *Os Lusíadas*, Sidney's *Arcadia*, Spenser's *The Faerie Queene*, Camden's *Britannia*, Ortelius's *Theatre of the World*, or Hogenberg's *Civitates Orbis Terrarum*. Each of them sees society, history, and the world in terms of perceptual myths that they use to transform a cultural geography. The generic barriers between such works need to be lowered, for their aesthetics and objectives are largely the same.

It is in this literature of national self-awareness, with its mixture of poetic and historical truth and with its overriding national and cultural self-consciousness, that the rivers most often appear. This is no doubt partly because the river partakes of both the historical and fictional dimensions of the European world: the rivers of myth and literature were also the rivers of the continental landscape. But the world in fact and fiction looked quite different in (and to) the

Renaissance than it had in preceding centuries, and the rivers quite naturally shared in the transformation. Writers were aware that changes were taking place, and this awareness is reflected in this body of literature. In this sense, Ralegh's *The History of the World* is immeasurably more modern and catholic (and not simply more sophisticated) in its understanding of world history than Isidore's *Etymologies*, for example. While the Renaissance perceived landscape in terms of reflexes acquired from the past, it also responded to the immediacy, the uniqueness, and the potential of the present. The result for the river is that its classical and medieval features (in landscape and literature) were assimilated into a current, humanistic conception of cultural unity. Our present concern is with Renaissance images of its landscape and its rivers, mainly in the topographical literature of the period, and how the geography of Europe (mainly Britain) contributes to and demonstrates them.

As the prose works of the topographers suggest, Europe was increasingly cognizant of its growing cultural and geographical integrity, and nations were developing the individual strengths of their various natural and political divisions. Europe had actually become a different sort of entity, had experienced an Ovidian metamorphosis which did not escape the notice of contemporary political theorists. It was a change in which the rivers played an important part, for in every way they were thrown into even greater prominence after the irregular growth of the Middle Ages.

An oversized peninsula, Europe was looking inward; periodically isolated by the Muslim world to the south and east, it consolidated its own resources and relied less on the Mediterranean. Its internal trade routes, as they became more familiar, became more frequented and embraced their regions more firmly. The Elbe in the east joined the Baltic and Black seas; the Rhine in the north brought together east and west and disembogued toward Britain; the Seine, Meuse, Moselle, Loire, Garonne, and Rhône valleys, connecting regions of France, together formed the principal trade routes across the face of Europe, linking Renaissance cities, urban centers on long-established sites, but whose populations, physical size, and sphere of political and economic influence had been considerably enlarged. Between 1500 and 1600 the number of towns with populations over 100,000 increased threefold, from four to twelve, and the growth of population and affluence, and the increasingly regular and reliable communications spread residual benefits to smaller centers as well.[35] In many cases a city's expansion amounted to the imposition of a new, more symmetrical order on its original plan, thereby reshaping the city according to Renaissance priorities for trade, defense, and magnificence. While it is impossible to define the order of priorities—although concern for commercial development and for displays of civic grandeur generally had as much influence on the shape of a city as did questions of defense—cities were being subjected to a new aesthetic superimposed upon the original foundations. Public and private building projects such as the Royal Exchange and Nonesuch House in London (completed in 1569 and 1577, respectively) were part of a burgeoning, competitive civic spirit and contributed to the sharpened awareness of landscape. Indeed, this "appetite for fame" through architectural monuments was so great that it was compared to the civic ostentation of antiquity which produced such prodigies as the Tower of Babel and the pyramids; the authors of the *Gesta Grayorum* (1594) observe ironically that "the plain and approved Way that is safe, and yet proportionable to the Greatness of a Monarch, to present himself to Posterity, is . . . the magnificance of goodly and Royall buildings and foundations."[36]

Statistics and isolated examples, however, cannot communicate the real changes that took place. In the considerable urban development along the rivers of France and Germany, and in the emergence of such major financial and commercial cities as Antwerp and Amsterdam, which were largely creations of the Renaissance, what is noticeable is the inland and northern growth of Europe. As Henri Pirenne argues, the Low Countries assume an importance in the north comparable to that which Venice, Genoa, and Pisa once had in the south,[37] although there is a significant difference. The Mediterranean ports imported from outside Europe and traded primarily along a network of coastal cities. The Low Countries, on the other hand, drew their resources from within Europe and from England, and thus served an essentially European community; even their trade with the East had first to be absorbed into the European trade routes.

Europe, then, experienced what might be described as a phase reversal. What had been perceived as a world with a sea at its center—a world traversed by boats and fringed with a border of coastal ports—became a world with a continental center, traversed by cart and barge, and surrounded by seas which threaded their way inland in the form of rivers. The sea was subservient to the land, rather than the land to the sea. The commercial and economic activity which before had been drawn to the coastal regions now had its gravitational focus inland—paradoxically, at what were often, in fact, internal ports: Paris, Antwerp, and London, for example. This geographical metamorphosis is part of the general transformation of modern Christian Europe to a cultural self-centeredness with a political ethic of self-sufficiency.

A very similar phenomenon occurred in England, although as an island country it always had at least the tendency to turn in upon itself and to work toward self-sufficiency. But during the Reformation and Renaissance, nationalism, coupled with comparative affluence and a sense of political isolation, intensified the tendency. England saw itself less in terms of France, Rome, and the sea than it saw Europe and the sea in terms of itself. An island battered by a sea which tosses up wave upon wave of invaders, Britain becomes an island embraced by a sea that provides protection and ready trade routes to Europe. Events such as the defeat of the Armada in 1588 and the panic of 1599 served to unify the nation rather than to unglue it as such events had done in the past. And while this is admittedly somewhat simplified, it is merely the description in geographic terms of certain creditable commonplaces about England's changing political and historical importance during and after the Reformation.

England, in fact, figures in miniature the changes that were influencing Europe's self-image; it was more obviously undergoing a process of self-realization. The ground plan of English landscape had long been laid; its principal towns and cities, its roads, field systems, and markets had been established for centuries and were also being enlarged and developed according to the greater scale of the period. But what is important is that England was very much a land drawing upon its inner resources and increasingly aware of its national topography and geographical unity, and this, in part, accounts for the immense popularity of the river as an image of the nation.

As in Europe, the rivers were unifying agents bringing the markets and resources of the land closer together: in a very real way they figure the reconciliation of the elements of land and water. Very much in the way that Europe became a smaller, more compact world compressed between the Baltic and the Atlantic, the North Sea and the Mediterranean, England was a nation that strove to bring together, through its rivers, its geographical extremes, so that Augustine's axiom that the world is "like a confluence of waters" acquires a new and different meaning in the Renaissance. England was as aware of its geographical rivers as it was of the rivers of literature. They were an ever-present consideration in matters of internal trade and travel, and relatedly, in the development of cities, towns, estates, and manors. Consequently a subtle but very important change occurs in the conception of the geographical river, and it is one which is reflected in the literature of rivers. Because of their close interrelationship, the rivers and the sea became inseparable and indistinguishable. As we will see, this geographical fact is the perfect analogue to the prevalent Neoplatonic conception of the world's unity.

Rivers carried the bulk of English produce and commodities; the principal markets were river towns whose sphere of production was generally within a radius of one day's journey. Many towns usually regarded as riparian were actually inland ports, so that the rivers in fact merged with the seas. Thus, in the sixteenth century, Shrewsbury, Gloucester, and York were riparian markets, the first two located on the banks of the Severn, and York on the Ouse. However, they were regarded as seaports, since they had an extensive coastal trade which extended beyond the range of their rivers. Indeed, since London was the nation's principal market, the many rivers which did not serve the Thames were adjuncts of the sea and were part of a coastal trade which served the metropolis. Newcastle, York, Peterborough, and Shrewsbury, to name only four, served London through a network of inland river, coastal traffic, and finally, the Thames. The coastal waters became something of an honorary river system: an expansive tributary of Thame's own tidal waters. England had virtually no exports other than wool, and so the circulating and orbiting traffic was the movement of internal bounty through the nation and around its perimeters in an intricate system of communication. These routes, essentially unchanged from the thirteenth through the sixteenth centuries, were worked with a growing regularity and frequency which necessarily contributed to the sense of geographical and political unity. Toward the end of the sixteenth century, efforts to improve the river traffic increased: there were plans to unite the south of England by joining the Severn, the Avon, the Great Ouse, and the Thames; the Exeter Ship Canal was dug between 1564 and 1566 and became a popular subject for West Country poets; the channel of the Lee was improved in 1571—altogether there were eight Acts of Parliament designed to improve the rivers.[38] Interestingly, the plans to develop the river traffic through canals, locks, and deepened channels, preceded efforts to improve the highways, although legal and financial considerations impeded most such schemes. Thus, although the seventeenth century really marks the era of river development—between 1600 and 1700 the number of navigable miles increased from 685 to 960—the interest in the rivers in the sixteenth century goes far beyond what is suggested by actual achievements.

There are other ways as well in which the river served as a unifier. As water itself seeks an even level, so the river is a kind of equalizer, joining literally and metaphorically the royal hill and humble vale.[39] In the Renaissance no less than in antiquity, the waters of rivers and wells were thought to have been created for everyone, rich and poor—although the lands along their banks were not. Water tends to defy rights of private ownership; the common need for it makes it, to a degree anyway, common property. One Renaissance correspondent speaks approvingly of the Muslim custom that "no money nor fee should be exacted for the use of water which God had freelie bestowed on poor and rich."[40] The universal solvent reduces social barriers in other, more sophisticated ways as well. It provides pleasure and profit for both rich and poor. Its piscine bounty was shared by all classes, if not by choice—the London poor complained that poverty constrained them to a diet of Thames's salmon—then by law, in the form of some 153 fasting days in the course of the year. The rivers provided both food and work, particularly for the poor. Fishing, hauling of barges, mill work, and countless other jobs were produced by the rivers, to say nothing of the farming industry's debt to them; watermen on the Thames derived a rakish pleasure from having their social betters in the same boat with them for a time. The rivers generally provided opportunity for all, and they figured in the leisure as well as the working life of both rich and poor. They were the stage for all kinds of religious festivals and public and private celebrations whose spectacles provided entertainment for all classes. Thus, through the extravagant river festivals celebrating the marriage of Cosimo de'Medici and Maria Madalana of Austria in Florence in 1608, or those on the Thames for Princess Elizabeth and Prince Frederick in 1612–13, the whole city seemed to participate in the historic moment.

However, the river also functions naturally both as a unifier and a divider. It customarily forms borders—between Asia and Europe, England, Scotland, and Wales, and between counties, manors, and estates. But in thus separating and establishing a recognized dis-

tance between neighbors, it also joins them. It brings their commodities together, forms an avenue of communication, creates
shared interests and the basis for common development—as Ralegh
realized in his discussion of Nimrod. European and English rivers
are landmarks, identifying cities and nations and their people. But
paradoxically, they also reduce these differences, make the landscapes they cover a unified and integral whole, and erode the
cultural distinctions between populations. This geographical fact is
true of modern Europe as well as of primitive societies,[41] so that the
river even seems to reduce the differences between periods of
history, as Ralegh also realized.

The political and geographical influence of the rivers did not
escape Renaissance authors. In field and folio, topographers identified their cities and nations with their rivers. Like the speaker in
Ovid's third *Amor*, they praised them and anatomized their u-
niquenesses (all rivers are in some way unique in the eyes of their
inhabitants) and the advantages that they confer on the surrounding
landscape and its society. As we have seen, these writers use a
language which joins literary *topoi* and classical associations with
that of the practical husbandman, the traveller, and the scientific
observer.

Authors in fact used the diversity of the rivers to unify their
political and geographical perspectives, and in this way the river
continues to reflect the nature of the world it inhabits. Thus, while
the topographical literature that poured forth during the sixteenth
century commonly promises descriptions of all of Europe's rivers,
writers conventionally perceived their own nations in terms of the
river, as we can see from the title of Gilles Corrozet's and Claude
Champier's *Le Cathalogue des villes et citez assises es troys
Gaulles . . . avec ung traicte des fleuves & fontaines* (Paris, 1539).
The first book describes the principal cities, their history and Trojan
origins, while the second is a treatise on French rivers. As the
authors say, "*La chose que plus anoblit une province sont les
fleuves*"; their objective is to show that "*Gaulle a des fleuves aussi
nobles, & aussi grand nombre que province ou nation qui sont en
Europe.*"[42] Following the chorographic form of the *descriptio urbis*,
the authors describe the major rivers of France, the cities and
mansions which adorn their banks, and the ancient noble families
which have brought fame to the country. Their narrative gives a full
sense of European and national self-consciousness; it brings
together myths of national identity and observations on the natural

and artistic beauties of the realm within a more or less geographically coherent view of France flourishing on the banks of her noble
rivers.

Travellers were encouraged to take particular notice of the rivers
of foreign lands, to note their situation, their qualities, the cities
they give rise to, how they are used for trade and defense, and
finally, to compare them with those of their native land. But as
Robert Johnson demonstrates in *The Travellers Breviat* (1601), the
rivers which serve to proclaim individual national identity also
remind the traveller how all people share in the world's bounty, and
how a city's wealth is the product of an entire kingdom's united
efforts:

> There is nothing in France more worthie the noting then the number
> and pleasure of the navigable rivers, whereof some . . . ' gird the
> whole realme. . . . Some others cut through the middle, as Sequano,
> Loire, Garonne. Into these three rivers fall so many other rivers,
> some from the uttermost bounds; some from the inmost parts of the
> realme, that it maketh the whole countrey commodious for trafique
> and exchange of each others wants: insomuch that by this facultie of
> carriage & entercourse of merchandize, all things may be saide to be
> in common to the inhabitants of this Kingdome. . . . The goodness of
> the soile, and easie transporting of commodities, is the cause that
> there are so many cities and so many townes, and these most
> commonly seated upon the bankes of the rivers.[43]

Notwithstanding its various material benefits, the river here is
primarily the agent of geographical and political unity, and it both
distinguishes the nation and unites it inextricably with the larger
world.

For these authors, very thoughtful as they are about the nature of
their society, the river is a topic which involves the ideals of an
essentially secular Christian humanism. In the rivers of Europe they
perceived ideas about civilization, its potential and its divinely
inspired objectives. Among those who make most use of the river to
develop these ideas is the sixteenth-century Italian political scientist, Giovanni Botero, who clearly apprehends a divine purpose in
the interrelationships between geography and human society.

For Botero, the city, in its reciprocal, harmonious relationship to
the world around it, is the fulfilment of human and natural potential; it must "vent forth those commodities, which are superfluous . . . and return such as are wanting."[44] His ideal city is not
a self-sufficient one; it must be so placed that it maintains a perfect balance between its inevitable deficiencies, whatever they

may be, and the excesses of its production or other assets. That is, the city depends upon its link with the rest of the world, and particularly with communities which can supply its needs and absorb its excesses.

Botero's conception of the city is based on the recognition of human and geographical limitations; indeed, he makes a virtue of necessity and embraces society's inadequacies as agents of universal concord. Thus he rejects the ideal of self-sufficiency, stressing that a city has to "participate in the extremes" of all aspects of life. It must have an equal share in the consumption, distribution, and production of goods and services. A commercial center such as Derbent, for example, fails as a city because "it participateth not of the extremes, but serves only for Passage; receiving onely that travel backward, and forward."[45] Because it is merely a commercial and economic cipher, it can never become more than a town and is incapable of enjoying all the variety of urban life. Moreover, when Botero speaks of the need to "participate in the extremes" of society, he is not merely speaking of the transfer of material goods but also of less tangible, but no less important things, such as attractiveness of situation, artistic and intellectual advantages, a comfortable and healthful environment—in short, those things which make a productive life also a pleasurable one, thus turning the city into a new Eden united with an ideally harmonious world. While there are many distinctive features about Botero's political science, his belief in the humanistic potential of the city is characteristic of the Renaissance.[46]

Botero's world is one of extremes and of movement, and in his essays he repeatedly returns to the rivers as a key factor in the creation and maintenance of the city for the very reason that they participate more than any other geographical feature in the defensive, economic, aesthetic, and intellectual needs of life.[47] A city without a river is almost inconceivable; in fact, Botero is obsessed with rivers and writes of them with a pleasure, interest, and rhetorical fervor that go beyond scientific concern. For example, in one particularly involved and conceited passage in his *Relation of the Most Famous Kingdomes throwout the World* he delights in a grotesque description of nature's most beneficial gift, clearly enjoying the disparity between image and meaning:

> Of all creatures in the world a River most resembles a monster. The
> head (like that of Rumor) is often times not to be found; the mouth

farre bigger than the head, and withall farthest off from it; The head hath no motion; the veines feed the bodie; the mouth serves not but to void the superfluities; How monstrous notwithstanding soever it be, yet most beneficiall it is. The next advantage to that of the Sea being the commodoty of great, navigable & unpassable Rivers.[48]

Aside from suggesting Botero's obvious delight in his subject matter, the passage tells us something important about his perception of the unity of the political landscape. In his broadminded and practical view of the world he perceives the rivers and the sea as extensions of each other. There are differences in the range and specific utility of each: in particular, the sea is more useful for the expansion of kingdoms, while the river provides more commercial and defensive advantages. But basically they are the same divine gift serving in varying degrees the same benefits: maritime trade extends to river trade, inland traffic on the rivers overflows into the maritime markets. Botero provides a good illustration of the phase reversal we have been discussing: his world is very particularly urban and land-based, but it is also large and diversified in its commodities. The seas and rivers serve the cities; they unify the social and geographical structure of the world, providing unity through diversity.

As natural features in a divinely conceived geography, the rivers provide Botero with a *topos* in which he can locate his conception of society and nature. His understanding of the world's diversity (and divinity) supports his view of human purposefulness—he is the neoplatonist of the commercial world. "Assuredly, it seemeth, that God created water" for the perfection of transport, he argues, and commerce is an extension of Divine Unity—it is the social manifestation of the *concordia discors* that is reflected in landscape:

> For his Divine majestie desirous man mutually should embrace one another, as members of the same Body, distributed commodities in such sort, that to no one Countrey gave he all things: to the end the one needing the other . . . communitie should arise: from community, love; from love, union. And the better to facilitate this meanes, the East is combined with the West, the South with the North.[49]

Botero is the Ficino of the merchant class. Not only does he perceive that the world in its divinity is but one body, not many, he, like Ralegh, sees that the microcosm and macrocosm are one, that the rivers of the larger world are tributaries of the individual's inner being, and they all are subsumed in a divine order:

> True it is, that the Rivers here are many, and very faire, and so fittly
> serving one the other, and all the whole, as it seemeth, Nature in the
> framing of our bodies, did not shew more wonderfull providence, in
> disposing veines and Arteries throughout the bodie, for their apt
> conveyance of the blood and spirit from the Liver and Heart, to each
> part thereof, than She hath showed in the placing of these waters, for
> the transporting of these commodities, to all her severall Provinces.[50]

With all its diversity then, or even because of it, the river, as it continues to be part of its physical geography, suggests to the Renaissance an underlying unity representing a cultural and social ideal, the components of which are classical and secular, Christian and, in their materialism, modern. The European geography brings together past, present, and the future. The divisive effect of a post-lapsarian rationalism serves a larger idea of Concord in which all the world is restored to harmony. The modern myth of geography, then, looks to universal concord, rather than self-sufficiency.

From these geographical contexts we can see, first of all, how closely related the rivers of landscape and rhetoric are, and secondly, how completely the external geography is also that of the mind. The river motif, figuring unity in diversity and here fixed in the landscape, was equally popular in its abstract, purely rhetorical form. The *topos* brings together a distinctly Renaissance historical perspective on modern Europe and its landscape—and one which is equally mindful of its cultural past. Thus, in a somewhat different manner, Sidney's translation, *A woorke concerning the trewnesse of the Christian religion*, contains a meditation on the river as an analogue to divine oneness, or tri-unity, and on the river-like condition of continuous being in which all things flow without interruption from their source in the universal *logos*:

> Likewise, in waters, we have the head of them in the earth & the
> spring boyling out of it, & the stream which is made of them both and
> spreadeth itsself out farre of from thence. It is but one self same
> continuall and unseparable essence, which hath neither foreness nor
> afternesse, save onely in order and not in tyme, that is to say,
> according to our considering of it, having respect of courses, and not
> according to truth. For the Wellhead is not a head, but in respect of
> the Spring, not the spring a spring, but in respect of the wellhead, nor
> the stream a stream, but in respect of them both, and so all three be
> but one Water, and cannot almost be considered one without
> another, howbeit that one is not the other. It is an express mark of
> the original relations and persons coessential in the only one essence
> of God.[51]

The passage is an interesting one. Rhetorically, it resembles, at least superficially, the passage from Epiphanius, or the river simile with which Bernard of Clairvaux opens Sermon 13. The author here, however, is clearly meditating on the physical realities of the landscape and what they tell us about knowledge. Philosophically, the passage has more obvious and important similarities to Botero's Neoplatonic and Ralegh's historical views of the world. What is most striking here is the way in which the passage, with its emphasis on the teleological fact that the river flowing from wellhead to outlet is necessarily one water (obviously it is a perennial river from a northern, Reformation country, not an Italian torrent!) is a *topos* for unity parallel in thought to Botero's perception of the metaphysical meaning of the commercial landscape. Despite the highly rhetorical quality which links it with medieval writers, the passage—especially as the translator has rendered it—retains a characteristically Renaissance concern for the geography behind the metaphor—the difference rhetorically between "likewise" and "like."

Clearly Renaissance writers recognized a coherence behind the diffuse literary and geographical dimensions of their rivers. Using them rhetorically to structure their prose and intellectually to focus their perceptions of the physical world, they saw in the rivers a complex but coherent and conventional topic. Of course there are radical differences in the river motif as it appears in Sidney, Botero, and Ralegh: the first associates it primarily with Truth, the second with Love, and the third with Knowledge. Yet the common ground between them is fairly obvious, and the river crosses it without difficulty; I have identified it with the idea of Unity. And so, notwithstanding the differences in emphasis and objective, these authors have a shared understanding of and response to the river's geographical and literary significance, and recognizing this, we can discern the distinctive character of the motif in the Renaissance without demanding that it always mean the same thing.

Although we have been examining the Renaissance response to landscape, the rivers, nevertheless, have echoed with the wisdom of the ancients. Thus, when Botero speaks of the rivers as agents of love and community, and when Sidney speaks of their coessential truth, they are both thinking of the flowing waters in terms of a unifying knowledge, and the weight of their learning is brought to bear on their arguments. Even when treated most rhetorically, the river captures the mysteries of nature and the intellect and focuses the author's attention on this world, on the human condition. René de Lucinge in *The Beginnings, Continuance, and Decay of Estates*, for example, adopts quite a different aspect of the river, the torrent, to locate his lesson about the precarious nature of governments:

> So have they [monarchs] many times lost it all in a moment: such conquests resemble torrents tumbling downe the mountains, which in less than an hour, by reason of the great slauter of waters they bring with them, become fearefull and dangerous; when soone after in an instant we see them fallen and shallow, so as a childe may wade throw them without trouble or danger.[52]

It cannot be stated whether the river here has geographical or literary origins, but one can say that Lucinge treats it literarily. It retains its naturalness for the very reason that he is speaking about the nature of human society: his mundane interests prevent the rhetoric from becoming completely disembodied. Yet his models could be entirely literary; he may simply have had Hesiod, Homer, or Plato in mind when composing the image.

But he too looks to the river, in nature and literature, for knowledge and wisdom. In a similar way, when Pierre de la Primaudaye addresses Henry III about the need to know nature's variety if one is to govern effectively, he thinks in terms of the fount of knowledge: "And trulie for Wisdome and Philosophie, as from a livelie fountaine floweth the gift of governing as by good lawes and good example."[53] Here the river taps both literal and metaphoric meanings and joins the classical and biblical traditions with the lessons of nature.

The rivers have an unusual place in the Renaissance imagination, one that is best defined by Augustine's identification of them with the earthly presence of the angelic hosts (*De Civitate Dei*, 11.34). Indirectly, if not directly, Renaissance writers give rivers just this significance. As Primaudaye suggests, in a unique way the river is an agent of divine wisdom and revelation; it behaves "as if it had some sense and understanding, and that God had caused it to heare his voice, and had commanded it, as he commanded man, to obey his ordinance, although it be a senseless creature and without life." Unlike Augustine or the medieval writers, who look beyond the river to a transcendent world, barely seeing the geographical reality of the river, Primaudaye's vision is fundamentally mundane—he is concerned with the world's reality. For him the rivers "have as it were a secret feeling by nature of the majestie of God their creator," and as God's earthly hosts, He sometimes "causeth them to rise up against men for their rebellion and wickedness." The river for Primaudaye is the epitome of nature, and therefore the natural mirror for people, and when he speaks of their deluges, saying that "it pleaseth God that they should overflow to chactice men, by deluges and flood," he himself has learned from Genesis and the *Iliad*, as well as from nature, although he is speaking about the real rivers of Europe. The traditional features of the river *topos* exert a covert influence on the author's perceptions of nature. His river torrents are very much those of Homer and the Bible, but they are made into something totally different, something which is fully part of the Renaissance. Because he perceived nature in terms of the shaping influence of humane learning, he regards them as a source of human understanding. When he says that "we shall therein finde goodly mirrors wherein to contemplate his [God's] majestie and greatness," he draws equally from the well of commonplace literature (Seneca in particular) and nature, and he has perfectly formulated a traditional aspect of the river *topos*, but his use of it to coordinate a humanistic view of divine concord in nature is very much the product of his own era.[54]

These writers, then, perceived their world in terms of their literary experiences, so that their rivers, as natural images of wisdom, flowed with mixed waters which were the confluence of streams originating in nature and in the divine intellect. In this way, they quite literally figured man's place in the natural order—between the angelic and the animal, directed by divine purpose, while confined to the lower world—and they do so more overtly and fully than in previous centuries. And the river emphatically retained its meaning for this world: it was a humanistic motif, and its waters crossed a human landscape bordered with meadows, palaces, cities and ruins, whose reflection in these waters offered a vision of human society, its character and potential, and thus showed the relation between divine and mutable nature, for the river itself seemed to draw from both these sources. For historians, topographers, and poets, the river was in a special way supernatural: it showed how all we know of nature and the world is an accumulation of our long-flowing intellectual history, what we have been taught to see in the world around us and what we know from diviner sources of our intellect: the grace which flows from unperceived sources. In this we can see how the river, and to a certain extent the entire landscape for the Renaissance, is perceived in terms of a cumulative sensibility: that is, one which resonates with many different aspects of the response to geography as it has evolved over the centuries. The secular learning and cultural ideals of the ancients and the religious ideals of the Middle Ages seem to come together in the Renaissance river to suggest a cultural myth which has the characteristics of a Christian secularism. As a passage from Bacon's *Advancement of Learning* suggests, the river seems to promise the confluence of two distinct streams, and was therefore a suitable image not only for society's but also the individual's pursuit of order and understanding in the spiritual and in the material realm.

> The knowledge of man is as the waters, some descending from above, and some springing from beneath; the one informed by the light of nature the other inspired by divine revelation.
> The light of nature consisteth in the notions of the mind and the reports of the senses: For as for knowledge which men receiveth by teaching, it is cumulative and not original; as in a water that besides his own springhead is fed with other streams. So then according to these two differing illuminations or originals, knowledge is for all divided into Divinity and Philosophy.[55]

4. Literary Contexts: Public and Private Landscapes, Poets and Topographers

> It *Troynovant* is hight, that with the waves
>   Of wealthy *Thamis* washed is along,
>   Upon whose stubborne neck, whereat he raves
>   With roring rage, and sore him selfe does throng,
>   That all men feare to tempte his billowes strong,
>   She fastned hath her foot, which standes so hy,
>   That it a wonder of the world is song
>   In forreine Landes, and all which passen by,
> Beholding it from far, do thinke it threates the skye.
>
> (Spenser, The Faerie Queene)

> Sure there are Poets which did never dream
> Upon *Parnassus*, nor did tast the stream
> Of *Helicon*, we therefore may suppose
> Those made not Poets, but the Poets those.
>
> (John Denham, Cooper's Hill)

Such, then, are some of the ways in which Renaissance writers thought of the rivers of geography, and it is clear that the process of "reading" or analyzing the landscape was well advanced. I want to turn now to some of the intellectual and imaginative, primarily literary contexts dominated by the river. These will not necessarily be fictional landscapes, but landscapes that should be looked at from a literary point of view. Read against the previous section, these examples should illustrate how fully nature was subsumed into art in the Renaissance, and how closely the maps of the imaginary and the physical worlds resemble one another.

More specifically, though, I want to observe how authors transform their landscapes, and how, in the process, they inform them with national or personal myths. Indeed, it is in terms of different kinds of public or private mythology that we must often read landscape literature. In identifying these two generic extremes I hope to prepare the way for examination in the next chapter of how myths of geography evolved in the course of the Renaissance: how authors' identification with a national geography and a public world yielded to an interest in private settings having meaning for the individual. As we will see, as national myths became fragmented, literary traditions, including the river poem, were adapted to ideals that were more relevant to the individual.

At this stage, though, it will be useful to take a step back and look generally at the authorial process of myth-making and how it is reflected in the literary landscapes of the Renaissance. From what we have said so far, we can see that all landscape is implicitly transformed by the imagination and naturally mythologizes the self and one's culture. In this section on literary contexts, I will formulate more fully this somewhat unorthodox approach to Renaissance landscapes and their rivers by illustrating the relation between the individual and literary geography in two very different kinds of literature. First, aside from some general illustrations, I will look at how personal and national myths enter into the highly literary but also very "real" landscape of Sannazaro's *Arcadia*. And second, I will look at the literary transformation of landscape by English topographers.

In these two sections it will become clear how closely art and nature mirror one another: "imaginative" and descriptive literature both reveal the same myth-making process. In the Renaissance, as in any other period, the creation of a literary geography or landscape inevitably reflects the author's self-conception and his perception of the public world and the individual's place within it. Whether creating a historical geography or a fictional one, authors explore their own psychological relation to it and to the world at large. In this sense, no geography is free from the influence of the shaping imagination. All settings contain in varying degrees a social and private vision; all have implicit values in which one can find fulfillment in social or individual terms, where the topography is organized in primarily communal or personal social structures. It is largely the art that has been imposed on geography that converts it to landscape and thus gives it meaning.

Thus all geographies are perceived according to imaginative constructs, are to greater or lesser degree archetypal. Their inhabitants, either historical or fictional characters, or the figure implied by the narrative voice of the author, have their meaning in their psychological relation to their environment, all settings thus being in some degree symbolic of the individual's mind, knowledge, and potential for self-realization. We strive to be accommodated in our landscapes, and because of accidents of time and history, because of personal shortcomings or greatness, we find them appropriate or inappropriate. The geography must match the mind of the individual and its society; when it does not, the disparity itself becomes the subject of the author's analysis, and this is equally true for history, poetry, and drama. Historians examine the difference in terms of social time and human events, and the contrast between times past and present; their own voices are the measure of that distance between the archetype of the past and the present. Similarly, "fictional" settings reflect particular relationships between the individual, geography, and time. For instance, in *Richard II* there is an incongruity in Richard's personal response to the national landscape when he returns to Wales in Act 3. The landscape is perceived in terms of the dramatic moment: it is political and social, appropriate for a king returning to a land beset by rebellion. Richard's response is as to a private geography in which the individual seeks a personal identity: "I weep for joy/To stand upon my kingdom once again . . . greet I thee, my earth,/And do thee favours with my royal hands" (2.2.4–11). In seeing himself alone in the national landscape, and seeing it as his private domain, Richard's response to the world is continually at odds with its dramatic representation in historical terms.

All landscapes, then, contain implicit or explicit cultural and psychological ideals. Whether it is a historical or fictional setting, whether it is primarily a public one as is that of *Henry V*, for example, or primarily personal or psychological as is that of *Para-*

dise Lost or *The Faerie Queene*, they all define in one way or another the relation of the individual and society to the world itself, and in so doing establish either a social or private set of values. The balance between the two is implicitly there, in the author's description of the scene. In many cases, perhaps even most cases, the psychological and public archetypes are complementary and overlap as in *The Faerie Queene* or *Gerusalemme Liberata*: personal and public goals and achievement are one and the same. The presence of time's influence, advancing or inhibiting the characters' self-realization, is felt in each kind of landscape. But as we will see more particularly, in the early decades of the English Renaissance, the public landscape is also psychological and personal, while in later decades, the private landscape emerges and asserts its values on the lives of its characters.

Commonly, the river brings together these dimensions and helps define the full significance and potential of the geography. As an extension of the self, the river also has both personal and public associations. It flows from the realm of private experience to that of historical epoch, and so it illustrates their relation to one another. Thus, it shares in the life of the individual and society, and suggests the goals common to each. In so doing it provides a convenient conceit in which the relation between the individual experience, society, and history can be represented and the ideals of the landscape can be scrutinized.

It is in terms of such ideas that the landscape had meaning for the Renaissance.[56] They are, after all, but the expansion of the commonplace that in the Renaissance, man was regarded as a public being, and the environment—historically, socially, and as we have seen, geographically—as his mirror. He, in turn, figures the larger world *in parvo*, in himself. Thus, while most river literature is primarily public, it resonates with a private voice, and its public themes also have significance for the individual. If Whitman can write of the world by addressing himself, the Renaissance poet, let us say Spenser, can write of himself by addressing the world. In his writings, the Renaissance author also creates a psychological world, a domain that is coextensive with his imaginative vision. In his *Britannia*, Camden marks off a psychological realm which reflects his own imaginative scope, defines the potential cultural arena for his conception of individual, as well as social achievement. He creates a national image of Britain which is also an intellectual world, and which defines his own public and poetic identity as one immeasurably grander and more significant, for example, than that which William Lambard can lay claim to in the *Perambulation of Kent*, and the difference is conveyed through the imaginative geography.

Authors, like imperialists, conquer imaginative territory and expand their control; their inner empire is always somehow, directly or indirectly, related to their ability to subdue the world beyond the self. Joyce's world, like Spenser's, embraces all the rivers of the world, with their cultural and personal myths. Lesser figures annex smaller territories. More dictatorial authors bring dimensions of both space and time within their imaginative control, reaching into the cultural or mythical past to embrace the first efforts by which humanity began to order the world and submit it to its will. They master its historical as well as its physical contours, subjecting as much as their imagination is able to, perceiving it either in terms of society's or the individual's potential for order and perfection. But by its very nature, all literature which has a major concern for topography raises questions about our ability to master the natural world and assert our place in the created order. The author's objective, in the Renaissance as in other periods, is to create an image of the world subdued by the powers of the intellect, and the dimension of that world, often defined by its rivers, is the measure of the author's poetic vision and of mankind.

a) Sannazaro

> No, fair Arcadia cannot be completer;
> My praise may lessen, but not make thee greater.
> My Muse for lofty pitches shall not roam,
> But homely pipen of her native home;
> And to the swains, love rural minstrelsy;
> Thus, dear Britannia, will I sing of thee.
>
> (William Browne, *Britannia's Pastorals*)

> When the raw blossome of my youth was yet
> In my first childhoods green enclosure bound,
> Of *Aquadune* I learnt to fold my net,
> And spread the sail, and beat the river round,
> And with labyrinths in straits to set,
>   And guide my boat where *Thames* and *Isis* heire,
> By lowly *Aeton* slides, and *Windsor* proudly fair . . .
> But when my tender youth 'gan fairly blow,

I changed large *Thames* for *Chamus* narrower seas:
And now my pipe the better sort did please.

(Phineas Fletcher, *Piscatorie Eclogs*)

Thus all landscape literature is reflexive, and while it may describe the public domain, it also involves the author's psychological identity as well. The prevenient unity that is figured in Botero's rivers relies on a coherent sense of the individual without which the world would be meaningless. The Renaissance topographer's perception of the external world depends at least in part on the assumption of an equally coherent inner world. Realizing this, we can better appreciate that the literary impulses driving Ortelius, Camden, Ralegh, and countless others are not very different from those driving Spenser, Drayton, Daniel, or William Browne. They are all Daedalian poets in the sense that they are image-makers creating a world from both the realm of ideas and that of images and relevant to both the inner being and society. As Sidney says in the *Defense of Poesie*, the poet "lifted up with the vigor of his own inventione dooth growe in effect, another nature, in making things either better then Nature bringeth forth, or quite a new, formes such as never were in Nature."

If we look at works of Renaissance poets, historians, and topographers, we see that this response to landscape takes the form of a national self-consciousness which incorporates the private self and that it often involves a process of classicizing the geography and creating a vernacular literary tradition. In the literary contexts that we will be examining, then, the writer's world is, in some degree, seen in terms of an implicit classical ideal. This aspect of Renaissance literature has, of course, been much discussed, but it should be mentioned here that the use of the river setting is one way in which public and private myths are made to overlap in a national landscape having at least a vaguely classical identity. The process involves the poet, who is the individual analogue to the classical poet, and whose duty to society is identical to that of his ancient precursor.[57]

Such thoroughgoing Hellenism was carried to its greatest extreme in France, though the impulse was strong throughout Europe. As many critics have recognized, the Pléiade poets attempted to recreate the very milieu out of which classical literature grew. They regarded themselves, their society, their political geography, as well as the poet's métier as analogous to their ancient equivalents. The fêtes at Fontainbleau, which we have already mentioned, offer sufficient illustration of the extent of this metamorphic national vision; what is important is that poets did not merely imitate the literature of antiquity, they tried to remake both its social and psychological context. This fashion was carried to such an extreme that English critics complained of preposterous violations of decorum. Histories which combined fact and fiction, they said, should strive for a "judicious collation" of their events, settings, and heroes; but some authors, argues Richard Brathwait,

> observe no methode, Planting an Arcadia in a Britanny; as if by some super natural accident there was a transplantation of Regions or some Earth-quake in the Authors braine, whence this immane [sic] colosse of an irregular Discourse proceeded. Which strange representation be not unlike to your Lanskip; where upon the Seas, whatsoever we see, by land, by land seemes in our sail to go with us; Even so do these vain Histories make strange objects unto us . . . transiting whole countries to make an impolished straine of pastorall musicke.[58]

What we can perceive here is that much of the transformation of landscape is effected in the cause of creating a national literature. History and literary archetype merge in the author's brain. More than any other group, the Pléiade poets, especially Ronsard, set the fashion for acting out the roles of their classical forebears, and this is a self-fulfilling poetic fiction that goes beyond the national landscape and absorbs the poet's own persona. As Ronsard forges his poetic identification with his native Loire, he aligns his personality with the national image while keeping a private and vernacular voice: poet, landscape, and poetry share one prophetic destiny. To mold the nation's image through the realization of its poetic potential as heir to Greece, is also to find self-fulfillment as the successor to the classical poets writing in Greek and Latin.

In varying degrees this goal of recreating the classical ideal in a national landscape and language pervaded Europe. Edmund Spenser, for example, achieved a similar confluence of the cultural and personal resources of his rivers, which he treated as classical authors treated theirs. Whether speaking in his public voice of the Thames or in his private voice of the Mulla, he is always in a way representative of the nation as a whole; his relations to his rivers always, in one way or another, reflect on the state of the realm.

But many other poets saw what the Pléiade poets were doing and asked, along with Thomas Watson (the arch-imitator of Ronsard), if

the "sacred nymphs . . . take . . . no delight in change of air? Is
Helicon your only Paradise?"[59] "Are there swans in Thames?" was
a question that was asked persistently, even as late as Milton, and
while it became a conventional act of poetic posturing, in the
present context we can see that the question addresses legitimate
historical and cultural issues: can the golden age of verse be recreated and how? Can the time and place ever again be right for the
poet to capture the mythic nature of his world? For Ronsard,
Spenser, Milton, and others, the questions "can our northern,
European world sustain the myths of the Mediterranean past, can it
create new ones when our culture derives from them?" were not
meaningless poetic mannerisms, certainly not for the Frenchman
writing in the vernacular nor for Spenser experimenting with "English versifying" or Milton as he reconsidered his plans for a heroic
British epic. These questions go to the very heart of literary creation
in the Renaissance, and they are commonly and conventionally
framed in the context of the river motif, for it conflates the historical, national, poetic, linguistic, and personal dimensions that are
implicit in them.

One of the results of this surge of national self-consciousness is
that the river assumed a greater literary range. In fact, it became
identified with the quest for a personal and national voice, the
search for a cultural identity in terms of the myths and literary
motifs of antiquity. This popularity is not surprising when we
remember that the literary Renaissance in Europe is part of the
same cultural revolution that sees the emergence of the importance
of the individual. Not only in France but throughout Europe, as
nations developed their vernacular traditions, they also acquired
self-proclaimed laureates who tuned their personal pipes to the
nation's waterfall. What I am describing here, of course, are several
aspects of the Renaissance itself, and these materialize at different
times in different parts of Europe. We see it as early as the quat-
trocento in Italy, where the river was an important trope in humanist repertoire.[60] It is helpful, however, to recognize that this literary
golden age is partly the result of geographical and political changes,
and that the political autonomy in Europe at this time is contemporary with the growth of a literature noteworthy for its distinctive
national and personal voice; across Europe we can see the popularity of topographical imagery which is at once traditional and yet
drawn from the modern political landscape. Relatedly, Renaissance
writers cultivated their national identity (even if they were political

victims). One way of doing so was to identify themselves, personally, physically, and historically, with the local or national river: Petrarch with his Sorgue; Boccaccio with the streams of Fiesole; Ronsard with his Loire; Montemayor with the rivers of Spain and Portugal; Spenser with the Mulla and the Thames; Phineas Fletcher with the Cam; Milton with the Thames and Grant.[61] The river, used in the rhetorical shorthand of synecdoche, was not only an abbreviation for the author and his locale, but also for the times, to allude to political complexities of the day, to the struggle of the humanists against the philistine, or to the literary, political, and intellectual conditions of writers. It was part of the witty posturing of authors, but this should not be understood pejoratively, for it involves the complex question of literary self-identity in the Renaissance, and the development of the arts and learning in various parts of a rapidly changing Europe.[62] The river was a motif which was suited to the somewhat hypersensitive literary sensibility, and as a result it appears in a wide variety of genres in different national literatures. It crossed different literary landscapes, helping to dissolve generic borders and to soften the distinctive voices and styles which distinguished regions such as the historic highlands or pastoral plains, while continuing to carry the alluvium of national self-consciousness. Thus, the river motif brings certain common literary and cultural ideas into heterogeneous settings, and even acts as a levelling agent, bringing in its waters hybrid forms of *genre mixte.*

While I will be concentrating on the river's place in the personal and national myths of the English Renaissance, it will be useful, partly for contrast and partly for illustration, to look in some detail at one very influential example of a mythic yet real river landscape in continental literature. Jacopo Sannazaro's *Arcadia* is a particularly good illustration of how a cultural ideal with public and private significance is imposed on a political, European setting, and it served as a model for English writers who attempted to transform their national geography in a similar way.

In the *Arcadia* the realms of political history and psychological biography share adjacent and similarly tinted quarters on the literary map, and they are joined by the deep waters of the river motif. Sannazaro examines the myth of an arcadian ideal that has been transmitted from antiquity, and he questions its reality for his world. Sannazaro is no literary *naif*; he was fully aware that the ideal of arcadia eluded Theocritus, Virgil, and Horace before him. But the ideal and the idea of a pastoral utopia seemed to exist for them even if they did not enjoy (or describe) such a life, and Sannazaro transplants this cultural myth into his own Neapolitan landscape, measures it against the reality of his age, and tries to redefine its meaning, to adapt it. He develops a political landscape in ways that use external nature to explore the psychology and cultural identity of his characters. Thus, although the archetypal world of Arcadia is presented to us first of all as the mental landscape travelled by the shepherd-poet, it is a social world dominated by the special virtues of the river, and (in the last chapters) Sannazaro uses the motif to transform its psychological values to those of a recognizable public realm, of Naples and King Frederick. Thus, if we look at the use of the motif in the *Arcadia*, we see a perfect example of its suitability for the public and private dimensions of the Renaissance sensibility.

Each major episode in the *Arcadia* is identified with the rivers; significantly, entry into the arcadian life of love, poetry, and solitude is gained by following their course:

> My friend, I was between Baiae and great Vesuvius,
>   in the pleasant plain where drawn into a little flood
> the lovely Sebeto joins himself with the sea.

> Love, that is never from my heart disjoined,
>   was making me then to seek out strange river regions,
>   whence my soul thinking on it is stricken still.[63]

And it is also by a similarly real, localized, very precisely identified (though psychological) river route that the poet eventually leaves Arcadia and reenters the world. These psychological transitions are set in a quasi-naturalistic landscape where the real rivers are transformed into metaphoric analogues for the poet's mental state.

If the rivers define the psychological nature of this literary province—set as it is, though, in a distinctly Neapolitan valley—it is also through them that we learn of its deficiencies. Quite literally, Selvagio and Ergasto, in physical and psychological exile, pursue self-knowledge along the rivers. In the last chapters the personal plaints of the conventionally tormented shepherds admit more and more to public concerns, and reader and shepherd together become aware of the world beyond their private emotions. True to the conventions of pastoral verse, Sannazaro's Arcadia cannot protect the individual from the greater world of public affairs. Thus we and Ergasto slowly awaken to the limits of Arcadia and to the fact of his mental and geographical displacement. The development of this realization is Sannazaro's primary theme, and it gradually unfolds

through the pursuit of the rivers. Ergasto, a stranger on the banks of
a strange river, begins to think of home, and his native river:

> For indeed, while these verses lasted, I was firmly persuaded that I
> was standing on the lovely and happy plain . . . and seeing the
> tranquil Sebeto—or rather, my Neapolitan Tiber . . . passing softly
> under the arches of a tiny bridge and without any turmoil blending
> itself with the sea. (p.117)

Sannazaro is analyzing the very nature of this archetypal, poetic
Arcadia in terms of conflicting ideals figured in the landscape. As
Ergasto's riparian reflections shift from the pastoral to the national
river, he is mentally retracing his steps and returning home. The
Arcadian world, which has proved to be morally ambiguous and
emotionally troubled, gives way to a conventional vision of the
public river decked with the "magnificences of my native land, most
proud and noble . . . with . . . lofty towers . . . rich temples . . .
proud palaces, the mighty and respected Sees of our patricians"
(p. 118). For the exiled romance figure, home is the real Arcadia,
whether it is an urban or a green world, and the understanding that
he achieves in the course of his travels is, in Ergasto's case, directly
related to the river. In the last section of the romance, he listens to
the elegy on Massilia, and realizes that he has fled into exile, not
away from it, and the lament, like a roundelay between the Arcadian and Neapolitan nymphs, is a farewell to pastoral; Ergasto
wakes up to his Arcadian self-absorption, "For I seemed to find
myself, exiled . . . in a solitary place I had never seen before,
among abandoned tombs" (pp. 133–34). Such is the vision of the
exile awakening to his solitude.

Sannazaro has completely internalized his very particular Neapolitan landscape, and used it to explore the poet's place in society.
Ergasto must withdraw from an Arcadia that has become a dream-
like mental torment, and unsure what to do, he impulsively heads
for the river, whose torrent reflects his own haste: "not knowing
where I should go—I came at last to the lower slope of a mountain
whence a great river ran with a marvellous rumbling and roaring"
(p. 134). What follows, comprising most of Chapter 12 and the
entire final section of the work is a sudden expansion of all the
various river motifs that have been developed throughout, and thus
it serves as a coda to Ergasto's decision to leave Arcadia. As he
stands in confusion on the banks of the Arcadian river, there arises

from its waters a Hesiodic nymph who takes charge of the youth. She addresses him sagely, "Follow my steps, for I am the Nymph of this region," and her words "implanted in me so much of veneration . . . that struck with astonishment . . . I set myself to follow her" (p. 134). And so, as for many another exile in later centuries, the way home is both ways along the river.

His return is marked by a general change from a private to a public setting, as Ergasto meets with his local river, the Sebeto. In a characteristic piece of Renaissance allegory, he must choose between two river routes, one leading to "the ornaments of the city" and the other "spreading out over the fields"; and in an eclogue sung by three shepherds, he hears that neither alternative offers a painless or innocent future: these visions vouchsafed Ergasto by the river nymph are those of experience and the vanities of the public world. Thus, the idealized conception of the city's splendor which drew Ergasto out of Arcadia proves to be a myth as unreal and ambiguous as his original naive expectations of Arcadia itself, and it too is modified by a vision which is realistic and mature.

Ergasto's final awareness is wholly enveloped in the river theme as, still beset with confusion, he is led beneath the nymph's waters to the cave of the rivers. The classical *topos* is brought into the Renaissance as the nymph, aid to travellers, healer, source of knowledge, youth's caretaker, restores a stronger and wiser Ergasto to his psychological and literal homeland. Thus, in a passage that draws on Homer and Virgil, and that influenced Spenser, Camden, and Drayton in their treatment of subterranean caves, Ergasto is brought to the cave-source of all rivers and granted knowledge that transcends the simple antithesis between the public and the private, active and contemplative lives: he is shown the source of all things, the mysterious unity that orders nature. In the river cave, then, "by the will of heaven," he is shown that place

> from which the rivers that run over the earth take their first beginnings.
> O marvellous handiwork of almighty God! The earth, that I thought was solid, encloses in its womb so great a hollowness! Then did I begin to feel no amazement at how the rivers should be possessed of such abundance and how with unfailing current they should keep their courses forever. (p. 136)

The river motif has been carried to its logical extreme. Ergasto, seeking understanding, has followed the guiding nymph to her underground source, where he beholds the significance of the hydrologic cycle for the order and unity of all things. As in Virgil and Ovid, the river god tells the legends of cosmic overreachers of the past, of cyclopses, giants, and the Encelades, and thus prepares for his reentry into the corrupt political world of modern Naples and for his final private grief, the death of Massilia.

Thus enlightened, Ergasto at first wishes himself dead and regrets ever leaving Arcadia, but his disillusion is the price of knowledge of the world. He has learned of the nature of life in its personal, public, political, historical, and mythical dimensions, and the price to be paid for this wisdom is departure from the introverted and muddled world of Arcadia. And what is particularly interesting about Sannazaro's treatment of the pastoral theme is the thoroughness with which he adapts the classical and Renaissance forms of the river *topos*, and his ability to turn the Neapolitan geography into a mental landscape in which we see the development of his character's world. To follow the use of the motif in Renaissance literature, we must be aware of both these dimensions, not only in the river setting, but in topographical literature generally. In this, however, Sannazaro is more than just an illustrative author, he is an influential one, for many authors saw in the *Arcadia* a model for modern pastoral forms and, more specifically, for ways of treating character and landscape. His influence has been generally recognized but not very thoroughly examined.[64] Taking the single example of his use of the river theme, we can see that, in England alone, Leland, Spenser, Camden, Drayton, William Browne, and Milton learned from his precedent. Relatedly, but more important, authors across Europe saw in the *Arcadia* the possibilities for generic variety and for a greater emotional and psychological range for political and national themes, and this is inextricably linked to his handling of landscape. In the *Arcadia* poets in particular were able to recognize a revolution in the use of myths of landscape; they saw the rewriting (and therefore reassessment of) the arcadian myth in terms of contemporary political geography and the peculiar pressures faced by the modern poet, and in this they perceived a renaissance of classical myth, and not just the perfunctory echo of classical lore. Ergasto, as a symbol of his culture, suffers from the burden of the past as he turns to, and ultimately flees from Arcadia, and in his anxiety we see Sannazaro's distinctly modern adaptation of the myth of Arcadia to his own culture.

b) Westcote and the Topographers

> Of famous cities we the founders know;
> But rivers, old as seas, to which they go,
> Are nature's bounty: tis of more renowne
> To make a river, than to build a town.
>
> (Edmund Waller, *On St. James Park*)

But to understand the peculiar nature of the river in the Renaissance, particularly in England, one must also be aware of the other manifestation of this literary impulse to shape the modern landscape: that is, the public voice in which the social world stands foremost. Here, the author's voice is identified in its public setting which is also dominated by the river, but a river which is first of all historical, political, or national rather than personal in its significance. This is a kind of landscape literature best illustrated by British authors: it dominated British perception of landscape until the seventeenth century, when the individual voice began to be heard in private settings. Continental authors combined the personal and public earlier and more successfully than did their English counterparts. Certainly, their greater formal variety and psychological range was felt across the Channel, and English rivers did occasionally rise on romantic and pastoral landscapes in direct imitation of such poets as Petrarch, the Pléiade poets, Montemayor, and Sannazaro,[65] but they do not reflect the mainstream of English response to landscape during the early stages of its renaissance.

This other manifestation of the myth-making sensibility is more immediately concerned with landscape itself. It is dominated by topographical and chorographic forms and is often preoccupied with aspects of cultural and political history, although it has the imaginative or intellectual objective of creating a coherent literary image of the landscape. Some examples of the form are more obviously imaginative or poetic than others, but the chorography and topography must be recognized as literary, rather than exclusively "scientific"—a distinction, after all, which was not firmly established until late in the seventeenth century.

In its form and its influence, topographical writing was an important literary genre in the sixteenth and seventeenth centuries, one which complemented the less topographical literature (such as the *Arcadia*) which also relied heavily on the representation of a political landscape. In this literature public and cultural myths rise to the surface, and the authorial identity is suppressed and absorbed into these larger themes, as we can see in two somewhat prosaic but representative models: Thomas Westcote's *The View of Devonshire* and William Harrison's *Description of Britain*. Both illustrate the river's growing importance for literary form, and the second example, the earlier of the two, is especially interesting because its recognized influence on poets such as Spenser and Drayton testifies to the generic affinities between topographical prose writers and poets.

This public topographical literature consistently reflects the desire to perceive a historically and geographically coherent landscape. The river's formal influence derives from its recognized unifying effect on history and geography and these qualities naturally bring it into the service of topographers whose narrative objective is to see individual regions "divided in themselves." The river motif shares in the basic chorographic form and unifying principle of topographical writing: "Chorography, sheweth the partes of th' earth, divided in themselves. And severally describeth, the Portes, Rivers, Havens, Fluddes, Hilles, Mountaines . . . yea and every particular thing in that part conteined."[66] As we will see, the river, as a *topos* and an aspect of geography, that is, as *topotheseia* and *topographia*, adds resonance to this chorographic design.

Chorography, the description of the physical divisions of an area, is based on the principle of unity and regional integrity. It recognizes the natural, geographical, rather than political identity of a landscape, and although the two are often inseparable, it is the topography that legitimizes the political order. Chorography also provides a natural link between literary form and subject matter, and for Spenser, Drayton, and Marvell no less than for Leland, Camden, and Harrison, the river was the convenient organizing feature in the landscape, and therefore in their topographical prose and verse.

If we consider the influence of chorography on literary form, we can see how writers drew on the ideas of geographical unity which we discussed in the last section. Whether describing a segment of a river between two cities (as Leland does), or a region defined by a network of rivers (as Westcote does), or an interconnecting system of roads, rivers, and the sea (as Camden does), the chorography puts art and nature into a coherent relationship, and in fact gives limits and shape to the narrator's (or cartographer's) art in a way that political divisions do not. Because it is theoretically confined to an area that can be surveyed by the individual, chorography also establishes a human—and humane—scale for a work; a county or estate is within the scope of a chorography, but an entire nation is not. While a country like England has its geographical integrity, for the chorographer it comprises many autonomous regions. In a work like the *Britannia* we are aware of the human scale of the individual units of the work, the separate counties and the geographical regions within them. The national landscape is always, in some degree, transformed into manageable divisions which reflect the relation of the individual to his environment. Thus Leland's *Itinerary*, as an attempted description of all England, lacks a coherent divisible order; it is peripatetic rather than perambulatory, and it remained a confused set of incomplete notes as Leland's wits succumbed beneath the burden of his task. The *Itinerary*, of course, consisted of Leland's firsthand observations, based on his own travels, but he attempted too much and failed to organize his material according to a coherent order. And even works of a more pretentious dimension (the descriptions of the world, for example) attempt to present their subject in units having chorographic and topographical integrity. As we will see, Camden ordered his *Britannia* according to an intricately designed balance of topographical and political divisions; Drayton's *Poly-Olbion* and Spenser's river pageant both adapt principles of chorographic description to order their treatments of the nation's rivers, and Norden's *Speculum Britanniae Pars* was to be a compendium of county descriptions. In each case the individual's perspective determines the sense of topographical integrity and brings the larger political or continental spaces within aesthetic and natural limits. William Lambard, for example, hoped that chorographic descriptions by individual authors in each county could be gathered together to "compact one whole and perfect bodie and booke of our English Topography," thus producing a volume at once unified and diverse.[67]

The river's natural importance in this body of literature was of course reinforced by literary precedent—in Pausanias's *The Description of Greece*, in the descriptions of the Holy Land, in the *descriptio urbis*, which had renewed popularity in the Renaissance, and most important, in literary works having an implicit geographical order, especially, the *Aeneid* and *The Moselle*. Renaissance cultural self-consciousness also looked to the river for its contemporary as well as historical interest.

Increasingly, the river became the principal interest of these writers: they identified their subject matter as well as their craft with the river, and so, as it had been for Ausonius, the river reemerged as a defining generic feature. For example, in spirit and in structure Thomas Westcote's *View of Devonshire* relies on the rivers. Not only is his description organized by them but his prose is enriched by their imagery, by river digressions, verses, and *encomia*; the more he can say about them, the higher his praise of the county. Briefly, his method is to follow the principal river, the Exe, describing along the way the scenic views of city and countryside, and the important antiquities. The Exe, however, runs from north to south, nearly through the center of the county, and so a thorough description requires much lateral movement along its tributaries:

> By following the river Exe in his progress and those other rivers, brooks, and streams, that have added their best subsidy and store to the augmentation of his small beginnings, when we fetched him out of Exmore, to raise him to that largeness, and profundity and strength, we left him at Exmouth, and 3 or 4 easterly rivers . . . and now by this time, I suppose, you can answere whether Devonshire may not say with Acheloüs in Greece, that famous river, which speaks by Ovid's pen,—Of many rivers, Lord I stand,/With crooked ways that cleave my land. (p. 248)[68]

We can see here how the river dictates form. Just as he must leave the Exe to travel the tributary waters, so too his narrative is necessarily digressive, and these excursions are developed as narrative ornaments deviating from the mainstream of his description. Thus he presents us with tales of personified geography—of the Tamar, and Tavy, of the impetuous Mole, and of the nuptials of Torridge and Taw. The view that we get of Devonshire is one of countless individual but interrelated rivers leading a mazy path across the county. Literally and figuratively, they are characters whose behavior originates in nature. Narratively, then, we are given a series of encounters between these animated river personalities in a topographical *carmen perpetuum* of successive tales having their beginnings in landscape—it is a topographer's version of a popular collection of histories, such as Painter's *Palace of Pleasure*.

Westcote thinks of his narrative style in terms of the river. At one point, when his narrative is getting bogged down in questions of etymology, he urges himself to "swim with the stream, the better to hasten our speed"; as Spenser occasionally does, he thinks of his craft as a writer in terms of a bark on the waters, and its difficulties are those he has encountered in travelling the rivers:

for in this journey through this city [Exmouth] I have rowed my simple bark (full fraught with desire to manifest to the world the esteem I have for it) against wind and tide, and endured the cross currents of slighting, the storms of neglect, the rocks of opposition . . . [yet] with my private strength, I am now disembogued and clear out at quay-gate. (p. 185)

The metaphor, homely as it is, is the rhetorical country cousin of Cicero's *flumen orationis*, and in it Westcote makes unpretentious but traditional use of its association with the fickle world of public opinion.

In his river obsession, Westcote is quite literally riding the streams of eloquence. His prose and his county's rivers are wholly bound up together, and they are developed like a conceit which both liberates and directs the author's imagination. And when he quotes other river poets, such as Alexander Neckham or William Browne, he speaks of their contribution as tributary to his mainstream: "We shall have a large subsidy from the river Tavy: of which fair though brown swan, Mr. William Browne, the poet, hath lately sung so sweet a note, as it hath caused more large and portable rivers to envy the glory and renown of it" (p. 365). This introduction of some lines from *Britannia's Pastorals* indicates how the river was regarded not only as a literary topic, but also as a metaphor for poetry and literature itself, and many others, including William Browne himself, shared Westcote's conception of the river.

Likeable, learned, witty and unpretentious, Westcote and his *View* are good examples of a certain type of English gentleman and his love of landscape. But we can see in these passages more than the odd illustration of how the river unifies both the geography and the narrative. Countless examples of this kind of chorographic description could be offered in which we see the intelligent country gentleman with regional pride describing a landscape that is private but that is also his link with something that all but subsumes the self. In some authors, usually of the sixteenth century, the link is with a national myth, so that regional pride, a personal myth, is absorbed into a larger identity, although for Westcote in 1630, the private myth resonates against a vague love of nature rather than nation. But in a strange way, we can see in these river narratives, whether early or late in the Renaissance, how the author's identity is absorbed by the process of description. Just as the mind becomes temporarily the thing that it contemplates, and the thing itself exists in the mind alone, the county here becomes the river and the meditation on rivers. It is an act of memory in which the mind, enveloping its watery subject matter, calls it forth in a re-creative act. For Westcote this process by which the thing described and the act of describing merge and become all consuming, is something he himself is aware of. For him, his native landscape becomes all that is implied by the name itself: it is the product of nature and language as is his *View of Devonshire*: "de Avon," "the river." Thus a conceited tautology lies at the center of his conception of the description:

> Nay look not strangely, I speak in our old vulgar speech: for Avon, in the Old British language, is a river . . . and the name for all fleeting waters, as wells, rills, becks, brooks, riverets, streams and rivers: and this province . . . De Avon, or Devon, [is] the county of rivers or waters. (p. 21)[69]

William Harrison's *Description of Britain* provides an example of the topographical description on a national scale, a form which was popular earlier in the Renaissance. In it we see the author's preoccupation with the myth of a national landscape. It is particularly interesting because in his thorough dissatisfaction with the work, he illustrates how the genre was conceived in terms of the rivers, for he assesses his achievement and its shortcomings in those terms. He thought of the work as a glorified chorography, and he consented to the project very reluctantly, he says, at the "yrksome sute" of some fellow antiquaries, and on the condition that they would provide descriptive accounts of regions he could not visit himself. Predictably, his colleagues left him in the lurch, no doubt with an impending publication date and an irate coauthor, Holinshed, hounding him to get the first part of their joint project completed. Thus Harrison, who had not been more than forty miles from London, was expected to provide a description of all Britain. In his distress, he had recourse to Mr. Simonson's maps and the neglected manuscripts of Leland's *Itinerary*, "utterlie mangled defaced with wet and weather." Harrison's desperation must have been great, for Leland's handwriting is painful reading at the best of times. It is hardly surprising, then, that Harrison, the untravelled chorographer, stuck with an impracticable project begun years before by Reginald Wolf, would be genuinely dispirited about his "foul frizeled treatise" (p. vi).

But what he actually accomplished in his *Description*, despite his limitations, tells us what was considered necessary to the chorographic form. Virtually all the topographical description consists of the enumeration of rivers, and the outline of their sources, courses, and outlets. Harrison obviously felt that his descriptive task was inseparably linked with the rivers, and he simulated the chorographer's art by using Simonson's maps and Leland's notes. Modern editors usually remove these sections, leaving a very distorted view of what the Renaissance readers, such as Spenser, evidently perused with interest and pleasure. They amount to six chapters (one hundred folio pages) of river routes, organized around a principal river, as in Chapter 11, "The Description of the Thames, and Such Rivers as Fall into the Same," or Chapter 12, which tells "Of Such streams as Fall into the Sea, Betweene the Thames and the Mouth of the Severn." As best he can, he traces their courses, and those of their tributaries and makes whatever observations he can on local antiquities and topographical details.

As he makes quite clear in his repeated apologies and complaints, it is on these chapters of chorographic description that Harrison felt his work most relied for its form and content, and it is because of their deficiencies that he concluded it to be an abysmal failure:

> And even so it happeneth in this my tractation of waters, of whose heads, courses, length, bredth, depth of channell (for burden) ebs, flowings, and falles, I had thought to have made a perfect description under the report also of an imagined course taken by them all. But now for want of instruction, which hath beene largelie promised & slacklie perfourmed, and other sudden and injurious deniall of helpe voluntarilie offered without occasion given on my part, I must needs content myself with such observations as I have either obtained by mine owne experience, or gathered from time to time out of other mens writings: whereby the full discourse of the whole is utterlie cut off, and in stecd of the same a mangled rehersall of the residue set downe and left in memorie. (pp. 78–79)

As for others before and after him, the national landscape proved too large to be encompassed by an individual's descriptive efforts. Nevertheless, we can see that he conceived of the description in terms of the rivers which bound together the sinews of the nation's natural strengths and history.

In the context of this complaint, Spenser's description of his "Epithalamion Thamesis" in his letter to Harvey, and his well-intended acknowledgment of Holinshed's aid sound like a courteous effort to soothe the antiquarian's wounded feelings; the phraseology of the letter even resembles Harrison's own. Unfortunately, Spenser could only have deepened the wound by naming Holinshed rather than Harrison. Nevertheless, that much discussed literary ghost, the "Epithalamion Thamesis," provides a convenient link between these prose materials and the verse which is also primarily concerned with the rivers: in both we see a common literary impulse to use the rivers to come to terms with the myth of the national landscape. In prose writers and poets alike there is a desire to find their literary identity in a public place and they used their rivers first of all for their geopolitical, rather than their personal associations, and in this they differ greatly from the example we found in Sannazaro. At the same time, they recognized in the river a literary motif which predicated a certain formal and thematic treatment which derived unity and coherence from generic requirements which seemed to be mirrored in nature itself. Thus, their river narratives were creations of the literary imagination whose focus was a national, rather than personal myth and in which, appropriately, the private voice was stilled. But from these two different kinds of literature represented by Sannazaro and the topographers we can see that, in the sixteenth century, the rivers had an intellectual identity that made greater literary demands than simple, topographical descriptions might seem to suggest.

[FIGURES 11–18]

In the sixteenth century the landscape asserted itself in the secular vision of topographical artists. They too presented the world according to implicit ideals; descriptive and figurative representation contributed equally to the formation of landscapes which were metaphors for civic and social, rather than religious order. For men such as Bruegel, Durer, Hoefnagel, and Ortelius, the worlds of myth and map, art and science were one and the same. Landscapes were perceived, charted, and described according to their literary and intellectual history, as well as their physical characteristics. The travels of Odysseus and Aeneas, the Vale of Tempe, were mapped out in landscape perspectives in the same way that contemporary sites such as Tivoli and Arnsberg, or imaginary scenes like Bruegel's were (figs. 11–15). Neither is wholly "topographical" nor wholly "imaginary"; each both pleases and instructs. The geographical descriptions designed for atlases were generic precursors of landscape drawing and painting, and Saxton's maps were embroidered into decorative wall hangings.

Thus, the topographers' atlases share the same imaginative and aesthetic impulse that shapes the landscapes of the perspective painters. The city-views of the *Civitates Orbis Terrarum* (figs. 12 & 13) are presented in terms of different visual and aesthetic perspectives. Each city is perceived according to a "kind" of urban ideal determined by the aesthetic of its situation (hill-town, river-town, or coastal-town) as much as by its logistics — by how one sees it, as well as what one sees. Artists and urban designers both had to make the town live up to its setting. Even when not the most important physical feature, the river defines these scenes: their elevation, contours, their economic and military potential, no less than their aesthetic potential; it harmonizes the landscapes.

Similarly, European and national landscapes were often conceived in terms of a shaping idea based on the exaggerated perception of reality (a method of "sur-realism"), as in van den Keere's "Leo Belgicus" (fig. 16), or on the literalization of a metaphor, as in the "Ditchley Portrait" (fig. 17). In these fanciful views and maps we see how the self-consciousness of the age visualized nations in ways that embody cultural ideals (the heroic emblem of fig. 16, the magnanimity of fig. 17) that accord with the classical and Christian elements of Renaissance humanism. Unlike the rivers of medieval art and design, these define the extent to which humanity has impressed its cultural vision on nature: unlike the other-worldly mood of the scene of Charles D'Orleans in the White Tower (fig. 9), that of Visscher's London (fig. 18) places the viewer within a scene which is both real and ideal. They are scenes that we live in rather than aspire to.

Figure 11. Vale of Tempe. From Abraham Ortelius, *Theatrum Orbis* (1610). The atlas contains maps and views of modern European, as well as classical landscapes.

Figure 12. Tivoli. From Georg Braun and Franz Hogenberg, *Civitates Orbis Terrarum* (1572–1617).

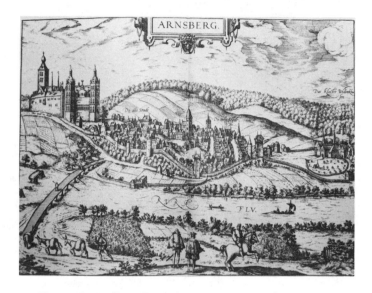

Figure 13. Arnsberg. From Georg Braun and Franz Hogenberg, *Civitates Orbis Terrarum* (1572–1617).

Figure 14. Peter Bruegel the elder. *Solicitudo Rustica*, etching (1588). Bruegel's landscapes commonly synthetize real and imaginary scenes.

Figure 15. Peter Bruegel the elder Alpine landscape, etching (1555).

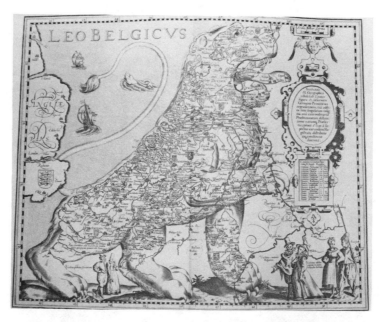

Figure 16. *Leo Belgicus*. From Peiter van den Keere, *Germania Inferior* (1617).

Figure 17. M.Gheeraerts the younger. Queen Elizabeth, the "Ditchley Portrait" (c. 1592).

Figure 18. View of London Bridge. From J. N. Visscher's *View of London* (1617).

IV. *Poets and Historians:*
The River Poem in England from Leland to Spenser

Rome now of *Rome* is th'onely funerall,
And onely *Rome* of *Rome* hath victorie;
Ne ought save *Tyber* hastning to his fall
Remaines of all: O worlds inconstancie.

(Spenser, tr., *The Ruines of Rome*)

1. *Leland: The Shaping of Landscape and the Making of History*

Here should my wonder dwell, & here my praise,
But my fixt thoughts my wandring eye betrays,
Viewing a neighbouring hill, whose top of late
A Chappel crown'd, till in the Common Fate,
The adjoyning Abby fell: (may no such storm
Fall in our times, where ruine must reform.)

(John Denham, *Cooper's Hill*)

Swans about to die sing their dirge sweetly, a thing to which all testify, poets and painters from Aeschylus onward, as well as the very leaders of the Philosophers, Plato, Aristotle, Chrysippus, Philostratus, Cicero, and Seneca.

(Jean Bodin, *The Method of Writing History*)

ARGUABLY, INTEREST IN LANDSCAPE, OR ENVIRONMENT, is fairly constant from age to age, although the nature of our responses to it and the aspects we find to be of interest may change. The world was pretty much the same size and shape for Caesar and Ausonius, but,

181

for a wealth of reasons, each had a different sense of spatial values, each perceived different things in his environment. The world for colonialists and imperialists in the nineteenth century may appear to be the same size, but their attitudes toward it were very different, as different as the writings of Doughty and Conrad. Interest in landscape may be local, national or international in scope, sometimes it is historical, apolitical, or geographical, but whatever an author's focus may be, it tells us something about cultural perspective. In looking at the cultural and literary past, it is possible (if risky) to generalize about the different voices and visions with which authors respond to the physical world and to understand in some small degree the rationale behind them, but it would be foolish to say that any period was indifferent to its environment.

The English Renaissance has left a remarkably large body of literature reflecting interest in the cultural landscape; it has a coherence that can add to our understanding of the period and its authors, and I have tried not to go too far in finding correlations between the literature and its milieu. In the remaining chapters I examine the extensive poetic response to the national landscape, how and to some extent why it focused on the river, and how this response evolved in the seventeenth century. It is part of an ongoing literary response to a cultural geography, and we will see that it too resonates with an awareness of other geographies in other times and literatures. Like the Renaissance poet and topographer we too must see their world in terms of the intellectual and literary traditions that they inherited: in trying to comprehend it in this literature, they did not describe their world, they invented it.

It is clear that the process of "reading" geography for insights into the past, present, and future was well established in the sixteenth century, and that it is not a product of the next century, as is usually suggested by literary critics.[1] Indeed, we have seen that it is a fundamental aspect of the European literary tradition. More specifically, in the sixteenth and seventeenth centuries, poets, historians, and topographers worked with shared literary and intellectual objectives; they thought of landscape much as they thought of time and history: it was not just to be observed but must be molded and used. But in the sixteenth century they looked to their world, with its ancient, medieval, and contemporary history, with a cultural, national self-consciousness that reflected their sense of the future. In this, as we will see, their myths of landscape differed from those of the next century. While the environment held profound personal meaning for the Englishman in the sixteenth century (much as it did for Sannazaro), this meaning was formulated in terms of settings and literary roles which were distinctly public in nature. Authors' responses, personal as they often were, succeeded in harmonizing individual and national destiny. It is in this literature and cultural context that the tradition of English topographical verse assumes its distinctive character, and it is in response to it that we must understand the genre as it evolves in the next century.

To an extent that it was not elsewhere in Europe, in England after the first quarter of the sixteenth century, the river was inseparable from the historical landscape and from the national myth which looked back to the past, the ideals of which it strove to realize in the present and future. We have seen that the river continued to be a popular motif throughout Europe at the time of the revival of learning, and English authors, turning it to national and historical themes, drew on the model of Virgil rather than Horace. It was also a more popular topic in England than in Europe, and the poetry of the river developed with a greater degree of literary self-consciousness than it did elsewhere. Sometimes interspersed in a larger work of prose or verse, sometimes appearing in suspiciously fragmentary form, and sometimes dominating a work in which prose commentary is subordinated to the poetry, the river poem was not only a recognized genre, but it also offered a kind of distillation of the author's response to landscape and nation. I want to define the English river poem and its particular literary concerns and examine it as a major component in that large body of literature which is concerned with the creation of a cultural and national mythology.[2]

In speaking of cultural or national myth, I am not referring to the infertile theme of the Tudor myth, but to a body of literature which explores the nature and potential of human society and its cultural, intellectual, and artistic expressions and institutions. As I have tried to suggest, the literature which looks to landscape often tends to look to the past, to impose on the landscape ideals that authors identified with a classical or an indigenous past. But this historical perspective notwithstanding, it first of all reflects an attitude to the present. In their settings authors invariably reveal their sense of his culture and themselves, what we can call a national or cultural myth. With its wealth of associations, the river captures this peculiar quality of landscape literature in which past and present seem to be afloat together in the current of time. Naturally part of a nation's self-consciousness, the river is especially sensitive to historical and attitudinal changes, and this is in part what makes it such a useful critical tool: it shows authors responding to time and the times.

The river poem took shape as English cultural self-consciousness intensified during the Reformation, and it evolved as this sensibility evolved over perhaps a century. The literature of the river shows us authors questioning the social significance of historical material— old and new—that was contained in the landscape. It reflects an acute responsiveness to the paradoxical contrasts of the land, with its magnificent ruins betokening the past, and the stately new architecture heralding modern achievement. As we will see, between 1530 and 1625, the landscape struck significantly different chords for different authors, and these suggest much about the English self-image during this time. For example, medieval ruins might supply material for the antiquarian, and monuments of the nation's prosperity might provide impetus for the poet's *encomia*, while the contrast of the two settings, juxtaposing decay and growth, might feed the sober moralist with food for reflection and prudent *sententiae*. The three emblems, fixed in the national landscape—of the past, the auspicious present, and the future adumbrated by the other two—are distinct, and an author's preoccupation with one to the neglect of the others tells us much about his mind and writing. What an author sees and stresses in a landscape is a clue to his thoughts, not only about a specific setting, but about history and his conception of his own art. Thus, depending on the author, a setting such as Verulam may suggest the heroic past, or the vulnerability of civilization, or it may simply exist as a landscape which pleases the eye and stimulates the imagination, although this aesthetic reaction is likely to lead us back to the other two. Understanding this dependence of the aesthetic imagination on history and cultural reflexes in the Renaissance is part of our objective.

A ruined abbey, set off by the quiet movement of a river, may evoke from Leland a sharp sense of loss and grief, but from Lambard, Carew, or Drayton, a more diffused sentiment of regret, nostalgia, even anger, not so much at the destruction as at the awareness of the presence of time and its inescapable effects. The emotions are of course very different and suggest radically different relations to landscape, ones which have been modified by the authors' own historical contexts. The river, having both past and future, is often the vital feature in such settings, and in the way that it accentuates these displays of human art and wit, it enables us to read the landscape and its impact on these authors. Although a landscape may contain vestiges of time, then, the river embodies the meaning of time, and the essence of its relation to the observer.

Considering the closeness of the river's association with trends in English historical thought, it is possible to sharpen the focus of our discussion by referring to four rather symbolic events which help to outline more clearly the changing response to the English landscape. The events provide a narrative and historical context for our survey of the river literature, and will even foreshadow its direction, while at the same time, as historical "moments" in the Renaissance, they themselves illustrate the perspectives on history which we have been discussing, and involve many of the authors of river poetry.

The first is the Dissolution of the Monasteries, the curious and depressing years of "unbuilding" and demolition during the 1530s, and their counterpart in the era of construction, with its haughty, extravagant monuments erected under the auspices of Cardinal Wolsey. The second is Robert Cotton's petition to the Queen (c. 1602) for the establishment of a Royal Society of Antiquaries, and the third is the effort of his friend, Henry Spelman in 1614 to revive the society which, though never chartered, flourished during the last two decades of Elizabeth's reign. The fourth is Edmund Bolton's address to the general public in 1621, promoting a "Academ Roial" for antiquarian pursuits.

We will return to these events separately, in their proper chronological order, but for our present purposes, we can see how they mark different stages in English response to history and landscape. On the one hand, the first was an act which shaped landscape and altered the course of (and perspective on) history, while the others reflect attitudes toward the past and landscape, and actions undertaken for their preservation. Actually, as is implied by the language of their documents, they indicate three stages in the antiquarian's changing view of history and national topography. For example, the words "foundation" and "revival" of the society designate very different relations to historical study, the objectives of the first being quite distinct from those of the second. Thus, the Dissolution has its immediate effect on the nation's historical topography and its archives; the early society is concerned with the preservation of the materials of history; the spirit of revival is concerned with historiography and the idea of history. Actually, Edmund Bolton's proposal is twice removed from the original initiative to preserve the records of the past; it is, as we will see, an effort to idealize the very idea of the past. Thus, the initial impetus begun during Henry VIII's reign becomes more and more rarefied in each succeeding phase.

The four events also suggest dates and people, and together they provide a chronological and thematic classification of closely related men and their work, extending over roughly four generations and consisting of much of the river literature we have been and will be discussing. In this way the Society of Antiquaries further defines the historical and literary context of the river poem. As John Harington states, "historians learned and poets rare" are the "swans" whose songs help keep oblivion at bay, and the unchartered society brought these two flocks together. Either directly through authorship or indirectly through one form or another of sponsorship the society and its members perpetuated the river poem.

Nowhere is the relevance of these events for the river more conspicuous than in the relation of the first English river poet, John Leland, to the Dissolution and in the way that he reflects its impact on the perception of history and landscape. It is misleading to speak of Leland's response to the national geography as "the discovery of Britain," as intellectual historians are wont to do, when what we really see, a new phase in cultural (and therefore topographical) self-consciousness, is the evolution of historical and national myths based in landscape. Leland's innovative antiquarian work would not have developed as it did without the chaotic influence of the Dissolution: his imagination became possessed by the nation's history, scenery, and archives.

Reformation, a process of revival, and the Dissolution, one of destruction, go hand in hand. As if by chemical reaction, what had been monasteries and religious houses became monuments of antiquity and as such, vestiges of history to be preserved in their ruin, not destroyed. Overnight, the present became the past, and the nation's relation to the landscape was irreversibly changed. Whatever people's religious sentiments, their reactions to the destruction were greedily negative: expropriation of the Catholic Church's properties and chattel was committed with shamefaced guilt, as we can see in a not very convincing exculpatory letter that one father, who shared in the looting of Roche Abbey in Yorkshire, wrote to his son: "What should I do . . . might I not as well as others have some profit of the spoil of the Abbey? For I did see all would away; and therefore, I did as others did."[3] The expensive, methodical process of destruction left horrific mutations as evidence of a nation's abuse of its own power and abilities. Buildings were systematically maimed, so that they could neither be restored nor adapted to other architectural uses, and frequently the demolition was so contrived that it was impossible even to salvage materials and examples of fine workmanship.[4] The result was a vast number of slowly decaying architectural corpses, repugnant to the practical layman as well as the historian. The decomposing shells symbolized for many their own sense of corruption and guilt in these events, and the *sententiae* on the ruins of time or the house of pride pronounced over these scenes must have been numerous. The destruction was a self-inflicted national disaster which resulted not only in the vast ruin of buildings which were suddenly perceived to be worthy of preservation, but also of books, archives, and other forms of the practical and decorative arts. Accelerated decay was the seed for rebirth.

The effect of the Dissolution on English historical thought was extensive; the landscape never had the same innocent promise. It compressed the effects of time into a few turbulent years and revealed to a generation, as in a prophetic glass, their own imprint on the national landscape. The sudden acquisition of antiquities was, as Margaret Aston says, "effective in stimulating consciousness of the past and in promoting historical activity."[5] While Leland is often cited as the father of modern English history, perhaps the title should be accorded with some irony to Henry VIII. With the willful destruction of history's treasures began a period of intense acquisitiveness; a spirit of profligate waste went hand in hand with the urge for preservation. Appreciation of aspects of the past—in societies as well as in individual lives—is only possible when they have been irrecoverably lost. The loss and ruin of quantities of manuscripts and other of the arts through neglect and systematic destruction inaugurated the period of the great libraries and collections, and the publication of the massive histories and topographies which strove to memorialize an image of Britain.

The Dissolution changed English perceptions in other ways. As the past came into focus, so did the landscape. These events intensified people's perceptions of and sensitivity to the landscape—and its rivers. Leland, very much a product of the times, set out to gather a visual impression of the nation's topography in much the same way that he gathered the facts and fictions of English history. He was consumed with a desire to *see* the historic landscape. He himself links this new perspicacity to his sudden obsession with this

newfound history when he explains the origins of his project to the
King. For him it was quite literally a consuming passion to see all of
England before it was too late:

> Wher fore after that I had perpendid the . . . studies of these Histor-
> iographes, I was totally enflammid with a love to see thoroughly al
> those Partes of this your opulente and ample Reaulme, that I had
> redde of yn the aforesaid Writers: yn so muche that al my other
> Occupations intermittid I have so travelid yn yowr Dominions booth
> by the Se Costes and the midle Partes, sparing nother Labor nor
> Costes, by the space of these vi. Yeres paste, that there is almoste
> nother Cape, nor Bay, Haven, Creke or Peere, River or Confluence
> of Rivers, Breches, Waschis, Lakes, Meres, Fenny Waters, Montay-
> nes, Valleis, Mores, Hethes, Forestes, Chases, Wooddes, Cities,
> Burges, Castelles, principale Manor Placis, Monasteries, and Col-
> leges, but I have seene them; and notid yn so doing a hole Worlde of
> Thinges very memorable.[6]

After Leland and Henry VIII, there was a steady increase in the
joint interest in landscape and history, and in the awareness of the
growing remoteness of the past, and this continued at least until the
end of the first quarter of the seventeenth century.

The desire to see the realm and its monuments was also a desire to
celebrate them and to arrest the effects of time, and for Leland and
succeeding generations, this was to be accomplished by the creation
of an artistic and coherent image of the nation in which history and
topography, art and nature harmonize. Leland, speaking of his
artistic intentions in his *New Year's Gift* to the King, provides one of
the clearest statements of this process of literary image-making. The
work that he promises, what would presumably have been the
finished version of the *Itinerary*, was to have preserved all the
magnificence of England in a description more wonderful than the
"thre large and notable Tables of Sylver . . . one of the Site and
Description of *Constantinople*, another of the site . . . of *Rome*, and
the thirde of the Description of the World," that were among the
treasures of Charles the Great. But what is interesting, and characteristically English, is that Leland promises Henry a "Description . . . of your Reaulme yn writing"; knowing the transience of
other monuments, he chooses a literary description "that it may be
more permanente" (p. xii). Leland has a clear conception of the
kind of literature his historical description is to be, and it is one
which was to be very popular in the Renaissance. It is the genre
which the *genius* of Verulam speaks about in *The Ruines of Time*,
and which Spenser adapts in *The Faerie Queene*.

Leland, of course, was never able to finish his "Description . . . of [the] . . . Reaulme yn writing," for he lost his sanity while his work remained mere notes. But from the *New Year's Gift*, the *Cygnea Cantio*, and the *Genethliacon*, we get a clear idea of what his artistic intentions were. We also know from the occasional laments interspersed throughout his prose that he felt sharply the irony of his situation, that while he was at work as the king's antiquary,[7] gathering English archives, Henry was busily destroying them. This paradox lies at the heart of English historiography and response to landscape, so that appreciation of history and of the nation's natural and cultural bounty is colored by the sense of willfulness, negligence, folly, and loss, as well as by pride and patriotism, and this paradoxical quality intensifies over the generations.

Leland's writings, as well as the very peculiarity of his position as king's antiquary, are strong evidence of the simultaneous sharpening of English awareness of history and landscape, and if the depiction of the effects of the Dissolution did not fully emerge in the graphic arts until the eighteenth century, it was very much a part of the literary consciousness in the sixteenth. Examples of settings dotted with ruins and other architectural details abound in the Renaissance, from Spenser and Churchyard to Marvell. Throughout this period, Leland's direct and indirect influence is to be felt.

But an important difference distinguishes Leland's perspective on historical topography. Leading the first wave of antiquarian enthusiasm, he was immediately involved with the collecting of archives, and while on tour with the King's warrant, he witnessed the events of the Dissolution. Inspired by the "Historiographes" he had read to see the land and its history, when he embarked on his pilgrimage, he encountered newly made ruins and the unmistakable lesson that history is not just discovered but also made and carefully preserved like a perishable viand. And so, some two years after beginning his travels and seeing the monuments of human achievement recede sinisterly before him, he petitions Cromwell (16 July 1536) for the extension of his commission to include specifically the collection of manuscripts for the King's Library. For him, then, there was an aura of discovery, an antiquarian's sense of enthusiasm and wonder; his awareness that, as the first semi-official antiquary to the King, he was saving history from neglect surpassed his feelings of nostalgia or regret. While it is certain that Leland's patriotic enthusiasm was occasionally put to the test, the element of discovery that pervades all his work far transcends that of loss. For him, to a degree that was impossible for his successors, there was a queer feeling of beginning: that history starts here.

What Leland learned so suddenly about history and topography was conveyed to later generations as a sad fact of life; an inescapable *sententia* about time and mortality was planted on the nation's terrain. Patriotic boasts about new architectural wonders and about venerable antiquity were tempered by an awareness of their mutability and by warnings against credulous pride. The legacy of the Dissolution was the acquisition of history, but in a form that reminded one at the same time of its lessons of willfulness, vanity, and impermanence. The inheritance of such a past, then, also results in loss of self-esteem: the landscape reflects folly as well as noble aspirations. Throughout the Renaissance there is a tension between these two extremes, and it would take the mythologizing imagination behind *The Faerie Queene*, rather than the tragic muse of *The Ruines of Time* or *Poly-Olbion* to reconcile the two and to harmonize history's relation to topography. Nevertheless, the ambiguous relation between them is a vital one, and efforts to resolve them produced the large body of historical and topographical literature of which the river poem is a part.

Leland's own work embodies this legacy; suppressing any criticism of the King, he conveys a sense of discovery in which the landscape stands out as its own witness to the past. In all of his major verse, he uses the rivers to animate a prophetic view of England which reverberates with the immediacy of his own involvement in this sudden surge of history. By raising the various *genii loci* in this way, he is able to reconcile landscape and history, and to have them work in concord rather than against one another. In this, Leland was a man of his age, an early product of the Reformation, steeped in the spirit of the revival of learning. Educated at St. Paul's School, where Erasmus's influence was most strongly felt, and at Cambridge, Oxford, and Paris, Leland's patriotic antiquarianism is part of his discovery of the ancients and his desire to bring the ideal of humane learning to England. We can see his discovery and preservation of British antiquities and ancient manuscripts and his own literary output as attempts to realize a positive ideal, and as part of his desire to thwart the forces of destruction: that is, they are as much an affirmative creative act for the future as they are a retrospective reach into the past.

His poetry reflects these qualities together with his desire to Hellenize Britain. Written in learned neo-Latin interspersed with

Greek phrases and influences and modeled on Greek and Latin epideictic forms, his work, like that of his counterparts in France and Italy, attempts to revivify the classical ideals in the modern world. More particularly, Leland's most ambitious poems, the *Genethliacon* and the *Cygnea Cantio* are epideictic, or occasional verse, strongly indebted to the Latin silver poets and in which he acknowledges the influence of Virgil, Ovid, Statius, and interestingly, Alexander Neckham—all poets who turned to nature and the physical landscape to create a cultural mythology. This is precisely what Leland does with the raw materials of his setting. He hopes to emulate the ideal that he sees in the ancients by doing to his landscape what they did to theirs—that is, transform it through a combination of poetic description, history, praise, and prophecy. It is he the poet, not the historian, who will, like Virgil, reshape the historical geography through the historical myth of poetry.

The landscapes of these poems are encrusted with fragments of a long and violent past, monuments which, for a later generation, someone like Thomas Churchyard, for example, would be society's *memento mori*. However, as for Virgil, history for Leland is not moribund, and in this we see the complementary cultural forces of the Dissolution and the revival of learning at work. The historical landscapes are revitalized by their relation to the geography: nature (most particularly the rivers) is given an active role in the presentation of history, not only in the literal sense that it announces history as revelation, in the present tense, but also in the sense that it denies the negative aspect of history as time past, rendering it instead as time present and therefore creative. Using his epideictic mode in the most positive manner, Leland presents history rather than points to it. By describing both the past and recent events of Henry's reign (such as the building projects at Hampton Court), he transcends a limited vision of history and emphasizes the affirmative relation between human achievement (the cities, arts, history itself) and the eternizing *genius* which nurtures it.

Leland's encomiastic verses, then, are not just politic praise; they present a coherent view of history, and the river, as part of the local geography and the classical tradition, is one of the most important devices he uses to create his national myth.

His design is most evident in the paean celebrating the birth of Edward, where diverse voices from distant regions of the realm are harmonized in their joy. Together the celebrants comprise an "*amoenus/Nympharum chorus*" (11.16–17); they are the nymphs of

England's Helicon, flowing from its own Parnassus. Of the individual choruses, some are Christian, some are classical, some are geniuses of the cities and Edward's principalities, Cornwall and Wales, and others are rustic deities of the soil and nature; all are sanctified in the Christian British landscape by a song on baptism; they form Apollo's troupe of muses, and as Leland says, Christ is his Apollo.

The songs of the Dryades, the Nepeae, the Oreades, the Oceanitides, and of individual river nymphs are those of nature celebrating the fulfillment of England's destiny; they are led by Thames, the *"nympharum gloria prima."* They are all descendants of the ancient nymphs of Hesiod and the Homeric Hymns, and they too look after youth and generally perform the *"officium nympharum."* Complementing their songs are those of the cities and palaces, those manifestations of man's art which seem to grow naturally from out of the animated landscape, as in the description of Hampton Court:

> Est locus insolito rerum splendore superbus,
> Alluiturque vaga Tamesini fluminis unda,
> Nomine ab antiquo iam tempore dictus Avona,
> Hic Rex Henricus taleis Octavius aedes
> Erexit, qualeis toto sol aureus orbe
> Non videt. (lines 90–95)

The river, backed by proud towers, often figures rather ambiguously as a reminder of mutability and of fortune's wiles. It is difficult to say conclusively just what is suggested by the evanescent, cloud-capped towers of *The Tempest*, for example. Here, however, the image is one of art, nature, and history in harmony. The river sets off Leland's view of history. The vision of the tower-capped river does not have the stoic skepticism that informs Janus Vitalis's description of the Roman Tiber, which the Protestant English later used to warn against their own moral complacency—"Learne hence what fortune can. Townes glide away;/ And Rivers, which are still in motion, stay."[8] Rather, it is one of fierce optimism transforming England's towered towns into an impregnable City of God:

> Arx antiqua, potens Tamesinae margine ripae
> Est sita, Bellini decus immortale tyranni
> Aerea terribiles basilisci hinc monstra tonabant
> Innumeris vicibus: colluxit fulmine coelum. (49–52)

Leland's use of the rivers in the *Genethliacon* is quite effective in showing the unanimous response to Edward's birth, and the perfection of art and nature that his succession promises. The harmonious rivers rise to the occasion, just as they rise to Aeneas's cause, and Rome's in the *The Civil War*. From them too flow the divine benefits of a potent nation: peace, law, justice, the arts, and prosperity—the traditional gifts of Apollo's sisterly nymphs. Through them Leland, like Virgil, suggests geographical and cultural diversity brought together in unity; there is a sense of expansiveness somehow joined naturally by a concordant spirit—the technique is also that which Spenser will use in Book 4 of *The Faerie Queene*. For Leland, the central river *topos* defines the spirit of the poem as one which transcends history by finding its animated voice in nature.

This coming together of harmonious voices celebrating a new dispensation is, of course, appropriate for a Christian nativity ode, which this is. Likewise, the stately river pageant and swan song of the *Cygnea Cantio* meets the demands of decorum for the praise of a king. Appropriately, the most obtrusive difference between the two poems is the greater coherence of the unifying river motif in the *Cygnea Cantio*; the river passage from Oxford to Greenwich concentrates the royal image and gives it a topographical integrity which reinforces the ceremoniousness suitable for Henry's praise.

Here too Leland demonstrates how thoroughly he has thought out his use of the river motif; as he suggests in his dedication to Henry, the swan's (and by implication, the river's) association with prophecy and poetry makes the journey of the cygnets the best vehicle for his own inspired vision of Britain. "*Thames, fluviorum omnium, qui Britanniam alluunt tuam, facile princeps, mihi in mentem venit*," he says, and to him the river nymph revealed the form and nature of his poem. For Leland, Thames is the modern descendant of the classical muses, and the poem, addressed "*ad Sacrosanctae Antiquitatis amatores*" and "*ad cultores Isidis*," brings together themes of poetry, history, and prophecy under the aegis of the native river nymph. The river motif, enabling Leland to present some of the antiquarian learning he had gathered in his perambulations, and to offer in small his projected description of Britain's cultural and natural bounties, also provides the opportunity to realize the nation's role as successor to antiquity through literature by showing us Roman presence in the national landscape. The river motif, then, is the principal means for shaping the landscape and molding the reader's cultural perceptions.

Naturally enough, the voyage down the Thames has a more rigorous control than the spontaneous polyphony of the *Genethliacon*, but it too has the immediacy of observation and description of

that poem. In the *Cygnea Cantio*, however, we are made aware of
the poet's controlled vision of the setting through the progress down
the most civilized and most historical segment of any river in
Britain, and the result is that in the descent the landscape seems to
pass radiantly before us:

> Decursus Tamesis celer profundi
> Iam me ducit, & impigre ad sinestram
> Ripam, fulget ubi velut corona
> Sedes aethereus Sion decora. (132–35)

The Roman Britain Leland describes joins easily with the contemporary landscape which Henry adorns with additional monuments.
Leland has emphasized the swan song's prophetic truth, not its
dirge-like qualities. History is not something lost, but a cultural
ideal still alive. This is not only Leland flattering Henry, but a way
of reading classical literature in the light of English experience and
evoking Rome's cultural influence. The *Cygnea Cantio* stands out as
a Reformation Englishman's rereading of the *Aeneid*.

The unified voice and design of the *Cygnea Cantio* also emphasizes the presence of history—in all senses of the allusive phrase.
However, movement along the river simulates the effects of time;
rivers and palaces rise before our view and pass before our sight in a
sure and natural progression, rather than in a sepulchral vision from
the grave. They are the creations of time, not its victims. The
river-scape in this last poem before the advent of his madness is
ethereal and metamorphic rather than mutable; he perceives it
through the eyes of a prophet rather than an encomiast, and judging
from the occasional lines which Philomen Holland translates for the
Britannia, this evanescent quality did not escape the notice of
Leland's seventeenth-century readers:

> How glittereth this place of great request,
> Like to the seat of heaven by welkin hie?
> With gallant tops, with windowes of the best.
> What towres that reach even to the starry skie:
> What Orchards greene, what Springs ay-running by.
> Faire *Flora* heere that in this creeke doth dwell,
> Bestowes on it the flowres of garden gay.[9]

As in the paintings, city views and miniatures of London from the
middle of the sixteenth century, there is a delicate balance of
accurate detailed observation, and stylized, idealized interpretation

of the setting; the realistic topography is presented with an artificial intensity which turns it to symbol. The result is that the scene is "enamell'd o're," refined; it seems to have an internal energy that makes it transcendent.

This kind of visionary landscape which is at once worldly and divine, historical and prophetic, draws on the thematic and formal potential of the *topos* and its classical associations, as well as on its Renaissance and Continental contexts, which Leland was familiar with from his studies in Paris. Leland's poetic persona has a far more public voice than Sannazaro's has, but as in the *Arcadia*, the riverine perspective of the poem removes the poet from direct involvement with time. The distant past, contemporary history, and nature all pass by together. The poet-cygnet on the river seems to exist in a quintessential realm, removed from and untouched by these vicissitudes; he can view them objectively and without fear. The river perspective creates for the poet a semblance of immortality which enables him to see history as a divine comedy, rather than as a tragedy. And although Leland's affirmative view of history soon yields to the less sanguine one of later generations, his understanding of the potential of the river motif carries on with other aspects of his legacy. Thus, by adapting his modern and classical models in prose and verse, he rediscovered the poem in which both form and content are dominated by the river, and those who succeed him continue to experiment with its possibilities, drawing both directly and indirectly on his example in the use of the British rivers to locate the image of the nation's historical and literary identity, and to establish the poet's own place in the landscape. Leland has succeeded in combining all aspects of his river poem to create a vivid and mythical image of the landscape which is genuinely timeless in effect. His is a major literary achievement: it amounts to the creation of a new kind of poem with a new vision of the landscape, its history, and the present. As such, it is something that did not and could not have existed before in British literary history.

Spenser will join the two different techniques of Leland's poems in the marriage of the Thames and the Medway, where the spontaneous variety of the world's rivers is ordered by the chorographic control and processional movement from Oxford to Thames's confluence with Medway; there too the progress, with the bringing together of the two rivers, seems to metamorphose the landscape and to bring order from the surrounding cacophony. Ultimately, Spenser will give even greater impetus to the motif and supplant

Leland as the principal river poet. It was Leland who identified the most fundamental contexts for the motif in Britain, and who began the fashion of creating a national literary image which would be immensely popular until after 1600, so that if he is eclipsed by Spenser's greater influence, he remains the invisible source for this flood of British river literature.

2. Geography and the Myth of History: Camden and the Rivers of Concord

> harmonie is on all sides so great among the elements, that it is no marvell if in their proper places . . . they maintaine and repose themselves with very great and friendly Concord. Whereby it appeareth, that none can induce a goodlier reason, why the water doth not overflow the earth . . . then to say, that it will not swerve from this agreement. (Pierre de la Primaudaye, *The French Academie*)

> One fayre Par-royall hath our Iland bred
> Wherof one is a live and 2 are dead
> Sidney ye Prince of prose & sweet conceit
> Spenser of numbers & Heroick Ryme
> Injurious Fate did both their lives defeate . . .
> Camden thou livest alone of all ye three
> For Roman stile & English historye;
> Englande made them thou makest Englande knowen
> So well art thou ye prince of all ye payre
> Sithence thou hast an Englande of thine owne
> Lesse wealthy, but as fruitful and more fayre.
>
> (Joseph Hall, "To Camden")

> CAMDEN, most reverend head, to whom I owe
> All that I am in arts, all that I know . . .
> What name, what skill, what faith hast thou in things!
> What sight in searching the most antique springs!
>
> (Jonson, "To William Camden")

> and justly might the stream of his commendations run broader whence meeting with a confluence of desert and friendship in the same party.
> (Thomas Fuller, *The Holy State and the Profane State*)

Leland's death in 1552 left a complex legacy to his nation. Among other things, it initiated the proliferation of his various literary and historical designs, officially installed "antiquarian" in the vocabulary, and set the strenuous standard that would inspire that peculiarly English being. On his death, his friend and publisher, Reginald Wolf, acquired his notes and manuscripts while also inheriting his unyielding obsession with grand topographical and historical projects which, like something Proustian, could not be finished before his death. It was, in fact, some years before Leland's death, about 1548, the time of his insanity, that Wolf began work on his "Universal Cosmography"; the notes acquired from Leland in 1552 were put to use on the sections dealing with the British Isles.

Wolf continued work on his master plan for twenty-five years before failing beneath the burden in 1573. Among those in his employ at this time were Raphael Holinshed and William Harrison who, much to the regret of the latter, took the task upon their own shoulders, eventually, however, reducing its scope to a description and history of Britain—ironically, the compass of Leland's original scheme. The final product is no doubt largely a posthumous edition of the *Itinerary*.

The first edition of the *Description of Britain* appeared in 1577, and we know that by 1580 Spenser had made particular use of it in organizing his "Epithalamion Thamesis." Spenser, "setting forth the marriage of the Thames," and describing "all the Rivers throughout Englande" and "their right names, and right passages," derives as much from the *Genethliacon* and the *Cygnea Cantio* as it does from Harrison, although as a sign of the changing sensibility of the times, Leland's neo-Latin yields to the reformed meter.

By 1580, then, Leland's influence was consecrated by the publication of the extremely popular work of Harrison and Holinshed, and by the announcement of a major river poem, the publication of which would keep readers like William Vallans expectant ten years later. Wolf and his assistants were not alone in their antiquarian pursuits; Lambard was busy on his perambulations before 1570, the date of the completion of the manuscript, Humphrey Lhuyd was working on his *Breviary of Britain*, and other topographical works less dominated by the river were also in progress. Lambard evidently originally intended to write a larger, nationwide description, and one reason for not continuing with the project was that even at this early date Camden's *Britannia* was taking shape. The two friends worked simultaneously on their separate projects, and the cult of the perambulating antiquary following the rivers was well established.

By the end of the first generation after Leland the contours of the modern, post-Reformation landscape were already familiar as the process of describing national and regional geography evolved and became more popular. This does not mark the age of the discovery of Britain, as modern critics describe the period, but a new phase in the evolution of perceptual myths, one which is greatly influenced by the Dissolution. Furthermore, the process of literary shaping of landscape after classical models, which combines accurate topographical description with a transforming moral vision—conventions which literary critics commonly associate with the second quarter of the seventeenth century—was not only well developed by the 1580s, it was also recognized as part of the classical tradition. If we see more of such topographical writing after the middle of the sixteenth century, it is largely stimulated by the heightened awareness of landscape and history after the Dissolution and the revival of learning, which taught authors how to impose their classical ideals (and literary forms) on the landscape.

All the literary devices usually found in seventeenth-century "loco-descriptive" poetry are conspicuously present, for example, in a rough but genuine chorographical poem by Thomas Churchyard called *The Worthines of Wales* (1587), a modest work but very interesting from a historical point of view. Old Palemon (as Spenser called him) illustrates how fragile the humanist's vision of the animated historical British landscape was and how soon these contrasts that Leland described were turned into static emblems of mortality in a world of novelty and change. His is not a vision of the glories of the past matched by those of the present; he looks on the ruins of Wales with a more modern nostalgia. But interestingly, his descriptions, which are mainly river scenes, impose moral archetypes upon carefully observed physical reality, so that they are alive and contemporary. Organizing his chorography and his moral *sententiae* around the rivers, he invests his perambulation with ideas familiar to us from Botero's analysis of the modern landscape. With his Renaissance eye for commerce and trade, he perceives the unifying effects of internal and coastal trade and describes the organic unity of the realm which links inland ports such as Shrewsbury with London and the rest of the nation.[10]

But Churchyard's theme is destructive time; the grandeur that is nurtured by the rivers is also eroded by them. His method is to use his chorography to link contrasting landscape *tableaux* which juxtapose modern prosperity with scenes of medieval ruins, and to set them off by the ceaseless flow of the rivers:

The walls wereof, and towers are all to torne,
(With wethers blast, and tyme that weares all out)
And yet it hath a fayre prospect about;
Trim Meades and Walkes, along the Rivers side,
With Bridge well built, the force of flood to bide. (p. 99)

His imagination is more visual than literary, but he repeatedly uses
contrasts found in the historical landscape to juxtapose art (both
new and medieval) and nature, and to show the vanity of human
efforts "the force of flood to bide." His technique is as old as the
Iliad. His tower-capped river is an emblem of vanity very different
from Leland's. But what is interesting is that this *topothesia* (to use a
sophisticated phase for his unsophisticated moral landscapes) is
joined to a thoroughly modern world in a way that might be
compared with Denham's *Cooper's Hill*. For him, British history
has lost its novelty: the myth contained in the national landscape is
one of loss, and it reflects a rather facile "world-weariness" that
distances him from Leland.

Thus, within twenty years of Leland's premature death, his literary projects and his interest in history and topography had pervaded
English thought, although his moral perspective on the past had
already evolved. Indeed, his notes and manuscripts travelled the
nation like a spirit in search of rest. When Reginald Wolf died, John
Stow bought his entire library, and shortly thereafter Camden, no
doubt with a touch of jealousy, offered him an annuity of eight
pounds in exchange for a copy (in Stow's own hand) of Leland's
Itinerary. For about twenty years, this first generation of scholars,
such as Stow (b. 1525), Harrison (b. 1525), and Lambard (b. 1536),
fervently set about realizing his projects. Although his influence was
soon felt, it was thirty-four years after his death before his ghost was
finally put to rest, and the *Britannia*, the legitimate heir to his plans,
was ready for its first edition in 1586. The *Britannia*, already years in
the making, would occupy Camden for some forty years altogether,
and its ambitious scope would have made Leland's heart swell for it
conforms almost perfectly to the format set out in the *New Year's
Gift*:

And this Worke I entende to divide yn to so many Bookes as there be
Sheres, yn *England*, and Sheres and great Dominions yn *Wales*. So
that I esteme that this Volume will enclude a fiftie Bookes, wherof
eche one severally shaul conteyne the Beginninges, Encreases, and

memorable Actes of the chief Tounes and Castelles of the Province allottid to hit.

But in the *Britannia* Camden moved beyond his somewhat older contemporaries, set the pace for further historical ventures, and began a new wave of antiquarian enthusiasm. In it he also goes far beyond Leland's original plan for national portraiture. He adapts the loose descriptive and historical design and the general patriotic objectives of his mentor, but he turns them to a more coherent and sophisticated view of history which, in turn, reveals very different ideas about antiquarian pursuits and history itself. Similar as their projects are, they show how radically the historian's relation to the nation had changed over those thirty-four years. While we do not know what the completed *Itinerary* would have looked like, it is clear that it would have been a vision of history through landscape, artistically combining prose and verse, and probably integrating the *Cygnea Cantio* somewhere in its midst. Beyond this enlarged image of the nation, it seems unlikely that Leland had planned a very comprehensive organization for the *Itinerary*, and it is probably for this reason that it remained unfinished.

At every stage Camden is informed by Leland's spirit, although his understanding of the objectives of historical writing is far more complicated. He also perceived his mentor's interest in balancing prose and verse and understood how he used the river motif as a means of locating his conception of the nation and its history. Just as in the *Cygnea Cantio* Leland fuses the individual voices of history, landscape, and encomiastic, and (through the syllabus at its conclusion) uses prose commentary to set off his verse, so too Camden employs different voices to harmonize his national image, although to different ends. The *Britannia* is a highly structured work whose divisions, mixture of prose and verse, and narrative line interact to create a complex image of concord between English history and geography, or art and nature. Throughout the *Britannia* Camden develops the river's potential, not only thematically, but also as a structural device, using it in his verse (in the *de Cunnubio Tamae et Isis* in particular) and in his prose to reinforce the theme of concord and unity, and in his success, he fully identifies one of the river's most important themes in the Renaissance.

Camden's technique is to interweave the geographical and political influences in the nation's development. Thus, although he treats each county individually, and follows classical models for chorography by beginning in the west and moving east, his design is also

topographical—in that the narrative is shaped by the landscape—
and it is historical, based on the ancient kingdoms that divided the
nation. These multiple structures are coordinated by the river.
Instead of simply moving from county to county, then, there is a
subtle combination of influences at work in the narrative. The
overriding pattern of his description traces historical and demographic growth, beginning in the west with that area inhabited by
the Danmonii—"that tract, which, according to geographers, is . . .
the first of all Britain"—and heading toward Kent. Thus he establishes a counterpoint between history and geography which transcends the modern political county divisions. Narrative divisions are
geographically and demographically intact, although they go beyond the county borders. By the time he has gone as far east as Kent,
he has defined an area that is both historically and geographically
unified, and like an explorer, he uses his rivers to strike out into new
territory:

> Having gone over all the counties of the British Ocean on one hand,
> to the Severn sea and the Thames on the other, I proceed to take a
> view of the rest in the intended order; and crossing the river, and
> returning to the source of the Thames and the mouth of the Severn,
> shall visit the DOBUNI who formerly occupied the present Glouces-
> ter and Oxford shires.[11]

Camden uses his rivers as a geographer and a narrator, and here
they carry us back over three and a half counties without causing
narrative or geographical disorientation. The rivers give order and
meaning to history, and therefore to the structure of his description.
Throughout the *Britannia*, the rivers provide us with the needed
frame of reference for understanding such transitions. For example,
Gloucestershire and Oxfordshire were both occupied by the *Dobuni*. Gloucestershire is divided between the Severn's influence in
the west, and that of the Isis in the east, and as we cross the territory
of the Dobuni from west to east, the narrative follows the two
rivers, shifting from Severn to Isis, and thus from Gloucester to
Oxford. In this way, the rivers unify geographical, political, and
historical divisions: the ancient domain of the *Dobuni*, the modern
counties, and the geography itself, a subliminal natural unity thus
keeps the whole together.[12]

Camden cannot always put the rivers to such methodical and
symmetrical use, where the reader portages so conveniently from
stream to stream, county to county, nation to nation, but with rare
exception he uses the river to order his narrative method. Some-

times the technique is quite simple, as in the chapter on Hertford-
shire, where one river leads the prose in a straight line from border
to county capital to border. Treating a coastal county such as
Devonshire, Camden follows the coast, striking inland at each river
outlet, so that one is hard put to follow the narrative without a map.
But throughout the work, as we pass from county to county, there is
a clash between England and the past, which refuses to be aligned
with the modern landscape, and the discord is resolved by nature's
own evolving and flexible divisions.

The movement through these counties, along the various rivers,
and past the ancient kingdoms is characteristic of Camden's narrative method. What stands out in these examples is the interplay
between the kinds of unity, or geopolitical division that are at work
in Camden's narrative. The rivers are the natural and narrative
sinews which cross—and thereby reconcile—ancient and modern
political divisions. Camden's technique calls attention to the dis-
crepancies between the modern and historical borders. His is certainly not the most likely approach to the material, and the territorial
disputes that are implicit in his narration are harmonized by the
natural topography.

This structural organization establishes a strong political undercurrent in the *Britannia*. The author's principal concern is historical
description, a reconstructed, primarily Roman landscape containing
accounts of heroics, human folly, and achievement. This same
prevailing sense of tension and resolution rises naturally from the
structural strata into the history itself. In this sense, then, it is
important to remember that the *Britannia* is not exactly history, but
history seen through descriptive topography, so that the landscape
establishes an enduring context for the human events.

Thus, Camden too presents us with an encomiastic image of the
nation, but it is one in which the descriptive topography is used to
clarify our political and historical perspectives. He does this by using
the landscape to make us reassess our knowledge of the past. The
landscape and authentic historical documents are used to recreate
an image of prehistoric Britain, that is, the Britain that the
Romans saw when they travelled up the Thames, much as Aeneas
and Carmentis made their voyages of discovery up the Tiber.
Historical and literary texts and verifiable empirical and geographical evidence are the two methods he uses to test our understanding
of the myths and history of the British past. His is a re-creative
methodology meant to question our myths in order that we may

understand them better. Far removed from Leland's objectives, Camden's *Britannia* is concerned with the relation between myth and history and the kind of knowledge provided by each. Historians have recognized it as the first historical work in Britain to use such methods. More important, though, is its place in an intellectual tradition that includes *The Defence of Poesie* and *The Faerie Queene* and that compares the kinds of understanding available through history and myth, and assesses the place of each in our cultural identity.

Throughout the *Britannia* Camden uses verse to focus his view of Britain, and he does so in such a way that he reinforces the structural harmony of the whole. The poetry is interspersed irregularly but densely through the chapters. Seldom does a page pass without the prose being elevated by fragments of verse, so that the tone rises and falls in a rhythmic reminder of the *de casibus* theme, and the texture of the whole becomes a verbal mirror of the landscape with its architectural fragments. The incomplete passages adorning the historical and topographical descriptions serve as brief phrases emphasizing the importance of historical verse, much as the nymph of Verulam calls for a poetic memorial in *The Ruines of Time*. Camden's point is underscored by the poets he quotes. Of the many verses, the only modern poets cited with any frequency are Alexander Neckham (if he qualifies as modern), John Leland, John Johnston of Aberdeen, and Camden himself—poets of the cities and rivers. The effect is a sharp awareness that the nation is better served by the poets of the past than by those of the present. Camden shores up this poetic legacy against oblivion; his objective is to revitalize poetic interest in Britain's history and topography, as we can see from his commission of city poems from John Johnston, and as he frequently tells us in the course of the *Britannia*. As we will see, his desire is to restore the spirit that is voiced in Leland's often-quoted and praised verses. However, the distance between the two, and the difference in their historical perspectives, is suggested by the very fact that Leland serves Camden as an *exemplum*.

The narrative function of the verses is to concentrate the structural pattern established by the geographical rivers in the prose, and not only are a large number of them about the rivers, but the most important ones are from his own *de Connubio Tamae et Isis*, which appears and disappears Arethusa-like throughout the *Britannia*. It is in these poetic shards that Camden gives us a compressed view of ancient Britain, and that we discern the difference between his and

Leland's image of the nation. Camden is far more concerned than Leland to put the landscape and its history into a moral perspective—he shows us history, rather than presents us with it—and if the whole of the *Britannia* is organized to accentuate these lessons, the verses locate them and carry them beyond the limits of history alone. Indeed, they stand in contrast to the history, for Camden uses verse to accentuate the points where our historical knowledge ends and our intuitive and mythic understanding begins. Thus, unlike any other historian in England Camden uses the juxtaposition of history and poetry to emphasize the relation between our empirical knowledge and that which comes from within. In this, Camden is even more emphatic than Leland about the importance of establishing a national poetic which will preserve our moral perspective. This is particularly clear in Camden's use of his own *de Connubio Tamae et Isis*, which identifies his prevailing concern with the theme of unity, and provides its most important illustration outside of Spenser. In fact, both structurally and thematically, Camden's use of the river resembles Spenser's own during this period.

While Camden's lines are themselves merely competent, they are integrated into the fabric of the work with considerable skill, and to dismiss them as mere fragments or as the triflings of an antiquarian is to be insensitive to the ways in which Renaissance history and verse served one another. Although it cannot be stated whether the *de Connubio Tamae et Isis* was completed in 1586 (before the first edition of the *Britannia*) or only by 1607 (when the last revisions and additions were made) or even if it was ever "completed" in the usual sense of the word and then perhaps dismantled for use in the *Britannia*, William Vallans had seen "it," whatever "it" was, by 1590, liked it, and deemed it fit for publication in its own right. Possibly Camden meant it to be an allusive, discontinuous poem whose fragmented nature paradoxically holds the large work together. It would not be the first Renaissance work designed as a fragment complete in itself. But what we can be certain about is that we have what Camden wanted us to have and in the form that he wanted us to have it.[13]

The poem, of some two hundred lines, is interspersed through those chapters dealing with counties crossed by the Thames and describes the source of the Isis, its union with the Tame, and their descent as the Thames to London. If Leland's *Cygnea Cantio* was

Camden's immediate source, which seems most likely, then the imposition of the marriage motif on the basic design of the river description was done to good purpose, for it establishes the theme of geographical and social unity. It is also quite possible that Spenser's "Epithalamion Thamesis" was an important influence; the relation between these two works will probably never be known. Nevertheless, both Camden and Spenser adapt the basic format of the river passage, developing it in terms of the common metaphor of the river marriage, and even more important, making it the organizing theme of an entire poem, and the *locus communis* for a larger, encompassing work. For Camden the marriage poem concentrates his political themes in nature, in the rivers; by stressing their inevitable confluence, it forces its order and by extension its political vision on the historical material, and in so doing it transcends the history itself.

Camden's technique creates a reciprocity between history and nature similar to that which he develops in the structural patterns of the prose. We have seen how the historical and geographical materials interact there to effect shifts from county to county and to call attention to the relation between society and the physical environment. As a result, the segments of the *de Connubio Tamae et Isis* do not appear in the proper order of the rivers' descent. Reading through the *Britannia*, we come upon the poem *in medias res*. We encounter it first in Berkshire; the rivers, already united to form Thames, enjoy the prosperity of their union in the form of Reading. The prose then leads us farther downstream to the next verse excerpt, describing Windsor's Thames-side beauties and praising Elizabeth; we then continue down the river to Richmond and more lines from the poem, praising both river and town. Knowing as we do that all of these excerpts are part of a poem on the marriage of Tame and Isis, we see the verse and the peerless structures that Camden describes not as the creations of any single monarch, but as the product of England's natural history and the union of Tame and Isis. The effect thus produced is that history and its monuments seem to be part of the ongoing present rather than of the foregone past; they are abstracted from a particular historical context and are seen within the dimension of time itself. Camden's objective here is to extricate the nation from history's confines and to give vitality to the nation's self-image by freeing it from the worship of the past, as we can see from the description of Windsor:

> Cease Windsor, cease to boast, and cease to paint
> The hounour of Saint George, thy patron saint . . .
> Yet cease thy joy and wonder at the past;
> All yield to one; by one is far surpast
> Thy every boast; for, now thy greater pride,
> Thy greater honour is, that here beside
> One banke with thee Eliza deigns reside. (1:219)

Elizabeth, herself a figure of unity and concord, is the true descendant of England's *genius loci*, who carries the past into the future. In Camden's need to extricate himself from the cult of history, we see the striking difference between his and Leland's relation to the past and present.

After the description of Richmond, the prose takes us on to Kent, and from there, as we have seen, we are transported to Gloucestershire, where there is "subjoined from the marriage of Tames and Isis a poetical description" of the source of Isis (1:384). Thus, we arrive at the beginning of the poem and the natural origins of the cultural bounty we have beheld on the banks of the Thames. From Gloucester we move on to Oxford, where the poetic marriage takes place, and then on to Middlesex and the verses on London, which is down-river from Richmond.

The geographical dislocation of the verses creates a cyclic order suggestive of natural union and increase, and in which human history participates. In a sort of mythopoeic circularity which imitates nature, we have been sent toward the sea and returned to our narrative beginnings. Thus, the *de Connubio*, in its very structure, asserts a topographical unity for the origin and development of the political and demographic organization of the chapters; it implies a natural order for history which supercedes all human motives. It acts on the reader in two ways. First, it calls attention to the human relation to nature simply by the presence of a river poem in the midst of the historical material, and by suggesting an organic unity which at least seems to relate contrapuntally to human history. The prose seems to lead one way, the river poem another; in fact, we learn that the river marriage not only leads in the same direction as the history, but, in a sense, gives it direction. And second, because the poem is conspicuously out of order, it forces the reader to reconstruct the fragments, so that natural order imposes itself on the political disorder, thus unifying the landscape in a way that the human geography appears, perforce, as a product of nature. The rivers' confluence seems to exist in a distant past—we meet the rivers already united as Thames and then go back to the time of their union. As the prose tells us of political and historical struggles and divisions, and of the evolving state of the nation, the rivers stay the same, remain fixed, the unmoved mover. As in Spenser's use of the motif, the reader must integrate the river poem into the larger work, and in so doing, come to terms with Camden's conception of history.

The structure of the poem, then, resembles in small that of the whole work, and thus enables us to perceive Camden's larger design more clearly. It is this obtrusive *tour de force* between the history and the poem that defines the cyclic interaction between human society and nature. The natural order of the poem emphasizes growth, and works against the regressive attitude which looks to the past and denies the future. Such a design is not as complicated as it sounds—the rivers have an implicit and undeniable order, and must take their own course. Camden simply excerpts from their description as his historical narrative requires—at Windsor, London, or wherever. And it should be said that such a literary adaptation of the nations' riverine unity is a perfect analogue to the geographer's conception of England and its network of rivers; Camden has simply used the geographer's schemes to support his view of history.

Camden's use of the river as a *topos* for concord and unity, then, draws on literary and geographical sources. In the *de Connubio* the river is the elemental beginning of all things. In it all elements meet in harmonious opposition. Camden stresses the river's symbolic role as the harmonizer of art and nature, and thus as a basic paradigm for history itself. The opening lines of the poem—which we encounter only after having read the descriptive praises and moral admonitions associated with such noble sites as Windsor and Richmond—describe the groom's (Isis's) source as the cavernous home of all rivers, where earth and water mingle in fruitful opposition, and where nature is most artificial. Here, at nature's androgynous center, is the source of history and knowledge, the secret of all earthly order:

> Where spacious Coteswold feeds her fleecy care,
> Rising in gentle hills, and from mid air,
> O'er Dobuni looks, a cavern lies
> Siding the Foss; the broken tops that rise
> By the hill's margin the recess disguis'd
> With gilded tophus shines the door, the halls
> Resplendent iv'ry boast upon their walls,

> Glitters the pendent roof with British jet,
> Alternate piles of pumice-stone are set.
> Yet Art with Nature's rich materials vies,
> Tophus, jet, pumice, iv'ry yield the prize.
> Queen of the glassy realm, the silver moon
> Art here has painted in the highest noon;
> Ocean and Earth in close embrace confin'd,
> Art here in endless wedlock has combined.
> Here rise in streams of common brotherhood,
> Nile, Ganges, and the Amazonian flood,
> Ister with double name, and neighbour Rhine;
> While interwove with their streams does shine
> Britain whom Phrixus' golden spoils adorn
> Victorious over Gaul, and crown'd with corn. (1:384–85)

This is the cave that Sannazaro's Ergasto visited to resolve the problem of the poet's relation to the mutable world of public affairs. Camden, however, visits it to capture an image of concord in nature, where opposites are bound "in endless wedlock" and streams rise "in common brotherhood." This theme of *"fide concordia sancta"* lies at the center of the marriage of the English rivers. There, as "Zephyr cloaths the verdant flow'ry meads," we see the union of the ethereal and mundane in a symbolic marriage of heaven and earth, offering the possibilities of a new Golden Age in a united, sea-girt Britain. It is nature's womb, containing the seeds of the civilized arts which the "poet-historical" has already described for us.

The *de Connubio* does not celebrate any mortal's marriage, and Camden's lines, unlike Leland's, are not directly associated with a patron or monarch. His stylized hymeneals never lose their contact with the crucial historical themes of his *Britannia*. In his image of confluence or concord, he reduces the course of history to its elemental beginnings, bringing the springs of our sacred arts into contact with their origins in nature. As the bride, Tame, descends the Cattechlanian Hills to Dorchester, the river nymphs, the "British bridesmaids," in procession cast upon the couple their blessings and gifts. Instead of flowers and herbs which grow upon their banks, they offer the blessings of a turbulent but honorable legendary history. The lines are an effective adaptation of the conventions of the epithalamion to the historical themes of the *Britannia*:

> For here each nymph in beauteous order throws
> From Greece what Brutus and what Brennus won,

From Ireland Gurmond fierce, our Amazon
From Rome, the English spoils,
Our Arthur bore memorials of his toils,
From Scotland what victorious Edward bore,
And British valour from the Gallic shore. (2:10)

All the ambiguous history, the doubtful legends, the violence, treachery, and heroics, are seen as the natural product of this marriage, as the nymphs celebrate the union with the *flores historiae* of Britain's mythical identity. Their offerings are part of an evolving pageant which constitutes the single stream of British history:

And in one connected stream,
With hearts united now, Isis and Tame
Arose exulting in united name;
And onwards moving in harmonious boast
Join Father Ocean in the Eastern Coast. (2:10)

Unity through myth and geography is Camden's reiterated theme. Here more conspicuously, Camden's history forms the perfect complement to the national geography. The bridesmaids sing of "Britannia sever'd from the world," and the literary *topos* and the geographical image of the nation come together as the landscape is shaped by Camden's coherent and transforming imagination. In Camden's mythologizing view, past and present, myth and geography join; history is not idealized, but is placed in a natural perspective. The legendary national image is as British as the waters of its rivers.

But in a related sense, in this marriage song Camden is suggesting to his readers the proper place of history and myth in the national consciousness. Thus, when the poem is reconstructed in its proper geographical order, there emerges an impression of orderly decline and deterioration that gives more pointed meaning to Camden's lesson about history and nature. For example, the verses before and during the marriage ceremony present nature in terms of stylized images of a golden age and the reconciliation of opposites. The bridal songs treat events and heroic deeds of antique legendary Britons. Nature and the mythical past are in harmony: nature is "primitive" and people are heroic. In the lines following the marriage, nature is richly adorned with the civilizing arts—it is almost lost beneath the cities, palaces, ruins, and other monuments which are the products of human history. There is also a sense of being brought up to date: "Now to the right is lofty Richmond seen,/Call'd in past ages for its lustre shine./Its modern name to the sage

prince it owes/Whose ancient style and title that name shows."
Complex personalities rather than deeds are presented, and simple
nobility yields to more ambiguous motives, pastoral *otium* to urbane
negotium:

> Then Thames to Hampton runs, whose stately space
> A city sees. The founder of the place
> Was Mitred Wolsey, a great ill-fated priest
> For whom his fate prepared in honey'd feast,
> Mingled with gall. Such were her Treacherous gifts. (2:85)

Camden's design here is unmistakable; the lines, simple and
sententious as they are, become more significant when we are
aware of their relation to the whole poem in its proper order.
Nature and human affairs are put in a moral context and are
perceived quite differently when they are measured against the
world of the bridal song. Thus, as the rivers descend to the sea, so
human nobility declines from its first estate; nature is obscured and
at odds with human achievement. Quite literally, the rivers rise
from their source and descend to the sea in a course which is
followed by the rest of nature and human history. Both, however,
like the river, have the restorative power to return to their begin-,
nings in nature and myth, as is suggested by the circular structuring
of the river poem, which does actually send us back to the recreative beginning. The technique is identical to that used later by
Ralegh in *The History of the World*.

Thus, in pointing to this common theme of the decline from
virtue, Camden is not just denouncing the times; nor does he
idealize the past, which is also a rather ambiguous affair. But by first
showing the origins of history in nature, in Isis's cave, Camden
identifies human character and potential in its undiminished state,
and it is from this beginning that all events flow. They are all one
continuous water, unbroken from its source, affirming the same
paradigm of unity and oneness that informs Ralegh's image of the
river of history, and Sidney's river of divine unity in his *trewnesse of
the Christian religion*. Thus, for Camden, the inspiriting waters
which feed Tudor Britain are those which fed Albion—all history is
unified, one, corruptible, but renewable. In thus basing his myth of
history in geography, Camden has, in fact, adapted a common river
motif to his own culture, as Plato did for his, and as the exegetes and
Neo-platonists did for theirs. He has turned its teleology to history,
rather than to myths of creation or metaphysics.

Camden uses the river poem to teach us to read and shape the landscape. It is, in fact, a unique and essential part of the *Britannia*, for it treats history as the larger work does not, and in a way that transcends the historian's methods. Camden, "nourrice of simple verity," renowned among his peers for his sensible, down-to-earth view of history, takes on the more exalted role of poet here, and addresses higher truths beyond the scope of the *Britannia* itself. Thus in the cave of Isis, and in the songs of the British bridesmaids, he invokes the full array of questionable myths of British ancestry—Albion, Brutus, Ulysses, Arthur—and he allows them a veracity which he could not give them as an historian. He gives them a legitimate place in British culture and the development of the nation, but it is the place of myth, not history. The poem, then, offers them as exemplars which history itself does not (and perhaps cannot) provide; they are as important and as legitimate *genii* of the realm as any historical figure is, and in this Camden, like Spenser and Sidney, perceives a creative means of defying time through myth. It is in the marriage poem that Camden attempts to establish a creative relation between his reader, time and history, and it is one which involves poetry itself. Poetry transforms history in order to urge us to virtuous action; through it, society frees itself from the past, renews itself, and this is what Camden's poem does for the *Britannia*. Camden is warning against the lugubrious complaints about the decline of the times which are popular in every age and which we have seen in Thomas Churchyard's *Worthines of Wales*, and in this respect he looks at landscape with a more discerning eye than most of his contemporaries.

3. The Consent of Rivers: The Consolidation of the National Image and the Death of Sidney

Come forth ye Nymphes come forth, forsake your watry bowres,
Forsake your mossy caves, and help me to lament:
Help me to tune my dolefull notes to gurgling sound
Of *Liffies* tumbling streames: Come let salt teares of ours,
Mix with his waters fresh. O come, let one consent
Joyne us to mourne with wailfull plaints the deadly wound
Which fatall clap hath made.

> (Bryskett, "The *mourning* Muse of Thestylis")

Return *Alpheus*, the dread voice is past,
That shrunk thy streames; Return *Sicilian* Muse,

And call the Vales, and bid them hither cast
Their Bels, and Flourets of a thousand hues.

(John Milton, Lycidas)

The appearance of the *Britannia*, then, marked the arrival of a second and larger wave of scholars at their intellectual majority. It was about this time, 1588 at the latest, that Robert Cotton, aged only eighteen, began the extraordinary library that would be such an . invaluable aid to so many historians, poets, and topographers. No doubt he had been one of Camden's favorite students at Westminster School, and he alone would rival his friend and master for influence on the study of antiquities during this period. And by 1586, through Cotton's and Henry Spelman's initiative, some forty-two young men were meeting regularly, like an informal group of graduate students, to discuss their research in the field of British history, and in effect institutionalizing the discipline that Leland pursued rather eccentrically. This group became the original Society of Antiquaries.

The nature of this group—its interests, activities, and membership—suggests much about the changing attitudes toward history as they are reflected in the river motif. It consisted of a young and ambitious group of gentlemen, many of whom were in Parliament of were attached to the Inns of Court. Cotton, born around 1566, was not yet twenty when the society began to flourish. Henry Spelman was twenty-four; the poet John Davies, born around 1565, was twenty-one. Many, slightly older, were coevals of William Camden, now thirty-five: the well-known historian, Francis Thynne, was born in 1545; John Doderidge and Lancelot Andrewes in 1555, Richard Carew in 1551, and William Lambard in 1545. John Stow, born in 1525 and the oldest and the humblest in origin, was something of an outsider.

The society was a collegium of gentlemen and was organized according to their tastes. The calendar of meetings coincided with the law term, suggesting that it was at least loosely linked with the Inns of Court,[14] and the papers that were delivered, on matters of title, privilege, laws and institutions, remind us that these were generally titled, propertied men of law and politics, whose interests were closely linked to their social rank. It is noteworthy, then, that with few exceptions these were not men of letters but men of action. They were moved with the same nationalistic zeal that inspired men such as William Warner, for example (whose *Albions England* also first appeared in 1586), but their place in society led them to forms of expression other than literature. The comparatively few literary men in their membership—Stow, Lambard, Carew, Thynne, Hartwell, Camden, and (for his influence rather than for his writings) Cotton—are important, for they evidently did most of the work and they form the connection with the literature we have been and will be discussing.

Under the scholarly supervision of Camden the society set out to ensure "the perseverance of history and antiquity" in England; their intentions were a mixture of those of Leland and those of Camden. Hoping for a royal charter, their objective was at once to preserve and to promote history: it was both archival and patriotic. Thus the society was not exempt from that image-making obsession we have spoken of, but it remained low-key. They were a sober and unfrivolous lot in their desire to mold an image of the nation, and they eschewed such materials as might be construed as poetic, confining themselves to more businesslike matters.[15]

Nevertheless, they prosecuted their studies with a quiet, but rigidly exclusive, nationalism. In fact, their view of history was nationally self-centered to the extreme of isolationism, and it provides an intellectual analogue to the social, political, and geographical insularity that distinguishes the period. In their eyes, of all modern nations Britain was blessed with the greatest antiquity, and therefore, it was argued, members should use only native materials in their researches, allowing nothing but British precedents and authorities in the arguments of their weekly discourses. In one colloquium in 1600, Francis Tate urged that "nothing be spoken but of this realme," although, as might be expected, the stricture requiring British content made scholarship rather difficult, and some months later, Francis Leigh admitted to some problems in researching certain points, "more especially as it is confined to the limits of our country; in experience of which, wee are most commonly ignorant, as having therein less help from reading and history, then we have in regard to other countries."[16] Unreasonable as the requirement was, and unsuited as it might be to sound scholarship, it had to be borne, since the resurrection of national materials was their very objective. And so their study continued, and the past was shaped according to their patriotic designs. In a manner not unlike that of many modern nations and groups suffering from a similar identity crisis, the healthy impulse to preserve the nation's past merged with a national narcissism, an egomania which is consistent with the tendency of the river poets to fabricate a national image, although the poets tended to have a more critical view of the nation. As Joan Evans says, the society's demand for British content

> inevitably resulted in insularity and even parochialism. Their true aim was to establish a "cultural longevity" for their country: Parliament had to date from the Roman era; the bearing of arms to go back to Caesar, and Christianity to have been brought to Britain by Joseph of Arimathea.[17]

The character of this well-intending society allows us to measure how much the antiquarian impulse had changed since Leland. While they identified their work with Leland's, they had unwittingly wandered far from him; he had hoped to capture the historic landscape of the realm, and to preserve its archives; they had a much more abstract idea of history in mind, as we can see from the spirit of their petition to the Queen and their account of Leland's and Henry's initial historical objectives: "Also when the Pope's authority was abolished out of England by King Henry the Eighth, there was special care had of the search of ancient Books and antiquities for manifestation unto the world of these usurpations of the Pope."[18] Antiquarian study has subtly evolved from the preservation of national archives to the use of them to rewrite history on the basis of their supposed importance.

The connection between the society and William Camden's career suggests much, not only about his importance, but also about the evolution of historical perspectives at the end of the sixteenth century. Linda Van Norden and Joan Evans have shown that the life span of the society covers the years from 1586 to 1610, that it was most productive between 1598 and 1602, and that it met regularly until 1607.[19] The twenty-four-year period of its activities coincides with the six Latin editions of the *Britannia*. If we look at the large collection of discourses prepared for the society, some of which were collected by Hearne and Ayloffe, although many remain unpublished, we can see how heavily the members relied on Camden's work. They drew on the *Britannia* as from a primary source; researched questions raised by Camden, and entered into academic exchanges in which Camden took the final stand. Camden assumes a respected professorial role among his serious and unpoetic protégés, and it is possible to detect in the *Britannia* and other of his writings subtle and sagacious warnings against intolerant nationalistic zeal which obscures sound judgment and good history. His undemonstrative treatment of the *de Connubio Tamae et Isis* may derive from the society's ban on poetry and poets, and it is significant that it is in his treatment of verse in the *Britannia* that he warns against the narrow-minded cult of history.

If these amateur collectors of the past were not the sort to write national epics, or to write much at all—the Camdens and Stows among them did most of the serious work—the society does tell us something about cultural self-awareness during the last decades of the sixteenth century. History for them was fuel for their patriotic fervor, but it was a personal matter, and they explored questions of title and legal precedents, and matters of ancient authority which were relevant to both personal and national identity. In their parochialism they may have worshipped the past, but they did not look at it as distant and irrecoverable. Although they strove to form a library[20] (and Cotton was much involved with his collection), this was still a secondary consideration. Their first priority was one of civic and personal pride, the revival of ancient rites, customs, and prerogatives.

While the members of the Society of Antiquaries were not inclined to voice their patriotism in verse, after the appearance of the *Britannia* in 1586, poetic national portraits which figured British history and geography in harmony became more popular, and they too shared the same uncritical enthusiasm evident in the society's work. They are national images, largely urban in setting, and in which London and her *genius* the Thames often figure as recipients of history's and nature's gifts. A work such as Peele's *Device* for the Lord Mayor's pageant for Wolstan Dixi, in which the nymph of the Thames expresses the concordant spirit of nature and the civic good will of the entire nation, is fairly typical. The myth of landscape is (to use Matthew Arnold's phrase) adequate for the age. The Thames expresses the myth of harmony, unity, and prosperity with which many in the sixteenth century were content to view their world:

> With silver glide my pleasant streames doo runne,
>   Where leaping Fishes play betwixt the shores:
> This gracious good hath God and kinde begun,
>   For Londons use with helpe of Sailes and Ores.[21]

This view of time and nature is the appropriate urban analogue to the much more private vision that would take its place a quarter of a century later, in Jonson's *Penshurst*, for example. It is as though, once Camden identified the nation's literary boundaries in the

1580s, it became more feasible to give its *genius* a coherent and credible voice, and the process of creating an image of the realm in verse became increasingly popular.

Nothing fixes a nation's (or an individual's) attention on itself so assuredly as a crisis, and during these years two events, the Armada and the death of Sir Philip Sidney, helped to consolidate this image of the nation in harmonious concord with itself, turning the river into new literary channels, and giving it a stylistic variety not yet achieved in Britain. The effect of the repulse of the Armada in 1588 was indirect, more on the mind of the nation, taken by surprise by its own temerity and good fortune, than directly on the river motif itself, although it was no less real and immediate. It confirmed the Protestant maritime images of Britain as the Fortunate Isles, with Thames in benevolent complicity with Neptune, and as the Protestant ark afloat on the waters of life. The event, in which divinely inspired nature seemed to work to defend England from her Catholic invaders, provided the perfect occasion for allegorizing her role as a chosen nation. It was just the sort of grist for the epic mill, and Thomas Campion's Latin epic fragment *Ad Thamesis* (1595) is typical of what might be expected from such a heightened state of national self-consciousness. Drawing on Virgil for prophetic and national themes, and Tasso for religious epicity, Campion "congratulates the Thames for the rout of the Spaniards." The anti-Catholic sentiments are conveyed in terms of Thames's and Neptune's efforts to keep the temples on the river's banks inviolate. The unnaturalness of the Catholic intentions and Thames's innocence and mystical knowledge and ability to restore natural order suggest Virgil's Tiber and also Lucan's Nile and Rubicon, and his floods of civil war.[22]

Campion's verses remained fragmentary, though, and no epic on the Armada was ever completed. Strangely enough, the event received comparatively little significant poetic attention, although it was addressed regularly from the pulpit and in ephemeral literature. Nevertheless, the event did raise the river to heroic status, or rather, it elevated the nation's self-image, and the river swelled with it. After 1588 Thames's and Neptune's rapport was taken for granted, and it suggested England's naval might and place in a providential order. At times their alliance was shaky, as in E. W.'s *Thameseidos*, and either a menacing Neptune threatens the vulnerable Thames with further unnatural invasion, or England has fallen from her exalted position through some sort of moral or political turpitude.

The aquatic image, however, remains the same within this range of meanings.

Yet full-scale epics inspired directly or indirectly by the Armada never materialized, unless we think of the various allegorical alexandrines on the Dutch wars late in the next century as descendants of this event. Its direct influence is felt in a few minor works which resonate with pride in British naval heroes, such as Fitz-Geoffrey's *Sir Francis Drake* (1596) and Thomas Kidley's "Hawkins" (1624),[23] but even in these the Armada is of secondary interest. The real importance of its influence is for the national image itself, in the consolidation of that emblem of insular solidarity which brings together both sea and land, and perhaps the most suggestive illustration of this is in Spenser's and Ralegh's figure of the Shepherdess of the Ocean and her aquatic flock.

If the Armada helped the river to regain some of the epic resonance of the *Aeneid*, the death of Sidney gave it Theocritan lyric grace, renewed its access to the middle style of *Georgics IV*, and generally had a far greater impact on the development of the motif. In either case, the river, while retaining its national associations, was emerging from its primarily historical contexts and assuming some of the qualities it had on the Continent. The change would no doubt have occurred naturally, but in these verses we begin to see the appearance of the poet's persona in a river setting that is at once public and private.

Why Sidney's death should inspire river elegies when he himself did not make much use of the motif is not exactly clear, but the possible explanations suggest something about the Renaissance understanding of the river and bring us nearer to the most important river poet, Edmund Spenser. The aquatic associations surrounding Sidney's death in a battle for an island fortress are hardly sufficient to explain the regularity with which poets tune their elegies to the sound of the rivers. On the other hand, many of the elegies adapt the conventions of the pastoral complaint from Theocritus, Bion, and Moschus, and expand the river's importance there, naturalizing the nymphs and muses through the local rivers and a native setting. This in itself not only gives a new dimension to the river motif in England, but also confirms that poets realized that the river figures very centrally as the voice of nature in the Theocritan tradition.

Here too, however, the prominence of the motif is greater than such literary echoes would seem to warrant. Moreover, the expanded Theocritan elements often conflate with echoes of Spenser, and so suggest that another reason for lamenting Sidney in terms of the rivers is his known friendship with the rising literary star, Spenser, the river poet. The two men were acquainted, if not in fact close friends (as is more likely). Spenser's contacts with Henry Sidney, Leicester, Edward Dyer, and Lodowick Bryskett (who travelled on the continent with Sidney between 1571 and 1574) all argue a more than casual acquaintance. Even more important than the relation itself, though, is that many other writers considered the two to be closely allied and that Spenser himself either felt it to be so or was content to let it be thought so by others and perhaps even promoted the idea. Thus, when he writes to Sir Philip's sister of his duty to her brother, he repudiates those who upbraid him for his long poetic silence at the time of Sidney's death, speaks of the "straight bandes of duetie" with which he was "tied to him," and otherwise works the connection throughout his poetic career.[24] Whether it had its basis in fact or in rumor, posthumously Sidney's name was linked with the poet's.

And as I have argued elsewhere, Spenser's own poetic identity was increasingly associated with the rivers. His early translations contain conventional riverside visions on the world's vanity; the poet's Theocritan affectations in *Aprill*, when Hobbinoll sings Colin's song, tuned "unto the Water's fall," the announcement (and evident circulation in manuscript) of the "Epithalamion Thamesis" all contribute to the poet's early identification with the aquatic voice of the nation.[25] The rumored association between the poets, then, and Spenser's own reputation as a neo-Theocritan river poet, make it natural and appropriate for Sidney's elegies to be tuned to the nation's rivers.

One very interesting example of this somewhat circuitous route by which the rivers entered the Sidney elegies is a late sixteenth-century Bodleian Library manuscript, MS. Rawl. Poet. 85, "Upon the death of S^r. P. Sydneye," later published with modifications in Davison's *Poetical Rhapsodie* (1602) and ascribed (or not ascribed), depending on one's opinion of the initials) to the mysterious A. W. The poem, which has been virtually ignored by critics, happens to be a fine example of Spenserian imitation, and is written with considerable skill and charm. But what is important for our immediate purposes is how much the rivers help to create its literary landscape, and how, by intoning the watery dirge with Theocritan and Spenserian echoes tuned to distinctly local melodies, the poet forms a close connection between Sidney and Spenser.

Indeed, the poem is as much lament for Spenser's bereft condition after Sidney's death as it is an elegy on Sidney. It is in the traditional form of the pastoral eclogue, particularly as it is adapted in *The Shepheardes Calender*; not only do we have the customary meeting of two shepherds who sing the song of a third, but many of the shepherds were familiar to Spenser's readers at least by name. It is Thenot and Perin who meet and discuss Willy's death; they tell how Colin's songs are best suited to such an occasion, and speak of hardships which keep his pipes silent; and they finally decide to sing one of Colin's songs as a tribute to both poets. Throughout, the pastoral contains general and specific likenesses to Spenser's *Aprill*, as well as allusions to other of his works and, even more interesting, to his life. For example, when Thenot requests one of Colin's songs, since they alone are "fitt our sorrow to fulfill," Perin excuses Colin on the grounds that

Tway sore extremes do Colyn press so neere
(Alas that suche extremes should press him so)
The want of welth and loss of love so deere
Scarce can he breath from under heapes of woe
He that beares heaven beares no suche wayght I trow.

To bring the literary and biographical allusion fully before the reader, Thenot then paraphrases to Perin the question of Spenser's Thenot to Hobbinoll in *Aprill*, lines 19–20:

Hath he suche skyll in makyinge all above
And hath no skyll to gett or welth or love?[26]

The situation around which Spenser's *Aprill* develops, the need to sing for Colin in his absence, is turned here to the need to commemorate Willy's death with his friend's song, and in his behalf.

The poet repeatedly interweaves references to Spenser's life, phrases from his poetry, and the theme of Sidney, who is almost left behind. The method of allusion frequently turns upon Spenser's Apollinian and aquatic nymphs and muses. Indeed, the song that Thenot and Perin sing is explicitly "tuned . . . unto the Waters fall" and has the same nymphal troupe that Colin had when singing of "Fayre Eliza." The echoes of Spenser's *Aprill* ring clearly:

Ye Nymphes that bathe ye bodyes in this springe:
Your tender bodyes whyte as dryven snow
Ye virgins chast that in this grove do synge

W^{ch} neither greefe of love nor death do knowe
  So maye your streames run cleer for aye . . .
  Depart apace . . .

And thou my Muse that whylomes wontst to ease
Thy masters mynde wth layes of deepe delyght
Now change these tunes.[27]

The elegist's design here and elsewhere in the verses is to capture the distinctive qualities of Spenser's verse and thereby to convert all the elements of the elegiac mode into a completely British form. All of nature and the society of shepherds share the loss of Willy, and the naturalization of the poetic form through Spenser intensifies the sense of shared grief. Later in the poem he expounds upon Colin's loss of "grace" by Sidney's death, and magnifies the loss, while also making it more personal, by invoking a distinctly Spenserian feature:

What Thames, what Severne, or what western Seas,
Shall geve me floods of trycklynge teares to shedd,
What comforte can my restless greef appese
Oh that myne eyes were fountaynes in my head
  Ah Colyn I lament thy case
  For thee remaynes no hope of grace.[28]

The poem demonstrates most effectively that the poet used the rivers to link Sidney's and Spenser's names, although exactly why remains difficult to say. From a literary point of view, the design is quite understandable; praise and lament of the nation's paragon can best be sung by the paragon of praisers, the author of the *encomium* on Elizabeth, and to convey the formal as well as the personal sense of Spenser's presence in the poem, the poet resorts to the river motif. For various reasons Colin's pipes remain still, and he himself is in need of some looking after. Someone else must therefore either sing one of his songs, or feign one by adapting his trademark; either way he will be doing Colin a good turn, while paying his obsequies to Willy. With all the biographical associations of the rivers, though, the poem is concerned with a national event and recognizes Spenser as something of a British Orpheus who can harmonize all the country's streams.

Two other Sidney elegies, dating from 1587, are especially important for their use of the rivers to join the names of Sidney and Spenser, and more particularly, for their use of the river as a *topos* of concord in a way that is not uncommon in the Renaissance, and that is most thoroughly explored by Spenser himself. The verses are Lodowick Bryskett's *The mourning Muse of Thestylis* and his *A pastorall Aeglogue upon the death of Sir Phillip Sidney*, and they were published in the collection which takes its title from his neighbor's *Colin Clouts come home againe* (1596).[29] Both poems were completed before Spenser had finished his elegy on Sidney, and in them Bryskett preempts his poetic device of the rivers to localize the Theocritan convention and to draw on the implications of Sidney's friendship with Spenser and himself. In the *pastoral Aeglogue* he uses them to address Colin directly on the theme of their shared grief:

> Hear'st thou the *Orown*? how with hollow sownd
> He slides away, and murmuring doth plaine,
> And seemes to say unto the fading flowres
> Along his bankes, unto the bared trees;
> *Phillisides* is dead. Up jolly swaine,
> Thou that with skill canst tune a dolefull lay,
> Help him to mourn. (11.4–10)

The mourning Muse, however, is a monody and the poet calls upon the Irish rivers to tune his song of grief as Spenser called upon his rivers for his song of praise:

> Come forth, ye Nymphes come forth, foresake your watry bowres,
> Forsake your mossy caves, and help me to lament:
> Help me to tune my dolefull notes to gurgling sound
> Of *Liffies* tumbling streames. (11.1–4)

What is more important than these invocations, though, is how Bryskett uses them to explore his elegiac theme. Conventionally the elegy describes the universal woe that results from the person's death, and strives to find meaning in it, and thus relief from it. In the Christian elegy the understanding reached is usually that he who is mourned is in a better place—"Having affixt . . . [his] eyes on that most glorious throne," as Bryskett says in *The mourning Muse*. In both of Bryskett's poems, the descriptions of nature's grief concentrate on the rivers, their nymphs and muses, and therefore associate the rivers with both knowledge and nature. Thus in each, Bryskett de-emphasizes the theme of Sidney's ascension and examines the public and private significance of death and grief in terms of nature's consent—the bond of nature that is affirmed through suffering.

Death strengthens nature's harmony, as we see in the poet's petition to the nymphs of the rivers in *The mourning Muse*:

> come let salt teares of ours
> Mix with his waters fresh. O come, let one consent
> Joine us to mourne with wailfull plaints the deadly wound
> Which fatall clap hath made. (11.4–7)

Largely through his use of the rivers, Bryskett broadens the implications of this idea of consent. All the rivers of the world—and by implication, all the nations—are in accord with *Mundus*:

> The *Thames* was heard to roare, the *Reyne* and eke the *Mose*
> The *Schald*, the *Danow* selfe this great mischance did rue
> With torment and with grief; their fountains pure and cleere
> Were troubled, and with swelling flouds declar'd their woes.
> The Muses comfortles, the Nymphs with paled hue . . .
> O help, O help ye Gods, they ghastly gan to crie. (11.36–41)

The private voice of grief joins with that of nature and the world at large; death's harmonizing is already felt, and ultimately poetry is its only antidote.

Their plaint rouses "old father *Ocean*," who here is the voice of restraint and understanding, and whose knowledge has its origins in the very heart of nature. The rivers' concord with Ocean, "full of majestie," is itself a pattern of natural order, the understanding of which is the subject of their lament. Their flow into him is itself a figure of death, and so his words enjoining them to resignation, and pointing out that all life comes from death, are the *anagnorisis* to which the poem works: "Such is his will that paints/The earth with colours fresh." His words, nicely turned to have the most meaning for a group of river nymphs, answer the private grief of the Medway and the public sorrows of the Thames by showing how death is part of mutable nature, although it cannot diminish the sorrow or lessen the loss. The shared grief of nature, then, is itself part of the order that is illuminated by Sidney's death, and that has its idealized form in the remote, celestial realm that Sidney now occupies after death. Bryskett's image of the world is one of incipient confusion, and through nature's sympathetic response to death, one which is echoed in the plaints of the rivers, ocean, and of the elegy itself, there emerges an order which integrates death into nature herself.

Death is shared and thereby understood in a similar manner in the *pastorall Aeglogue*, where, in Colin's and Lycon's songs, Neptune and the English rivers, in their cavernous dwelling, behold the passage of Sidney's funeral procession:

> Loe father *Neptune*, with sad countenance,
> How he sitts mourning on the strond now bare,
> Yonder, where th'Ocean with his rolling waves
> The white feete washeth (wailing this mischance)
> Of *Dover* cliffes, His sacred skirt about
> The sea-gods all are set; from their moist caves
> All for this comfort gathered there they be
> The *Thamis* rich, the *Humber* rough and stout,
> The fruitfull *Severne*, with the rest are come
> To help their Lord to mourne, and eke to see
> The dolefull sight, and sad pomp funerall
> Of the dead corps passing through his kingdom. (11.95–106)

Bryskett creates an image of the grief-stricken, "Unhappie *Albion*," her rivers joining in their lament with Neptune, and finding comfort in their concord. The shepherds on the banks of their Irish rivers are brought into the universal movement as they tune their own laments to the sound of the Orown. The rivers, joined with Neptune in their grief, represent and even participate in the process of death and dissolution. Lycon's song has its echo in Colin's descriptions of the wasting of nature, of the "widow world" and "fountains now left desolate." The world of the poem is primarily aquatic, and all its inhabitants, the muses, nymphs and rivers, all reenact Sidney's death, disappearing like the rivers themselves beneath the ocean:

> Ye Nymphes and *Nyades* with golden heare,
> That oft have left your purest cristall springs
> To harken to his layes, that coulden wipe
> Away all griefe and sorrow from your harts.
> Alas who now is left that like him sings?
> When shall you heare againe like harmonie? (11.118–23)

The "like harmonie" is that of nature itself and the sympathetic voices of grief, of which Bryskett's elegy is one. Thus, the poem works toward a cathartic integration in which nature, if it does not defy death, at least embraces it within its own order and compensates somewhat for the loss by making it its own. The poem expresses the central idea of concord and understanding, and Bryskett's theme is unfolded through the harmony of the rivers. Albion bereft and the Irish shepherds are all subsumed within the image of concordant nature, and in their participation in nature's grief they understand its order.

As any good elegy must, these verses transcend their immediate occasion and explore the human relation to nature and death. It is often the case that elegies turn to the theme of poetry itself just as Bryskett here uses the rivers to express the communal impulse that finds its most important expression in the shepherd's own songs. In this way, Sidney's death brought together certain literary conventions, and called up in the self-consciousness of the occasion certain motifs which were current in the national poetic, thus providing the context for poets to address the theme of England's cultural and literary identity. As vehicles of a national myth in the sixteenth century, they reflect their age and suggest the ideal of concord. Great as the loss may be, the elegist in the sixteenth century generally felt up to the task of elegizing, or knew someone who was. As we will see, this is less often the case in the seventeenth century, when a comparable degree of harmony seemed impossible and the rivers sang separately.

The elegiac mode, then, naturally involves certain themes that are often located in the river. Acquired literary myths and modes suddenly seemed suited to the time and place, the landscape and the event, and for reasons which cannot finally be defined—whether from Spenser's influence or from the river's growing popularity generally—the motif emerged in these elegies with a coherence, an immediacy, and an emotional range which it had not had before in England, thus having more striking cogency as a national image. And while Bryskett's river poems are good but not great, there is a rightness and naturalness about them that tells the reader that the poet is comfortable with these poetic materials.

After Sidney's death, English rivers commonly figure as the organizing feature and national voice in elegiac verse. Elegies on Elizabeth, James, Prince Henry, and Queen Anne are frequently tuned to the rivers, and they are not only the voice of the nation and nature, but significantly, they are also Spenserian rather than Theocritan, and they call up an image of the nation's poetic legacy in their efforts to measure the effects of time. They are more clearly linked with time and verse, and they help to identify a Spenserian standard for understanding these themes. As the rivers become more closely associated with the nation's poetic legacy, they add a new dimension to the elegy in the Renaissance. Any person's death is a death for the whole world, and the course of a river reminds us that in the death of the individual we see the demise of the world. Poetry, in its ability to draw the particular into a universal order, shares in that natural cycle. Thus, as it was for Sidney's poets, so too for Milton, in *Lycidas*, the river also adumbrates the full meaning of death, and for him as well, it also has to do with life and poetry.

4. *The Landscape Transformed: Rivers in Fairy Land*

> But know, that secret virtues are infusd
> In every fountaine, and in every lake,
> Which who hath skill them rightly to have chusd,
> To proofe of passing wonders hath full often usd.
>
> (Spenser, The Faerie Queene)

> Fayre *Thamis* streame, that from *Ludds* stately towne,
> Runst paying tribute to the Ocean seas,
> Let all thy Nymphes and Syrens of renowne
> Be silent, whyle this Bryttane *Orpheus* playes.
>
> (R. S. on The Faerie Queene)

> In waving Throne here sits the king of waters all and some,
> ISIS, who in that Majestie which rivers doth become,
> All rev'rend, from his watchet lap pour's forth his streame amaine
> With weed and reed his haires tuckt up that grow both long and
>   plaine. . . .
> Heere Zephyrus with fresh green grasse/The Banks above doth
>   spread,
> Faire flora with ay-living herbs/Adorneth ISIS head,
> Most lovely Grace selecteth forth/Sweet floures that never dy
> And gladsome Concord plats thereof/Two guirlands skilfully.
>
> (Camden, de Connubio, tr. Holland)

> Rivers, and Springs, and Bathes, and Pooles there beene
> That Beautifie the Mantle of this Queene.
> That flowen from the mightie Ocean
> Running again thither where they began.
>
> (N. Baxter, Sir Philip Sidney's Ourania)

Between 1586 and 1600 the English rivers took their place as the new Helicon. There is a self-fulfilling quality in this; to write of these native rivers was itself to demonstrate that the new golden age of literature was established on English banks, that Apollo and his troupe of nymphs could survive in Thames water. Although the river's topography continued to dictate the shape of works in prose and verse, it more often dominated individual works in less rigidly formal ways, so that it emerged as a recognizable and reputable topic susceptible to various forms. Such differences in the treatment of the rivers, then, reflect the changing perceptions in the nation's poetic and its cultural self-consciousness.

The enormous flood of river poetry during these years itself illustrates how thoroughly the landscape had been mythologized. In the natural evolution of English poetry, and stimulated by such events as the Armada and Sidney's death, the river found its way into every conceivable form, and having a tendency to usurp entire works, it emerged as a defining generic feature. Yet the river continued to have a primarily public voice. Poets used the river for its historical associations, to forge analogies between their own culture and the classical golden age, which used its rivers to express cultural ideals. As river poets begin to echo British writers who made use of the rivers we see literary allusion transform into literary tradition. In the hands of major and even very minor writers, the national landscape has become legitimate literary material: British rivers become sufficiently familiar to authors for them to acquire meaning; analogues found in other landscapes no longer eclipse the significance of the local rivers. The landscape can accommodate its own myths, so that the literary self-consciousness of Charles Fitz-Geoffrey's boast—that "Poe and Seine are sicke to thinke upon/ How Thames doth ebbe and flowe pure Helicon"[30]—reflects a more genuine change in English sensibility than its poetic merit might seem to suggest.

In some authors we can almost feel their sense of determination as they set about describing the local landscape. For example, William Vallans, in his dutifully sententious "topochronographical" river poem on the river Lee, *A Tale of Two Swannes* (1590), has made the generic link between Leland's *Cygnea Cantio* and Spenser's "Epithalamion Thamesis," and he humbly submits to publication in order to encourage Camden and Spenser to publish their river poems. In modernizing Leland, neo-Latin has been converted to the "reformed meter" of his other model. Instead of a chorus of nymphs, we hear a threnody of hoarse swans who look with despair and loathing on a wasted landscape whose lost golden age is, in fact, the age of Henry VIII and the Dissolution, and this adds an element of pathos to his poem and his view of his own generation. The iron age he deplores is modern, mundane, and dilapidated. Significantly, like Camden, he is responding to time and the times rather than to history. And yet, unlike Camden, for him the inevitable journey downstream is almost completed: his is the song of an old man in an old world.

Works such as Thomas Lodge's epyllion *Scillaes Metamorphoses* and his historical legend *The Complaynt of Elstred* (1589) are attempts to create English river poems in new forms and they show an increasing ability to naturalize techniques borrowed from Ovid and modern Continental writers. These and many other poems show the first real fruits of English interest in cultivating the river motif, and in them we see an awareness of the river's associations and a keen interest in the national landscape. These works rarely flow with the pure waters of eloquence but they are instructive illustrations of the creative process in the Renaissance. In looking at their handling of the river motif we can see authors attempting to use literary syncretisms to alchemize their world into one of gold. A poet such as Charles Fitz-Geoffrey tries to evoke a timeless mythic world for his English hero, Sir Francis Drake, by creating a setting in which the archetypal rivers of antiquity share the landscape with those of Britain. To develop Drake's heroic identity he defines aspects of his personality in terms of specific analogues—Neptune, Ulysses, and Hercules; significantly, this process also includes the creation of an indigenous geography for his hero, and in this he shows an awareness of specific links between culture heroes (particularly Hercules) and their rivers: "had he [Drake] surviv'd, Tempe had been our land,/And Thames had stream'd with Tagus golden sand."[31]

The process is often very artificial in effect, producing gold plate rather than something of truer metal. Nevertheless, one must recognize the importance of their efforts, for they are attempting to do what all artists must do: transform the quotidian into something universal. Their method is to use a kind of literary alchemy to blend specific "real" details from contemporary life with remoter "universal" features of myth. The result is often a pale alloy of a antique gold with the best of modern lead, but the aims and even the technique are legitimate and time-honored; they are Joyce's as well as Fitz-Geoffrey's.

There is a certain literary economy in this method of viewing the world in terms of geography, and it suggests the extent to which the national landscape had become the property of the imagination and was able to support this kind of vision. If lesser authors were not altogether successful, it is because they fail to blend their mythical and material worlds completely. They adapt the details of their classical and modern landscapes without reaching the human essence of the worlds they are trying to address. This required a profounder art in which the landscape participated in the author's view of reality and humanity.

It took a genuinely mythic imagination like Spenser's to perceive that the inner being must be transformed along with the landscape, and for this reason his river verse is the culmination of this process in which external and internal nature mirror one another. Spenser succeeded in bringing together the two streams of myth and history, using them in their deeper channels to reflect simultaneously the higher truths of poetry and the more transient images of human affairs. Few poets evoke the physical world of their verse as vividly as Spenser does, and it is always seen in mirroring streams where, through the imaginative vision of the mythologizer, the past, present, and future seem to merge. In this way Spenser transforms his reader's vision, and thus his world, as no other Renaissance poet does. He is interested in the psychological and the social being, and like Shakespeare, he realized that the historical landscape is a figment of our imagination, that our imagination is constantly changing that world, and that the greatest poetry has the power to remake the world in an act of the will: such is the meaning of the word poet,[32] and such is the objective of the poet who would "fashion a gentleman . . . in virtuous and gentle discipline." His landscapes and their rivers, therefore, constantly make us aware of our creative—and recreative—powers.

All of Spenser's major verse is concerned with recreating the world: that is, with the relation between the realm of fallen nature, where history takes place, time, with which we are continually at war, and the imagination, which is the enchanted shield and lance with which the individual and society wage the war. As he tells Ralegh, his method is not to recount events as "historiographer" would, but in the manner of the "poet historical," who thrusts into the midst of his material and presents things "forepast" and "things to come" and incorporates all time in his scope to make an "analysis of all."[33] Most obviously in *The Faerie Queene* but in his other verse as well he tries to identify the points of contact between the springs of nature's order, and the civilizing forces of the imagination which create society and which Spenser associates with grace. To achieve that condition, where art and nature are one, is to repudiate the long and violent history of our decline from grace. In the course of his poetic career, Spenser uses the river in different ways to locate his theme of the redemption of nature and to concentrate for his reader the larger plan of the individual work, so that in the muddled and misplaced river nymph of *The Ruines of Time*, in the uneasy but inevitable union of Mulla and Bregog, in the corruption of Molanna and her eventual union with Fanchin, in the marriage of Thames and Medway, and in the confluence of the pastoral Lee and the urban Thames, we are given distinctive episodes which figure the essence of the surrounding work by defining its world. Not only are they rhetorical devices unifying these works, but they are also images of Concord, or Unity.

From the early riverside visions adapted from Petrarch and du Bellay, and the experimental "Epithalamion Thamesis," to the *Prothalamion*, the last work published in his lifetime, Spenser systematically developed the way in which the river motif related to the surrounding context, and with the possible exception of *The Ruines of Time*, the motif consistently involves the poet's particular conception of concord and the way in which it locates the personal, moral, and social dimensions of love in the poetic landscape. When one is aware of this fact, it is evident that Spenser is very thoughtfully exploring the possibilities of the river's literary past, using and rejecting its conventions and forms, and generally adapting them to his own poetic terrain. Thus, like many other poets, notably Drayton and Milton, he serves a riparian apprenticeship, beginning with the uncomplicated dream vision before attempting more difficult waters. He experiments radically—and presumably unsucessfully—in attempting to enlarge Leland's design and versify Harrison's prose in the "Epithalamion Thamesis." In *Colin Clouts come home againe* and the *Cantos of Mutabilitie* he imitates the myths of local geography (such as Sannazaro's or more obviously, Boccaccio's *Nymph of Fiesole*) and the treatment of the digressive epyllion in Virgil's fourth *Georgic*. In Book 4 of *The Faerie Queene* the technique is expanded from its georgic middle style to the epic scope of the *Aeneid*. And in the *Prothalamion* he returns the rivers to the geographers, to Leland and Camden, thus paradoxically going back to his first native influences. All the while, in his experimentation the poet is refining his ability to concentrate his poetic world, so that in the *Prothalamion* the refrain is sufficient to define the moral climate of the poem.

I have examined these generic and formal features in some detail elsewhere.[34] What I want to concentrate on here is how Spenser's rivers, with their literary qualities and their sense of physical and geographical reality, are extensions of the poet's imagination—as all the world is—and how, in rather particular ways, they focus his meditations on time and mankind's transforming relationship to geography. We are encouraged to ask how the river defines the human relation to the world, how it reflects Spenser's view of the world as a geographical, historical, and, above all else, imaginative phenomenon. His riverine characters and settings have a mythical quality that makes them allegories of nature and humanity. In this, they figure both private and social myths simultaneously, so that Spenser is part of that culturally self-aware literature of the Renaissance in a way that, let us say, Milton, with his individual destiny and metaphysical concerns, is not.[35] Thus, Spenser's rivers reflect the essence of the poet's characteristically Renaissance secular humanism.

Spenser's earliest verse, his translations, reflects these preoccupations with cultural myths fixed in landscapes where the relation between nature, art, or civilization, and time is explored. Here, we see Spenser exposed to conventional forms where some of these ideas come together in Renaissance contexts: in Petrarch, du Bellay, and du Bartas, poets who made a cult of their national self-consciousness. The sonnets that he practices on in the *Complaynts* are, for the most part, meditations on time. Largely emblematic, they do not give much scope for the development either of setting or imagery, but in their brevity they capture most, but not all of the traditional features of the rivers that were brought into the Renaissance: the tower-capped river (usually the Roman Tiber) that rather ambiguously figures greatness and impermanence in worldly matters and the contrast between art and nature (*Rome* 3; *Bellay* 12); the use of particular rivers to suggest cultural history (*Rome* 31), or the more abstract notion of Time itself (*Bellay* 1); the association of the river (specifically the Nile) with primitive, amoral, fecund nature (*Vanity* 3); and the thematic links between the river, the poet, the enduring monument of poetry, or the poet's prophetic vision (often in the form of a river nymph in a dream vision; *Rome*, 31–32; *Bellay*, 1, 10, 11).

With all their differences in focus, these poéms illustrate the acutely self-conscious national identity of their authors; they exemplify a poetry which is intensely aware of the European landscape as a key to understanding the course of history, the possibility of redeeming nature through redemptive art, or grace. It is a poetry that looks at the broad sweep of time, the movement of culture from ancient Egypt and the East to western Europe and recent history. Their cultural myths are created with the uncomfortable awareness of the need for a myth of culture—that society is an act of faith and imagination for both the individual and the community. Obviously, the river is neither the only nor always the most important motif in these verses, but it is a recurrent one that Spenser found readily adaptable to his less emblematic, more complex exploration of these ideas in a British context.

It is clear, though, that these poets that we now look on as models of the cultural sensibility of the Renaissance provided Spenser with the abstract of many of his favorite themes, and their influence is quite plain in one of his earliest published poems, *The Ruines of Time*. Here, the theme of the ruins of Rome is adapted to the Roman ruins of Verulam.

Spenser's method of naturalizing his literary models is not unfamiliar to us: the local details from classical or Continental literature are given British analogues. The setting of *The Ruines of Time* is immediately recognizable and seems conventional enough, especially when read with Sonnet 1 or 10 of the *Visions of Bellay* in mind: "It chaunced me on day beside the shore/Of silver streaming *Thamesis* to bee,/Nigh where the goodly Verlame stood of yore,/ Of which there now remaines no memorie,/Nor anie little moniment to see' (11.1–5). However, Spenser's use of the prophetic river muse is far more complex than his models'; indeed complexity, moral ambiguity, and the obscurity (moral and otherwise) of history are to a large extent Spenser's theme in this poem. He adapts the conventional features of the complaint rather wittily, and the process begins with his treatment of the river nymph. Instead of a single-minded nymph rising from the river in a prophetic trance and delivering unambiguous truisms *de contemptu mundi*, which is the norm for the genre, Spenser's hysterical nymph suffers from an identity crisis, a kind of cultural amnesia that not only makes her pronouncements suspect, but also makes the reader wonder whether her forgetfulness conceals a morally uncertain past.[36] The ambiguity of the poem is introduced with the nymph (11.1–18). Also through her Spenser focuses the cultural dimension of his theme of literature as the moral force of history and the need for British literary tradition. In making his nymph a nameless amnesiac, Spenser draws on a fact of local geographical history, that the name

Verulam had been supplanted (as the town itself had been) by St. Albans. The nymph is a victim of history and neglect: "'Name have I none,' quoth she, 'nor anie being,/Bereft of both by Fates unjust decreeing'" (11.34–35).

Spenser implies that the uncertainty about her past results in our inability to learn the moral lessons of history. Thus, he has thrown the generic focus of the complaint off center; his subject is not the "vaine worlds glorie and unstedfast state" (1.43; whatever that phrase really means), but the need for cultural memory through literature. The river nymph provides the example (a paradoxical one) which clarifies the moral thrust of the poem by her contrast with the cultural, literary, and moral models of the poem, Sidney and Camden. Her anonymity arises from literary neglect, and it is this that distinguishes her from Sidney, who was himself a poet, as she herself points out:

> But me no man bewaileth, but in game,
> Ne sheddeth teares from lamentable eie:
> Nor anie lives that mentioneth my name
> To be remembered of posteritie. (11.162–65)

The obscurity of her past is contrasted with the light of historical learning which is immortalized in the *Britannia* and personified by Camden himself.[37] Her history has been allowed to drift into oblivion by all

> Save One that maugre fortunes injurie,
> And times decay, and envies cruell tort,
> Hath write my record in true-seeming sort.
> *Cambden* the nourice of antiquitie,
> And lanterne unto late succeeding age,
> To see the light of simple veritie,
> Buried in ruines, through the great outrage
> Of her owne people, led with warlike rage;
> *Cambden*, though time all moniments obscure,
> Yet thy just labors ever shall endure. (11.166–75)

Thus Spenser has more than naturalized the conventional river motif; he has mythologized his Verulam, made the reality of its history—the disappearance of the Roman town and the river that watered it—serve his literary and epideictic themes. The poem itself is not difficult to understand, but it is artful—the use Spenser has made of the river not only shows invention and imagination but it also shows us the poet's experiments in mythologizing his native landscape. The ambiguity with which he surrounds the river nymph becomes a characteristic feature of the Spenserian river. In using the river nymph to introduce the idea of the poem and act as foil to Sidney and Camden, Spenser has turned convention inward upon Britain and its literary needs, and upon himself, its river poet. The obscurity of the nymph reflects the historical and literary deficiency of Britain: she is, therefore, correctly described as the *genius loci*, and in this way Spenser uses her to define the world of his poem. In questioning the very nature and reality of the historical self-conceptions of nations and individuals, he adapts the river, in its traditional role as the repository of national identity and social values, to point to their origins in literary tradition:

> . . . such as neither of themselves can sing.
> Nor yet are sung of others for reward,
> Die in obscure oblivion, as the thing
> Which never was. (11.344–47)

Spenser's more mature work stands out as radically more imaginative than either *The Shepheardes Calender* or *The Ruines of Time*. This is the natural result of the poet finding his own distinctive voice. For Spenser it involves, in part, the development of his own brand of allegorical myth—extended analogy having its basis in the mutable nature of a recognizable fallen world. As in lesser poets, it is possible to watch how Spenser works to blend the particulars of contemporary reality with the universals of archetypal experience: with ideas of love, concord, and chastity, for example. Spenser is always concerned with men, women, and social ideals of his own world, where the future will take shape and where cultural regeneration through the individual must begin. Thus, in creating his myth of Fairy Land, the cultural myth that pervades all of his work, not just *The Faerie Queene*, he turns away from the specifics of history and does not attempt to idealize aspects of the past or to defend the historicity or nobility of a particular period or figure. Rather, he is interested in mythic patterns relevant to our cultural development and understanding, some of which come to us as history. The elfin history that Guyon reads and the book of "Briton Moniments" that is given to Arthur (*Faerie Queene* 2.10) represent two different *kinds* of history, two kinds of experience and learning that must be understood by the heroes and, more important, by the reader. Aside from the narrative and allegorical aspects of this episode,

Spenser is concerned to show that not only must we learn from the particulars of history but we must also learn by transforming history, and from the myths which teach us what should be as well as what is.

Throughout his poetry we can observe Spenser in the act of transforming his world so that its reality can teach us something beyond the particular, and this is part of his allegorical process: to make the reader an allegorist. In his careful and systematic treatment of the river we can see that he recognized in it a motif that could be used to cross the border from the particular to the mythic and universal. In *Colin Clouts come home againe*, Book 4, canto 11 of *The Faerie Queene*, and the *Cantos of Mutabilitie*, he continues to use the river to define the world of his verse. But we see him turning away from its static form in the complaint to experiment in more versatile structural treatments of it that he found in Virgil and Ovid. In short, he recognized the greater formal range of the river in the hands of those poets who were able to turn the particulars of history and landscape into cultural myths by making them part of the fabric of this narrative art: from them he learned to look to the world for illustration of his thoughts.

In those works where Spenser makes significant use of the river, he examines the natural landscape for the mainsprings of concord in nature and for a paradigm for social order: the river is both idea and object. In responding to these more important influences, though, Spenser adapts the river to his own personal and cultural myth as it is manifest in the idea of concord. The river, providing a composite image of the inclination in nature toward concord, imposes a myth on landscape which is private and public, and "natural," moral mythic and historical.

From Virgil and Ovid Spenser acquired a narrative facility which is very evident in his use of the river. As we will see, he learned to integrate the motif into the narrative in a way that forces the reader to interpret its relation to the poem as a whole. The river literally acts as an agent of concord joining, in the case of *Colin Clout* for example, the diverse but interrelated themes of love, friendship, and courtesy, the world of the shepherds, and that of the English court. As in *The Ruines of Time*, the reader must identify the relevance of the river motif for, in this case, the story of Colin Clout's return to his rustic society of shepherds. In the process, one is required to examine the river tale and is led to an understanding of the origins in nature of the two societies whose comparison constitutes the essence of the poem. Thus, while Spenser's Mulla and Bregog offer a mythological rather than historical setting, the poet still has on eye on England and its social order.

In each of these three later works, then, Spenser leaves the river episodes' links with the whole implied rather than stated,[38] and this structural strategem is part of Spenser's theme, one way that he instructs his reader. We see his mature ability to use the motif in this way in *Colin Clouts come home againe*, a poem that seems to fall into two parts (thematically, one concerned with friendship, and one with love; structurally, into an Irish and an English section) and a seemingly irrelevant river song. Spenser not only asks us to analyze the relation between these three sections, but he also uses the river episode to provide an essential link between the other two parts. Thus, *Colin Clouts come home againe* works subtly from the theme of friendship and fellowship, which dominates the first half of the poem, to the hymn of love (11.835–94); the universal harmony, or concord, which is common to both love and friendship is figured in one form in the river digression. In the first half Spenser develops his ideas through contrasts and negative examples. Fellowship in the face of hardship in Ireland contrasts with sumptuousness and strife in England, the one's *otium* with the other's *negotium*. As is often the case, Spenser's Neoplatonic themes are worked out primarily in scenes which are disarmingly unpretentious or mundane. Nevertheless, based as they are in the physical world, they adumbrate larger themes about social order, and in this they reflect Spenser's characteristically Renaissance interest in the ideals which are embodied in our institutions. As he develops the link between friendship and love through the contrast between Irish harmony and English discord, he digresses on the simple tale of a personified geography: the contours of the local topography—the inevitable confluence of two rivers which would seem to flow apart, rather than together—are presented in terms of human love overcoming social conventions which threaten to prevent its consummation. The tale tells how, despite the paternal topography, even as old Mole "warily still watch[es] which way she went," the two young rivers, Mulla and Bregog, manage at last to share the same bed. Notwithstanding the attempts to keep them apart and Bregog's eventual annihilation, we learn that "love will not be drawn, but must be ledde" (1.129).

The shepherd's simple tale is without pretension, although it is ostentatious in its self-consciously digressive placement. Colin's technique is to *impose* a human, moral order on the local landscape.

However, later in the poem a similar lesson on love is told, but it is transformed by the divine fury that inspires Colin to what is essentially a hymn to love. Here, in a higher style, we are shown that same principle of universal attraction. But the poet possessed has a different technique, and *draws* on the natural landscape for the moral order of human affairs. Thus, he explains love's power and importance in society in terms of geographical and elemental impulses, thereby inverting the strategy used in the river georgic:

> For by this powre the world was made of yore,
> And all that therein wondrous doth appeare,
> For how should else things so far from attone
> And so great enemies as of them bee,
> Be ever drawne together into one,
> And taught in such accordance to agree?
> Through him the cold began to covet heat,
> And water fire; the light to mount on hie,
> And th'heavie downe to peize. (11.841–48)

The two songs show us the power of love from two contrasting perspectives, one illuminating the other. The shepherd who saw nature (or love) in human terms reveals his diviner gift when he can see humanity in terms of nature; the reader who perceives the relation between Colin's georgic and divine verses is able to look on the humble world of Spenser's pastoral and apprehend its profounder meaning for the court and English society. Colin's two songs, then, explain the world of the poem and relate directly to its contrasting themes of love and its corruption in Ireland and England; the link is made clearest when Lucida justifies Rosalinda's feelings: "Or who with blame can justly her upbraid,/For loving not? For who can love compell?" (11.913–14).

In the river tale of *Colin Clout* Spenser gives us a *manifestation* of his idea of concord in the physical world; the Neoplatonic hymn teaches us how to *interpret* that tale and how to realize our ideal vision in the material world. For Spenser, to read the river is to examine one's own understanding of the worlds, and as in Bacon, this is a process which draws simultaneously on divine and natural sources. Spenser's Neoplatonic rivers always descend finally to the precincts of the city and human society, just as *Colin Clout* turns in upon the themes of English society and the need to recognize the concord that binds humanity together. In terms of the narrative structure, Colin's song about Mulla and Bregog is presented as an act of friendship and a manifestation of pastoral community (see, for example, 1.96), and so it naturally brings together the themes of friendship, love, and social order that are adumbrated in Colin's verses themselves.

Spenser's use of the river epyllion to define the nature and unity of the poem is both thematic and structural, as Virgil's use of the motif is in the fourth *Georgic*. For both, but perhaps more obviously for Spenser, the appeal of the river derives first of all from the fact that it seems to capture the author's sense of nature, and second, from its demonstrated usefulness as a literary motif. The two are, of course, closely related: our understanding of nature closely resembles our understanding of literature. In fact, Spenser uses the river epyllion to bring literature and nature together and into each other's service. His success in using the river in this way is perhaps most obvious in the *Cantos of Mutabilitie*, where Nature, post-lapsarian mutability, and the redemption of nature are Spenser's themes. The epyllion relating Molanna's plight contributes essential information about the nature of fallen nature. Here too, the tale is conspicuously digressive. Moreover, its relevance for the story of Mutabilitie is not obvious, although the link between Nature in the abstract, in the form of Dame Nature, and the geographical nature of the epyllion is perhaps evident enough. What is more important, though, is the way in which the poet meditates on physical geography to clarify his ideas about time and nature in the canto as a whole. The myths of Actaeon and Diana, and Astraea are revised and adapted to the geography around Arlo Hill. Through myth, then, the landscape is given meaning: Molanna is first of all an ideal landscape, a classical *locus amoenus* which, in the Golden Age, the gods visited "for pleasure and for rest:"

> For, first, she springs out of two marble Rocks,
>   On which, a grove of Oakes high mounted growes,
>   That as a girlond seemes to deck the locks,
>   Of som faire Bride, brought forth with pompous showes
>   Out of her bowre, that many flowers strowes;
>   So, through the flowry Dales she tumbling downe,
>   Through many woods, and shady coverts flowes
>   (That on each side her silver channell crowne)
> Till to the Plaine she come, whose Valleyes shee doth drowne.
>
> (7.6.41)

Later, we empathize with Molanna's very human temptation and fall, but we understand their significance because of her natural geography, altered but not changed from its first estate.

Thus, we can see that Molanna is truly a sister of Mulla; both are driven by imperceptible, subterranean impulses which have their origins in nature itself. So it is that, because of her attraction to Fanchin, Molanna, enticed by Dan Faunus's "Queen-Apples, and red cherries from the tree," deceives Diana, and is both physically and morally corrupted. Diana-Astraea never returns to her fair banks; the Golden Age is ended, the pastoral beauty defaced, and its serenity broken by Irish wolves and thieves. The landscape, still incomparably beautiful, it should be noted, unites dimensions of mythic geography and human reality. The relation between the two is thus set forth in terms of a literary topography, and we understand the world of Spenser's verse in terms of a marriage between myth and landscape.

The tale of Molanna's corruption is essential to the more metaphysical history of Mutabilitie's attack on Olympus. Faunus and Molanna are also overreachers, though on a humbler scale than the bold Titaness. Moreover, they tell us more about nature than Mutabilitie possibly can, and illustrate Dame Nature's verdict as words alone cannot; again, we require the physical manifestation which illustrates the intellectual ideas of Spenser's verse. In their punishment we perceive the full range of mutability in nature. And, as William Blissett says, "nature intervenes" in their punishment "to limit the consequences of the fall to suffering and discomfort, not annihilation."[39] However, the true difference between immutable and mutable, pre- and postlapsarian nature can only be seen in the story of Molanna. Mutabilitie herself cannot tell us of it, since she is, by nature (if you will), postlapsarian and likewise, the fallen reader can perceive it only dimly in the divine judgment of Dame Nature when she pronounces that things "are not changed from their first estate" (7.7.58). Thus for Spenser, the nature of fallen nature is best understood by a story based in the physical world; there we can perceive the true degree of change in the world, and that change is measured in terms of the disfigured but still beautiful and fruitful Molanna, bedded at last with beloved Fanchin as she had wished. The nymph gives us a new perspective on the harridan Mutabilitie; it is her story that finally humbles that bully for the reader and that teaches the full extent of grace in nature.

The rivers of *Mutabilitie* also draw on both divine and mundane sources. Here too Spenser's thoughts are on the workings of society, in the sense that he explores the limits of change and the possibilities for renewal in nature, and therefore the potential for creating an order which will resist the effects of time. The poet draws his sources together by taking the knowledge that goes beyond the individual's experience—the vision of Olympus allowed the Orphic poet—and embodying it in the physical landscape where it can be better apprehended and where the mythic vision is, in fact, realized. In this way, through the river episode, Spenser brings the visionary and the earthly realms nearer together. Thus, his brazen Ireland is "enamel'd o're" with a mythic recollection of a golden age, and the resultant vision shows Mutabilitie for what she really is and corrects our weakened and fallen judgment and that of Elizabeth's court.

The rivers of *The Ruines of Time*, *Colin Clouts come home againe*, and the *Cantos of Mutabilitie* do more than demonstrate Spenser's growing poetic skill and his ability to rival classical authors in making myths of landscape. He saw in them the essence of the poet's art as it is centered in the relation between the imagination and the world. As I have tried to suggest in my Introduction, the poet's objective is to realize his poetic vision in the world, to make the world conform to what he sees in his mind's eye. For Spenser this is the very basis of the unique allegorical technique that *is* his poetic, and there can be little doubt that in the rivers of the world he saw a way of approaching the rivers of the mind: in recapitulating one another they gave the poet and the reader he tried to instruct a unique route to travel from the one to the other. The rivers were part of objective, material reality, to be named and described, and yet inexplicably, mysteriously, they testified to a divine influence identifiable with transcendent ideas of concord, grace, and love. The development of Spenser's poetry would suggest that he felt that, perhaps by periodically using the rivers as a matrix for his art, he might achieve for his reader that perfect correspondence between idea and object that is the overriding analogy of all poetry. This correspondence is the poetic objective of Spenser's allegory: Isabel MacCaffrey speaks of it in terms very much like those which we have been using to discuss the relation between physical geography and myths of landscape. His allegory addresses the basic epistemological problems about the relation between knowledge and the material world. "Allegorical fictions develop," she says, "within a 'mental space' which is analogically related to the spaces realizing God's 'great idea,' the macrocosmic spaces of the universe." Allegory is a process by which the imagination "'makes' the object it perceives . . . by making sense of it, understanding and locating it. This process can occur because an intelligible 'outer' world and a sense-making 'inner' world are aspects of a single divinely-designed universe.''[40] If we see allegory, or more generally a work of the poetic imagination, as a process of making or unravelling this analogy, as a peripeteia between the realms of idea and material reality, we can see the river *topos* as one of the points where that correspondence is located, where the imagined world and the real world are reflected and their images are identical.[41]

Such a view of the river is not just a matter of individual poetic whim; another aspect of nature would not serve quite as well. As we have seen, the writers of the Renaissance, like their cultural antecedents, saw something unique in the river. So too did Spenser; his thoughts seem to coincide with those of Pierre de la Primaudaye (quoted above). He too seemed to see God's divine spirit as extraordinarily present in the river. For this reason, as an object in nature worked on by the interpretive imaginative faculty, it would seem to reward our study with understanding and insight.

With such an unusual place in the Renaissance myth-making imagination, and particularly in Spenser's poetic development, it is appropriate that the river should assume an important role in the poet's most comprehensive cultural myth, *The Faerie Queene*. And judging from what we have said about Spenser's other work, it is not surprising that it should receive its most coherent thematic and formal treatment in the Book of Friendship. Its appearance in Book 4, canto 11, in the extended tale of the marriage of the Thames and the Medway, is a unique episode in *The Faerie Queene*: in it the European landscape and the elements of nature become animated, enter the otherwise heroic narrative as nowhere else in the epic. Historical and mythic geography, physical and metaphysical nature come together here in a dance of the elements that is at once cosmic, prophetic, and historical in scope. That is, the "mental space" that Coleridge describes as the world of *The Faerie Queene* and that MacCaffrey speaks of as the allegorist's imagination, merges for once with our physical, historical world, and we can see the mythic reality of Spenser's Fairy Land in terms of a knowable geographic framework.

It is as though Spenser is trying to embody in this one episode the idea of his imaginative process, in order to make us see and believe in his vision. Spenser does tell us about his allegorical poetic. In the proem to the second book, Spenser admits that his "history" will by some be judged a "painted forgery,/Rather then matter of just memory,/Sith none, that breatheth living aire, does know,/Where is that happy land of Faery." He argues that the lands which we perceive only with our senses are not the only ones: "Why then should witlesse man so much misweene/That nothing is, but that which he hath seene?" Fairy Land is one of these "other worlds" forged anew from nature and extant more in the mind than in any discernible physical dimension, although, as he goes on to say:

Of Faerie lond yet if he more inquire,
　By certaine signes here set in sundry place
　He may it finde; ne let him then admire,
　But yield his sense to be too blunt and bace.

Thus, this mirror of Elizabeth's realm is variously one of myth, history, and the senses, informed by divine and material sources. Like the world of Molanna and Mulla, it is the incarnation of a mythical and imaginary realm, and in Book 4, canto 11, these "certaine signes" blaze forth all at once into recognition.

Like other theorists and poets, Spenser saw his art as drawing from the divine intellect and from the senses. It is clear throughout *The Faerie Queene* that he, like Primaudaye, felt that the river represents this dual inheritance. Throughout the work we encounter many rivers and their offspring, in the form of wells, springs, and unnamed rills of various sizes. However, they tend to be either emphatically of nature's (or history's) creative and destructive cycle—amoral, fertile, pagan in character, such as the monster spawning Nile of 1.1.21—or they tend to be divine waters, associated with redemption, Christian virtues (especially chastity), grace, and spiritual regeneration. These adumbrate a cycle of spiritual death and regeneration which is analogous to the mythic cycle of the river in physical nature, and we see one example in the "streame of balme" that restores the Red Crosse Knight in his combat with the dragon (1.11.48). This kind of divine river whose influence is invisibly present in our world is also suggested by Guyon's name, which is also the name of the river of Paradise which, we have seen, was associated with temperance. In him, at least potentially, is the presence of that virtue once manifested in the waters of Paradise.[42]

Spenser tells us quite explicitly of these two kinds of river and how they represent two kinds of nature in 2.2.5–7. Here the Palmer explains to Guyon (and the reader) the "secret vertues [that] are infusd/In every fountain"; one sort is associated with Dame Nature's "fruitfull pap" and the other is a "gift of later grace" and is able to repair fallen nature. Mythically, before the fall, these two aspects of the river would have been one as in the exegetical descriptions of Paradise, in whose rivers natural and spiritual virtues were joined. In Spenser's work the rivers of nature and of grace represent the two extremes of his mythic world, and they help to delineate the moral and natural landscapes of *The Faerie Queene*. Thus they provide a dominant image in which he can figure his poetic goals. In the marriage of the Thames and the Medway he brings these two extremes together, showing us the moral force of concord working through the natural and historical cycles of the rivers of geography. In this we can see his successful treatment of a theme that occupied river poets since the beginning of the Christian tradition.

As Spenser makes quite clear in the Palmer's speech, his rivers represent what in our fallen world are regarded as opposites but what should be and once were united: spiritual and material nature. The marriage of the Thames and the Medway can be seen then as a massive image of *concordia discors*. It is in many ways a unique episode in *The Faerie Queene*, but like other of Spenser's rivers, it stands out as having a conspicuously oblique relation to the rest of the work. As in the other river episodes, the reader is expected to engage the text critically in order to help integrate the episode into the larger work; that is, to participate in the process of bringing *concordia discors*. Ultimately, then, the episode is consistent with the rest of the work and its allegory, and the Spenserian reader can understand it "by certaine signes." The rivers' marriage has a climactic quality to it. It is, as it were, the culmination of the rivers of *The Faerie Queene*, the coming together of one strand of images in the work. The episode functions like the *theomochia* of the *Iliad*, and Spenser probably expected us to see it in that light. As in the *Iliad*, we encounter numerous rivers in our travels through the world of *The Faerie Queene*. In Book 2 the Palmer alerts us and Guyon to their nature, and the rivers that we meet along the way conform to one of the two models he describes. Other characters cross and recross waters; we are generally aware that their world is well watered. Most of these streams are anonymous, though: Spenser is saving the effect of naming for the culminating episode in Book 4. Gradually the major characters are drawn, like the rivers themselves, to the strand, where we see them come together in confluence for the marriage fête. The rivers and the sea have a magnetic attraction for the characters of *The Faerie Queene*; there, Spenser's heroes invariably have psychologically and morally significant encounters which amount to symbolic rites of passage. Thus, in the course of *The Faerie Queene* we learn to associate the rivers with significant symbolic moments in the history of that world and come to expect big things of them.

From this largely anonymous river-crossed landscape of *The Faerie Queene*, the rivers of the world suddenly burst forth in a fluid symbol of concord and diversity in nature. We have seen the device of harmonizing many rivers in song and in epic catalogue used to similar effect by Leland as well as by Virgil. Although the episode is not the logical culmination of narrative threads involving the major participants, the Thames and the Medway, it is unmistakably consistent with the movement of the rest of the work. Its rightness is poetic, natural, and imaginative, rather than logical, narrative, or historical. In this sense alone it validates the poetic mode of the allegorist. The narrative links through the histories of Florimell, Proteus, and Marinell are weak and do not justify a river marriage; but the unseen moral, psychological, and allegorical links—the force of concord, the union of opposites (sexual and elemental), the psychological breaking of resistance to love, the natural and spiritual influences that are represented by the rivers—make it as "natural" and inevitable as the union of Mulla and Bregog.

Spenser is able to use the epithalamic river procession and the reconciliation of elemental opposites suggested by Marinell and Florimell to illuminate the larger themes that are suggested in *The Faerie Queene*, particularly in Book 4. Here too his method of calculated incongruity helps us to understand what lies behind his narrative in this book. As he does elsewhere in *The Faerie Queene*, Spenser is creating a cultural myth which looks at the relation of public and private virtues to the workings of society, keeping as always one eye on the celestial order, and one on the world. Even his courtly romances address the realities of the political scientist, and if, as he says,

> The rugged forhead that with grave foresight
>   Welds kingdomes causes, and affaires of state,
>   My looser rimes (I wote) doth sharply wite,
>   For praising love, as I have done of late
>   And magnifying lovers deare debate (4, proem 1)

the marriage, by bringing forth the nation-founding rivers in a political geography, may be Spenser's attempt to illustrate more clearly how "kingdomes causes" and the praise of love are intellectually compatible.

In rerouting the rivers of the world and having them all harmoniously attendant on Thames and Medway and in so doing imposing a direction on history, Spenser magnifies the river's potential as a *topos* of concord as we have seen it in Hall, Bryskett, and Camden. Spenser's use of the motif remains very close to Camden's own conception of the "fide concordia sancta"; the confluence of waters in Book 4 brings together lovers, nations, and historical epochs, turning the world into a creative torrent. It is a political cosmography in which the principles of natural and human order are the same. As we descend beneath the waters with Marinell, we enter a cavernous source of all rivers vastly more capacious than that entered by Ergasto in the *Arcadia*, one that seems to be as large as the entire world, and in which we perceive the world's mythic origins and creative order. But it is important to note that the canto presents the watery world within the context of a transforming imagination; it *seems* commensurate with the world, but in fact it is contained, encompassed within Proteus's hall beneath the waters, restrained by a "more decent order tame." Spenser is careful to stress that the "banquet" takes place within the hall: it is not simply the subterranean mirror of our own world—the pageant transpires in a quintessential dimension while "halfe mortall" Marinell "walkt abrode" waiting for his mother. Thus, a greater art holds the torrential forces within its bounds, and this, coupled with Spenser's very compact verse in these stanzas, makes the vast pageant very crowded and busy.

It also contributes to the sense that, in all its magnificence, the river pageant is primarily an *image* of concord in nature. And, as in *Colin Clouts come home againe*, it is through the rivers that we see that behind love and friendship is a common natural impulse which in Book 4 Spenser defines as concord. Book 4, then, is not so much the book of friendship, or the continuation of the themes of love in Book 3, as it is a book of concord, subsuming the two. Moreover, it is a characteristically Spenserian vision of concord: it is the reconciliation of the discordant forces of love and hate, the "Mother of blessed *Peace* and Friendship trew" (10. 34).

Throughout the book Spenser returns to this theme. Its primary concern is to extinguish the sparks of discord so that love and friendship can be celebrated in the river marriage—the spirit of Ate, or discord, that opens the book, must yield to that of concord, as it is defined in canto 10.[43] Whether Spenser is dealing with lovers or friends (he alternates between the two much as he does in *Colin Clout*), common to both themes is the threat of discord and the bond of concord. And each of the three kinds of love that he explores here (see 4.9.1) is achieved or strengthened only by overcoming some kind of discordant resistance or impediment, either to friendship as in the case of Cambell and Triamond, or to love as in the case of virtually all the many lovers of Book 4, but most pertinently Britomart and Artegall, Marinell and Florimell, and Medway and Thames. Each episode in Book 4 is dominated either by Ate or Concord, who serve as touchstones testing the quality of the love or friendship, or showing the falseness of the hateful or invidious.

Life in *The Faerie Queene* is not an easy matter; there is little rest and unceasing frustration in the pursuit of ideals; where there is love, it is always troubled by misunderstanding, ignorance, inner fear or weakness, or a previous commitment. No virtuous couple can reach an understanding for long enough to consummate their love, to say nothing of getting married, although the less virtuous engage in all sorts of casual affairs which are not to be mistaken as concordant or loving. The marriage of Medway and Thames, which itself has been long in the planning, must suffice for them all; it does so in very specific ways for Marinell and Florimell by providing the narrative framework for their sudden accord. The rivers' marriage, then, is the image of concord that Spenser cannot depict through the actions of his characters because they would be too local and symbolically inadequate. No human manifestation of the theme can capture the mythic dimension of the ideals pursued by these lovers, as Spenser realized when he excised the androgynous union of Amoret and Scudamour. Spenser wisely chooses instead to show us the strength of this concordant impulse which drives his characters and makes them overcome external and internal obstacles. He uses the rivers to suggest its mythic dimension and has their marriage provide the occasion and setting for the watering of Marinell's heart with ruth and love, although he stops short of marrying the two mortal lovers. But here, and in the larger context as well, the rivers adumbrate the meandering but certain course of the several knights and their ladies, and their eventual union, and extend the promise of success despite the fact that the narrative topography usually has them going, like rivers, in different directions.

The Faerie Queene—indeed all of Spenser's verse—presents

something of a mundane comedy: an expansive, not very clear view of immanent social order being worked out in the same way that natural forces inevitably find their true paths and eventual harmony. If Spenser's vision of social order is not immediately clear, it is because it is quite literally adumbrated. The union of Arthur and Gloriana, Artegall and Britomart, Amoret and Scudamour, Marinell and Florimell, the friendly accord between countless knights, the vision of social harmony in the New Jerusalem and Cleopolis, are all but shadowed forth and can only be discerned (in Book 4) in the shadows cast by the ideal vision of Concord and perfect androgynous unity presiding over balanced opposition in Venus's Temple, and by its material, mundane version presented in the marriage of Thames and Medway. Perfect harmony in human affairs lies somewhere between these two visions of concord, just as in *Colin Clout* the idealized potential of Elizabeth's court is adumbrated by Colin's song of Mulla and Bregog and his paean on love, and in *Mutabilitie*, constancy in nature is figured in the *words* of Nature and the *reality* of Molanna.

We are forced, then, to bring together the dark conceit of Venus's Temple and the image of concord in nature in the rivers.[44] This process itself is one which imposes order on the disparate parts of the poem, and in perceiving their relationship one apprehends the presence of the ideal in the material world. Such is the perception that is granted Colin Clout; it is a godlike, ordering vision of reality: "None but a god or godlike man" (4.2.1) such as Orpheus can bring concord from discord in this way. The "godlike man" can, like Venus, command the waters and harmonize nature (4.10.44), and that shaping vision is precisely what is represented in the river pageant: the poet's ability to bring nature and myth, real and ideal, together.

This design has a more particular application as well. The rivers of the pageant figure a political geography, so that, as in the *Britannia*, there is a reciprocity between nature and human history which culminates in England. The marriage of the English rivers, the recalcitrant Medway and persistent Thames, suggests the ordering of the protean element, as they agree to have their banquet in that elusive god's house. Shakespeare creates a similar sort of mythic couple in Oberon and Titania, but he chooses to leave any historical frame of reference out of their characters. Spenser, however, having the entire course of history in mind, reaches back to the elemental origins of civilization to give direction and unity to its development. As in *Mutabilitie*, he returns to the hidden sources of our memory to shape his prophetic vision:

> Helpe therefore, O thou sacred imp of *Jove*,
>   The noursling of Dame *Memorie* his deare,
>   To whom those rolles, layd up in heaven above,
>   And records of antiquitie appeare,
>   To which no wit of man may comen neare. (4.11.10)

The image of the rivers of time, confluent in Thames and Medway, then, is a return to the beginning of time (and history, its recorded form), as well as a projection of its fulfillment, and as such, it presents history in terms of cosmography. Led by the elemental gods Neptune and Amphitrite and their brood, and followed first by the aquatic founders of nations—Albion and Inachus among them—and by Ocean and Tethys who "both sea and land possest" and then by the famous rivers associated with successive periods of human history, the procession brings the flow of history forward in one continuous, unbroken stream—one water with a common source and outlet:

> But what doe I their names seeke to reherse,
>   Which all the world have with their issue fild?
>   How can they all in this so narrow verse
>   Contayned be, and in small compasse hild?
>   Let them record them, that are better skild,
>   And know the moniments of passed age:
>   Onley what needeth, shall be here fulfild,
>   T'express some part of that great equipage,
> Which from great *Neptune* do derive their parentage. (4.11.17)

The wedding procession begins with Neptune and ends with the bride and groom, and Thames and Medway, once they are joined in geography, work their way back to the neptunian sea. Hexameral myth is, therefore, recapitulated in historical geography and the social ideal of marriage. As we move from Neptune to the sea, myth and reality correspond. Through the imaginative landscape history is presented in terms of the eternal present, within which, however, there is a loose but unmistakable chronology, as the rivers of history, the Nile, Scamander, Tiber, and newfound "Oranochy," follow in procession behind the elemental waters and nation-founders. The pageant is thus designed to show how nature is realized in history, just as the episode as a whole is meant to provide an image of the ordering impulse based in nature.

One empire succeeds another until we reach the paragons of the present age and the realm defined by Tame and Isis. The refinement of history continues as these rivers figure more and more clearly the images of human perfection of nature, with tower-capped Tame, bent beneath the burden of Oxford, appearing as the emblematic city-founder and the union of art and nature. The lesser rivers whirl obsequiously around the wedding party and outline a unifying order which is at once geographic and historical. The attendants on the wedding party are the rivers which join the Thames south of Reading before it reaches the Medway, and they are presented in the order that Harrison gives them in his eleventh chapter. Then, after brief mention of Thames's two greatest rivals dividing the kingdom, the Severn and Humber, Spenser begins his catalogue in the west, as Camden does, and spirals east and north, and then south along the west coast to the Dee and Conway. In the process of outlining the country in this way, he hints at its history and cultural development by mentioning historical and topographical details such as the tin mines on the Dart, the forests on the banks of the Rother, and the violent history associated with the Humber. As in Camden's *Britannia*, the rivers seem to determine the course of history.

Despite the undercurrents of an erratic and troubled history, the dominant image of the procession is of an ongoing, perfected order in which terrestrial nature and divine art become one and eclipse the vicissitudes of human affairs. Unity is the most important aspect of this view of history: these are all one water flowing from one source; it is a family event. Time and age here are arbitrary ideas, contrivances of the human imagination—the Orinoco seems younger than the Nile because it is 'but knowen late." Out of the framework of our ordering intellect they are all ageless; it is by virtue of the shaping imagination that some seem older than others. The history that these rivers outline is one in which age and youth are complementary: the wisdom of the past is renewed by the strength of the present, so that if old Tame stoops beneath his towers, his son Thames is an image of age and youth, art and nature combined:

> But he their sonne full fresh and jolly was,
>> All decked in a robe of watchet hew,
>> On which the waves, glittering like Christall glas,

So cunningly enwoven were, that few
Could weenen, whether they were false or trew.
And on his head like to a Coronet
He wore, that seemed strange to common vew,
In which were many towres and castles set,
    That it compast round as with a golden fret . . .

With such an one was Thamis beautifide;
    That was to weet the famous Troynovant,
In which her kingdomes throne is chiefly resiant. (4.11.27–28)

Thames is his father: has his history and wisdom, while also having the strength of eternal youth. The description recalls the Renaissance commonplace that "if old men were strong, and young men were wise,/There would be a new paradise."

This image of self-renewing time is also an image of the artist as he recreates from the past; as such, it is a figure of human potential. It is also, and more obviously, the dominant national image, an emblem of society's capacity for self-renewal and redemption through grace—a secular humanist's emblem of the celestial city. The marriage of Thames and Medway, then, promises the fulfillment of this potential, the bringing together of the ideal in the real, of the celestial in the mundane. They are themselves opposites lately reconciled. Thus, if Thames, bearing his urban garland and accompanied by retainers from every county of his domain, is a rather political figure, he is complemented by his bride. Paler and more celestial than he, she too has a cunning artifice about her:

Then came the Bride, the lovely *Medua* came,
    Clad in vesture of unknowen geare,
    And uncouth fashion, yet her well became;
    That seem'd like silver, sprinckled here and theare
    With glittering spangs, that did like starres appeare,
    And wav'd upon, like water Chamelot,
    To hide the metall, which yet every where
    Bewrayed it selfe, to let men plainly wot,
    It was no mortall worke, that seem'd and yet was not. (4.11.45)

She is distinctly otherworldly, with the beauty of an Aurora offering a "new spring," and her attendants, the fifty mythical nereides, continue her association with divine art. They return us to the cosmogonic dimension which began the procession, to Hesiod and the *Theogony*, and the realm of the muses and the divine fury, which enables the poet to recreate the order of the universe.

Medway and her nymphs, all deriving from their celestial sources, suggest both the wisdom of a divinity and the powers of the poet. The marriage of Thames and Medway, then, brings together on a grand scale the English rivers and the ancient muses, a timeless union of past and present, and the fulfillment of cultural myths, and in the bride and groom is the promise of the marriage of heaven and earth, and an eternal spring. We soon see the effects of their redemptive union in Florimell's release, after seven wintry months, from Proteus's hall, in the rejuvenation of Marinell by her love, and in the promise of the fertile union of the sea and land.

For the Renaissance, memory is the faculty that serves the poet.[45] As Spenser often reminds us in this canto, it is memory, or Clio, that he relies on in creating this river pageant. In a unique way, then, Spenser's art is in its purest form here, for he deals directly with the basic elements of his craft to write about memory itself: he is trying to remember and to order memory, to think and to organize thought at the same time. His material is all the known world—all that he can call forth from his mind: time, knowledge, and his world are coextensive. In the purest, most ideal manner, he creates through memory, as the author of Genesis or Hesiod did. And what Spenser does in the marriage of the Thames and Medway is of exceptional importance for *The Faerie Queene* as a whole, for not only is it the fullest expression of the extent of its world, but it is also a projection of time itself. Spenser comes closest here to realizing his godlike, Orphic capacity, for from the elemental waters he creates a mythical order which has its own organic and evolving sense of unified time, emanating from the mind of the poet himself. It is a time based in nature and geography as well as the mind, and it affords endless potential without the threat of death or mutability: the rivers always carry the waters uninterruptedly from their source. Thus, it is a sense of time based on unity and concord, and is coherent as human affairs can never seem to be. The rivers, then, define a world of order and time in a way that radically alters our perception of Fairy Land. It becomes recognizable, and its potential becomes less remote. The existence of these harried knights and ladies has a renewed meaning and sense of purpose, despite its frustrations; we see the promised end, and they are assimilated into it even as they disappear on yet another quest. What Spenser has done is to recreate geography according to his own myth as all world images and image-makers must strive to do. He has absorbed his heroes into the landscape by making them a part of that same myth of the rivers, products of the same unified imagination and the same order. By naming his world here, he gives a sudden substantiality to his struggling heroes and their ideals.

Characteristically, then, Spenser's landscapes subsume history in what we have called perceptual myths—imaginative constructs which organize the meaning of landscape. In this he recreates and revitalizes rather than creates anew; these are ordering devices which he has assimilated from historians, philosophers, and poets. His method is very much of the age. For this reason, their physical reality seems to merge with their literary ideality. The *Prothalamion*, for example, which seems so characteristically Spenserian, is also one of his most conventional works, and this tells us something about the poet's ability to rewrite history. Here again he marries perceptual myths of landscape and the physical topography to recreate his poetic world. It is this treatment of the rivers of the poem that makes it both Spenserian and conventional.

The river motif has always been recognized as flowing through the center of this poem, and its gently ambiguous murmurings as setting its tone. Interestingly, Spenser's adaptation of the swan's passage downstream, so completely different as it is from the treatment of the rivers in *Mutabilitie*, for example, reveals his continuing interest in the rivers of the historians and topographers, for the *Prothalamion* is almost identical in design to Leland's *Cygnea Cantio*, Camden's *de Connubio*, and Vallan's *A Tale of Two Swannes*. His choice of form for the spousal verses reflects his historical preoccupations around the time that he was completing the second part of *The Faerie Queene*. But whatever form he adapted for his rivers, he always used them to define the nature and potential of the world of his verse, imposing his intellectual ideals on the mutable and human landscape. While in Book 4 of *The Faerie Queene* the river marriage is the surrogate for that of Marinell and Florimell, the occasional nature of the *Prothalamion* reverses this format, and the marriage of the daughters of the Earl of Worcester expands and realizes the themes which are only implied by the confluence of the Lee and Thames.

Here too, however, the rivers suggest the potential for the redemption of nature through love and concord, and the possibility of arresting the effects of time, suggested in the refrain, "Sweet *Themmes* runne softly, till I end my song," through art. Spenser continues to develop the perceptual myths of his earlier work, and he is concerned with the problems of nature dominated by time, and the power of the social arts to embrace nature. The public world of the Thames, with its vanities and mutability, is described with conventional ambiguity as we approach it in the company of the cygnet-brides:

> There when they came, whereas those bricky towres,
> The which on *Themmes* brode aged backe doe ryde,
> Where now the studious Lawyers have their bowers,
> There whylome wont the Templer Knights to byde,
> Till they decayd through pride. (132–36)

But it is, as the lines that follow remind us, the world which the poet and lover must cope with and transform—the prime matter for their arts. Against this changeable world the *carpe diem* of the bridal song gains meaning, for in it is the promise of renewal and the hope of escaping from time. Both art and love seek to eternize the moment of order and harmony; the vision of nature which informs each is that suggested by the confluence of the pastoral Lee, a landscape shaped by an idealized myth of nature's beauty, and the precarious Thames, distinguished as a setting for the social arts *par excellence*. The ideal of the one must join the reality of the other in the spirit of national concord.

As in *The Faerie Queene* and *The Ruines of Time*, Spenser here emphasizes that the active life must not exclude the contemplative, that of urban *negotium* must not neglect the renewing *otium* of the pastoral. The social arts must find sustenance for their ideals in nature itself. Thus, as the lords descend from the "high Towers" along the Thames to receive their brides as emissaries from that other realm, the urban landscape itself is transformed, and the ideals implicit in it are affirmed; it is restored from that state of travail to a poetic and heroic dimension that reconciles eternizing art and fickle nature. The lines echo the descriptive verse of Leland and Camden:

> From those high Towers, this noble Lord issuing,
> Like Radiant *Hesper* when his golden hayre
> In th'*Ocean* billowes he hath Bathed fayre,
> Descended to the Rivers open viewing,
> With a great traine ensuing.
> Above the rest were goodly to bee seene

Two gentle Knights of lovely face and feature
Beseeming well the bower of anie Queene,
With gifts of wit and ornaments of nature,
Fit for so goodly stature;
That like the twins of *Jove* they seem'd in sight
Which deck the Bauldricke of the Heavens bright.
They two forth pacing to the Rivers side,
Received those two faire Brides, their Loves delight,
Which at th' appointed tyde,
Each one did make his Bryde,
Against their Brydal day, which is not long;
    Sweete *Themmes* runne softly, till I end my Song. (163–80)

The rivers here, bringing together the occasional and historical and the poetic and idealized, mythologize the landscape and give it the values that make human actions significant. Instead of the confluence of two rivers, offering the possibility of earthly perfection, we have the image of an ideal social marriage uniting the worlds symbolized by the rivers. The public world of active life descends to embrace the pastoral *carpe diem*, and the war against time stops briefly to celebrate the timelessness of love. The sources of the two rivers which define these worlds are at once in literature and in nature, and they figure a universal concordant spirit that is common to both love and poetry. For Spenser, love and poetry achieve the same thing: they transform the world by example, and they help to realize nature's potential for perfection. They provide moments when myth is incarnate in a mutable reality. For him, the river brought these two themes of love and poetry together and signified the very purpose of his verse by its ability to suggest the entire prospect of history and the ambiguities of the human condition, as well as the ideals which inform human actions and attempts to impose social order on nature. Interestingly, then, this poem, so similar to its historical models, does not address the past in any detail; rather, it suggests the power to determine history through society. Thus, in a strange way the *carpe diem* of the *Prothalamion* is also an exhortation to heroic action, and a reminder that the bridal day is no longer than any other. These timeless moments of poetry and love are always won through diligent struggle with the chaotic, protean material of the fallen world. The descent to the Thames must be followed by a return to the embanked towers; behind the lightness of the "spousal verses" is the echo of those other historical river poems with their reminders of human affairs. If for Spenser allegory is a means of making his readers seek the meaning behind the signs of language and history, then the river seems to have been a means by which he could remind us that we must use our understanding to realize our cultural, mythic ideals.

PART THREE

THE ENGLISH RIVER POEM
IN THE SEVENTEENTH
CENTURY

Then pardon me, most dreaded Soveraigne,
  That from your selfe I doe this vertue bring,
  And to your selfe doe it returne againe:
  So from the Ocean all rivers spring,
  And tribute backe repay as to their King.
  Right so from you all goodly vertues well
  Into the rest, which round about you ring,
  Faire Lords and Ladies, which about you dwell,
And doe adorne your Court, where courtesies excell.
               (Spenser, *The Faerie Queene*)

V. Spenser's Legacy:
Rivers of Time and the Times

We see which way the stream of time doth run,
And are enforced from our most quiet there
By the rough torrents of occasion.   (Shakespeare, *2 Henry IV*)

And had the king of rivers blest those hills
With some small number of such pretty rills
As flow elsewhere, Arcadia had not seen
A sweeter plot of earth than this had been.
  For what offence this place was scanted so
Of springing waters, no record doth show.
                          (George Wither, *Faire-Virtue*)

AFTER SPENSER'S DEATH IN 1599, the use of the river motif or the
river poem to form an image of the nation and its poetic and address
themes of concord or unity became a literary fashion. The art of
national myth-making gained generic focus and momentum, probably because it was increasingly concerned with the past, though it
was not necessarily historical. Spenser helped to consolidate the
form and themes of the river poem and provided an example of how
to metamorphose the quotidian world into mythic forms meaningful
for both the individual and society. In this he helped give poets a
private voice for their public themes.
   Spenser did more than just consolidate or influence aspects of a
sub-genre of topographical verse. Through him the river became
associated with the age of Elizabeth and her poets, and served to
mark the distance travelled from the golden age of British poetry.
His poetry rerouted the development of the motif by turning it away
from the realm of historical topography, the domain presided over

by Camden, and into one of poetic convention, which over the next
two decades became increasingly devoid of topographical immediacy. In successfully rendering landscape into poetry, he began the
process by which his imitators eventually divorced the river from the
realm of nature altogether. And in locating their model in the poet
most firmly associated with Elizabeth, the poets who wrote about
the nation and its rivers recognized the strong social, latently
political concerns of Spenser's verse. As we will see, their work
assumes a greater political stridency than that of Spenser's
mythologized landscapes. We see in Spenser's influence on the
motif, then, an instance of his impact on English poetic sensibility. In
the hands of writers such as Drayton, Phineas Fletcher, William
Browne, and John Milton the river was a Spenserian device that
readily evoked a poetic legacy that he seemed to represent personally, but their treatment of the motif shows their own strong perception of the difference between their image of the nation and his. The
poetry of national concord begins to resonate with individual voices
of discord and the national landscape soon seems to be less able to
sustain a national myth.

Nevertheless, in 1600, the landscape was very articulate indeed. It
was a repository for literary topics to be plucked up by enterprising
poets, as we can see from the full title of Robert Allott's miscellany,
*England's Parnassus: or the Choysest Flowers of our Moderne Poets,
with their Poeticall Comparisons. Descriptions of Bewties, Person-
ages, Castles, Pallaces, Mountains, Groves, Seas, Springs, Rivers &c*
(1600): The miscellany was really a compendium of topics which are
more literary than topographical. The landscape of the new Parnassus had been discovered and surveyed; it was now subject to a
full-scale process of poetic strip-mining, and the result is that the
original landscape is hardly recognizable beneath the generally
artificial literature that it produced. It is striking how much of this
poetry that makes extensive use of the nation's rivers is both
Spenserian and preoccupied with the development of a poetry of
politics. If Spenser took some of the antiquarian interest out of
Leland's and Camden's rivers, he seems to have muddied their
political waters. From 1600 to James's death in 1625 we see national
self-consciousness reaching new extremes, and in the parallel development of the river, we see what might be called political allegory
taking the place once occupied by a tamer antiquarianism. Thus,
there is a politicization of the landscape, and to a large extent poets
seem to have thought that this was one way of either being Spense-

rian or using Spenser as a political point of reference, and there is irony in this when we think that Spenser's poetic objective was to transcend the particular.

This evolution is accelerated after Elizabeth's death, but there are poems from before 1603 which indicate not only how quickly Spenser's example acted to bring the river into the service of political allegory, but also how carefully some poets had thought about Spenser's poetic techniques. In the best of these poems the national rivers continue to resonate with an immediacy which combines both the poet's public and private voices, and joins the geographical and literary landscapes. One interesting but little known example of Elizabethan Spenserianism is E. W.'s *Thameseidos*, published in 1600 to celebrate Elizabeth's birthday. As an early example of Spenser's influence, it shows sensitivity to his ability to mythologize the landscape, and yet already, in the manner of its allegory, we see the course that the national river myths will take. E. W.'s subject matter is the story of the Thames and the Medway. His allegory focuses on the tale of the royal nymph, Isis (or Thamesis; he employs the contraction to draw on the connection with the Egyptian goddess). He uses the river and its turbulent relations with Neptune to explore a national image in both psychological and political dimensions. It is striking for its Spenserian qualities, particularly for its ability to shift from topographical description to personification and characterization, so that his nymphs, Isis and Medway, reflect his very subtle understanding of Spenser's treatment of Molanna and Mulla, and the psychology of timorous Florimell. The work could be described as a romantic epyllion that sets out self-consciously to establish its native, British literary and geographical contexts. We are shown an elaborate progress in which Isis's bed is borne from Nile, past Tiber, and on to Thames, and a series of Spenserian, ekphrastic *tableaux* presenting histories relating to the deity, and effectively naturalizing her (in slightly humbler form) with her full array of ancient and native connotations. The excessive artificiality of this preliminary progress recalls not only various of Spenser's allegorical processions, but also his tendency to draw attention to his river episodes: E. W.'s account of Thames and Medway seems to be the narrative story behind one of the *tableaux* depicted visually in the progress—the technique, what Rosalie Colie called "unmetaphoring," is common in the Renaissance.

Notwithstanding these Spenserian qualities, the *Thameseidos* projects a complex national image which is very different from

Spenser's: one identifying the national psychology with Florimell rather than Britomart. The mood that is suggested by this difference is increasingly evident throughout the seventeenth century in such figures as William Browne's own sadly abused British maid, Marina. E. W.'s subtle, and not always clear allegory must certainly have outraged Elizabeth had she known of the work. His dark conceit, working on several allegorical planes, tells of a lecherous Neptune's repeated efforts to deflower Thames. Although the obtrusive political allegory remains vague and unspecific, it probably refers to the Spanish scare of 1599, the year before the publication of the work. What is most interesting is E. W.'s ability to conflate political allegory with sexual psychology, thus adapting the public and private dimensions of the river; national images, as we have seen, have their psychological sides as well. E. W.'s Thames suggests the particular sensibility of the last years of the Virgin Queen's reign, for the fear of sex and death are one in his strange aquatic world. Consider, for example, Neptune's rhetoric of *carpe diem* as he pursues Thames; he will have his way with her as surely as the rivers flow to the sea, and as surely as youth succeeds to age:

> . . . do not bost
> But think, that as thy flood bears to my realme
> With an indefatigable course his stream,
> Returning nere again unto his head,
> So the hours, the day, the day thy youth will lead,
> Till on it death, or wretched age will sease.[1]

The image of the threatening forces of sexual outrage, death, and naval invasion, all implicit in the rhetoric and camouflaged in allegorical polyvalence, could hardly have entertained the sensitive queen. E. W.'s integration of allegorical planes here shows an intelligent, if perhaps excessively political, understanding of Spenserian writing.

At times E. W. seems to be writing a *roman à clef*, and the particular events and characters he has in mind pose a provocative mystery. For example, Thames's vulnerability seems to be exacerbated by a strange and morose shepherd who has just returned from Germany and who stands in brooding and detached disapprobation on the banks of the threatened river. The identity of the shepherd, to say nothing of the identity and meaning of other characters and events, piques our curiosity all the more because of the sensational nature of the narrative. The drama intensifies considerably in Book

3, when Neptune, in pursuing Thames, is distracted by an innocent bystander—nymph Medway—and callously satisfies his lust with her. The cold brutality of the episode gives it an intense and stark dramatic quality, although it is also part of E. W.'s political allegory. Medway's rape is compared to Drake's invasion of the Spanish coast, and she is frequently described in terms of maritime images. When Thames learns that Medway is no longer a virgin, Diana-like, she expels her from her company, and the pregnant helpless nymph is likened to "a great ship in the wide Ocean Seas/Whose stately Mast being spent, and proud sayles lost/Is by each Wave hither and thither tost."[2] The simile is appropriate at least in a general sense, since the royal fleet was customarily moored in the mouth of the Medway, at Rochester, where it could thwart any neptunian incursion up the Thames, which, in a way, the nymph does.

Throughout the *Thameseidos* E. W.'s characterization of his royal river nymph presents not a militant and sufficient noble maiden, but an insecure spinster nauseated by the thought of sex and age, both of which, for the Renaissance, are agents of mutability and the world's decline. Thus, in another episode Thames is once again being pursued by Neptune, and as he nears his victim, she turns, beholds his face, and in a swoon of fear and sexual revulsion, she envisions the swelling seas and appalled, cries out, "What is this world but vanity subject to change; full of inconstancie." In another Spenserian episode, Medway stealthily enters a secret cell beneath the river and there sees the portraits of British heroes. One chamber contains the mysterious prophecy of the nation's future in the form of a magical portrait of Elizabeth, but she cannot penetrate this chamber because she is impure. An element of enchantment surrounds these submarine cells, and there is a mystic power associated with virginity which resembles aspects of Spenser's House of Busyrane. In an ominous scene which seems to be an elaboration on Spenser's Molanna, the innocent (if not virginal), indignant, and not very bright Medway tells Neptune how he can take Thames by surprise and finally succeed in raping her. The subsequent threat to Thames's chastity results in a burst of self-awareness and a recognition of the reality of age, death, and the inevitability of personal and national violation. The author gives us a sudden glimpse of the disparity between the Virgin Queen's humanity and her motto, *Semper Eadem*. Thames flees her pursuer, we are told, twice as fast as Florimell, and yet Neptune implacably nears his goal. As Spenser's threatened Cynthia calls on Jove to restrain Mutabilitie, and Jove in turn implores Nature's intervention, so Neptune's threat forces Thames to call on Nature's and Jove's assistance to preserve her integrity, to protect her from corruption and the death of Neptune's sexual attack. If E. W. is using Spenser here (as seems to be the case), in his more dramatic allegory the analogy with Muta- bilitie has been adapted to stress Neptune's maritime and sexual aggression. The change shows a sensitive understanding of the psychology of sex, not of Mutabilitie's, perhaps, but of Florimell's and Amoret's. The cult of virginity in the Renaissance receives one of its most complete expressions in E. W.'s treatment of the royal image of the river nymph.

Not only is E. W.'s insight into Spenser's psychological allegory very perceptive, but his literary techniques and objectives are also similar. He too uses an imaginatively conceived perceptual geogra- phy to develop a national image which enables him to explore the effects of time at psychological and cultural levels simultaneously. Thus, he too uses the river as a clue to the nature of the mutable world, seen in public and private contexts. His ability to transform his characters from nymphs to geographical rivers, and at times, to make them seem to be both at once, is uncanny and highly devel- oped Spenserianism. And yet his national image is wholly unlike Spenser's; it is that of a nation about to be cast into the waters of change and insecurity after forty years of Elizabeth's reign. Suc- ceeding generations will also use the river motif to reflect the decline in the nation since Elizabeth, but with far less searching psychologi- cal insight. As an early Spenserian, what E. W. has done is adapt this motif, as characteristically Elizabethan, even Spenserian, and use it to explore the temper and mentality of the age, and as we will see, this political self-consciousness will become characteristic of Spenserian verse.

1. The Poetry of Politics and the Politics of Poetry: The Royal Elegy and the Masque

> Yeeld tributary streames to Times vast Flood
> Work love, swell seas, may that muse ne're be blest,
> That drownes his Wit in standing Lake of mud:
> But Pegase Hoofes strike learned Helicon,
> Whose Rivulets now may run through Albion.
>
> (Christopher Brooke, "A Funerall Elegie on . . . Prince [Henry]")

Thou art a bountifull, and brave spring: and waterest all the noble plants of this Iland. In thee, the whole Kingdome dresseth itselfe and is ambitious to use thee as her glasse. Beware, then, thou render mens figures truly, and teach them no lesse to hate their deformities, than to love their formes.

(Ben Jonson, *Cynthias Revels*, "To the Speciall Fountaine of Manners: The Court")

It is interesting, though, that the Spenserian river appears less often in the narrative forms of epic, allegory, or romance, where decorum demands that the private voice of the poet be subordinate to a higher (perhaps national) theme, than in occasional and epideictic forms which allow the voice of the individual to be heard in a public context. Considering the river poem's English origins in Leland, it is appropriate that it should flourish in an epideictic form which is particularly sensitive to recent historical events—that is, the royal elegy. Here, in the elegy and related occasional, culturally self-aware forms, poets commonly employ a conventional image of nature—in this case the river—to explore the effects of the nation's loss, or some other important event. The epideictic poem is something of a generic grab bag, and as we saw in speaking of Leland, it encompasses poems on a multitude of occasions: births, deaths, marriages, commissioned encomiastic verse of different kinds.[3] We have seen it to be congenial territory for the river in Statius, Claudian, Leland, Sidney's elegists, and Spenser, and so it is not surprising that it offers an important opportunity for pointing out the changes in the motif after Spenser. As we will see, in the seventeenth century, the Spenserian river often provided the means for smuggling thematic and political nuances into verse ostensibly commemorating an important historical event.

The river gives a degree of generic coherence to much of this literature, and particularly to the elegy. Because they are so directly concerned with the national image, these elegies on Elizabeth, Prince Henry, and Queen Anne do much to hasten the changes in the *topos* by consolidating it, making it more conventional, and removing it from its immediate contact with the national landscape. In a sense the river's appropriateness as an image of the nation ensured its emergence from landscape to symbol. The change is precipitated by the element of imitation, particularly of Spenser, which inevitably hastened its removal from the world of nature to that of artifice. Indeed, the motif's very sensitivity to its society makes it a good gauge of the changes that were to occur in the nation's self-perception and its poetic.[4]

Interestingly, these poets frequently abandon the usual Theocritan model that was most popular with Sidney's elegists, for a looser form that is most conspicuously indebted to Spenser, or else, going one step beyond the Sidney elegists, they filter Theocritus through Spenser. The river then becomes an image not only of the nation, but of a particular age, and as the century advances, this form, looking to the Elizabethan past, resonates with greater nostalgia for the receding age. Thus, John Lane, in his Spenserian elegy on Elizabeth, invokes the watery muses, and while he sings his "April song by roate," they, with "learned instruments in hand," "lament the Lady of the Faiery-land." Richard Niccols, another poet who consistently introduces the rivers into his verse, complains that since Colin Clout's death and Rowland's (Drayton's) disfavor, no one is left to sing Elizabeth's elegy. He may even have Bryskett's verses on Sidney in mind when he says:

> You christall nymphs that haunt the banks of Thames,
> Tune your sad Timbrils on this wofull day;
> And force the swift windes and the sliding streames
> To stand a while and listen to your Lay.[5]

There is one aspect of the royal elegy in particular which reinforces its Spenserian and riverine elements, and that is the inescapable paradox of joy in sorrow, of grief accompanied by rejoicing at the prospects of succession. The paradox naturally sharpens the focus of the national image, and the river, with its inherently paradoxical quality, was obviously well suited to represent such a lamentably happy state. The titles of these works alone suggest the essence of the form, and as we can see in Phineas Fletcher's *Verses of Mourning and Joy*, the river perfectly locates the *anagnorisis* of the elegy:

> Ye goodly nymphes, that with this river dwell,
> All daughters of the yellow-sanded Chame,
> Which deepe in hollow rockes frame out your cell,
> Tell me nymphs, for you can surely tell;
> Is death the cause of life: or can that same,
> Be to my greatest blisse, which was my great'st annoy?
>   Eliza's dead, and can it be?
>   Eliza's death brings joy to me;
> Hell beeing the cause, why heavenly is the joy?[6]

The best elegies seek to understand the first causes of life and death, and as in Spenser's non-elegiac verse, the rivers continue to embody these mysteries of nature while putting them in a national context.

The sorrow's-joy motif was an essential feature of these elegies, and the formula was abandoned only at great risk as Drayton learned by his too joyful welcome of James. It also exerted its influence on the elegies on Prince Henry, who died at the peak of the celebrations of his sister's, Princess Elizabeth's, wedding. Throughout James's reign, Henry symbolized the nation's hopes.[7] He assumed a cult-like popularity, which was similar to that of Sidney and which reflected the people's desires and hopes more than it did the personality of the Prince itself. He seemed to promise a revival of the heroic past, an age of militant Protestantism (also associated with Sidney), and the casting off of the vanities of James's court. In effect, he represented the possibility of returning to that age of Spenser and Sidney, and his elegies reveal these hopes through their use of Spenserian river motifs.

As the very genuine sentiments of many of these elegies suggest, his death truly dashed the hopes of the nation, and of poets in particular although there is little evidence that Henry had much interest in promoting the arts. Nevertheless, his death served to focus the nation's fading hopes and growing fears on the self-image which represented the age that they had hoped to recreate. And yet, by inconveniently dying in the midst of Elizabeth's wedding festivities, he forced elegists to harmonize their grief with prudent expressions of joyful hope, lest the expensive festivities all go for nought. The result was a flood of volumes with titles such as *Teares of Joy* and *The Period of Mourning . . . together with Nuptiall Hymnes*, and echoing the anxieties of 1603.

Far more than the predictable death of Elizabeth, though, these events of 1612–1613 intensified England's introspection and sharpened its self-image while voicing its insecurities. Joy, however, must come from grief, and it was argued that Henry died to be born again of his sister and Prince Fredrick—and the first son born of this unhappy couple was named Henry and was celebrated by Henry Peacham in 1615 with his verses, *Prince Henry Revived*. The river was able to participate in both extremes of feeling, and the fashion of describing England as an island of sentient rivers becomes ubiquitous. Robert Allyne, in his *Funerall Elegies upon . . . Prince Henry*, hopes that greater unity and strength will result from the loss:

> Let never this small Ile, while Heavens remaine,
> Be dark'd with such a dire eclipse againe.
> And though the bravest branch be cut away,
> Yet seat the root most stedfast in his place,
> To shine from Thames, and Trent, to Forth and Tay,
> Eternal in his never ruin'd race.[8]

Christopher Brooke perceives the rivers which "run through Albion" as "tributary streames to Times vast flood." His coauthor in this volume of elegies, William Browne, concludes that England is no longer among the Fortunate Isles and calls for Thetis's nymphs to come to Isis's shore, where they can all "rend their hairs" together.[9] In many if not all of these verses the river motif puts the image of the nation in focus. Interest in geography, of course, hardly exists at all, and instead we notice the preoccupation with generic convention: the elegies echo with conventional features of the occasional river verse of Leland, Spenser, and Sidney's elegists.

Drummond of Hawthornden, the best and most important of these authors, shows the direction in which the river motif is moving in these elegies and shows how it evolves from Spenser. In his *Teares, On the Death of Moeliades* he presents the world's vast loss in terms of the sympathetic rivers, as the voice of nature itself. As in Spenser, they convey their physical reality while also serving the poet's allegory. The universal concord of the rivers suggests the limits and potential of nature, society, and the arts. Together they express nature's and Europe's loss:

> *Tagus* did court his *Love*, with golden *Streames*
> *Rhein* with his *Townes*, faire *Seine* with *all shee claimes*.
> But *ah* (poore Lovers) death did them betrey,
> And (not suspected) made their *Hopes* his *Prey*![10]

But for Drummond nature is incapable of transcending its terrestrial sphere. His rivers, very Spenserian as they are, have not the grace that enables them to rise from their natural realm; they are confined to futile cycles of death and decay, and not even poetry can elevate nature temporarily to a celestial sphere:

> When *Forth* thy Nurse, *Forth* where thou first didst passe
> Thy tender Dayes (who smyl'd oft on her Glasse
> To see thee gaze) Meandring with her Streames,
> Heard thou hadst left this *Round*, from *Phoebus* Beames
> She sought to flie, but forced to returne

By *neighbour Brookes*, Shee gave her selfe to mourne:
And as she rushed her *Cyclades* among,
Shee seem'd to plaine, that *Heaven* had done her wrong. (11.71–78)

And while this perhaps seems appropriate for the elegiac mode, the distance between heaven and earth is far greater here than it is, let us say, in the Sidney elegies and in Bryskett's use of the river, and it is much less easily crossed. Drummond's verses in fact have many similarities to Bryskett's *Mourning Muse*; in both nature can but realize its own capacities through its shared suffering, and death can only be adequately understood through nature's mirror in the celestial realm. But Drummond does not find any consolation in the image of concordant rivers; they represent the mortality rather than the immortality of the human condition.

For the popular elegists, to meditate on the nation's grief was also to meditate on nature and its relation to the arts and society. For Richard Niccols, in his *The Three Sisters' Teares*, England is "Halcyon like," a nest for nature's sons. But as his muse travels up the Thames in her grief, she beholds the fêtes celebrating the Lord Mayor's Pageant at the time of Henry's death, and she condemns the decadence that corrupts both art and nature:

So many varying and so vaine delights
Floating upon the floud, I then did see,
Such divers showes and such fantasticke sights,
That Thames the Idle-Lake then seem'd to be.

The allusion to Spenser's Idle Lake and the image of Thames transformed by effeminate entertainments demonstrate very clearly how Spenser was used as a convenient point of reference by which one could measure the decline of the times. And what is interesting in these verses is the difference between their attitude toward poetry and Spenser's and that of Sidney's elegists. As we have seen in *The Ruines of Time*, Spenser urges the importance of literature, argues the redemptive effects of poetry and its divinity, and calls for greater literary output. There was a confidence in the sufficiency of nature and the humane arts. For Prince Henry's Spenserian elegists, the future of literature is "rapt up in lead"; the understanding they reach in their complaints is not one that looks to the future, but one that accepts the loss as irreplaceable and irredeemable, and which despairs of the future. Significantly, poetry shares the fate of nature; it has lost some of its divinity. For Spenser death was an occasion for poetry; it confirmed its importance. For Stuart poets, death threatened the future of poetry and suggested its mortality and the uncertainty of the future.

Theoretically at least, the antidote to the loss of Prince Henry was to have been the marriage of Princess Elizabeth. However, a rift had entered the sorrow's-joy formula, and what were meant to be complementary verses became pairs of occasional poems on divergent occasions. Nevertheless, simply by appearing in both elegy and nuptial, the river motif often served as a border joining and dividing the two psychological realms of grief and joy, representing on the one hand nature's mutability and on the other its constancy.

The royal epithalamion, with its prototype in the Song of Songs and with its inevitable political significance is the natural setting for the river motif, and in those celebrating Princess Elizabeth's marriage to Prince Fredrick it appears regularly in the form of the marriage of the Thames and the Rhine. The special nature of this union of Protestant states accentuated the political and social significance that was implicit in Spenser's riverine image of concord in marriage. The concord of the two nations was figured as a kind of geopolitical harmony based in nature, as we can sense from Augustine Taylor's sorrowfully joyful lines:

> Well may she [Thames] boast she was of able power,
> To grace Faire Rhenus with an English flower,
> And when these two meet in great Oceans,
> Thei'l know each other by their native Swans.
> So by this marriage, Eccho understands,
> Twill make acquainted both Seas and Lands.[11]

The European geography has subtly assumed the voice of national policy, and the rivers reflect British destiny with un-Spenserian specificity.

The wide range of literary associations conveyed by the river gave many of these epithalamia greater imaginative scope than one might expect from their authors. James Maxwell's *A Monument of Remembrance Erected in Albion*, for example, uses the rivers to conflate national emblems and their political implications with aspects of the mystical nature of the Song of Songs. Glossing his verse with passages from philosophers, geographers, patristics and mystics of the past, he submits German and English topography to his own complicated Protestant myth. He describes the meeting of the Tam-Isis nymph and the "renowned Myrtle Nymph" of Heidelberg in terms of the fertile union of earth and water; the Tam-Isis nymph is not only the English Thames, but a descendant of Isis and Osiris and the mystical gods of the Nile. When the two nymphs meet, the Myrtle nymph pays homage to Tam-Isis, and the poem, with an abundance of religious imagery and gloss on the allegory, goes on to develop the theme of militant Protestantism and the redemption of Europe and of nature which will result from the marriage:

> Oh, if I had the hands to advance
> *Myrtilla's* state amidst as many Townes,
> As there are Myrtle-trees in *Spaine* and *France*,
> In *Italy*, or yet in *Germany* bound;
>   All should be to hers twise ten thousand
>   For why, Her worth deserves as much and more.
>
> Yet for a signe, I wish her all the hap
> Which this my Myrtle-emblems sence resounds;
> Lo how I lay into her lovely lap,
> As many berries as be Towers or Townes
>   Twixt purest *Rheine* and fruitfull *Nilus* Flood,
>   Abiun whose Bankes many Myrtles stood. (sts. 68–69)

If Maxwell's strange mysticism is imperfectly converted to poetry, his use of the range of river motifs to mythologize his landscape does, nevertheless, reveal both originality and an ability to give an immediacy to his allegory, and in this he demonstrates how thoroughly understood the possibilities of the river theme were. Indeed, his mythical nymphs are essentially nature deities redeemed by the political and religious concord offered by the marriage; his natural landscape, in which England becomes a fruitful Egypt on Isis's banks, is completely transformed by his curious syncretistic myth. His vision of aquatic concord, though, retains its basis in nature.

Thus, notwithstanding the conventionality of most of these occasional verses, it must be said that the Palatine marriage, by appealing to the two countries' common cause of Protestantism, encouraged poets to look at the real landscape with a vision that informed it with their hopes and revitalized it with a mythical potential. Many of these poems evoke a national image rather vividly in order to express the belief in the power of religious myth to transform reality and to shape the world according to mystical ideals, and in part this is a product of their Spenserianism. The more zealous among them conceived of the marriage in terms of nature's victory over dark necromantic forces, and as its refinement and access to the higher forces of reason. In this conception of the river as an image of natural and social harmony shaped by diviner power, we can perceive the development of conventional river themes under Spenser's influence.

Certainly the greater number of these occasional verses use the river for simple synecdoche, as an emblem of the nation united in grief. Yet, for the more capable poets, the river and its Spenserian features, instead of numbing their thoughts through imitation, helped to define their ideas about nature and society, while retaining an immediacy and specificity of reference. Recognizing the river as a national image based in geographic reality and having a literary tradition linking it with ideas of concord, history, and time, they developed its potential for raising rather pointed political issues. In effect, the Tudor myth of cultural geography handed down by Leland, Camden, and Spenser, became a point of contrast with Stuart political reality. These sixteenth-century poets saw the geography of the mind and of the physical world as a place for the discovery and the realization of the self and society; through their river poetry they transmitted to the seventeenth century a belief in the mind's ability to realize itself in nature. Theirs was a vision of concord and harmony which was as much political, social, and historical as it was philosophical. For their successors, the rivers continue to suggest this myth of geography, although it was recognized as the product of a different era; thus, the rivers perpetuate the national image but also accentuate a contrasting political reality. In the reflection of their waters, then, we see juxtaposed images of ideal and real, between Stuart politics and Tudor myth.

Joseph Hall's *The King's Prophecie: or Weeping Joy*, for example, uses the occasion of Elizabeth's death and James's accession to analyze the themes of concord and harmony and to warn against the dangers of discord between Scotland and England. His theme is rather delicate for such an occasion, and he approaches it circumspectly, in terms of the heroic future of the united Protestant nation and through various archetypes foreshadowing the harmony of England and Scotland. Hall develops an image of Stuart Britain culminating a process in which concord emerges from a long period of discord. As others had before, he uses the river as a device for making nature the touchstone for history. He argues that both history and nature teach not only the fundamental unity of Britain, but also the greater strength to be gained from a union which follows a period of discord:

> Well did this wise Creator, when he laid
> Earth's deepe foundations, charge the watery maine,
> This Northerne world should by his waves be made
> Cut from the rest, and yet not cut in twaine.
> Divided, that it might be blest alone,
> Not sundred, for this fore-set union.[12]

National geography testifies to their destined union, and to resist it is to impede Divine will. The idea of civil concord based in nature emerges as Hall's central theme, and it becomes clear that he is adapting his ideas from the river motif in Spenser and Camden. Elaborating on their conception of concord, he perceives political harmony as a "Double . . . powre" and as "Double . . . glory" founded on universal order, and he locates his ideas in a simile which alludes to both these authors:

> Like as when *Tame & Ouse* that while they flow
> In sundrie channels seemen both but small,
> But when their waters meet & Thames doth grow,
> It seems some little sea, before thy wall,
> Before thy towred wall, *Luds* auntient towne,
> Pride of our England, chamber of the crown.[13]

From this union of the rivers stems the thought of Lud's antiquity, the image of the city's towered pride and strength, and the suggestion of law and civil order—all conventional aspects of the river *topos*.

It would be difficult to determine whether the author derived his conception of the rivers and their connection with concord from Spenser or Camden. The rivers he chooses suggest Camden's rather than Spenser's influence, his interest seems to be more historical than mythical, and elsewhere he praises the *Britannia* as being more enduring than Spenser's or Sidney's national images. Yet his treatment of concord and its relationship to universal love and his use of the river to suggest the greater strength of harmony following long-standing strife and to encourage Anglo-Scottish peace seem to be Spenserian in inspiration:

> That where before scarce could a shallow boat
> Float on each streame: now many whole Navies ride

Upon his rolling waves; so shall this knot
Of *Love* and *Concord* that is lately tide,
Betwixt our Lands; double the wonted deale,
Our fathers had of honour strength and weale. (st. 62)

Hall has married Spenser's fairy mythology to Camden's historical geography to put into a political context the idea of a *"fide concordia sancta."* He too looks to the landscape to confirm his political vision of harmony and concord, and he reinforces this by his reference to the two major literary images of the nation. But he does so in warning, suggesting the incipient dangers of discord from the current political situation, rather than in a spirit of affirmation.

These examples of epideictic literature illustrate how the river began to be used to assess the suitability of Tudor national myths for Stuart Britain. As we will see, much of what is regarded as Spenserian verse is political in this way, as though the myth of landscape has been established and subsequent human events must now strive to conform to it. This sharpened political focus of the river grew directly out of its traditional (but primarily Spenserian) theme of Concord, and it was often used specifically to address the problem of Anglo-Scottish tensions. For example, in an elegy on Queen Anne in 1619, Patrick Hannay, a Scotsman who attached himself to James's court when it went south, uses the rivers ostensibly as an image of Scottish and English unity, but also, more allusively, to suggest latent animosities. Hannay's description of the Forth's journey to join the Thames in mourning emphasizes the rivalry of the rivers rather than their love, and his explicit theme of *concordia discors* conveys discord somewhat more vividly than concord. The Forth's torrential descent frightens the aggrieved Thames and reminds her of the rebellious past, and the poet unconvincingly tells the ghost of Queen Anne to "Feare not (*faire Queene*) it is not their ambition,/But swelling *sorrow*, that breeds thy suspicion."[14] Throughout the elegy, the image of riverine concord echoes with threats and warnings of discontent from the Scottish rivers. Nature is more than sympathetic in its grief; Neptune himself is wary of Forth's motives: "Great *Neptune's* selfe doth feare invasive wrong,/Seeing *her* strange waves through his *waters* throng." Thus, Hannay reiterates that his theme is the reconciliation of opposites, and how the late "*Wrath, discord, malice, envy, rapine, strife,/Thefts, rapes,* and *murderous mischieves* [which] were so rife" have been resolved, so that now "being *one/We* might love better: *Twixt united foes,/*

And separate friends, love and hate groes/To Greatest heights." Yet Hannay protests too vehemently; the superficial serenity cannot hide the undercurrent of strife and distrust that characterizes the Scottish rivers, so that the myth of concord reflects a reality of discord.

We can see from Drummond of Hawthornden's *Forth Feasting* how the Spenserian motif was adopted for its political potential in other epideictic forms. Drummond, an intensely personal man with a strong sense of national identity, refused to join the court in its exodus south and cultivated a poetry of retirement that drew on his response to his local landscape for spirit and subject matter. In *Forth Feasting*, written in 1617 for James's progress to Scotland, Drummond summons the Scottish rivers, led by the Forth, to respond to the monarch's return to his native land. Working from an idea fundamental to the river motif and expressed in the poem's epigraph from Ovid, "*Flumina senserunt ipsa*," it develops an image of the sentient river's natural sympathetic response to James's return. It opens, for example, with Forth being roused from a slumber that has presumably lasted since 1603: "What blustring Noise now interrupts my Sleepe?/What echoing Shouts, thus cleave my chrystal Deep?/And call mee hence from out by watrie Court?" (11.1–4).

As in Hannay's elegy (which might have been influenced by *Forth Feasting*) here, instead of using the Scottish rivers to pour forth undiluted encomiastics, Drummond too rather sensitively measures his rivers against those of England, and in so doing he gives voice to the sense of neglect that many Scottish writers felt:

> Ah why should *Isis* only see Thee shine?
> Is not thy FORTH, as well as *Isis* Thine?
> Though *Isis* vaunt shee hath more Wealth in store,
> Let it suffice thy FORTH doth love thee more. (11.183–86)

Into his subsequent roll call of rivers, suggestive of Spenser's in the marriage of Thames and Medway, Drummond infuses a national spirit that is expressive of more than the praises it professes. These northern rivers are as qualified as England's to pronounce on the virtues of love, concord, peace, truth, and justice, which distinguish James's reign. The rivers, which become rather impudent in their protestations, provide Drummond with a national image through which he can praise James and also express Scottish political sentiments. Furthermore, the river catalogue is an image of art and cultural identity as well as of sentient nature. It invokes a national image in terms of the Spenserian poetic; Drummond asserts Scottish pride and her political concord in terms of a distinctly English poetic myth, and he does so to show that he can do with the Scottish rivers what Spenser did with his. The effectiveness of his encomium, and the proof of his nation's harmonious intents, lie in his ability to assume the English river myth (and its language) and make it harmonize with the Scottish landscape—and it is not only a profession of loyalty, but a subtle act of poetic usurpation. Through the river, then, nationalism and poetic and cultural identity conflate, and Drummond attempts to make the Scottish poetic myth commensurate with the Spenserian.

Poets cultivated these images of concord with the hope of continuing Tudor myths of national identity and developing them into a distinct political image for James's reign. What emerged naturally from the geopolitical climate of the sixteenth century was thus processed for political ends in the seventeenth. And in many respects this aspect of the river motif that emerged from the changing sense of landscape during the sixteenth century seemed to encourage the smooth flow of the Spenserian river into the seventeenth century, although it also assured the motif a contrived and artificial quality, and in this we can predict some of its changes during the century.

Occasional poems, however, were more or less voluntary contributions to the national myth. Complementing them, even validating the ideal behind them (if not its political reality), were more official expressions of a national, or royal, self-image. These were the court pageants and masques that James enjoyed, and their imagery closely resembles that of the epideictic verse we have been surveying. Such entertainments virtually institutionalized the process of royal myth-making, and they are distinguished by an aritificiality and political purpose exceeding those of the sixteenth century. This trend is evident in Anthony Munday's rather simple pageant *The Triumphs of Re-United Britania* (1605). While officially a Lord Mayor's Pageant, it was in fact London's welcome to King James, and the extent to which it is informed by a coherent political design is clear from the title. Its setting was a triangular island figuring

Britain; placed alongside are its *nymphae loci*, Britannia and Troya-Nova, who call upon the rivers for encomia on James:

> Troya-Nova (Now London) invites fair Thamesis, and the rivers that bordered their several Kingdomes (personated in faire and beautifull Nymphs) to sing Paeans and Songs of Triumph, in honour of our second Brute, Royall King James.

The design is very close to that of Leland's *Genethliacon*, but the more pointed political message is Stuart in character. Their songs of history and heroics, of Thames's favored status with Ocean, of the legends of Humber and Severn, emphasize the fulfilment of Britain's destiny, the reconciliation of time and place in political and geographical concord throughout the kingdom. Munday is obviously exploiting the traditional range of the river's associations, and it is easy to imagine the setting as a rudimentary map, perhaps like those "stripped-down" Saxton maps in Drayton's *Poly-Olbion*, on which only the principal rivers are depicted and next to which stand their articulate nymphal personifications.

Munday was an experienced propagandist (he was an image-maker for Elizabeth as well); he knew exactly what he was about, and he coordinated all the components of this suitably static image of harmony to create the effect of control and order. The conspicuous artificiality here is not simply attributable to the pageant form; Spenser too made use of the pageant, but with very different results. Rather, what we perceive is a new phase in the taming of the rivers. As they become emblems of concord, they are raised from their natural beds and made mere hieroglyphs designating human mastery of the world. They are servants to the political ideal, rather than a means of discovering it.

This evolution goes even further as the pageant yields to the more complex masque, the very purpose of which is the creation of a heightened image of nation, king, and court, and the celebration of universal order as it is manifested in the microcosm of the monarch and his train. In these "complements of state," as Daniel calls them, there is a political sophistication beneath the simplicity of its message: the river becomes the emblem of what people know or assert, rather than an image of the natural mysteries that they strive to understand. The landscape has become wholly internalized and cerebral; the river is an expression of knowledge, rather than the pursuit of knowledge. This process of simplification is strikingly demonstrated in Jonson's early pageant, "The King's Entertainment through the City of London, 1603," where the Thames and London's *genius loci* are again used to express the nation's joy and to show the fealty that is expected of them. Jonson, however, provides a gloss to his allegorical figures, explicating the origin of his entertainment in the often-used line from *Amores* 3: "*Flumina senserunt ipsa.*" In Ovid, as we have seen, the line is a playful reference to the immense reverence paid to the unpredictable, seemingly human behavior of rivers. The poet mocks those who perceive the rivers unrealistically, in anthropomorphic terms as extensions of their own needs rather than as they are. Like many wits, Jonson is capable of remarkable humorlessness. His explication of the line so simplifies and vitiates the image that it has no power of suggestion and no naturalness. He explains "that rivers themselves, and such inanimate creatures, have heretofore been made sensible of passions and affections, and that he now no lesse partook the joy of his Majesty's grateful approach to this city, than any of these persons to where he pointed, which were the daughters of the Genius."[15] His words in fact sound very much like Botero's description of the geographical rivers, but it is one thing for a geographer to describe the rivers as sensible, and quite another for a poet to explicate Ovid's urbane poem in this way. Perhaps Jonson is doing just what a commentator is meant to do, that is, simplify his text. But Botero's geography has more interest than Jonson's factitious allegory, which is more concerned with what people say than what nature means, and the same abstract and static quality carries into the entertainment itself.

This rationalistic simplification, however, is appropriate to the masque's theme of order. Consider, for example, Jonson's first court masque, *The Masque of Blackness*, with its informing conceits of Aethiopia, the Niger river, and its Blackamores, intended as foils to England, the Thames, Anne, and her attendants. Although Jonson refers to the geographers who describe the Niger and its geography and though the river retains many of its conventional attributes, the work is at best a *tour de force*. It does show how thoroughly symbolic the river and its associations had become, but the image has its source in the mind, not in nature. Our interest lies essentially in the design of this courtly compliment; its form is its meaning.

The geographical rivers, with their unknown sources, unpredictable windings, and the litter of human history on their banks have

no place in the orderly court masque. These entertainments antici-
pate the neoclassical aesthetic with its emphasis on control. In its
symbolic mode of music and dance, the masque was by its very
nature an affirmation of the social order and harmony that the
Stuart court thought it epitomized. It is natural, then, that the river,
which from early antiquity had represented the presence of divinity
in nature and human efforts to create order and concord in nature,
should also be an image of the court itself. The *humanum genus* was
at the center of this mystic dance. Whatever superhuman mysteries
the river conveyed were suppressed, so that significantly, what
emerges from the form is above all an image of the human conception of the river, not of the river itself. Divine order was recapitulated in the image of the court, in the political and social harmony
that it represented. In this, denatured as the river might have
become, it continued to serve the basically Neoplatonic, symbolic
function that it was given by writers such as Alan of Lille. It joins
the celestial and material realms.

Daniel's *Tethys Festival* (1610), and his own objections to the
masque form, are good illustration of what is happening to the *topos*
as a national image. The entertainment in honor of Prince Henry's
investiture presents "Tethys, Queene of the Ocean, and wife of
Neptune, attended with thirteen Nymphs of Several Rivers." The
nymphs are ladies of the court and represent the rivers of their
county seats: the countess of Arundel is the nymph of Arun, Lady
Arabella is the Trent, Vicountess Haddington the Rother, and so
on, with Princess Elizabeth representing the Thames. In the topography is figured the social and cosmic order manifest in the ceaseless flow of the rivers into the sea. The masque is but the
choreographic form of this image of order. The meaning of this
"insubstantial pageant" is common to all masques, and is often
framed in terms of the rivers. Jonson expressed it in the address to
the court in *Cynthia's Revels* (see the epigraph above), where he
urges the nobility to live up to the symbolic image of their orderly
society.

In *Tethys Festival* and generally the river is mere synecdoche for
the perfected order or for the individual or city it represents, and the
pageant is the ritualized expression of the idealized image of concord. The political objective of the form is clear. No aspect of nature
is allowed outside the domain of royal order, concord, and wisdom.
The anti-masque is simply a device by which the limits of concord
and royal control are broadened, a method of expanding the scope

of compliment. Conspicuous is the change in attitude from the pageantry of Leland's verses, with their sense of discovery and revelation, and the very strong sense of the human place in a larger history and an encompassing world that goes beyond king and court. The court masque obscures these perspectives and allows no shadows or ambiguities; all is embraced within the mind of the individual, beyond which nothing is real. The exception of the wedding masque in the *Tempest* and the limitations of Prospero's control proves the rule.

These "pompous shows," despite their popularity in court, were not congenial to the English author, who harbored suspicions about things not first fixed in print and whose "onely life consists in show."[16] Daniel and Jonson have the same prejudice that Leland, Camden, and Spenser had; they too preferred books to spectacle, and they strove to extricate the form from the realm of ostentation and to raise it to that of literature. Nevertheless, they reflect the extent to which political image-making was practiced in literature and the arts. The river of the masque shows how much the national landscape was a figment of the mind and a product of the political imagination. In its evolution the river lost much of its vitality and meaning, being perforce no greater nor more suggestive than the wit of the author treating it and carrying less mystery and allusive association of its own. It is as though the river image, instead of reflecting the poet's response to the environment, was being forced to conform to a preconceived order.

This taming of the river is even evident in Milton's *Comus*. Sabrina figures the strength of grace in nature; there is an appropriateness in the river's treatment based in both literary tradition and legend, and it is arguable that here, in his most Spenserian work, Milton mined the religious and literary traditions of the river as a *topos* by making the goddess the voice of divinity in nature, as well as an image of nature's strength and perfectability. Obviously Milton saw the suitability of the river goddess for his theme, and was certainly delighted by the way in which she brought together—right up to the castle gates—the local lore and an image of chastity, thus providing him with a theme with which to compliment Lord Bridgewater and an image which linked it specifically with his host, and thus made the masque more personal. His choice of Sabrina was dictated as much by the location of Ludlow Castle as by anything else. Milton's mind is on human nature, not external nature, and his thoughts are elsewhere than on the landscape. One gets the impression that another abstraction would have served equally well. It is right and meet that the power of chaste nature should rise from the river, but one suspects that Milton would have been just as content with Iris or Psyche, and one wonders what he would have done had his host lived by a different river—or no river at all.

Formally, Milton's success in *Comus* is in evoking a household god to celebrate domestic virtue and nature's perfectability in a private dimension, in a form which customarily treats a national *genius*, public order and public virtues. The river, however, is an accident of his form and plan, not at its center. He sets out to make a public form private, and for various reasons he chooses the river as one of his principal images. What is important, although it is looking ahead somewhat, is that in this treatment of Sabrina in 1634, we can see the reaction against the contrived use of the masque for perpetuating political and national myths. *Comus* reflects his awareness of the discrepancy between the national myth and the reality, and he turns the form—and the river motif with it—to another, primarily personal dimension, and in this he participates in the movement from the public to the private landscape.

2. The Poet in the Landscape: Tudor Myth and Stuart Reality—Fletcher and the Spenserian Poets

> Yet cheerely on my *Muse*, no whit at all dismay'd,
> But look aloft tow'rds heaven, to him whose powerfull ayd;
> Hath led thee on thus long, & through so sundry soiles,
> Steep Mountains, Forrests rough, deep Rivers, that thy toyles
> Most sweet refreshings seeme, and still thee comfort sent,
> Against the Bestial Rout, and Boorish rabblement
> Of those rude vulgar sots, whose braines are onely Slime,
> Borne to the doting world, in this last yron Time,
> So stony, and so dull, that *Orpheus* which (men say) . . .
> He might as well have moov'd the Universe as these.
>
> (Drayton, *Poly-Olbion*)

In providing an index to the political sensibilities of the nation, the river also reveals the changing perception of its landscape. In this it announces not only the evolution of new myths, but also alterations in the relation between the individual and his environment. It is, in fact, quite remarkable how sensitive the literature of these years is to cultural changes. The poets of the first quarter of the seventeenth century were very political; they tend to brood on the social changes of the period. This is the effect of the dissolution, rather than the consolidation of the national myth and self-image. Increasingly the river crosses narrower, local landscapes; it less often captures an image of the nation and a sense of unity, although it continues to address national themes. It is more frequently an image of the times, rather than of time itself, and in this it reveals the decline of its mythical potential.

These changes are partly a reflection of James's efforts to shape the national image and to direct writers' imaginations, although his success in this did not always have the political results he had hoped for. Elizabeth also sought to influence the nation's imagination, but in the seventeenth century the world of public relations was more sophisticated, and the machinery by which public images were made was more intricate. Increasingly James worked to keep these mechanisms in his control through efforts to direct the activities of the court, by charging the nobility to return to their country seats after the disbanding of Parliament, through the control of historical and topographical studies and publication, and through the "media," such as the masque. Here again, the fate of the Society of Antiquaries helps to highlight the cultural changes that were affecting the river. For example, just prior to Elizabeth's death, John Doderidge and Henry Spelman had petitioned for a royal charter. Their request was received favorably; Elizabeth had always encouraged the society, but she died before the charter could be granted. But from the beginning of James's reign their days seemed numbered. Although topographers continued their anatomies of the nation, they fought royal indifference and even active disapproval. The society continued to make repeated requests for a charter, and although they promised to avoid discussion of "all Matters of State," their requests were met with James's stern disapprobation. There was a very strong sense that their meetings and discussions were conducted in direct violation of the royal will. In short, the climate was not conducive to the development of a national myth having its basis in historical lore and study. James perpetuated his own personal myths, but discouraged the independent pursuit of national images through the shadowy dimension of historical study. This was not simply a matter of aesthetics, but of the interrelationships between historical knowledge, social institutions, literary creation, and royal prerogative.

At the same time, changes were occurring in the society itself.

The young men of the 1580s had long before come into their estates; their parochial views had been tempered by maturity, and they were on the brink of rural retirement, which was encouraged by James's policies. A letter from Richard Carew in Cornwall to Robert Cotton, apologizing for being unable to meet with his "Sweete and respected Antiquarum Society" because of his "remote dwelling," indicates that already by 1605 it had become difficult for members to insist on mandatory attendance at the meetings as they had done.[17] Advancing age and growing interest in country life had its natural effect on London-based society. Sir Henry Spelman expresses as much when writing of the dissolution of the original society around 1607:

> Thus it continu'd divers Years; but as all good Uses commonly decline: so many of the chief Supporters hereof either dying or withdrawing themselves into the Country; this among the rest grew for twenty years to be discontinu'd.[18]

Thus, art and nature—or James's policies and the effects of age and time—worked their inevitable changes on the national sensibility, and the impact of this de-emphasis of London life on the national aesthetic was considerable. Nations age as individuals do, and like King Lear, so too lesser mortals begin to see their personal fortunes, rather than their nation's, reflected in the landscape. The river continues to be immensely popular—indeed, its popularity never really diminishes—but its vitality as a national image is lost. For that matter, as writers themselves began to realize, no image or form after about 1615 ever recaptures the nation's imagination in any encompassing way, with the possible exception of the drama. This is just the realization that Milton made, not only in choosing his epic subject matter, but also in the long course of writing his *History of Britain*.

The national landscape itself begins to disappear, and the river appears more and more frequently in local settings. What is interesting is that it continues to address political, even national themes in terms of its Spenserian past, but it does so obliquely, from the provinces, and with an individual voice, such as Jonson's when describing the "painted meades,/Through which a serpent river leades/To some coole, courteous shade, which he calls his,/And makes sleepe softer than it is!" at Sir Robert Wroth's estate in Kent. This change is emphatically not a rejection of a national perspective or a retirement from the public world as critics of topographical poetry suggest. Indeed, what is of particular importance is that this emergence of the local landscape and the river's removal from London took place in spite of efforts by poets to sustain a national perspective and myth, and to perpetuate a coherent image comparable to that of the preceding century. Thus, the response to local landscape that is commonly described as characteristic of the seventeenth century in fact developed virtually in spite of poets' attempts to resist it and to keep their eye on the national image as a whole. As Jonson makes clear in the opening line of his poem to Wroth ("How blest art thou, canst love the country, Wroth"), the private landscape is not to everybody's liking; nor, of course, is it the discovery of the seventeenth century. But that Jonson should even address Wroth in this manner suggests that the taste is being acquired by necessity if not by choice. Eyes which looked at the map and beheld Britain now perceive counties and private landscapes.

Thus, it is from a complex set of historical, political, and personal influences that the river motif acquired many tributaries from more rural landscapes during the period of Prince Henry's death. The river was distinctly the same body of literary water, but it had changed character, and its nymphs spoke to the nation with a different voice. It flowed through landscapes that were both public and private, that is, those with a political or social identity such as the Cam and the Isis, or those identified with the life or personality of the poet, such as Drayton's Anker or Browne's Tavy. As in the sixteenth century, personal and public identity are not easily distinguishable: self-fulfillment still lies in the public sphere. The meaning the river gives to the landscape is still based on a national perspective, much in the manner that Colin Clout, in his voluntary rustication, uses his tale of Mulla and Bregog to comment on the court of Elizabeth and on London life. But increasingly Stuart political reality clashes violently with national myths, making the angry voice of the poet sound louder than that of the patriot.

It is in this respect that the poets who continue to use the river motif as an aspect of physical nature, and not just as an abstract rhetorical image, are often Spenserian: they look at their landscape with a public vision which has been determined by their understanding of that poet, and by the place that he has assumed in the legendary identity of the nation. Thus, while they write with the same poetic that guided the sixteenth century (as Joan Grundy is wise to point out in her study of the Spenserian poets),[19] because of their awareness of their distance from Spenser they project a very different outlook on the nation and its image in the river. Their consistent use of the river to capture the Spenserian manner provides a contrast between their own world and that which is reflected in the river motif.

Following Spenser's lead, these authors use poetry as the standard by which they evaluate the nation. By means of it they hold their own poetic world up for comparison with the nation which produced *The Faerie Queene*. The national myth which forms their standard is not the world depicted in *The Faerie Queene*, but the poetic achievement it represents, as a work of art and a product of an age. For them it shows the poet in an ideal relation to his world. Thus the Fletchers and their coterie, William Browne and his West Country colleagues, and the poets associated with the Inner Temple, Drayton, George Wither, William Basse, and Christopher Brooke, all appraise the national myth in terms of the poet in his landscape. Through an implicit comparison with the Spenserian ideal in which the poet is one with the national image, and with remarkable frequency, the river is the image that locates their ideas.

Phineas Fletcher's very personal poetry about very public themes offers an important illustration of this second phase of Spenserian river poetry in which the poetry of politics degenerates into the politics of poetry. Fletcher was a true Stuart in sensibility: his self-image as a poet was first fed by the legend of Spenser and the Elizabethans, and it was subsequently starved by the reality of his own struggle for recognition.

For Fletcher, poetry is an ideal as well as an art, and as he and his friends write about writing poetry, they create a portrait of the artist, the background of which is a perspective on society. Borrowing from Sannazaro and Spenser for the biographical metaphors for his craft, he makes the river his world in place and time. It defines the poet's relation to his world. For the piscator-poet striving to find his place in the local and national waters, the river offers the potential for and impediments to achievement. It thus has national and personal significance. As with Spenser, the political myths merge with those of the poet's personal identity. But even more than Spenser, Fletcher makes his rivers serve simultaneously as a figure of autobiographical and historical time—of time and the times. His pastoral drama is the unfolding of basic myths of identity. The device, inherent to the river motif, was a common one as we can gather from the portrait of Sir Henry Unton in the National

Portrait Gallery. There, the river of his public and private life unfolds as though flowing from the *fons et origo* of his mind; the autobiographical portrait is a good visual analogue to our discussion of the river motif in the earlier part of the Renaissance.

But Fletcher does not recreate landscape through myth in the way that Spenser does; the mythic ideal is implicit in the criticism of the mutable world of the present. His Cam, the resting place of the muses, the setting for learning and poetry, can no longer support the poetic myth, and is inhabited by very worldly nymphs; its *otium* is corrupted by the atmosphere of *negotium*. In the first of his *Piscatorie Eclogues*, for example, he tells of his growth as a scholar and poet in terms of the river, and how, as he matured, he "chang'd large *Thames* for *Chamus* narrower seas."[20] Ideally, the world of the river is one of poetry and learning, one based on a state of concord and characterized by the virtues of courtesy, constancy, love, and friendship. As Thomlin, Fletcher's piscatorial colleague, says of Cam, "More sweet, or fruitfull streames where canst thou finde?/ Where fisherlads, or Nymphs more faire, or kind?/The Muses selves sit with the sliding *Chame*:/*Chame* and the Muses selves do love thy name./Where thou art lov'd so deare, so much to hate is shame" (2.5).

Contrasting with this ideal is the reality of Fletcher's world of strife, enmity, and inconstancy. Thus, Fletcher uses the archetype of the river as friend of poets and nurse of the virtues that poetry subsists on to understand the meaning of his own modest pastoral world. Cam is polluted and behaves in a most un-river-like fashion; as Thirsil (Fletcher's pastoral identity) says: "His stubborn hands my net hath broken quite:/My fish (the guerdon of my toil and pain)/He causeless seiz'd" (2.8). Thirsil's indignation with his local river resembles the complaint of the lover-poet in Ovid (*Amores* 3); here the river's virtues are introduced only to expose the Cam's unnaturalness, but the recent Cambridge graduate lacks the self-mocking wit of Ovid.

Fletcher's autobiographical fisherman-poet is psychologically and physically exiled much as Sannazaro's Arcadian figures were. Cam's ingratitude and perfidy make poetry, the repository of all virtues and the only career represented in the eclogues, impossible:

> Ungratefull *Chame*! How oft hath *Thirsil* crown'd
> With songs and garlands thy obscurer head?
> That now thy name through *Albion* loud doth sound?
>   He whom thou lov'st can neither sing, nor play;

> His dusty pipe, scorn'd, broke, is cast away.
> Ah foolish *Chame*! who now shall grace thy holy-day? (2.8)

We can see how Fletcher's local landscape draws upon and suggests a national image. Cambridge is seen in terms of Britain's fame and literary posterity as sharing in the Spenserian legacy. He has compressed his national image and moved it from London. The Spenserian echoes magnify the unnaturalness of Cam's behavior, which appears as a perversion of the national spirit, so that we are aware of an autobiographical voice addressing a public ideal.

Spenser, focusing on the river, sees the world's vices and mutability and presses on to remake the world and to develop its potential. Fletcher sees the individual in the landscape as it is; his vision is, in its modest way, tragic rather than comic. He struggles against obstacles instead of surmounting them. The understanding that he reaches is of the world's condition, not its potential for renewal, and he stubbornly renounces it in a spirit very different from Colin Clout's:

> But seeing now I am not as I would,
> But here among th'unhonur'd willows shade,
> That muddy *Chame* doth me enforc'd hold;
> Here I forsweare my merry piping trade . . .
> Thou *Chame*, and *Chamish* Nymphes bear witness of my vow.[21]

"Seeing now I am not as I would," Thirsil breaks his pipes. This line expresses a spirit that Spenser resists throughout his verse, one which despairs at the discrepancy between what is and what should be. The analogous incident in *Faerie Queene* 6.10.15ff, points out the dramatic difference between the two poets' visions. Colin Clout's momentary anger when he breaks his pipes results from the courtly Calidore's indiscretion, not from society's enmity. It gives rise to poetry, an ecstatic hymn to the muses which, in turn, moves Calidore and instructs him in the virtues of poetry. Unlike the episode in Fletcher, this is not a complaint against court and society, although its focus is on society. The clash between ideal and real that results in the disappearance of the graces yields to an even more hopeful mood in which we see society improved by the song of the poet. This important episode in Spenser looks toward the integration of the poet into society, while Fletcher's focuses on alienation and the frustration of poetry.[22]

Fletcher's local landscape captures the "spirit of retirement" as it often appears during these years; it is one based not on a preference for a pastoral idea, but on a search for involvement coupled with a sense of exile. These "pastoral" poets use their rural setting—for lack of a better one—to try to put the national image in perspective, to find a moral and cultural climate conducive to their ideal, which is poetry. They respond sensitively to landscape; however, the landscape (and its society) seem to reject the poetic myth that drives them. There is, then, in these verses—and this applies to Basse, Brooke, Browne, and Drayton—a kind of desperate homelessness; any setting will do so long as they can write, and to write is of national importance. Consider, for instance, Fletcher's dissatisfaction and ambivalence toward place as he tries to choose a suitable landscape in which to settle:

> Ah! might I in some humble *Kentish* dale
> For ever eas'ly spend my slow-pac't houres:
> Much would I scorn fair Aêton's pleasant vale,
> Or *Windsor Tempe's* selfe, and proudest Towers:
> There would I set safe from the stormie showers . . .
> Piping (ah!) might I live, and piping might I die![23]

His exile, which is involuntary, can be compared with that of Ergasto, his analogue in Sannazaro's *Arcadia*, which is voluntary. Fletcher is tortured because he is rejected by his world. Ergasto's plight is more psychological; he has the freedom to choose his landscape—his social milieu—but he is tormented by imperfect knowledge of himself and the world.

Fletcher's landscape is transformed by his own psychology and values. There is jealousy implicit in his words; he longs for those fairer, more noble (and public) settings from which he has been exiled. The decision between a public and private life is hardly a choice at all; retirement means getting out of the storm so that one can continue to pipe. Fletcher, like Jonson, longs for involvement, but the worlds of university and court are too corrupt for poetry. There is no delight in the rural landscape; it always reminds the poet of a nobler setting. In all the Spenserian poets there is this desire for involvement, to be part of the larger scene, as Spenser seemed to have been, and in this they share his sensibility. Forced into retirement, their minds continually revert to the public world:

> So much we sport, we have no time to grieve;
> Here do we sit, and laugh white-headed caring.[24]

Thus, from their Kentish and Devonian banks they give us a glimpse of the smaller rivers, but these springs are always tuned to the national Thames, the true source of these provincial waters.

To a large extent this pastoral posturing echoes *Colin Clouts come home againe*. But Spenser's character has a free hand in choosing his setting. He rejects the court; the court does not reject him. His voice is always admonitory, enjoining his fellow poets to further verse. After all, Spenser was a settler, and part of a bold (if rather risky) scheme, and his verse reflects a diehard pioneer's optimism. The Spenserian poets, between 1613 and 1620, move between London, the universities, and their paternal estates. These are historical settings and could not support a myth which looks to and symbolizes the future. In their retirement their rural leisure soon turns to urbane *ennui*. They wish for some sort of national anthem, but their songs are always solitary voices. Their verse, then, looks unrealistically on the past. For them the poet had lost his place in the nation; the *genius loci* was no longer Apollinian, his sisters were no longer muses. They took to the rivers as an avenue to the nobler past, not as a transforming image. They try to travel it to a false Spenserian ideal, but it offers no way back, partly because the ideal is a false one, partly because they allow it to fetter, rather than free their imaginations, and partly because the past cannot be recreated. Their verse, however, shares poetic and cultural ideals that Spenser held (and this is quite a different thing), although their technique is primarily autobiographical. They too attempt to see the poet in his world, but their vision is obscured by trivial details; they are unable to create an appropriate setting for the poet, as Spenser was able to do. In this sense, then, Fletcher and his fellow poets in dry-dock, and Brooke and Basse and the other shepherds fighting the encroaching swineherds, are all realistic in a way that Spenser was not. Emphasizing the close relation between courtesy, friendship, love, and poetry as their mentor did, they see the world for what it is—inimical to these virtues—and in this they are incipient satirists. Their rivers are those of the world and time, then, but their energies are spent in showing the changes of the times that have laid waste to their poetic traditions. Their rivers are too much of the times and not of time itself.

The differences that appear in these treatments of the river are the result of the merging of the myths of biography and history, the tendency to see time personally rather than nationally. As in the portrait of Henry Unton, there is too much foreground and a blurred background. The Spenserian poets, then, represent an unwilling shift from a broad public or national perspective on landscape, to a primarily private one which concentrates on the individual's place in society. It is a shift that seems to be belied by the public, epideictic literature which forged (in both senses of the word) an official image of national concord but within which we can also see evidence of the private voice of dissent. The poetry of Fletcher and others of the Spenserians reflects the fact that society was indeed more fragmented; there was no encouragement for poets to perceive the landscape within an encompassing national perspective. Thus, if these poets lament the passing of an ideal, it is because the society and the intellectual climate which supported it have changed. The image of the nation must evolve as the nation does. For the Spenserians the rivers were a constant reminder of the past embedded in the landscape, and for their readers as well they are an index of the incipient changes.

3. The River Divided: Public Rivers and Private Voices—Michael Drayton and William Browne

> O loyal father of a treacherous son!
> Thou sheer, immaculate and silver fountain,
> From whence this stream, through muddy passages,
> Hath held his current and defil'd himself,
> Thy overflow of good converts to bad.
>
> (Shakespeare, *Richard II*)

> O could I flow like thee, and make thy stream
> My great example, as it is my theme!
> Though deep, yet clear; though gentle, yet not dull;
> Strong without rage, without o'erflowing, full.
>
> (John Denham, *Cooper's Hill*)

Although the Spenserian poets indicate real changes in the perception of landscape during the first quarter of the century, seen in the context of their contemporaries (Donne and Jonson, for example), they are more easily recognized for what they are: distinct and important links with that Elizabethan sensibility, participating almost inadvertently in the changes in perspective, voice, and style that they wanted to forestall. But the changes that finally turned the river from its national and potentially epic dimensions to a particularly local landscape whose interest is primarily aesthetic, came about very gradually, so that the motif is a useful reminder of the limitations of certain commonplaces about distinctions between Tudor and Stuart topographical literature. Notwithstanding the changes evident in the river motif of these poets, they are closer to Spenser than they are to Milton and Marvell, although they tend to be studied in the context of the later poets. Once again, the river is useful: it puts into relief those continuities between Tudor and Stuart response to the national geography. Thus, the literary impulse that originally gave meaning to the river in the Renaissance, the grand plan to outline a national image in terms of the rivers and their historical and topographical associations, to create a national myth equivalent to that of antiquity, persisted to the end of James's reign, and sporadically thereafter, even as late as the Restoration. In several major works of the period, and in numerous manuscripts and publications which are now rare, the poem which creates a cultural myth from the nation's rivers and has its native origins in the revival of antiquity in the Reformation continues to be an obsessive but elusive literary goal. Although they show a dimming perception of the unified national landscape, their sensitivity to both the geography and the literary tradition carries the river motif as it first emerged in the Renaissance well into the seventeenth century, as we see in John Speed's *Theatre of . . . Great Britain* (1611). However, the most interesting examples reflect Spenser's influence on the myth-making mind and reveal the desire to harmonize myth and history by marrying *The Faerie Queene* and the *Britannia*. Two works in particular demonstrate this obsession with the essentially Tudor form of the river epic: Drayton's *Poly-Olbion* and William Browne's *Britannia's Pastorals*. Seen together, they illustrate the realization of the generic ideal and, at the same time, the inevitable cultural changes which make its literary success, as a national myth, impossible.

Ironically, *Poly-Olbion* is the most important illustration of the poetic use of the rivers to coordinate a historical and topographical image of the nation and also of the decline of the convention and its popularity during the second decade of the century. In his peculiarly self-conscious art and in his development of the river as a national *genius*, especially in *Poly-Olbion*, Drayton examines the adequacy of that image and its prospects as a poetic form in ways that Spenser does not.

Drayton was a professional Spenserian who continually (and on principle) worked in conventional Elizabethan modes, and so his poetry testifies to the conscientiousness with which the potential of the river motif was developed. Like Spenser, he served his literary apprenticeship with the rivers, experimenting with their possibilities in the sonnet and pastoral, and identifying himself and his muse with the rivers of his youth. He is the perfect example of that desire to create commensurate personal and national myths.[25] Personal as much of his verse is, there is no distinction between his public and private voice; it all contributes to the nation's poetic legacy. In the 1580s and 1590s, following the example of the Continental poets, he envisioned his future as a British bard in terms of a transformed personal landscape, hoping that his rivers would flow pure Helicon as his art took its place in the national poetic. Thus, his intentions were national rather than personal. No less than Spenser and Ronsard, he hoped to create a private world within a national topography that in the course of time would be coextensive with the public world and the national setting. Everywhere in his verse he mingles classical themes with local river settings, and identifies his muse with his own poetic growth, but all with an implicit patriotic design. Perhaps even more than Spenser's, Drayton's is a cerebral realm where his own identity merges with his nation's; he is a totally public poet in the sense that all his work is the product of England's *genius*, while at the same time he is very private writing about himself as a servant of the nation.

In his own lifetime he served as the prototype of the Spenserian, linking Spenser and his younger imitators. But born 1563, eleven years after Spenser, he must be seen as a contemporary Elizabethan and as a disciple who was trying to do with his collected work what Spenser was doing with his, not only in *The Faerie Queene*, but in his approach to all his verse. In a way he succeeded in making his poetry the perfect analogue to his mind, and therefore the expression of his total identification with his nation; he made his poetry his life, and through poetry he took his place in the affairs of the nation.

It is impossible to understand the essential nature of Drayton's verse without understanding this laureate quality. It is the professional poet's view of the progress from pastoral to georgic and epic. For Drayton, each stage of personal development is a stratum in the formation of the national poetic. There were others who shared this professional self-image: to a degree Spenser did; Jonson and Daniel did as well; Sidney did not, but should have. But for each of these poets it is necessary to understand the psychology behind the poetry, and while there are not very many such figures in the Renaissance, they represent the essence of what poetry stood for during the period.

Both formally and thematically, the river was unsurpassably well suited for Drayton's purposes. He took his self-appointed role as poet laureate seriously; he memorialized the forms of the period, and by writing so obsessively about rivers, he canonizes the form for us. They have the conventionality characteristic of all his verse, so that all his rivers have their frame of reference, one way or another, in the generic conventions of the day, although most particularly in Spenser. Thus Drayton's Elizabethanism is also his Spenserianism; this becomes increasingly true after Spenser's death, when he ceased to be an elusive rival and became someone to be imitated.

In 1598, two years after the publication of the second part of *The Faerie Queene*, Drayton caught the lingering infection of Leland's still-troubled spirit and was possessed with the desire to create a vast image of the realm in rivers. He, too, was cured only through death—the work occupied him for the rest of his life. And as the work, *Poly-Olbion*, progressed, over the years he saw its audience dwindle, realized that it was anachronistic, and grew to doubt himself and his faith in the future of his nation. However, his compulsion to complete the work was based in his poetic identity; the very nature of the work was representative of the age, and therefore it had to be written. The idea itself probably had its immediate source of inspiration in Spenser's "Epithalamion Thamesis," and no doubt Drayton was pleased that the prince of poets never quite succeeded with that work, so that in *Poly-Olbion* he could out-Spenser Spenser.

The idea, though, was generally in the air, and it was Drayton's duty to condense it into verse. As others had, he had practiced with the motif in its compact, sonnet form, the objective of which was to contain *multum in parvo*, to compress a river into fourteen lines.[26] But in *Poly-Olbion* his goal was amplification—Jonson would probably have said in order to contain *parvum in multo*. At the very least, though, he achieves what many others had failed to do, and he culminates a literary form and impulse that had been maturing for decades. Thus, when he says to Prince Henry that "my Poeme is genuine, and first in this kind" (iii*), he is both correct and incorrect. Genre in this case antecedes prototype—there is no other work quite like it, but it is generally quite conventional. It is at once very familiar and yet wholly unique.

This paradox is almost entirely due to the river motif. *Poly-Olbion* is the monument of river literature. So ubiquitous are the rivers that it is a wonder that no one has questioned their appearance before, and yet his use of them leads naturally to the conclusion that there was a form of river verse—to conclude otherwise is to grant too much originality to a traditionalist like Drayton. Once one is aware of the rivers, it becomes obvious that the poet develops all his themes of nature, history, and time in terms of them: every aspect of the *topos* is exploited here in a prevailingly Elizabethan nationalistic context.

And yet, in the Renaissance conventionality is not a bar to originality, and Drayton uses his rivers to present a conception of history in which geography and nature interact with time. Through his rivers, Drayton develops an image of England which lies somewhere between Leland's historical positivism and Spenser's Neoplatonic didacticism, and in this respect, as one writing from the convention itself, he takes a different attitude toward the period in which and to which he writes. His view of history develops from his knowledge of Leland, Camden, and Spenser. Drayton is reassessing the attitudes of his elders and contemporaries and the viability of their national judgments, and in so doing, even more than Camden, Drayton turns to the landscape for a perspective on history. While there are many similarities in their use of geography, Camden uses it to call our attention to the need for historical myth, to make us see legend in the landscape, while Drayton, with the more judgmental spirit of the Spenserians, uses it to measure myth against the moment, and so to appraise the adequacy of the one for the other. Thus, in *Poly-Olbion*, Albion's pride is put to the test of time, and during the poem's long gestation, Drayton perceives not only that it might fail, but also how much it is prone to the effects of time.

Thus, contrary to what is usually said about *Poly-Olbion*, Drayton does not idealize the past, fond of it though he is. His interest is in how historical myths relate to time. He sees their arbitrariness and contradictions and realizes that all myth is modern, turned to the tastes of the age. Critics writing about *Poly-Olbion* usually speak of his treatment of history, but they fail to distinguish between topography and history when in fact these are two radically different aspects of the poem and its image of Britain.[27] Drayton formulates a historic nationalism based in geographical nature. This is an encompassing myth of time itself, one which transcends the debilitating partisanship and factionalism that attends a more parochial sense of history, and provides the kind of friction that we see in the debates over the existence of Brutus, or over relative merits of British, Roman, or Saxon England. His concern is to go beyond the accidents of time to see Britain timelessly in a myth of geography.

Drayton's use of the national landscape is distinctly different from Camden's, for example. For the poet, the landscape reconciles the contradictions in historical myth and legend. Thus, only in a limited sense is it true that Drayton "conflate[s] history and geography."[28] Certainly they go together, as surely as history needs a setting. But we judge them differently, and they provide the reader with completely different moral (and narrative) perspectives. He sets out, as his full title tells us, to celebrate first the country and its wonders, its nature, and geography, and second, its people and history, and this is pretty much the moral hierarchy of the poem: nature has a higher moral purpose than does human history. It also embodies a myth which is greater than those of history because it embraces them. Drayton's priorities then are important; for Camden, geography ratifies the fictions of the imagination and history; for Drayton it puts them in perspective. Drayton is careful to emphasize that his muse is the *genius* of the land, whose principal residence is in the soil, though her perspective includes both time and space. Reinforcing this idea are the frontispiece and the verses which describe it and invite us to envision the "*Happy* Site" in Neptune's embrace; images of national achievement and antiquity circle the *genius*—the nation itself—like satellites in orbit. The opening lines reiterate Drayton's prime concern and his priorities:

> OF ALBIONS glorious Ile the Wonders whilst I write,
> The sundry varying soyles, the pleasures infinite.

All history is presented in terms of the landscape: we see and hear nothing of human events but it is told to us, or shown us by topographical personifications. His muse is a riverine *genius* who leads him through the land, following the course of the rivers. As a nature deity she is older than human history, the springs of which are to be found within her:

> Thou *Genius* of the place (this most renowned Ile)
> Which livedst long before the All-earth-drowning Flood,

Whilst yet the world did swarme with her Gigantick brood;
Goe thou before me (1.8–11)

The priority of the myth of landscape is further suggested by
Selden's illustrations at the end of each song of Part 1. As Selden
frequently tells us, Drayton is not greatly concerned with historical
precision; the illustrations are meant as clarification, to set straight
the facts that Drayton has taken blatant poetic liberties with.
Selden's tolerant notes on Drayton's "history" remind the reader
that historical facts are not the poet's prime concern, and this is
precisely what Drayton and Selden realized in their collaboration.
Even the specially designed maps reinforce the topographical emphasis. Landscape is razed of nearly all the usual signs of human
presence and achievement; only diminutive towers garland the
heads of the buxom river nymphs; otherwise, they depict an unem-
bellished topography. Missing are the signs of humanity's shaping
influence usually included on Renaissance maps, the symbols depicting the religious, military, and civilizing presence of society and
history. The full effect of these artificially primitive maps can best
be had by seeing them beside the standard Saxton maps, which
flaunt a humane geography gaudy with information about human
influence on the terrain; in them nature is wholly transformed by
art. Hole's versions of these maps, instead of being described as "of
little geographical use," might be seen as of only geographical use.[29]
Drayton expects us to see the maps, to read the landscape in verse,
and to understand the history in its context as serving it. Such a
comparison should reveal the uniqueness of Drayton's view of time,
history, and the nation. He is redefining the "right relation" between people and nature. He almost seems to be trying to escape
from human history and to find a voice which is finally an impartial
one. In thus separating history and topography, and reversing the
conventional method of viewing landscape in the Renaissance, he
explores the dynamics of man's relation to nature: instead of seeing
the environment as a product of human presence, he sees people as
a product of their environment.

"Dynamic" is a useful critical term for describing Drayton's view
of Britain. His animated landscape is in a state of continual flux. It is
copious, richly varied to the point of confusion. This nearly chaotic
material nature, consisting of rivers, plains, forests, and hills, where
individuals are but transient figures, is ultimately harmonious in its
natural state of incessant change. Thus, for him the national geogra-

phy has the qualities of a large *locus amoenus*, consisting of extremes in a state of perpetual reconciliation, of opposites constantly resolving themselves in moderation. This is his view of nature and the nation, as he makes perfectly clear in the early lines of Song 1:

> OF ALBIONS glorious Ile the Wonders whilst I write,
> The sundry varying soyles, the pleasures infinite
> (Where heate kills not the cold, nor cold expells the heat,
> The calms too mildly small, nor winds too roughly great,
> Nor night doth hinder day, nor day the night doth wrong,
> The Summer not too short, the Winter not too long)
> What helpe shall I invoke to ayde my Muse the while? (1.1–7)

Like Spenser, Drayton looks to nature for moral lessons, but his conception of *concordia discors* is entirely different—the difference between necessary strife and moderation. Likewise, Drayton perceives a harmonious spirit in nature, but his idea of concord also differs from Spenser's: it is one of accommodation rather than of the violent yoking together of opposites, and this extends to Drayton's very benign view of time, despite the violence of history. Thus *Poly-Olbion* is a long series of confrontations and conflicting passions, set in the landscape, and resolving themselves in an affirmation of nature's ability to persevere by accommodation. His technique at first seems to present an ominous sense of conflict in nature and history, but in fact it is one which emphasizes sanity and compromise, and the early songs in particular locate this lesson in nature rather than history. Song 3, for example, is rife with what seem to be foreboding conflicts in nature, but Drayton's Argument to the song establishes a comic, rather than tragic tone: "In this third Song, great threatenings are,/And tending all to Nymphish warre." The author never allows nature to become menacing. In this song we hear how Salisbury Plain kindles the love of two neighboring rivers, the Willy and the "Eastern Avon." The rivers contend in heated jealousy for her love, until report is "lately rais'd" that a third and matchless rival, "Bathes clear Avon," approaches to offer suit. Drayton's nature has its Machiavellian side, and with all due aquatic agility, the smaller waters temper their passion with policy:

> This when these Rivers heard, that even but lately strove
> Which best did love the *Plaine*, or had the *Plaines* best love,
> They straight themselves combine: for Willy wiselie waide,

> That should her *Avon* lose the day for want of aide,
> If one so great and neere were overprest with power,
> The Foe (shee beeing lesse) would quicklie her devour. (3.93–98)

This rather political conception of concord is Drayton's equivalent of Spenser's Platonic view of harmonious love and friendship in nature; as Selden sententiously explains, "This compendious contention . . . is aptly concluded with that point of ancient politique observation, that Outward common feare is the surest band of friendship." The poet goes on to elaborate on the political ramifications of this lesson of policy in nature which he derives from the geographic phenomenon of two lesser rivers flowing together to form one larger one.

The *exemplum* thus represented topographically is the creative principle of Drayton's world, and increasingly in the later songs it is carried directly into the poet's interpretation of history. For him history is not a myth imposed on the landscape, but one extracted from it. In Songs 8 and 9, for example, historical motifs emerge from topographical contentions. When the Severn, with a full consort of tributary rivers, sings the praises of the British kings, the *genius* of Merionethshire complains that her British worthies were not also celebrated, and she goes on to praise her own rivers which have graced and protected the country. The numerous river nymphs become rowdy, and the surrounding mountains also become jealous and commence their own song, until the confusion, which reflects the rough and chaotic landscape of the area itself, approaches violence. But Mount Snowdon looks on in grand superiority to the confused terrain, and attempts to reconcile them by uniting them in a common nationalistic cause:

> So, when great *Snowdon* saw, a Faction they would make
> Against his generall kind; both parties to appease
> Hee purposeth to sing their native Princes peace. (9.167–69)

Drayton's conciliatory landscape teaches us that when rivals stand on common ground, so to speak, their opposition should be of a complementary (and complimentary) rather than antagonistic nature. The rivers are then joined in harmony, and each individually removes toward the Irish Sea, singing Snowdon's praises (9.371–78). The episode here is meant to address, among other things, the nature of historiography itself. Supporters of historical myths and factions should not allow their rivalry to assume more importance than the patriotic objectives for which their parties and debates exist. Drayton tries to go beyond the factional issues of British and English history and attempts to find an enduring and shared identity and moral perspective on nature.

Both Drayton's history and his landscape are preeminently natural; both are interpreted in terms of nature's order. The usual critical opinion, that his description of Britain is historical,[30] does not go very far and distorts the narrative itself. While British history is certainly one of Drayton's favorite topics, it is put into perspective; he subordinates it to his view of *concordia discors* in external nature. British, Saxon, and Norman, to say nothing of Scottish and Irish, are all factions assimilated into British history, and all are participants in the inevitable process of change in nature and so must submit to the prevailing authority of his *genius loci*. In the same manner, Drayton's complaints about contemporary problems, the dangers of pollution, deforestation, enclosure, and the spoliation of the national landscape all assert the precedence of the land over the exclusive claims of separate parties.

The principal historical rivalry of *Poly-Olbion* is, of course, between proponents of the English and the British factions, but to argue Drayton's Welsh bias is to misread his topography and hence his history. In this matter he uses his landscape much as Camden does, to reinforce his view of history, but if the technique is similar, the objectives are very different. He does not submit the landscape to the same severe structuring principle that Camden does.[31] There is a kind of simultaneity in Drayton's historical geography in which events happen as though all at once, and this "equalizes" each faction by removing the superiority that is accorded by antiquity alone. As Drayton's muse carries us from county to county, she also takes us through various stages of British history, but not in a strictly chronological order. Nature and History as well as individual histories vie for her attention. For example, as we move to the extremes of Wales and cross the Dee and Severn rivers, there naturally arises a clash between Welsh and English sentiments. The "English" river Weaver angrily compares himself to the holy Welsh river Dee and objects that the English riparian worthies deserve no less praise than the Welsh. Drayton takes an intelligent and unbiased view of the usual complaint that the British past remains uncelebrated and suggests that the same is equally true of the English past. As the debate between the local rivers intensifies, topography again intervenes in the form of the Severn, who (being a border) is of both parties. It is she who delivers the lesson that there is a higher order determining history and that the "celestiall Powers" decided "when o're this generall Ile the Britaines rayne should end" (11.154). The end of British rule is seen as the inevitable result of time, nature, and God's purpose.

Song 12 continues the process of mediation by pointing out the common interests of both factions. Drayton's use of the national landscape for a view of history becomes clearer. Here again, a river which rises in Wales but which is an English ally (that is, it passes into England) is called upon to mediate. As old Wrekin says;

> The *Britains* should not yet all from the *English* beare;
> Therefore, quoth he, brave Flood, though forth by *Cambria*
>   brought,
> Yet as faire *Englands* friend, or mine thou wouldst be thought,
> (O Severn!) Let thine eare my just defence partake. (12.37–40)

The river consents, and in the ensuing perorations Drayton skillfully dramatizes the river's conventional role in legend and landscape— that of mediator.[32] The river judiciously praises the Welsh in order to compare the English to them. In some nicely poised rhetoric, the river's symbolic significance is acted out as the river makes each faction's esteem of its rival essential for the basis of its own self-respect. The topography thus demonstrates how the complementary elements in Drayton's historical dialectic are separate but equal.

As is inevitably the case in such a compromising view of history, individual issues become unimportant in themselves. What *is* important is the larger pattern of change itself, and the recognition of the past in the present. For Drayton, then, an understanding of nature's patterns is necessary for an understanding of history. The landscape teaches people how to live with time and how to accommodate it. The details of history are made unimportant beneath the natural pattern of growth; in short, the lesson of time and nature is that of the relation between art and nature, history and time. This is put most clearly in an episode which stands out as the *locus communis* for Drayton's major themes—the musical strife between the Welsh and English river muses for possession of the Ile of Lundy, dominating Songs 4 and 5. The *débat*, having a general (and generic) resemblance to similar Ovidian contests involving rivers, locates Drayton's concern for the way that the conflict between art and nature is itself a reflection of *concordia discors* in both nature and

history. Although the episode is superficially concerned with historical themes, Drayton is careful to make sure that the particulars do
not obscure his point. Thus, we are not much concerned with what
becomes of Lundy, "a Nymph to idle toyes inclin'd." Our interest is
rather in the nature of the strife itself, which is conducted in
the watery court of Severn—yet another river cave and source of
wisdom.

Drayton's treatment of this contest between the muses, in which
each faction again sings its nation's history, emphasizes the theme of
poetry and history and their relation to nature. The entire episode is
an expansion of the *topos* of the pastoral *débat*, and its every detail,
in all its artificiality, stresses not so much what is sung or why, as
how—the poet is here exploring the nature of his own art, not only
its subject matter, but also its formal qualities.

The episode begins with an epic call to arms and a catalogue of
the rivers drawing together to join the contest; even in this watery
convocation the harmonizing process is evident, as the rivers gather
from distant parts of the nation, coming together in response to the
summons to defend their nation. But what is particularly germane
about Drayton's treatment of this *topos* is the importance that he
places on the kinds of music that are performed and their relative
naturalness, and in this he goes back to the orginal significance of
the contest in antiquity.[33] Each faction is distinguished by its own
musical mode which both contrasts with and is similar to its rival's.
Thus, the Welsh nymphs' songs are presented as seeming to be more
natural, an expression of the "sacred rage" articulated without
obtrusive form and accompanied only by the simple harp. And yet
their songs (we are told) are no less varied, skilled or profound for
this seeming simplicity:

> So varying still their Moods, observing yet in all
> Their Quantities, their Rests, their Caesures metricall.
> For to that Sacred skill they most themselves apply,
> Addicted from their births so much to Poësie.   (4.185–92)

A paradox informs their art. It is a reconciliation of opposites:
ironically its naturalness is the product of ancient tradition and
practice.

The English nymphs, on the other hand, display their skill in
highly formal songs richly adorned with instrumentation. Despite
this apparent artificiality, their remarkable enthusiasm, and the

agility of their performance and use of their instruments make their music seem more natural. Thus their songs too show art and nature in harmony:

> But th'*English* that repyn'd to be delay'd so long,
> All quicklie at the hint, as with one free consent,
> Strooke up at once and sung each to the Instrument;
> (Of sundry sorts that were, as the Musician likes)
> On which the practic'd hand with perfect'st fingring strikes,
> Whereby their height of skill might livliest be exprest.
> The trembling Lute some touch, some straine the Violl best
> In sets which there were seene, the musick wondrous choice:
> Some likewise there affect the Gamba with the voice,
> To shew that England could varietie afford. (4.350–59)

Both the "sacred rage" of the Welsh and the "learn'd strife" of the English are the natural products of their separate historical traditions—their art is the expression of nature and history together. Their contrapuntal music is the varied and satisfying song of England's past, and from it we learn that "England could varietie afford." Both kinds of music are traditional, and both are natural. Nature and history accommodate both and benefit from both. History thus serves nature. More particularly, the *débat* shows the importance of the poet for preserving the past, for keeping it alive and in touch with nature; the poet is nature's agent, as well as history's. Poetry and all its forms are part of the natural process of continuity, of order emerging from chaos. It celebrates concord not just because it imitates the music of the spheres (a conventional motif Drayton also emphasizes), but because it shares in the uninterrupted flow of time. Poetic kinds are like the rivers of *Poly-Olbion*, for they are self-perpetuating and eternal, although the singer and the specifics of the history she sings of are mortal. There is, in both factions, a "free consent" which draws the nymphs into a poetic order which transcends the individual and particular. In this, the dynamics of poetry are the same as those of nature.

The example of the music itself supports the point of the episode as a whole, expressed in Sabrina's judgment concerning the insignificance of Lundy, and her exhortation to unity and concord: "Why strive yee then for that, in little time that shall/(As you are all made one) be one unto you all" (5.76–7). Sabrina's solution to the problem of history and time reflected in Lundy's fate—and it resembles at least one of Hamlet's problems—is comic rather than tragic. The river, then, as a body continuous in time and space, is a device that enables Drayton to look forward in time and perceive the common destiny shared by both factions. From the diverse concord of Britain comes a vision of both the unity of time and the community of individuals, and Botero's political science finds its full expression through the metaphor of poetry itself. Poetry is the voice of unity and continuity which transcends the accidents of history, time, and place.

Drayton has fully assimilated the sense of unity that covertly exerted its influence on Renaissance historical writers. For both poets and geographers, "consent" and "concord," used within the context of time, were essential words in the rhetoric of rivers. The contest in Songs 4 and 5 explores the theme of the relation between art, nature, and history in a coherent, almost theoretical form. His conclusions, that artistic form and kind share in nature's processes and are themselves a celebration of the importance of the myth of history, are certainly consistent with his own poetic techniques, in which form is often more important than poetic content. And they are radically different from those of Spenser and others who used the river to explore these themes. Drayton attempts to reconcile art, nature, and history. He is concerned with poetry's role in absorbing history and assimilating it into the social order; poetry overcomes the limitations of history. But Spenser had a greater belief in the creative faculty of the imagination. He saw poetry as creating myth and directing history, his mythic rivers are Hellenic while Drayton's are Roman.

The rivers' musical lesson in these songs informs Drayton's view of history generally. Through the landscape he perceives the need for accommodation and moderation. He embraces historical lore with an open-mindedness that piqued his annotator; all history and its transformation into myth are the expression of a natural process. There is a tolerance, even a passivity in Drayton's verse; he loves history but is impatient with historians and their strife. But in presenting history and poetry as nature's agents, he hopes to order change and minimize human folly. There is an element of distrust in his view of human affairs, and in the course of *Poly-Olbion* he gets more and more bitter about the decline of the times, the vices and vanities and anti-intellectualism of the period. This does not alter his benign view of time, only of man. Nevertheless, in the rivers' musical strife for Lundy, he is able to formulate his ideas in a way that suggests, at least theoretically, an ideal rapport between the poet and society, and this myth-making quality makes him a poet of considerable importance.

Notwithstanding their different views of society, then, for both Spenser and Drayton, rivers serve as the voice of nature. This becomes increasingly important for *Poly-Olbion*, as humanity becomes distanced from nature and is seen as more and more unnatural. Through them Drayton is able to distance himself from human follies and to accentuate the unity of history and nature and to de-emphasize the particulars of human behavior. Interestingly, in the course of the century poets look more and more frequently to nature as an antidote to history. This is most conspicuously the case in Drayton's adaptation of the Spenserian motif of the marriage of the Thames and Medway in the concluding five songs of Part 1. Drayton uses poetic form (built into the river poem) in harmony with the landscape to evoke an image of a creative union and order which extends beyond human affairs. As Homer does in the opening of Book 12 of the *Iliad*, he uses the rivers to adumbrate a future which surpasses the vision and memory of mankind.

The marriage of the Thames and Medway dictates the shape of these four books in the way that we have already seen river topography determining the form of prose and verse. And throughout the very circuitous narrative of Thames's course to the Medway, Drayton continues to digress on history and topography and to personify his landscape. In this relation between the landscape and the narrative Drayton further qualifies his Spenserian image of concord in nature. His treatment of these personified rivers, particularly the Thames, stresses the indirect, seemingly willful pattern of history, and this circuitousness is reiterated in the verse. Drayton's narrative is discontinuous; he digresses from and returns to the story of the river marriage, making his verse exaggerate the irregularity of the river's course. Historical and topographical details that enter Spenser's river descriptions as a brief epithet are here enlarged to whole episodes interrupting the flow of the story. Thus, he indulges in frequent conventional city descriptions in which art is seen to garland nature, in enthusiastic visions of human achievement, qualified by the violence of history. He often digresses on the effects of mutability, and the lamentable changes of the present age: "the angry Muse, thus on the Time exclames,/Sith everything therin consisteth in extreames" (16.359–60). This conspicuously erratic narrative presents an ambiguous view of history, one which wavers between patriotic enthusiasm and misanthropic despair, but Drayton joins these varying moods in a conception of the reconciliation of opposites, as part of nature's dialectic.

As Thames works his willful way toward his chosen bride, exhibiting every kind of youthful impetuosity and rebellion and resisting his parents' authority and their right to determine the course of his married life, we know that his marriage is, nevertheless, inevitable. The passions, follies, and whims that Drayton attributes to the young river are as nothing against the certainty of the landscape and the course of nature and time. This contrasts sharply with Spenser's treatment of the union of rivers. Social order and convention in Drayton's river marriage are in harmony with nature and figure the inevitable pattern of human affairs, while in Spenser love takes its own course. But we know the outcome of Thames's resistance not only because of nature, but also because of art through the inevitability that is conveyed by Drayton's use of literary form. So it is throughout *Poly-Olbion*: the human attributes of his rivers—their pride and willfulness—finally yield to natural inclinations and the tendency toward confluence, which are also presented in terms of social order, restraint, reason, and convention. Drayton's myth of geography, then, is one of order and reason; he uses it to draw his themes of history and nature together and set an example of naturalness—or concord—in human affairs. It is in this way that *Poly-Olbion* too seeks to fashion gentlemen to "gentle and virtuous discipline." The rivers humanize history; by making it personal, they give Drayton's reader a humane perspective on events which are usually removed from such a personal context. Thus contemporary events, which Drayton laments, and the past, which he both praises and dispraises, are seen as part of the same encompassing natural and temporal process.

But the river marriage which dictates the structure of these last five songs of Part 1 is perhaps of even more interest for what it suggests about Drayton's view of his art and literary form. As we have said, the marriage of the rivers is as certain poetically as it is naturally; poetic convention as much as topography necessitates their union despite Thames's resistance. In protracting this episode and amplifying it as much as possible when its outcome is foreseeable, the poet shows us the harmony between nature and literature. But he also makes an important point about the how they work together to resist the effacing effects of time. Poetry is one of Drayton's major themes in *Poly-Olbion*, and his treatment of it offers us an important insight into Renaissance aesthetics. Like the delayed union of Thames and Medway and their fulfillment of society's and nature's will, then, Drayton's verse, in its very conventionality, will survive as the natural product of its age and thus as a monument withstanding time because it is part of time's workings. This belief in form itself legitimizes Drayton's work. Written against a background of inescapable cultural change and a mood of indifference, *Poly-Olbion* is an immense repository of history, rumor, fable, and descriptive topography. It is a testament to change, a record of the mutability of human values and social truths, and a compendium attesting to human inconstancy. At the same time it is a memorial to a prevalent convention, symbolized best by the river poem, with its origins in the national topography. As such, it defies time and the times, denouncing them and the effects of change while embodying them, capturing them in its very form and subject matter—aesthetically, it resembles an artistically designed documentary. Thus, it assents to change as inevitable while attempting to resist it. Its form captures both convention and change, past and present, and in this way, through convention, Drayton perceives the world in a momentary order and submits it to a harmony which is both transient and enduring.

Drayton, unlike Spenser, is essentially passive beneath the influence of time. He retains a tenacious belief in the need for tradition and for the importance of an intellectual and historical sensibility, although his own view of time as gradually but certainly eroding them points to their inevitable futility. He does not argue that things remain unchanged from their first estate. Holding desperately to his sense of order, Drayton's cultural self-consciousness is both greater than and different from Spenser's. He increasingly argues for an intellectual tradition, not so much out of a belief in its durability, as in an effort to hold off barbarism and ignorance for as long as possible. Literature alone will not preserve the past and its values; an intellectual tradition, based on the belief in the importance of the transmission of ideas, is essential—what he calls the "memorable act" (10.274):

> . . . when we lay it up within the minds of men,
> They leave it their next Age; that, leaves it hers agen:
> So strongly which (me thinks) doth for Tradition make,
> As if you from the world it altogether take,
> You utterly subvert Antiquitie thereby.
> For though Time well may prove that often shee doth lie,

Posteritie by her yet many things hath known
That ere man learn'd to write, could no way have been shown.
(10.275–82)

How close to, and yet so very far from Spenser's ideas this is! Drayton is not concerned here with literary monuments or history's "simple veritie." All things transmitted from the past are of value in resisting ignorance. Drayton, resigned to time's omnipotence, is concerned with the power of the mind itself and with retaining the place of rational human endeavors—a somewhat more desperate position than Spenser's.

More and more certainly in Part 2 even this dim belief in what sounds like a primitive oral tradition fades. His river nymphs, who have repeated their local histories so often in earlier songs, seem to perceive their own and society's incipient idiocy, or senility, and lapse into a state of despairing apathy: "'Tis but in vaine to tell, what we before have been/Or changes of the world, that we in time have seen" (17.397–98). As natural images of change and continuity (note the nymphs' delight in change), history, and evolution, the river nymphs are self-consuming, creating themselves out of existence. Drayton's patience in the face of time in Part 1 yields to an acknowledgment of the processes of devolution that go to the heart of the poet's humanism; man is more slave than master. Yet, in its willing bondage to tradition, Drayton's art springs from a greater depth of understanding than is achieved by the private complaints of most of the other Spenserians. And interestingly Drayton's world, based on a modest aim to preserve tradition and a principle of accommodation, is far more vulnerable than Spenser's world, boldly recreated as it is by a transforming imagination, resisting any compromise with time, and insisting on human mastery over nature.

This disillusion and sense of futility are built not only into Drayton's conception of time but also into his understanding of his role as a poet and his sense of form. In this he is in part a product of his age. With a realistic awareness of the character of the age that is typical of the Spenserian poets, Drayton addresses himself to the age and its flaws. There is something rather fatalistic, even masochistic about his determination to create an epic portrait of the realm when the taste for such historical works was clearly past. But like other of the persevering Elizabethans who are determined to speak of the "Rarities and Historie of our owne Country delivered by a true native Muse," he intends to perpetuate the tradition against all odds. As he says to Prince Henry in his Dedication, just prior to the Prince's death, he is fully aware in 1612 that this is "such a season, when the Idle Humerous world must heare of nothing, that either savors of Antiquity, or may awake it to seeke after more, then dull and slothfull ignorance may reach unto" (V*). And although he overstates the case—he had many intelligent and industrious readers—this is something that Spenser could not have said in 1596. Even those who admired *Poly-Olbion* respected it, as Jonson did, more as a monument to an idea than for itself.[34]

Poly-Olbion, then, erected on a vicarious foundation of ideas alone, all but culminates a tradition, and between 1613 and the publication of Part 2 in 1623, Drayton's national river muse is kept alive only through artificial means. He continues his work because it must be completed, knowing full well that even the audience that he had in 1613 had largely disappeared. And yet, Drayton's headstone to the tradition remained in a curiously fitting way incomplete. The essential books on Scotland—essential for any "unified" view of Britain after 1603—remained not quite finished, unprinted, and the object of his friends' searches for several years after his death. Yet, to some considerable degree, Drayton has been vindicated, and his work has retained a modest popularity continuously since his death, and has exerted a quiet influence on authors of industry and imagination (not the least of whom was James Joyce) who perceived the rivers as an enigmatic link between cerebration and perambulation.

William Browne

> See in what wanton harmless folds
> It ev'ry where the Meadow holds;
> And yet its muddy back doth lick,
> Till as a *Chrystal Mirrour* slick;
> Where all things gaze themselves, and doubt
> If they be in it or without.
> And for his shade which therein shines,
> *Narcissus* like, the Sun too pines. (Marvell, *Upon Appleton House*)

Despite the general similarities between Drayton and his older contemporaries, *Poly-Olbion*, between 1612 and 1623, marks a definite bend in the river, away from the public and historical landscape, into one which is private and aesthetic in nature. Not only in *Poly-Olbion* but elsewhere as well, we see that the landscape acquires a value of its own, apart from its historical credentials, often in spite of them. The poet's response to the landscape, with its variety of attractions, becomes dissociated from its national context. The setting takes on an aesthetic rather than political meaning, and the river no longer captures a sense of the nation as a whole. This is not to say that it loses its conventional symbolic attributes or that it does not address political themes, but rather that it draws its meaning from a set of values existing in a private dimension. The rivers of *Cooper's Hill* or *Appleton House*, for example, certainly have their significance for their authors' political themes, but they are symbols of a form and order which contrast with the political world rather than national images emerging from it. Denham's river of moderation is an ideal of form which is indirectly applied to the political allegory (and the author's verse). Marvell's Denton, running through Fairfax's estate, defines the world of that poem in a Spenserian manner; it identifies the complex interrelationships of earthly values, of retirement and public involvement, and shows them subject to the limitations of a fallen world, which contrasts sharply with the celestial order defined by Maria at the end of the poem. But it too is an image figuring an idea reinforcing a moral order based first of all on private rather than public virtues. It is a matter of form; it may figure the nature of the place, but it is not the *genius* of the place, and its pertinence lies ultimately with Fairfax the individual, not Fairfax the lord general. The image is private, not public, representing an idea, not embodying it.

Such is the trend that is foreshadowed by *Poly-Olbion* in the second decade of James's reign, when the river motif meanders between the public and private dimensions. In Drayton we see the dutiful laureate suppressing his private identity to give voice to a national muse and to create a heroic setting for the *genius loci*. Generically, Drayton is fairly successful. But, ironically, the real energy of the work is in its quirky, eccentric individuality. The other work which seems to complete the evolution of this epic impulse to anatomize the nation in terms of its rivers, William Browne's *Britannia's Pastorals*, tries to develop and maintain a national voice but fails; it is begun as an act of duty and ends as an act of poetic imagination. Thus, William Browne approaches his task from a different perspective than Drayton. Initially reaching back beyond Drayton's influence, he attempts to perpetuate the Elizabethan and

Spenserian river motif, but perceiving his failure in Drayton's, he eventually abandons his task and turns to the private rivers and a personal landscape that is more beautiful than historical.

Together, William Browne and *Britannia's Pastorals* show how clearly Drayton stands as the last direct link with Spenser. Drayton, fifty-seven years old in 1620, was an elder among the writers and poets of the period. Since many of them, like Browne, were too young to have any real sense of the previous generation, he helped them to focus their own sense of change. Thus Browne's comment, that "All met not Death,/When wee intoombed our deare *Elizabeth*./Immortal *Sidney*, honour'd *Colin Clout*,/ Presaging what wee feele, went timely out,"[35] tinged as it is with precocity, articulates the very clearly formulated sense of change over the years, and Drayton is the link with Sidney, Spenser, and the late queen. Browne himself did not have much hand in burying "our dear Elizabeth," being only twelve at the time, but with Drayton's help he locates his own sensibilities in that age.

Thus, just before Prince Henry's death, both Drayton and his protégé were working quite independently on very similar projects, both having their inspiration in the encompassing "topochronological" national images of the previous age, the one a massive pastoral epic of the rivers, the other an epic pastoral equally dependent on river settings, although the younger poet's work finally dissolves into the landscape of the West Country. At least initially both authors intended a largely historical context for their poems, and John Selden, while he was preparing the "Illustrations" to Part 1 of Drayton's *Poly-Olbion*, was also answering questions for William Browne, and providing gloss for his pastorals. Although the first book of the pastorals appeared in 1613, most of it was written before Browne was twenty years old, that is, before 1611. *Poly-Olbion* was only entered with the Stationers' Register in 1612. And while Browne certainly knew of Drayton's work, as Joan Grundy points out, Spenser's influence is most conspicuous in the first book,[36] with its discontinuous narratives, sensuous allegory, and its rivers. In Browne too, then, the original literary impulse to create a vast image of the nation fixed in the landscape was still alive and asserting itself and had not yet been displaced by the immediate influence of *Poly-Olbion*. For the first five songs Browne develops his own conception of the Spenserian style and the national myth, taking his place as Tavy's poet much as Spenser had been Thame's and Mole's. Succeeding songs in Book 2 reflect more of Drayton's influence, as the poet turns more to the landscape until finally he assumes his own voice and seems to abandon the original conception of a national image altogether and with it his principal models and influences. With Browne, as with other Spenserians, it is essential to read his poetry in terms of the poet and his landscape.

In its inception, though, *Britannia's Pastorals*, with its preoccupation with the rivers and the landscape, and its fundamental affirmation of Britain's *genius loci*, if not its *humanum genus*, tries with considerable success to transform the landscape, to blend physical reality and poetic myth to make it conform with its reputation as the reincarnation of the classical world, and in this he is more successful than most Spenserians. The early songs, poetically less successful, have an unnatural quality in their rather conspicuous effort to create a national myth which seems compatible with the landscape. The imitative poet here seems to be suppressing the private voice which, in the later songs, finally asserts itself.

As decorum requires, Browne's Britannia has a pastoral landscape which has less of the heroic than does Drayton's Albion. But the young poet's intention to shape the image of the nation is clearly similiar; he is

> Drawn by time (although the weak'st of many)
> To sing those lays as yet unsung of any.
> What need I tune the swains of Thessaly?
> Or, bootless, as to them of Arcadie?
> No, fair Arcadia cannot be completer;
> My praise may lessen, but not make thee greater.
> My Muse for lofty pitches shall not roam,
> But homely pipen of her native home;
> And to the swains, love rural minstrelsy;
> Thus, dear Britannia, will I sing of thee. (1.1.7–16)

Although Browne's intention is to *create* an image of Britain as a pastoral world, what he ends up doing is *looking* for a pastoral world in Britain. Thus, despite his objectives, he does not convey a coherent image of Britain as having a landscape with some informing quality or myth which gives it meaning. Unlike Drayton, he never develops a unified conception of the nation; on the one hand, his narrative is too fragmented, and on the other, it is too personal in feeling and localized in perception. Moreover, his political observations conflict with the patriotic *sententiae* he inherits from his Tudor models. He does, however, go through the necessary motions of recreating Britain as the new Arcadia. In doing so, he uses the popular device of describing the removal of the classical deities, Thetis in particular, to Britain, and her reception in Thames's court. The motif is by nature well suited to the evocation of a national landscape. In Book 2 he tells "What afterward became/Of great Achilles' mother," and we hear of her migrations and eventual residence in Britain:

> But let us leave, fair muse, the banks of Po;
> Thetis forsook his brave stream long ago,
> And we must after. See, in haste she sweeps
> Along the Celtic shores; th'Amorick deeps
> She now is ent'ring: bear up then ahead,
> And by that time she hath discovered
> Our alabaster rocks, we may descry
> And ken with her the coasts of Britany.
> There still she anchor cast to hear the songs
> Of English shepherds. (2.1.955–64)

The motif is a familiar and old-fashioned one, redolent of Spenser, Watson, Harvey, Vallans, and others; classical in origin, it was rather predictably adapted to England's self-conscious cultivation of a poetic identity early in the Renaissance. Browne too uses the motif to explore the theme of England's fulfilment of its poetic legacy and the promise of a literary golden age, and he combines specifics of the national geography with classical themes. Browne reworks the conventional image of the confluence of the diverse rivers in their rush to the sea to describe how the land itself responds to Thetis's arrival: "At Thames fair port/The nymphs and shepherds of the Isle resort" to welcome Thetis to "Nereus' Court" (2.1.973–74). Browne's treatment of the episode bears resemblance to many possible models, but most of all to the gathering of rivers to contend for Lundy in Song 4 of *Poly-Olbion*. But Browne always responds to the Spenserian elements of the mythological geography. All the English poets—"Ye English shepherds, sons of Memory"—gather to serve Thetis, and appropriately, this leads Browne to an *encomium* on Spenser. Perhaps because of its very conventionality there is a sense of all England's involvement in Browne's pastorals here—of the unified nation, and not of the individual in a local landscape. Yet, as he meditates on Spenser's death, the myth collapses beneath the reality, and the poet's contrived (but poetically fairly successful) national fiction succumbs to bitter, disillusioned satire that echoes with the poet's private voice:

> For my own part, although I now commence
> With lowly shepherds in as low a verse,
> If of my days I shall not see an end
> Till more years press me, some few hours I'll spend
> In rough hewn satires, and my busied pen
> Shall jerk to death this infamy of men. (2.1.1039–44)

As in other Spenserians, the poet's legacy becomes a spur to satire.

Browne's harmonious vision of England is dispelled as abruptly as the vision of Gloriana, though it is replaced by the poet's anger, an image of the nation in strife, and the poet's reaction against the nation itself. This change of voice, where the poet promises to abandon his national myth for social satire, demonstrates the tension between the assumed Spenserian voice and the incipient personal voice of satire dominated by the present reality. Throughout *Britannia's Pastorals* one feels that Browne keeps up the Spenserian imitation as long as he can and that his lapses are expressions of the genuine feeling, not mere posing. The borrowed tune, however, does not last long. The dominant allegory of Thetis's progress suffers from the discontinuity which is characteristic of Browne's narrative verse. As though the Spenserian manner simply did not suit his personal geography, it is abandoned and renewed irregularly, as the poet indulges in digressions on the diverse rivers associated with a more harmonious private life. Indeed, Thetis herself retires from Albion's larger scene and escapes into the more peaceful confines of the West Country. Her travels give a vague direction to Browne's muse,[37] and they consist of a series of isolated meetings with Browne's favorite rivers:

> At *Exe*, a lovely Nymph with *Thetis* met;
> She singing came, and was all round beset
> With other wat'ry powers, which by her song,
> She had allur'd to float with her along. (2.3.623–26)

His use of Thetis in this way, to traverse the landscape, loosely resembles the movement of *Poly-Olbion* and of other works which receive their topographical structures from the rivers. For Drayton, though, the move from setting to setting gives rise to historical narratives; it is a way of elevating his geography, and is the essence of his unified vision of Britain. Thetis, however, leads us farther from the national scene into a remoter, humbler setting whose beauties are natural rather than man-made. It cannot be said that this is the essence of Browne's vision of Britain's pastorals, at least not as begun in the first book; it is Browne's rejection of the national theme altogether. And the course that Thetis traces is that of the river motif itself from historical to aesthetic interests, and her retirement suggests Browne's own realization that he has attempted a literary mode that is not suited to his personal sensibilities and his understanding of the nation, and which is even inappropriate for the age itself.

When in the national setting, Browne's characters all travel a confused and dangerous world, and there is little sense of direction until the second book, when he suddenly understands how to coordinate his narrative and the geography. But even in their erratic movements they are familiar pastoral romance figures with literary first cousins in Montemayor and Sannazaro, and perhaps nearer relatives from the more threatening English literary landscape of John Fletcher's *The Faithfull Shepherdesse* (see, for example, 3.1). But Browne, as a Spenserian, submits his long-suffering heroines— Aletheia and Marina in particular—and the landscape itself to a greater degree of allegory than these authors do. Marina encounters Famine and Riot and Oblivion; Aletheia, or Truth, is the daughter of Chronos, while the landscape harboring them is recognizably Britain itself. In this sense, all of Browne's characters emerge as ominous figures of the national *genius* or, in Thetis's case, of her experiences in a promised land which fails to live up to its initial welcome. All of these figures in this decadent arcadia are as culturally disoriented as Ergasto was.

Browne's technique here is an expansion of what we have seen in Phineas Fletcher, for example. He explores his image of Britain in terms of the character in his landscape, and indirectly, Marina, Browne's principal heroine, becomes associated with the poet and his poetry. Marina in her innocence is pursued through an inimical world, harrassed by Famine, Riot, and Oblivion, so that she appears as an imperiled *genius* hounded by the corruption of her own nation. Thus, while she resembles Spenser's Florimell, she is experiencing the hardships to be met in a more particularized, Stuart England. And as in Drayton, there is a contrast between the native landscape and the humanized world. When Browne discontinues his narrative, as he frequently does, he turns to the landscape—which is to say, the rivers—for solace and moral perspective. A sharp distinction emerges between nature and human affairs. Browne returns only reluctantly to the painful tale of Marina, and the conventional device of the poet apologizing for so long abandoning his heroine becomes all the more effective in exposing the split personality of Browne's verse:

> Alas that I have done so great a wrong
> Unto the fairest maiden of my song,
> Divine Marina, who in Limo's cave
> Lies ever fearful of living grave. (2.3.1–4)

He grows into the role of the *poète maudit*; he is perpetually burdened with an awareness of the times and how they take the pleasure out of his poetry.

> Here full of April, veil'd with Sorrow's wing,
> For lovely lays, I dreary dirges sing. (1.5.1–2)[38]

The corruption of the times is inescapable for Browne. It is as though Marina, Fide, and Idea, as images of the present state of England, were subjects too painful to treat without the relief of his digressions on nature. The poet's sensitivity is echoed by nature and the rivers, as we can see from Browne's variation on Spenser's view of Verulam:

> When Verulam, a stately nymph of yore,
> Did use to deck herself on Isis' shore,
> One morn (among the rest) as there she stood,
> Saw the pure channel all besmear'd with blood;
> Inquiring for the cause, one did impart,
> Those drops came from her holy Alban's heart;
> Herewith in grief, she 'gan entreat my sire,
> That Isis' stream, which yearly did attire,
> Those gallant fields in changeable array,
> Might turn her course and run some other way,
> Lest that her waves might wash away the guilt
> From off their hands which Alban's blood had split:
> He condescended, and the nimble wave
> Her fish no more within that channel drave:
> But as a witness left the crimson gore
> To stain the earth, as they their hands before. (1.4.315–30)

Inspite of all its Spenserian parallels, the passage reveals how greatly changed is the response to the historical landscape.

We begin to see how nature almost inadvertently takes on a new

importance in Browne's verse. Like Drayton, he turns to the national landscape for the real spirit of his verse, and for each it is
associated with time. But Drayton's is a historical geography, while
Browne's is one that has a private frame of reference and leads away
from human affairs. His poets, it will be recalled, are the "sons of
memory," and as Browne says, his quest through the landscape is
also through time:

> Thus, gentle Muse, it happens in my song:
> A journey, tedious for a strength so young,
> I undertook by silver streaming floods,
> Past gloomy bottoms and high-waving floods,
> Climb'd mountains where the wanton kidding dallies,
> Then with steps enseal'd the meekn'd valleys,
> In quest of memory. (2.1.17–23)

Browne's rivers lead him beyond a sense of historical time to a
dimension of remembered simplicity; his quest through memory
takes him finally to "A pleasant garden for a welcome rest." These
rivers of the mind are also of nature, though. Browne's journey,
then, is like Ergasto's: it is psychological, but it passes through the
natural landscape away from the public, contemporary world
figured by Marina.

Indeed, time is no less Browne's theme than it is Drayton's, but it
and nature take on quite different meanings. For Browne, too, it is
the poet's task to preserve the past in verse, and like other Spenserian poets, he sees the past nostalgically, as irrecoverable—such as
when he sings of the heroes of his native Devon soil, of Davies,
Greville, Gilbert, Drake, and Hawkins: "Time never can produce
men t'oertake . . . [their] fames." But Browne looks to poetry,
nature, and time more optimistically (and abstractly) than Drayton;
he has a youthful confidence in the poet's powers:

> For there is hidden in a poet's name
> A spell that can command the wings of Fame,
> And maugre all Oblivion's hated birth,
> Begin their immortality on earth. (2.2.337–40)

Both nature and the poet are time's agents, and it is through his
repeated use of the river *topos* that Browne brings these themes
together. Nature is, like poetry, the repository of moral order; it
preserves the virtues which society seems to have destroyed. It is in
his rivers that Browne explores the recollections of these virtues.

Thus he reads his landscape while describing it; there is no distinction between the metaphoric and physical worlds. In describing the pure water that springs from the source of one Devon river, he says that

> . . . the rock did first deliver
> Out of his hollow sides the purer river,
> (As if it taught these men in honour clad)
> To help the virtuous and suppress the bad
> Which gotten loose, did softly glide away. (1.2.659–63)

Throughout *Britannia's Pastorals*, as Browne indulges in the pleasures of describing the topography, he perceives in the rivers the moral order that is absent from the world that torments Marina, and this is fundamentally different form Drayton's rivers, which embody the narrative. It serves as the poet's deep, cultural memory just as the poet is society's. Thus, for Browne, the rivers in nature, like poetry itself, work with time to preserve the memory of things past:

> As men from earth to earth; from sea to sea;
> So rivers run: and that from whence both came,
> Takes what she gave: waves, earth; but leaves a name.
> As waters have their course, and in their place
> Succeeding streams will out, so is man's race:
> The name doth still survive, and cannot die,
> Until the channels stop, or springs grow dry. (1.2.664–70)

This is not just Browne turning the rivers to sententious capital. It is his response to time and the physical world which, for him, embodies the possibility of continuity in nature, the perseverance of a natural order despite the mutability of historical accidents. This is similar to Drayton's view of nature, but he attributes nature's order to history—Browne sees it as separate from, even existing in spite of history. As rivers pass through landscapes, they leave a name; there is a residuum of meaning which lingers in the setting, just as the individual is assured the posterity of a name—and time and the poet find them out. In this way, Browne perceives nature as the embodiment of a moral order and a promise that things of lasting value will persevere; with a view such as this one, a poet does not need a national myth.

Time, then, for Browne, is the discoverer, the revealer of truth—precisely the opposite of Drayton's "injurious Time" (10.272). It preserves things as they are rather than as they seem, and in this,

also very different from Drayton, it is the nation's scourge and the
exposer of the folly of the times. Thus, Browne looks to the future
as Drayton does not. The allegory of Book 1, Song 5, expresses
Browne's thought quite clearly, if a bit abstractly. Aletheia, or
Truth, the daughter of Chronos, or Time, in her plight is rejected
throughout Britain, by all except Idya, the *genius* of Britain herself.
Aletheia urges Idya to preserve the memory of Elizabeth. Time and
Truth hold the secret and promise the preservation of the true
honor of Britain during the period of oblivion, ignorance, and strife.
The image of Time victorious over the times is vividly invoked by
Aletheia when she describes the glories of her father, Chronos:

> What mariner is he sailing upon
> The wat'ry desert-clipping Albion,
> Hears not the billows in their dances roar,
> Answer'd by echoes from the neighbour shore?
> To whose accord the maids trip from the downs
> And rivers dancing come, crown'd with towns,
> All singing forth the victories of Time
> Upon the monsters of the Western clime,
> Whose horrid, damned, bloody plots would bring
> Confusion on the laureate poet's king,
> Whose hell-fed hearts devis'd how never more
> A swan might singing sit on Isis' shore:
> But croaking ravens, and the screek-owl's cry,
> The fit musicians for a tragedy,
> Should evermore be heard about her strand,
> To fright all passengers from that sad land. (1.4.365–380)

For Drayton there is no such promise that the "sad land" might be
redeemed by time from its present debasement. This passage is
Browne's direct answer to Drayton's and the other Spenserians'
vision of the poet exiled from his landscape and nationless. It is his
myth of time restoring harmony between the poet and his geography—returning the laureate to his seat by the nation's rivers.
It is a mythic vision that many of the Spenserians were incapable of,
and it transcends national identity.

   This allegory extends directly into the descriptive narration,
where nature and the rivers are the real evidence and manifestation
of Britain's nobility and worth which kindle the poet's patriotic
spirit. It is there, rather than in history or society, that Britain's
genius is preserved. And increasingly, the delight in nature alone

feeds the poet's patriotism, as the allegory is abandoned because of the debased national image it presents. Book 2 is wholly devoted to the tale of the rivers associated with Browne's landscape, the Walla and the Tavy. They come to dominate landscape where Limos (famine) and Riot are rampant, and where Marina suffers so persistently. In turning to these rivers, Browne finds personal rather than national myths adequate for his experience and suited to his poetic voice, and in this he differs from Fletcher, for example, who persists in his longing for a public voice and a national muse.

In the last book, which was not published in his lifetime, Browne's muse disappears into the landscape altogether, abandoning the painful tales almost entirely, drawing her poetic spirit from the rivers and the topography, and from their beauties rather than from the recollection of the British worthies. And while to the end, Browne's pastorals are alive with nationalism, it is one which is nourished by and find expression in regionalism and a personal response to nature.

The differences in Browne's historical perspective, his resistance to his own national allegory and his contentment with a private poetry focusing on natural settings appealing to his aesthetic sense rather than to his concern for a political destiny, is partly his acceptance of his individual identity defined by his own sense of time and place separate from the nation's as a whole. His humanism drew its resources from very different springs than Drayton's did. In many respects Browne's career seems to resemble that of his mentor, and *Britannia's Pastorals* seems to share the fate of its avuncular *Poly-Olbion*. It too occupied the poet for many years, from approximately 1611 to Browne's death around 1645. After 1613 Browne reluctantly continued the work, publishing the second book in 1616, and only under great pressure consenting to have the two published together in 1625. The incomplete third book presumably occupied him intermittently through the remainder of his life, and the increasing bitterness and the poet's reluctance to write—or at least to publish—lead one to believe that Marina's tale would never have been told in full.

But the differences in the poets' sensibilities are more striking than the similarities, and they reflect their essentially different relation to the age. Browne, an inveterate and gifted writer, was not a professional poet as Drayton was. He suffered more keenly the criticism and abuses that clearly harassed poets during these years, and which finally drove him to all but abandon his muse. Unlike

Drayton—or Spenser or Fletcher, for that matter—he did not have a mission to add to the national literature. While Browne had to be exhorted to publish *Britannia's Pastorals*, Drayton was exhorted not to publish *Poly-Olbion*. However dispirited he was, Drayton was not reluctant to publish and was hardened by a generation of criticism. Browne was content to settle for his retired life in Devonshire and later in Oxford as Robert Dormer's tutor. His prospects for promotion and as a poet were very good indeed; he had very enthusiastic and important friends, but he clearly did not feel the obligation to enter the world as a professional and public figure, and in this he stands in complete contrast with Drayton.

4. Conclusion (1): The Inadequate Image—Poets, Historians, and the Denatured River

> Like the vain Curlings of the Watry maze,
> Which in smooth Streams a sinking Weight does raise;
> So Man, declining alwayes, disappears
> In the weak Circles of increasing Years;
> And his short Tumults of themselves Compose,
> While flowing Time above his Head does close.
>   (Marvell, *The First Anniversary* . . .)

> But I, retiring from the Flood,
> Take Sanctuary in the Wood;
> And, while it lasts, my self imbark
> In this yet green, yet growing Ark.
>   (Marvell, *Upon Appleton House*)

> Thus *Poets* (like the *Nymphs*, their *pleasing themes*)
> Haunted the *bubling Springs* and *gliding streams* . . .
> *Poets* (like *Angels*) where they once appear
> *Hallow* the *place*, and each succeeding year
> Adds *rev'rence* to 't, such as at length doth give
> This aged faith, *that there their Genii live*.
>   (Vaughan, *To the River Isca*)

After 1625 there is no work on a comparable scale with these that reflects the impulse to create a coherent national image and employs the river as a crucial *topos* locating the author's ideas about nature and the nation, and embodying myths of cultural and individual identity. There are a number of minor works, mostly in manuscript, which show that the tradition persisted until roughly 1642, after which the political mirror reflecting the unified image of the nation was, perforce, broken. Most of these are vestigial, and the poet's themes and landscapes are determined by a lingering Spenserian influence which also shows the signs of inevitable change in the form of a growing regionalism—often focusing on the West Country— and an increasing debt to the early Spenserian poets.

They often bear witness to the genre of the river poems, either in the form that Leland and Camden used it, or in Spenser's more mythic, Neoplatonic mode. Some of the poets, quite aware of the many examples of the form, echo or imitate other river poems now as obscure or minor as their own. In virtually every case, the poet's pretentions to a national voice of concord fail, betrayed by regional interest, political cynicism, or a general sense that the vision of the nation that he attempts to incarnate in his verse is not based in his own cultural experience, but is simply a thing of the past. A work such as J. M.'s "The Newe Metamorphosis," for example, which in its conception and development is nearly the exact contemporary of Part 1 of *Poly-Olbion*, originally had a contest between the nymphs of the Thames and the Rhine at its center.[39] Alluding to Spenser and Drayton and inspired by such nationalistic enterprises in historical and topographical forms as John Speed's *Theatre . . . of Great Britain*, J. M.'s work is overtly concerned with the disappearance of a national myth. It is bitterly satirical; its fragmented landscape and the geniuses that reside in it are corrupt and ugly, overt parodies of their literary ancestors.

A regional poet such as Thomas Kidley, from Devonshire, turns enthusiastically to the river motif to give his "Poetical Relation of the Voyages of Sir Richard Hawkins . . . [and] History of 88" (1624–1636) a genuine flavor of "those Times (during the raigne of B: Q: Elizabeth)."[40] The result, more a historical imitation or memorial than an attempt to revive or continue the ideal supposedly located in the Tudor past, shows the distance in time and tone from even the previous generation. However, Kidley knows all the pertinent river poets: his models include Spenser, Fitz-Geoffrey, his slightly older contemporary, William Browne, and even the elusive J. M., but his true mentor is, significantly, Drayton: "show me to this stream which did infuse/Such influence to Drayton's phoenix-Muse" (p. 8). Furthermore, encouraged by friends at Exeter College, Oxford, the usual haunt of Devon men, his heroic river poem is really inspired by his youthful loyalty to his private world of

Devonshire, and aiming for the heights of Ossa and Olympus, his muse rarely rises above her own Tempe, the valley of the Taw.

To a large extent the river motif traces the evolution of Spenserianism in the seventeenth century. We can see that poets continued to perceive it, with or without its national topographical context, as distinctly Spenserian. Around 1640, for example, Samuel Sheppard ventures into a shadowy world of Spenserian allegory with a poem called *The Faerie King*,[41] and in his use of a river pageant modelled on the marriage of the Thames and the Medway, he reveals his own rather perceptive interpretation of Spenserian allegory. Love, or concord, is Sheppard's central theme, much as it is in *The Faerie Queene*, and it is presented in terms of the reconciliation of opposities, Cupid and Zelota, or love and hate, the concupiscible and irascible passions. These allegorical figures are manifestations of the psychological development of Sheppard's Spenserian hero and heroine, Byanor and Olivia, and their relation to the allegory is elucidated in a river pageant described and explained by the figure Metanoia. She and the pageant represent the power of "harmony ineffable" in nature, a less subtle variation on Spenserian Concord in which all the rivers congregate in Nereus's palace, and "where/all Floods receive their Lawes for peace or Warre" (5.5.16). As we have seen in other river poets, the author uses his principal model—Spenser in this case—to interpret other treatments of the river. Sheppard's pageant also seems to echo analogous episodes in Homer, Virgil, Ovid, and even Sannazaro. While mainly concerned with the psychology of love, his pageant is also, like Spenser's, about the emergence of law, peace, and social order from harmony in nature.

Significantly, though, it lacks the national and historical context that is implicit in the marriage of the Thames and the Medway. Its images are intellectualized, the sensuousness of its allegory is disembodied, its form is rigorously symmetrical. As a reading of *The Faerie Queene*, the work is very interesting; as an imaginative or mythic evocation of forces in nature it lacks the protean, metamorphic quality that makes Spenser's image seem true to nature and experience. Sheppard has done to *The Faerie Queene* what Purcell did to *A Midsummer Night's Dream* in his opera *The Fairy Queen*. The river here has moved away from the landscape into a realm of abstraction which does not come in contact with either the rivers of nature or those of nation. Spenser's art is a mirror to his society in fairly evident ways, while Sheppard's looks inward on the lovers' souls, and the Fairy King is in no discernible way identified with Charles.

In these and other works of the period between 1625 and 1640 we continue to see spasms of that Spenserian sensibility, with vestiges of national and historical interest, but the world has become narrower and its meanings are for each one of us, not all of us together. The response of these authors to Spenser and the Tudor poets is intellectual and analytical rather than imitative, and in this we can see the growth of an incipient neoclassicism. And perhaps surprisingly, there is less political animus in this second generation of Spenserians, as though their interest in their antecedents is more purely literary than nationalistic: they may idealize the Elizabethan past, but they seem not to perceive it as a national myth to be sustained or revivified. The changes that they see in their own world, for good or ill, are not the violation of a cultural legacy that they locate in Sidney or Spenser and regard as their birthright as Drayton or Fletcher did. Increasingly, the mythic dimension of the river—its image of concord and harmony—is that of the soul and psyche of the individual as he exists outside of society in a geography whose values are spiritual rather than political.[42]

Indeed, the growing infrequency of the river's appearance in historical and topographical settings is part of the marked decrease in historical writing after about 1620. The historical studies which were *de rigueur* in 1600 had become unfashionable by 1621 and were the pastime of a fairly small circle of zealots and anachronistic antiquarians. There is a hiatus in such historical and topographical writing until approximately the Restoration. Those who continued to be interested in such literature in their defensiveness idealized it; those who were not, ignored it. This is the situation that Drayton recognized and deplored in 1622. In his indignation, he casts a Shakespearean curse on history's detractors, and it suggests the changes he has seen in two decades:

> And some of our outlandish, unnatural English. . . . sticke not to say, that there is nothing in this Island worthy studying for, and take a great pride to bee ignorant in any thing thereof; for these, since they delight in their folly, I wish it may be hereditary from them to their posteritie, that their children may be beg'd for Fooles to the fift Generation, untill it may be beyond the memory of man to know that there was ever any other of their Families.[43]

English perspectives on history had, in fact, changed over the decades. It was looked on as something remote and moribund rather than as a vital part of the culture itself: it was something of the past, rather than of the present. Such changes parallel and even involve the evolution of the river motif, and so one last look at the Society of Antiquaries will be appropriate here.

This new phase in Renaissance historical sensibility is evident in 1617, when Henry Spelman attempted to revive the original society. As we have seen, lack of interest, compounded by the death or dispersal of its members and royal disfavor, defeated Spelman's efforts to have what would have seemed like an old-boy's reunion, and which would have included such dignitaries as Camden, Jonson, and Cotton. His failure marks the end of the society as it was first conceived, by men for whom British history and historical thought had a sense of immediacy and timeliness and who felt that its ideals might still be revived.

After this, in reaction to this drying up of the fount of antiquarianism, attitudes toward the past entered another phase whose spokesman was the intransigent Edmund Bolton. As the past became more remote, its loyal adherents regarded it with greater reverence, and Bolton was their priest in sackcloth. At the end of James's reign Bolton's imagination became possessed with the desire to create a new society, an "Academ Roial." In many ways his obsession with British history resembles the parochialism of the original society, but their desire to research and preserve historical materials among themselves has evolved into a fanatical process of myth-making and of packaging history: Bolton would turn history into the material of popular romance. Although Bolton was a man with a penchant for getting into politically embarrassing situations, men such as Robert Cotton, William Camden, Ben Jonson, and John Speed took him seriously enough to try to keep him out of prison.

In Bolton we can see the Stuart reincarnation of the possessed spirit of John Leland. Using his distant family connection with the Duke of Buckingham to pave the way, he initiated a series of petitions to Parliament and the King to promote his project. His proposals have a conspicuous hyperbolic and heroic rhetoric which suggests far less concern for history than for myth. The fervent rhetoric of his scheme stands in utter contrast with the sober, practical objectives voiced by the founders of the original society. Bolton envisioned that his society would "celebrate the memory of the secularly noble of Great Britain that the history of our country may rescue itself from the shears and stealths of tailors . . . thereby to correct the errors and repress the ignorance and insolencies of Italian Polydores, Hollandish Meterans, rhapsodical Gallo-Belgici and the like."[44] Not only is there something strangely anachronistic about his attacks on Stow, Polydore Vergil, and other historians from previous generations, but there is an unmistakable encomiastic quality to his view of history. Preservation of the nation's antiquities and the propagation of knowledge have given over to a loud beating on the drum of nationalism.

Bolton's enthusiasm was irrepressible, and his petitions to Buckingham and the King get more and more extravagant. The society was to meet annually at Windsor, on St. George's Day; on their seal would figure the heads of James and Solomon; it would be called the "Academ Roial or College of Honor." In the court transcript of one proposal that Buckingham presented on his behalf to the King in 1620, the bombast is almost self-parodic:

> He says that it is "after long debate & the demurrer of many years" that the Supplicants ask his Ma[tic] "to found an Academ Roial" or College of Honor where lectures & exercises of heroick matter & of the antiquities of Great Britain may be had & holden for ever; . . . "although to many it will appear little more than a glorious dream" . . . because the maidenliness & inaudacitie "of our island's genius, which is reputed cold to sodein singularities . . . is alone enough to quash this affair in the embroin."
>
> Then at great length, and ranging from an Agon of Olympus to the judgment of Daniel, he shows that the example of King Solomon countenances "the magnificent handling of magnificent knowledges."

The passage is virtually a caricature of the historic sensibility of the last years of James's reign. The scheme aims at heroic poetry rather than history. In 1603 James thought the original founders of the society were too sober, practical, and independent, and for that reason frowned their society out of existence. But if ever a king was a lover of national images, James was one, and during the 1620s he warmed up to Bolton's plan. Ironically, while the original society made a cautious promise to avoid matters of state, Bolton's untrammelled plan, which all but promises to provide propaganda, found acceptance, and in 1622 the King encouraged Charles to promote this "publicke worke."

The essential differences between the two societies are obvious enough. One was a reserved and exclusive set of gentlemen pursuing their personal interests as they intersected with national history, while the other was the project of a man with a poetic conception of a heroic past and a desire to mold history to a basically literary design. This extends directly to the organization and membership of the society, where Bolton's literary objectives become clear and where their relevance for our subject emerges, for his plan had the spirit which infused the poets who used the river motif.

He envisioned three categories of members, the first being the "Titularies," consisting of Knights of the Garter and other high-ranking luminaries. The second were the "Auxiliaries," potential patrons chosen from the peerage. The third were the "Essentials," consisting of "able and famous laymen" who would do all the work and who would be the antiquaries who legitimized the society. While the society is clearly meant to be a microcosm of the nation in the manner of the Italian academies,[46] when one considers its organization and its purported scholarly objectives, it stands out as a semi-official source of literary propaganda rather than a body designed for the exchange of ideas and information. The antiquarians were its drudges, stagehands to draw before the luminaries the pageants of history. But for our purposes, the eighty-four members Bolton proposed for membership among the "Essentials" are more interesting than the categories themselves, for among them are the writers figuring in this last phase of that disappearing sensibility represented by Bolton's scheme itself. In fact, the membership of Bolton's "commonweal of witt" consists largely of "poets historical" and historians who form a link between Tudor and Stuart antiquarian thought.[47] Bolton's determination to bring antiquarians and poetical makers of national myth together says much about his perception of history and how it differs from that of Cotton's group. Bolton obviously thought that the objectives of the society would be well served by the bards, and their presence here is as telling as their absence was from the original society. The literary and historical activities of many of these men are associated with the development of the original "topochronological" form of the river poem and with its evolution in the seventeenth century, and so, some discussion of them and their shared interests is in order.

Two key figures on the list, Jonson and Selden, help to bring together the extremes of the mythopoeic and the historical; Jonson was (among other things) a respected scholar-historian, while Selden was known for his regard for poets and was himself an amateur versifier, although not one to mistake myth for history. These two men bring together other familiar personalities associated with our subject. Both Jonson and William Alexander used the river motif, and both had close connections with the poet of *Forth Feasting*, whose residence in Scotland excluded him from the list. Drayton, also a nominee, was acquainted with these men, and whatever we conclude about his relations with Jonson, they both held William Browne in high regard, although because he was just below the minimum age of thirty which Bolton set for the academy, he was not included among the "Essentials." Although Camden died in 1623, he is represented on the list by his protégé, Hugh Holland, an author of river poetry and city descriptions and a man with extensive connections with personalities associated with the motif. He is best known for his verses in the First Folio, and included among his closest friends are Jonson, Spelman, and Bolton. Another, river poet, John Lane, author of a work called "Triton's Trumpet" (B. M. MS. Royal 17 B. XV; 1621) and a very close friend of Holland, identifies him and his work with Sidney and Spenser. In fact, Holland's connection with Lane creates an interesting set of associations involving authors who used the river motif and extending from Spenser, Churchyard, and Lodowick Lloyd ("Spenser would not have had any funeral honours paid him after being suffered to die of want, but for my loving friend Lodovic Lloyd"), to Milton; indeed, Lane was a close friend of Milton's father, and the two joined their households together in a business venture.[48]

Numerous other strands of acquaintance could be spun from the list, joining authors with historical and topographical interests from the period of Spenser to the middle of the seventeenth century. Cotton, Selden, Spelman, and Jonson alone provide a web of friendships which incorporates nearly the full range of authors using the river *topos* and sharing the sensibility which it reflects. The authors and poets are the most coherent group in Bolton's list: Drayton, Jonson, Chapman, Alexander, John Beaumont, Holland, Thomas Roper, and Wotton, to name only some of the most obvious figures. Directly or indirectly the membership involves individuals who participated in that world that was evolving rapidly during and after the third decade of the century. Bolton's list reflects his own romantic sense of the past, and contains those venerable figures who had a part in that idealized Elizabethan age. Significantly, while the original society was markedly youthful, Bolton's was distinctly mature—all were over thirty, and most were considerably older. Cotton, we will recall, was only eighteen when he helped establish the original society. Bolton's selection shows a desire to resist the changes of the times, to hold at a distance the youth who

might be ignorant of or indifferent to the past. The original youthful
society, for whom history served to foreshadow their own future,
would have been transformed to a group of elders intoning the
glories of the past, intent upon preserving its own mature historical
outlook.

Obviously, one must be careful not to superimpose Bolton's
obsessions on all of these authors. Nevertheless, the connections
between them were very close, and Bolton's list gives a strong sense
of a nation having an aging literary intelligensia. His historical point
of view was certainly congenial to many of his nominees, such as
Drayton, Jonson, Spelman, and Holland, and one senses that in
many respects he is the voice of his generation. There is something
desperate in his stridency. He and others looked to the past with a
"clinging gaze," hoping to prevent its retreat. But as we have seen
in the river literature, the decline of this national sensibility was inevitable, and the prospects for a new antiquarian society and what
it represented continued to diminish. In 1629 Robert Cotton was all
but helpless to resist Charles's confiscation of his library, and
antiquarians such as Selden were less and less able to separate
historical pursuits from political entanglements. And, again as the
river has reflected, a unified and affirmative national image became
all but inconceivable in the 1630s and 1640s, when the individual's
identity was repeatedly thrown into conflict with the royal image of
the nation. A greater distance separated private and public life,
personal myths became distinct from political myths and were
sought outside the public domain. No longer could one find a
satisfying and complete identification with the images of the nation.
These efforts we have seen to recreate those national myths which
proliferated only two generations before were but pale reflections of
their models. The myths no longer suited the landscape, and after
1642 the landscape was no longer suited to the myths.

Indeed, the geography had created its own cyclical myth, as it
turned back on history and cast up the reflection of ruins and
destructive willfulness which signalled the beginning of the historical
national self-consciousness during the Dissolution. Just as the impulse which focused the attention on the river geography began in
destruction, so it ended in the destruction of the Civil War. The
paradox implicit in the historical myth that informed the river
literature in the Renaissance—that history began with the destruction of history—reechoed in these years and seemed to suggest that
the cultural ideal which was generated by human folly was a spuri-

ous one, or rather was interpreted incorrectly by Leland and his successors. The mythic vision of the tower-capped nymph who seemed to rise on the landscape of the 1530s and promise a glorious future growing from the ashes and ruins of the present, rose again from the river banks in a self-fulfilling process of historical recurrence, looked backwards with corrected vision, and seemed to say that the myth created out of Renaissance cultural self-awareness, which was built upon a scene of ruin and which transformed that landscape to one of nobility, was a figment of the imagination, the product of the creative mind, and had ignored the lesson of the landscape itself. The vision of the past in *Cooper's Hill*, looking back on the Reformation, seems to acknowledge the failure of the Renaissance myth: "May no such storm/Fall on our times, whose ruine must reform."

Essentially, the culture which was roused to a socially oriented humanism by the discovery of its own history and landscape, and which believed in the revival of an idealized antiquity in Europe and England, manifesting its self-image in the transformation of the landscape, saw that same landscape returned to the ruin with which it began, giving the lie to—or perhaps setting the limits to—the original mythic vision and its ability to recreate the world through the powers of the mind and imagination. As though the landscape were reasserting its own reality beyond human imagination, the monuments of royal aspiration were razed, returned to the general state of disorder of the 1530s, ready for a new cycle of mythic invention. The patriotic humanism of the period could not sustain its self-conception. The northern landscape rejected the imposition of the ideal like a body rejecting a radical transplant.

5. Conclusion (2): Bend in the River: The Rejection of Myth—Poets in Search of a Landscape

> for me there shall be a sufficiently ample reward, a sufficiently great glory . . . if only fair haired Ouse shall read me and he who drinks of Alan and eddying Humber and all the woods of Trent; and if above all the rest my own Thames and dark-metaled Tamar . . . shall commit my verse to memory. (Milton, *Damon's Epitaph*)

> I am housed in the city which the Thames washes with its refluent waves and am well content to be in my dear native town. No longer am I interested in returning to Cam and its reeds, nor am I tormented with longing for my room there from which I have long been debarred. (Milton, *First Elegy*)

What then happened to the river after 1642? Obviously, it did not dry up; it did not even disappear underground. On the contrary, some of the best known Renaissance rivers have their course through these years. *Cooper's Hill* takes shape between 1642 and 1655; the elusive Denton of *Upon Appleton House* dates from around 1650; Milton's early verse was being published in the 1640s; the Thames figures prominently in the poems on the fire of 1666 and on the Dutch wars and the invasion of 1672. Then why stop in the Renaissance, or why with Pope, or Wordsworth, or Coleridge? Why stop at all? The river certainly continues as a crucial image without interruption.

The answer at this point is not too elusive. The rivers of these succeeding decades of the Renaissance are unmistakably the products of what went before, although they are, with equal certainty, very different from them. Generally, they either lack that cultural self-consciousness that the river possessed at the height of the Renaissance, or more particularly, they represent reactions against it, as Milton's do. In either case they tend to be associated with private rather than public virtues and defined either by a personal voice or setting. The river-crossed landscape begins to nurture personal rather than national myths—or rather, it is the former that defines the latter. Some of these are rivers of the poets of retirement, or of the meditative mode, or of poets of the *via media* addressing affairs of state, and as such they are well known to students of the topographical poem. Their dominant features—a distinctive personal voice responding personally to a landsape whose moral significance is defined in terms of that voice—clearly have a different mood to them than do the settings of the earlier decades, with their public voice, historical geography, and cultural or national themes. The mood is different, the myths have evolved but the topographic techniques of imposing perceptual myths on our geographies are the same. The differences are there; the curve in the river is unavoidable, but it is the same river.

What I have tried to do in following the rivers to this particular bend is to suggest continuities rather than differences, to suggest that these better known rivers of the later Renaissance have hitherto unexplored affinities with the previous generations, and that the topographical poem of the seventeenth century is very much the direct descendant of that earlier response to landscape. In short, I have tried to suggest that it is all one river, but one which, because of cultural changes, takes a sharp turn in the seventeenth century. In the rivers' frequent appearances during these years we discern clear, though often muted echoes of what has gone before. The use of the river by Milton, Herbert, Vaughan, Denham, and Marvell, all show an awareness of what (or where) the river has been; they show their knowledge of its use as a *topos* and of the generic form of the river poem: and they recognize its cultural origins, in antiquity and in the Renaissance impulse to reroute Helicon to Thames, to translate cultural values of antiquity to the northern latitudes, and to make them flourish in the native soil. These later examples of the river, then, are not the manifestation of a new and original perception of landscape, but the continuation of a response that is based in the Renaissance tradition. They are the last phase of that transforming act and fading cultural self-consciousness as they yield to the individual sensibility which dominates these years.[49] The river, then, goes through another phase reversal similar to that of late antiquity and the Middle Ages: the river of the physical world is supplanted by the metaphoric analogue of the inner being. In its own transformation, the river locates that changing perception wherein the cultural and personal exchange places in the poetic conscious. For all these authors, then, the river continues to reecho the past while finding its place in a new poetic landscape; in this we see literary history repeat itself.

Milton, for example, reacts against the river motif of the previous generation, although in his thoroughly self-conscious adaptation of literary forms he illustrates its conventionality. If Milton uses a topic, it must be accepted form. It is interesting, then, that the river appears repeatedly in his early verse in the context of his desire to write a British epic or when he is meditating on the significance of his cultural inheritance. In his foreign correspondence, he and his correspondents invoke the rivers to establish national identity and to explore themes of poetic development. Paradoxically, this is the Italianate Milton, ruminating on his destiny as a British poet.[50] And at the same time, as we can see in *Comus* and *Lycidas* it is also the Spenserian Milton, thinking of his place in the national poetic legacy, and wondering how he will unseat Spenser. In these early verses, then, the river helped Milton to explore the very goals of poetry. In *Lycidas* the local and classical rivers mingle freely, and ultimately bring together his themes of poetry and prelacy in terms of the poet's obligation to society. Chamus's denunciation of the clergy draws on the river's literary past and on Fletcher in particular. The rich literary allusiveness by which the poet defines his theme of

Christian poetry is indebted to the rivers of classical and Continental literature but is ultimately concerned with the *genius* of Britian and *his*, that is Milton's, relation to him.

Milton repeatedly shows an awareness of the conventions attached to the river, for example, in *Comus*, where the Attendant Spirit tells us that Sabrina is "sprung of old *Anchises* line" (1.922), thereby making a cultural link in the conception of love and chastity that extends back from Spenser to Virgil. Yet Sabrina is also a national image, though drawn more from its poetic than its landscape. Her tower-capped brows reflect her native poetic heritage from Dunbar through Spenser and Drayton. And, although it is unemphatic, Milton does make use of the river here to suggest Britain's cultural identity, but it is an image of Britain subdued by Comus and finally liberated by Sabrina. Milton's perspective on the national image is, as we have seen, oblique; he has a private rather than a public voice. He uses Sabrina to reform a corrupt cultural identity. Thus, to a degree, all of Milton's verse is directed at this "old, and haughty Nation, proud in Arms," and is meant to reform it, to find a new image for it. In this sense, when he rejects his British epic—for reasons he makes very clear in his *History of Britain*—he rejects the national image and its informing myth. For him, his place in the national literature will be assured by his rejection of the cultural legacy that is represented in, among other places, the river. He clearly understood the river as a national image, associated it with its poetic, and put it aside when he moved on to his Christian theme. And it was always for him an image, not an aspect of the landscape, but a poetic fiction that Britain had discovered in the Italians. For him, as for others of these decades, the river, while associated with its national contexts, existed in the mind rather than in nature.

Even when poets took to meditating on their private landscapes, the rivers were a link with tradition, their poetic craft, and with myths of identity. The motif reveals how aware poets were of the changes in their place in society. The response to the riverine topography, then, was not a novel one, but one which has its basis in the response to tradition itself. In "To the River *Isca*," for example, Vaughan, thoroughly aware of the literary significance of his choice of a retired life, reflects on the poet's treatment of his landscape in terms of conventions of river poetry. The local river makes Vaughan's reflections on poetic tradition more personal. Vaughan stresses that his response to genre originates in his response to nature: that the springs of poetry come from within. The result is a poetic *tour de force* between public and private definition of genre and setting:

> When *Daphne's* Lover here first wore the Bayes,
> *Eurotas* secret streams heard all his *Layes*.
> And holy *Orpheus*, Nature's *busie* Child
> By handlong *Hebrus* his deep *Hymns* Compil'd.
> Soft *Petrarch* (thaw'd by *Laura's* flames) did weep
> On *Tybers* banks, when she (*proud fair!*) cou'd sleep;
> *Mosella* boasts *Ausonius*, and the *Thames*
> Doth murmure *SIDNEYS* Stella to her *streams*,
> While *Severn* swoln with *Joy* and *Sorrow*, wears
> *Castara's* smiles mixt with fair *Sabrin's* tears.
> Thus *Poets* (like the *Nymphs*, their *pleasing themes*)
> Haunted the *bubling Springs* and *gliding streams*
> And *happy banks*! whence such *fair flowres* have sprung,
> But happier those where they have *sate* and *sung*!
> *Poets* (like *Angels*) where they once appear
> *Hallow* the *place*, and each succeeding year
> Adds *rev'rence* to't, such as at length doth give
> This aged faith, *That there their Genii live*.[51]

There could hardly be a clearer statement of the awareness of a genre of river verse and of all its thematic associations. Even in his devotional verse, such as the *Mount of Olives*, he perceives his meditation on a topographical phenomenon in terms of his secular predecessors. Similarly, when, in his two *Jordan* poems, George Herbert reflects on his decision to write devotional verse, he is adapting an image which draws on conventional religious and secular themes and traditions to explore the meaning of the poetic vocation and the poet's place in society. The river, however, has become an emblem, a device to serve the poet's meditation.

Even the poet who is reputedly the originator of the new topographical poem, John Denham, combines this element of conventionality and altered sensibility. Indeed, *Cooper's Hill*, with its stylized description of the Thames Valley, combining observation and poetic archetype, topography and history, is the most old-fashioned of all these poems. He comes closest to using the motif as a national image in the British tradition deriving from Leland, but how different is his response to the landscape of rivers and ruins:

> But my fixt thoughts my wandering eye betrays,
> Viewing a neighboring hill, whoe top of late
> A Chappell Crown'd, till in the Common Fate,

The adjoyning Abby fell; (may no such storm
Fall on our times, *where ruine must reform.*) (113–17)[52]

But, of course, his Thames is not really such an image. It represents a moral and aesthetic idea of moderation, seemingly reflected in nature. It defines the ideal nature predicated by the poem, and in this Denham is true to the Spenserian manner. However, it is decidedly not a national image or part of a cultural myth. It is the function of the didactic, occasional nature of the poem. Its moral depths draw on primarily personal, individual resources—we must each achieve this mean in our own being—rather than on a sense of public order, although it is toward that larger end that his moral aims. Denham's river, as a political image of the monarch, is, by its very nature in the poem, representative of the inadequacy of the national image. It gains its symbolic significance from its identity as an ideal set in nature but violated by political reality.[53] The myth of geography, preferred didactically, is meant to reveal the unnaturalness of Charles's enemies. Nevertheless, it remains an aesthetic principle, the distillation of the traditional meanings and uses of the *topos* as it is found in Virgil, Lucan, and Spenser. For all its conventionality, the motif, used to support the deposed king, is itself paradoxical and reflects the process of continuity and change; it summons the poetic past to support the present, literary artifice to reinforce an idea of nature.

Thus, the river continues in its identifiable forms, and with its network of meanings, but the times required that poets find new ground for it. Poets repeatedly reveal their knowledge of its native and classical traditions but reject them or try to adapt them to other poetic modes. The ideals it represented in the national landscape become disembodied, abstracted, pass through the realm of the intellect and the soul rather than external nature. A work like Walton's *The Compleate Angler* seeks contentment in the physical world and the retired life, and studies how they nurture the spiritual graces and virtues of friendship and courtesy. It too "internalizes" or "psychologizes" the river's Spenserian attributes. His work is the Commonwealth's answer to *The Courtier*, and the virtues he emphasizes are those of the ideal, private life, freely chosen. Ironically, the piscator retires into the national setting that is rich with cultural and literary associations—he moves into the mythologized landscape and discourses on courtesy, moderation, friendship, and

harmony, while plying the rivers. The river becomes the background for, not an image of these virtues. Walton literalizes the
setting that for Fletcher was metaphoric or mythic. Seeking the ideal
in the real world, he retires quite literally to the piscator's life,
rather than trying to bring its ideals into the public domain.

Even Andrew Marvell, the arch confounder of conventions, the
one who most represents the seventeenth-century topographical
poem, and who therefore seems to exist on the very frontier of our
topic, employs the river with an awareness of the potential of its
traditional themes in order to develop his "survey" of Nunappleton
as an image of Fairfax and the world.[54] Its landscape mirrors the
mind of the individual much as that of *The Faerie Queene* mirrors a
mental and social world. And the Denton is the essence of nature in
Marvell's poem, and as such, flowing as it does from the purlieus of
the estate, through the abyss, the meadow, and the forest, it is the
key to his thoughts about the retired and the active life, and to his
larger themes concerning the limits and potential of human knowledge.

Marvell stresses the river's importance as the lifeline of the estate
and as the basis of its, and therefore Fairfax's self-sufficiency. Quite
literally, it reflects the identity of the estate. It is the mirror, the
principal natural feature of its setting, the one that embodies the
questions preoccupying the poet. Thus, for Marvell as for Spenser
the river in nature, as well as in its poetic associations, represents his
principal ideas and defines the world of his verse. Both literally
and metaphorically, the river of Nunappleton manifests the metamorphic, impermanent, ambiguous nature of the world, not only of
the microcosm of the estate, but also of the political world at large,
which it adumbrates. It is, therefore, essentially ambivalent: it is the
foundation of Nunappleton's self-sufficiency, and its link with the
world beyond the estate; its flood is described as both the nilotic
flood of abundance, and the threatening flood of civil war and
destruction, that of Lucan.

The phrase "perceptual myth" is particularly well suited to describing Marvell's treatment of the Denton. The poet is careful to
link the metamorphic qualities of the river to his central themes.
The river is one means by which we recognize the impossibility of
distinguishing between retirement and public involvement: they are
interdependent, just as the meadow and the flood are conflated. The
political world pervades that of the estate, so that the flood best

symbolizes the arbitrariness (and ambiguity) of our moral perspectives:

> See in what wanton harmless folds
> It ev'ry where the Meadow holds;
> And its yet muddy back doth lick,
> Till as a *Chystal Mirrour* slick;
> Where all things gaze themselves, and doubt
> If they be in it, or without. (80)[55]

In Marvell's world there are no absolutes; all things depend on our point of view.[56] Neither the ethic of retirement, nor that of commitment can be held as universally applicable.

But in a more encompassing sense, Marvell points out the limits of knowledge, and of our efforts to submit the world and its landscape to perceptual myths. It is to this end that he examines the relation between art and nature. While "nature"—the world of mutability—is very much present in the poem, it is always "vitrified"—we perceive it beneath a thick enamel overglaze which is meant to arrest for a moment its incessant movement. Thus, the speaker, in walking through the estate, creates richly artificial metaphors which seem to "fit" the landscape but which are eventually "overtaken" by reality itself. Nature thus seems to mock the speaker with the artificiality of his conceptions, pointing out their distance from nature, and the limitations of their appropriateness in ordering the world. This is most obviously the case in the elaborate flood episode, but the pattern pervades the poem, where intellectual formulations of the world—metaphoric constructs—are thrown into contrast with, even threatened by, the literal or natural manifestation of what they describe, just as the estate itself, a microcosmic, and therefore metaphoric image of the world, is threatened by the world it tries to replace. But this pattern also shows the struggle to bring art and nature together. Thus there is also a process of fulfillment, when nature merges with the arts and conforms with our perceptual understanding of the world:

> Then to conclude these pleasant Acts,
> *Denton* sets ope its *Cataracts*;
> And makes the Meadow truly be
> (What it but seem'd before) a Sea.
> For, jealous of its *Lords* long stay,
> It tries t'invite him thus away.

> The River in itself is drown'd,
> And Isles tho' astonish'd Cattle round. (59)

The world defined by Marvell's river is very Spenserian. It is *Mundus*, a fallen, mutable realm in need of being shaped by human imagination. Yet this material world is more fluid than Spenser's and less lastingly transformed. Each of the speaker's efforts to come to terms with nature is interrupted, or otherwise only partly successful—not because of the intrusion of a Calidore figure, but because nature will not long submit to the spell of the Orphic poet. But Marvell clearly recognizes in the river a motif which focuses the theme of human struggle to perfect nature, to achieve understanding of the world. Marvell's art is extremely self-conscious, but not in the specifically cultural sense that Spenser's is. He too is thinking in terms of humanity's potential for understanding, for creating order in nature, and achieving a degree of self-sufficiency, although he explores the problem in the context of the individual.

The speaker's relation to the river is one way in which Marvell explores the power of the individual intellect to embrace nature and to be in accord with it. Marvell's is basically a Senecan, stoic ideal in which the individual's knowledge of and rapport with nature enables a self-realization which results in a transcendence beyond the self, and an integration within the natural order. The moment of such an insight is one in which art and nature, our thoughts and our world, are one, and the image that Marvell chooses to figure this is that of his speaker metamorphosing into the *genius* of the land, resolving into that watery element that defines the nature of Nunappleton, and identifying with the river god, the keeper of the river's secret knowledge:

> Oh what a Pleasure 'tis to hedge
> My Temples here with heavy sedge;
> Abandoning my lazy Side,
> Stretcht as a Bank unto the Tide;
> Or to suspend my sliding Foot
> On the Osiers undetermined Root,
> And in its Branches tough to hang,
> While at my Lines the Fishes twang! (81)[57]

Art, in the form of the classical river god, merges with nature, and the speaker, for a moment, becomes a part of the river-scape that was so elusive and mutable in the course of his perambulation.

What Marvell describes here is a process of self-realization, a loss of self in nature. It is this understanding of "Natures mystick book" that leads the speaker to a vision of divine knowledge, the celestial river of grace that descends from above and gives meaning to the lower world of nature. Marvell presents the vision of Maria specifically in terms of the correspondence between the ideal, celestial sphere and that of the material world.[58] The result is a harmonious vision which reconciles the forces of transcendence and incarnation in an image that other poets as well have located in the river *topos*:

> Tis *She* that to these Gardens gave
> That wondrous Beauty which they have;
> *She* straightness on the woods bestows;
> To *Her* the Meadow sweetness owes;
> Nothing could make the River be
> So Chrystal-Pure but only *She*;
> *She* yet more Pure, Sweet, Streight, and Fair.
> Than Gardens, Woods, Meads, Rivers are. (97)

As it winds through Marvell's landscape, then, the river helps to define the poet's image of our epistemological and moral confusion in a mutable world. In the poem we have an anthology of river motifs. He draws on the wide historical and literary range of the river to underscore the poem's generic richness and to reinforce its interest in polyvalence: we have the fertile Nile flood, the river's links with material and commercial bounty, the flood's association with rebellion, the river themes of nature's mysteries and the quest for knowledge, and the contrast between public and private life. From stanza to stanza, these varied themes flash briefly into recognition on the shimmering surface of the Denton. In the poem the river is all these themes: it is as fluid and ambivalent in meaning as it is mutable in form, and in this it defines the ambiguity which is the world of the poem until the arrival of Maria, who "vitrifies" nature, tames it by making its opaque meaning clear, by making the *raison d'être* of Fairfax's estate comprehensible.

We have seen how for centuries authors have used their rivers as a topic in which they can explore their relation to the world, as a way of understanding what it means to tame nature. In the river we have seen the fluctuating myths of meaning that writers found in nature. Marvell has instinctively recognized the significance behind our geographical myths and used the variety of river associations to illustrate the human need to understand nature and control it intellectually. More than any other of the authors we have discussed, he is interested in the problem of knowledge itself, and in the disparity between belief and knowledge. He shows us the subjectivity that informs our response to the world; he recognizes the intellectual origin of our cultural values and realizes that they are projections of the self. But he is preeminently concerned to make us see the limitations of our myths of knowing, to recognize the fallibility of the intellectual, moral, and scientific dogmas with which we try to stabilize the world of uncertainty so that we can draw on the simpler grace represented in Maria.

In this he resembles Spenser but differs greatly from him. Spenser perceives these limits to our knowledge, but he is determined to redeem nature. Not content with understanding, he wants to urge us, through his poetry, to virtuous action. Close as he is to Spenser's view of mutable nature, Marvell has a greater sense of the need for the individual—in this case Fairfax—to find his own harmony within the natural order, to achieve his own transformation which will identify him with nature's *genius*. The bend in the river, then, is there and inescapable. Looking back beyond it, you can still see the ruined towers and the abbey across the meadow, but hereafter the river's monuments have their resonance in the individual, not the national or social consciousness. Its pleasure domes are our own, it speaks to us about ourselves, exists for ourselves as our culture is reflected in us, not as we are reflected in it:

> . . .Was it for this
> That one, the fairest of all rivers, loved
> To blend his murmurs with my nurse's song,
> And, from his alder shades and rocky falls,
> And from his fords and shallows, sent a voice
> That flowed along my dreams? For this, didst thou,
> O Derwent! winding among grassy holms
> Where I was looking on, a babe in arms,
> Make ceaseless music that composed my thoughts
> To more than infant softness, giving me
> Amid the fretful dwellings of mankind
> A foretaste, a dim earnest, of the calm
> That Nature breathes among the hills and groves.
>
> When he had left the mountains and received
> On his smooth breast the shadow of those towers
> That yet survive, a shattered monument

> Of feudal sway, the bright blue river passed
> Along the margin of our terrace walk.[59]

The river continues to cross the barriers between the individual and society, but it draws from a smaller landscape having a private range of knowledge and meaning. Yet, a source of cultural memory, it continues to carry a traditional knowledge that enables one to understand one's place in the world and society. It thus continues to serve as a reminder of essential human impulses in our relation to the world: the process of formulating myths by which one can understand the world and subdue it through a cultural, or social order:

> riverrun, past Eve and Adam's, from swerve of shore to bend of bay, brings us by a commodius vicus or recirculation back to Howth Castle and Environs . . .

and an individual one, in which personal myths embrace the world, and are embraced by it, sharing its profoundest memories:

> My leaves have drifted from me. All. But one clings still. I'll bear it on me. To remind me of. Lff! So soft this morning, ours. Yes. Carry me along, taddy, like you done through the toy fair! If I see him bearing down on me now under whitespread wings like he'd come from Arkangels, I sink I'd die down over his feet, humbly, dumbly, only to washup . . . . First. We pass through the grass behush the bush to. Whish! A gull. Gulls, Far calls. End here. Us then. Finn, again! Take Bussoftlhee, mememormee! Till thousendsthee. Lps. The keys to. Given! A way a lone a last love a long the

[FIGURES 19–24]

If not actually intensifying, the interest in landscape develops a different focus during the seventeenth century. Perceptual myths that emphasized civic virtue yield to ones which present an order identifying the individual with the landscape. Figure 19, with the allegorical river of the mind and life crossing the personal landscape in the background, behind Sir Henry Unton's portrait, might be an emblem of the changes to take place.

City views, like those of Hollar (fig. 20), in the tradition of Hogenberg's or Visscher's (figs. 12 & 18), place the city literally and figuratively at a distance from the viewer — the individual looks on, set apart emotionally from the social scene. The public perception of the landscape persists, in Speed's *Theatre of . . . Great Britain*, for example, but there is increasing and self-conscious development of alternative responses. Drayton replaces the myth of history with one of nature. The maps designed for *Poly-Olbion* (fig. 23), based on Saxton's originals (fig. 22), have been dehistoricized to create a natural geography in which the nymphs speak with the voice of individuals rather than as historical characters.

The rivers of these settings pose the same questions and aesthetic challenges as in previous periods. The essence of landscape must be adumbrated and its physical characteristics described; point of view must be defined, and aesthetic problems of integrating foreground with background must be dealt with as before. The problems are less often resolved in terms of historical frames of reference; aesthetic rather than social myths are what order the settings. Claude Lorrain's "Tiber Valley" (fig. 24) juxtaposes the natural setting with the classical river god in the foreground — sets the river against the image of the river, and contrasts the emerging romantic tradition, with its aesthetic response to the landscape, with the classical tradition, in which the metaphor for the river looks over the setting, at once disembodied from it, and part of it. The river god surveys an undulating landscape that is given definition by the Renaissance and classical architectural details that dot the banks of the river. The perspective that we share with the deity, a nearly depopulated expanse, could be the backdrop for books eleven and twelve of *Paradise Lost*.

Figure 19. Sir Henry Unton (artist unknown; c. 1596).

Figure 20. Wenceslaus Hollar. *View of London* (c. 1635).

Figure 21. England. From John Speed, *The Theater of the Empire of British Empire* (1611).

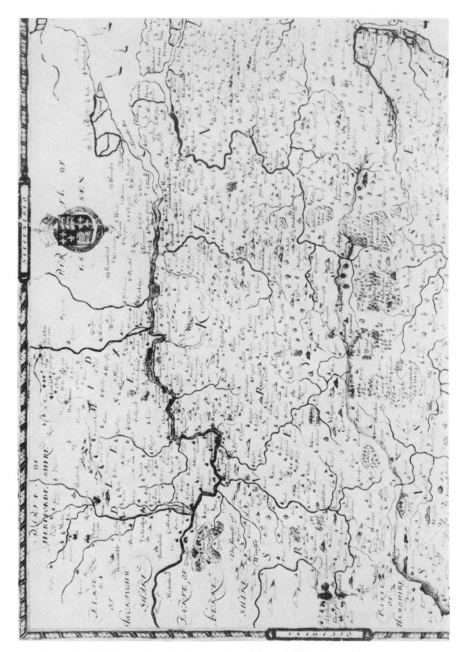

Figure 22. Middlesex (detail). Christopher Saxton (1579). Saxton's county maps became the prototypes for Speed and Norden. Their historicized landscape an iconography
of man's cultural presense; symbols for cathedrals, castles, manor houses, towns, enclosures, parks, fragment the setting and are outgrowths of the rivers.

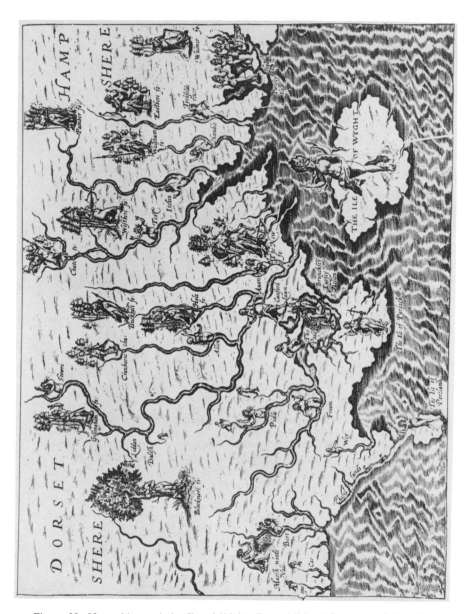

Figure 23. Hampshire and the Ile of Wight. From Michael Drayton's *Poly-Olbion* (1622). Based on Saxton's maps, Hole's engravings for *Poli-Olbion* remove the social boundaries placed of the landscape in other ways. The rivers are restored to nature.

Figure 24. Claude Lorrain, Tiber valley with river god; drawing (1660). Geography and the myths of geography are used to comment on each other.

Notes

Notes

[INTRODUCTION]

1. Carlos Fuentes, *Terra Nostra*, trans. Margaret Sayers Peden (New York, 1976), p. 766. I should mention at the outset that in the course of these pages I will occasionally discuss passages referring to streams, springs, moving waters generally, and even fountains as well as rivers. These other waters were regarded as the products, or offspring, of the rivers, and as part of the same geographical and symbolic configuration—in a most obvious way, for example, in Bernini's *Fountain of Rivers* in Rome. They are all tributaries to the larger, more encompassing literary motif.

2. William James, *The Principles of Psychology*, 2 vols. (New York, 1950), 1: 239.

3. Augustine, *De Civitate Dei*, 7 vols., trans. William Chase Greene (London and Cambridge, Mass., 1960), 6:29.

4. E. R. Curtius, *European Literature and the Latin Middle Ages*, trans. Willard R. Trask (New York, 1953), p. 8.

5. Coins, for example, which were religious objects and kept in holy sanctuaries, bore the images of the gods, and those of the river deities were especially common.

6. See Ovid's *Fasti*, 1.509–14, for an account of Carmentis's vision of Rome rising on the banks of Tiber.

7. See Ferdinand Braudel, *The Mediterranean and the Mediterranean World in the Age of Philip II*, 2 vols., trans. Sian Reynolds (London, 1972–1973), 1:282.

8. Curtius, *European Literature*, pp. 9–10.

9. E. C. Semple, *Geography of the Mediterranean Region: Its Relation to Ancient History* (New York, 1931), p. 130.

10. See Frances A. Yates, *The Art of Memory* (London, 1966), p. 8, for a different interpretation of this passage.

It is necessary to reemphasize the range and use of *topoi* and the extent of their importance not only in classical but also medieval and Renaissance rhetoric and literature. Current use of the term, as it has been influenced by Curtius's revival of our interest in it, is much too narrow and even misleading, for it misrepresents the variety of *topoi* and of their use in prose and verse, particularly in the Middle Ages and the Renaissance. The term requires a thorough reexamination and redefinition. Sister Joan Marie Lechner, in *Renaissance Concepts of the Commonplaces* (New York, 1962) offers the fullest view of the subject.

11. Philip Sidney, *Apologie for Poetrie*, ed. J. Churton Collins (Oxford, 1907), p. 8.

12. For exegetical descriptions of the Holy Land, see W. H. Herendeen, "The Rhetoric of Rivers: the River and the Pursuit of Knowledge," *Studies in Philology* 78 (1981), 107–27.

13. Petronius, *Satyricon*, trans. Michael Heseltine (London, 1913), 2:8 and 5.

[CHAPTER 1]

1. The distinction between the perennial and torrential rivers was recognized even in antiquity, as we see, for example, in Plato's *Timaeus* (21e–23c), and it continues to inform geographical study of Mediterranean lands. For the river in Roman law, see the *Institutes* of Justinian (2.1., 1–4 and 20–24): wherever it flows, the river is public domain: "*Riparum quoque usus publicus est juris gentium, sicut ipsius fluminis*" (4). Useful studies of Mediterranean geography are: Ellen Churchill Semple's *The Geography of the Mediterranean Region: Its Relation to Ancient History* (New York, 1931) and *The Influences of Geographic Environment* (New York, 1911); H. H. Scullard and A. M. Van der Heyden, *A Shorter Atlas of the Classical World* ([Amsterdam], 1962); M. Cary, *The Geographic Background of Greek and Roman History* (Oxford, 1949); J. L. Myers, *Geographical History in Greek Lands* (Oxford, 1953), particularly pages 24–33 and 108–32; and Michael Grant, *The Ancient Mediterranean* (London, 1969).

2. See, for example, the descriptions of the Nile in Herodotus (2.14) and Diodorus Siculus (1.36.8).

3. Semple, *Influences*, p. 360; J. Simmons, *The Geographical Texts of the Old Testament* (Leiden, 1959), p. 69; and Jack Lindsay, *Men and Gods on the Roman Nile* (London, 1968), pp. 39–40.

4. Diodorus Siculus, *The Library of History*, 12 vols., trans. C. H. Oldfather (Cambridge, Mass., 1933), 1.36.1–4. Subsequent references to Diodorus are from this edition.

5. Semple, *Geography of the Mediterranean*, pp. 159–65.

6. For the Nile as unifier, see E. A. Wallis Budge, *The Gods of the Egyptians*, 2 vols. (London, 1904), 2:40–46, and Lindsay, *Men and Gods*, pp. 40–42; for the Nile as "land builder," see Semple, *Geography of the Mediterranean*, p. 107.

7. Diodorus, *Library of History*, *1.12.6.*

8. Plutarch, *Isis and Osiris*, trans. F. C. Babbitt (London, 1936), p. 66.

9. Budge, *Gods*, pp. 42–43; Lindsay, *Men and Gods*, pp. 42–43; I am indebted to Budge's researches for much of my discussion of Hapi.

10. Plutarch, *Isis and Osiris*, pp. 32, 33. J. Gwyn Griffiths, *Plutarch's De Iside et Osiride* (Aberystwyth, Wales, 1970), p. 58, argues for Plutarch's intention to present the myth in its authentic, Egyptian form. For fuller discussion of Isis and Osiris and their importance see E. A. Wallis Budge, *Osiris and the Egyptian Resurrection*, 2 vols. (London, 1911), especially 2: 283–306, and R. E. Witt, *Isis and Osiris in the Greco-Roman World* (London, 1971).

11. Plutarch, *Isis and Osiris*, p. 13.

12. Griffiths, *Plutarch's De Iside et Osiride*, p. 70. Osiris's dependence on Isis's wisdom recalls the sage clemency of Spenser's goddess:

> "For that same Crocodile *Osyris* is,/That under *Isis* feete doth sleepe for ever:/To shew that clemence oft in things amis,/Restraines those sterne behests, and cruell doomes of his" (*Faerie Queene*, 5.7.22).

Spenser seems to have been familiar with both Plutarch and Diodorus.

13. Diodorus, *Library of History*, 1.15.4. H. and H. A. Frankfort, John A. Wilson, and Thorkild Jakobsen, in *Before Philosophy: The Intellectual Adventure of Ancient Man* (Harmondsworth, Middlesex, 1949), study the growth of speculative thought in the ancient world and the relation between the experience of the physical world and the structure of thought. Many of these characteristics of historical geography and their influence on the ancient world are discussed here, particularly the influence of the Nile on Egyptian thought (see pp. 39–103). One

pertinent detail that they record is that the Nile and its flood represented a kind of covenant with Egyptian society, and each year sacrifices to the river involved an expression of the "Nile's obligations" (p. 24) to its people, and this suggests the interdependence that Egyptians perceived between the nilotic mysteries and human society.

14. Plutarch, *Isis and Osiris*, p. 3; see also Diodorus, *Library of History*, 1. 18. 4–6 and 1. 25. 2–7. For the river nymphs, see Percy Gardner, "Greek River Worship," *Trans. Royal Soc. Lit.*, ser. 2, 11 (1878), 204–5.

15. For Hesiod's modification of the cult of the muses, see M. L. West, ed., *Theogony* (Oxford, 1966), pp. 32–33; Floyd G. Ballentine, in "Some Phases of the Cult of the Nymphs," *Harv. St. Class, Phil.* 15 (1904), 77–119, identifies their cult more fully; and Griffiths, *Plutarch's De Iside et Osiride*, pp. 364–65, offers additional documentation for the association of Isis and the muses.

16. For detailed examination of the torrential waters of the Holy Land, see George Adam Smith, *The Historical Geography of the Holy Land* (London, 1894); Nelson Glueck, *The River Jordan* (Philadelphia, 1946); Denis Baly, *The Geography of the Bible: A Study in Historical Geography* (New York, 1957); Yohn Aharoni, *The Land of the Bible: A Historical Geography* (London, 1966). It is generally accepted that the greatest cultural influence on the Jordan Valley came from Mesopotamia: see, for example, the *Oxford Bible Atlas*, ed. Herbert G. May (London, 1962), pp. 24–25. For more particular discussion of similarities in their cosmogonic myths, see Alexander Heidel, *The Babylonian Genesis*, 2d ed. (Chicago, 1951). As Heidel says, the Euphrates "was to Babylon what the Nile was to Egypt" (p. 75). The roles of the two rivers in their respective societies were very similar; compare for example the hymn to the Euphrates (Heidel, p. 75) and the "Hymn of Thanksgiving to the Nile," reproduced in E. A. Wallis Budge's *From Fetish to God in Ancient Egypt* (London, 1934). In *Before Philosophy* (p. 137) the authors contrast the physical worlds of Egypt and Mesopotamia and describe how they helped produce very different cultural attitudes, the one "trusting, the other distrusting, man's power and ultimate significance." The river is the single most important geographical feature influencing these attitudes; see pp. 139–69 for further characterization of the physical environment of Mesopotamia. *The Epic of Gilgamesh* is the best known cosmogonic text from Mesopotamia, with material predating 2000 B. C. Its primitive conception of life and death as concrete, material realities identifies the river and its deific forces with both. See A. Heidel, *The Epic of Gilgamesh* (London, 1957) and Idem., *The Epic of Gilgamesh and Old Testament Parallels* (Chicago, 1946).

17. See, for example, *Hippolytus*, 5.9.18: "This Euphrates . . . is the water above the firmament" and Simmons, *Geographical Texts*, pp. 32–33.

18. The extent to which the legends and landscape of the Old Testament are direct responses to those of Egypt is, of course, considerable. The frequency with which the river is used to focus this response is remarkable, and it is instructive to read Simmon's *Geographical Texts* in this context, for it illustrates how often Old Testament landscape, and the rivers in particular, are used to define politico-religious identity. I use the King James version of the Bible throughout.

19. George Herbert, *The Bunch of Grapes*, in *Works*, ed. F. E. Hutchinson (Oxford, 1941), p. 128.

20. E. H. Warmington, *Greek Geography* (New York, 1973), p. xxv, offers this date for the relaxation of Greco-Egyptian tensions. Greece relied upon its imports to supplement its own, very inadequate wheat crop: of the Greek states, only Thessaly and Boeotia were self-sufficient in their grain production. Their trade generally took the Greeks to North Africa and Asia Minor, but relations with their "suppliers" were very uncertain. In the fifth century B. C. the situation was greatly

improved by access to the Egyptian resources. Indeed, in 445 B. C. the Egyptian king came to the rescue of the hungry Athenians in their moment of need with a generous gift of wheat. These facts of agricultural and commercial life inevitably had an influence on Greece's political dealings with Egypt. See Semple, *Geography of the Mediterranean*, pp. 342–75, for fuller discussion of the grain trade at this time.

21. As well as being religious sites, Greek temples were also storehouses for money and grain. For Egyptian influence in Greece, and particularly the popularity of the cult of Isis, see Witt, *Isis and Osiris*, pp. 46–58; V. Tran Tam Tinh, *Essai sur le cult d'Isis à Pompéi* (Paris, 1964), especially pp. 18–19, and his *Le culte des divinités orientales à Herculanum* (Leiden, 1971); and the extensive work of Françoise Dunand, *Le culte d'Isis dans le bassin oriental de la Méditerranée*(Leiden, 1973), particularly vols. 1 and 2, *Le culte d'Isis et les Ptolémés* and *Le culte d'Isis en Grèce*.

22. The passage from Diodorus, *Library of History*, is from 1.19.1–3; Anne Burton, *Diodorus Siculus: Book I, a Commentary* (Leiden, 1972), p. 85, points out that this strange myth "is totally divorced from the usual Greek tradition," although she does observe (pp. 11–12) that there are hints of such a variant in the second and third century B. C., and she mentions Apollonius in this connection. For Hesiod on the muses, see *Theogony*, 11.337–62; for the Nile's numerological significance, see Heliodorus, the *Ethiopica*, 9.22.5–6, and Lindsay, *Men and Gods*, pp. 39–40. For Diodorus, "Isis" meant "ancient" (1.2.4).

23. Diodorus Siculus, *Library of History*, 1.36.8.

24. Gardner, "Greek River Worship," p. 191.

25. H. F. Tozer, *Lectures on the Geography of Greece* (London, 1873), pp. 310–11.

26. Strabo, 10.2.19; cited in Tozer, *Lectures*, pp. 95–96. For an early version of the myth of Acheloüs and Hercules, originating from Aetolia, see Sophocles, *Trachiniae*, 11. 1–50. In the *Phaedrus* (230, 239, 241–42), Plato makes interesting use of the Acheloüs not only as the prototype of the river god, but also, in connection with the *nympha loci*, to reinforce his ideas about love as nature's perfection and intellectual and moral goodness.

27. See Tozer, *Lectures*, pp. 86–91, for further examples of the geographical origins of Greek philology, as well as Pierre Chantraine, *Dictionnaire étymologique de la langue grecque, histoire des mots* (Paris, 1968–1980). The river's importance for Greek cosmogonic myths is amply demonstrated in Jean Rudhardt's *Le thème de l'eau primordiale dans la mythologie grecque* (Berne, 1971). Rudhardt's monograph is a useful supplement of Károly Kerenyi's very general study, *The Gods of the Greeks*, trans. Norman Cameron (London, 1951).

28. Semple, *Geography of the Mediterranean*, p. 446.

29. *Timaeus*, 21e–23c; the translation is that of A. E. Taylor (London, 1929).

30: Gardner, "Greek River Worship," p. 197; for Prodicus's comment on the Egyptian gods, see M. P. Nilsson, *A History of the Greek Religion*, trans. F. J. Fielden (Oxford, 1945), pp. 272–73.

31. *Odyssey*, 13.353–60. Passages from Homer are from A. T. Murray's translation of the *Odyssey* (London, 1919) and the *Iliad* (London, 1924), The lines on the river nymphs as the offspring of Apollo and Tethys are from Hesiod's *Theogony*, trans. H. G. Evelyn-White (London, 1904), 11.337–47.

32. Tozer, *Lectures*, pp. 103–4.

33. See for example Pausanias, *Description of Greece*, 10.30.5. For the variant interpretations of the Marsyas legend, see the *Dictionary of Greek and Roman Biography and Mythology*, 3 vols., ed. W. Smith (London, 1850), 2: 962–63; the *Oxford Classical Dictionary*, ed. Cary, Denniston et al. (Oxford, 1949),

pp. 541–42; Georg Wissowa, *Paulys Realencyclopädie der classischen Altertumswissenschaft* (Stuttgart, 1966), 14: 2, 1986–2000.

34. See also: Theocritus, *Idylls*, 7; Plato, *Phaedrus*, 241–43; Sophocles, *Trachiniae*, 1–50.

35. C. H. Whitman, *Homer and the Heroic Tradition* (Cambridge, Mass., 1952), especially pp. 248–88, demonstrates the presence and importance of symmetrical design in the *Iliad*, and his insights enable us to make further critical observations on the art and objectives of the *Iliad*.

36. Although my reading differs greatly from Whitman's (*Homer and the Homeric Tradition*, pp. 139–50), he too is part of that critical tradition which views the *theomachia* in elemental terms. The tradition begins with Homer's first commentator, Theagenes of Rhegium, when he "interpreted the war between the gods in . . . the *Iliad* as a contest between the elements, the wet and the dry, the hot and the cold, the light and the heavy" (Nilsson, *History of the Greek Religion*, p. 271).

37. The mosaics, dating from around 80 A. D., have aroused considerable controversy; Witt (*Isis and Osiris*, p. 88) regards them as a simplified map of the Nile's delta region. A discussion of them from quite a different point of view than my own is to be found in Jean Charbonneaux, Roland Martin, and Francois Villard's *Grèce héllenistique (330–50 avant J.-C.)* (*[Paris]*, 1970), pp. 176–81. Essentially, they regard the mosaics as a stylized view of the "*vallée du Nil, grouillante de vie, et de ses rives a demi désertiques, domaine des animaux sauvages.*"

There are numerous other well-known illustrations of the artistic conflation of Egyptian, Greek, and Roman river deities, such as the *Farnese Cup* (Alexandrian, Roman provenance) and *Cleopatra's Cup* (? Pompeii, first century A. D.). See notes 1 and 21, above, for materials on Italian geography and religious and cultural influences.

38. Horace, *Odes*, 3.29.31–40, tr. C. E. Bennett (Cambridge, Mass., 1914); see also Ovid, *Amores*, 3.6.1–6.

39. Wilhelm Sigismund Teuffel, *Teuffel's History of Roman Literature*, 2 vols., rev. and enlarged ed. by L. Schwabe, trans. G. C. W. Warr (London, 1891), 1: 28–38, 150–52, 198–200, provides extensive illustration of this highly cultivated historical sensibility in Roman literature.

40. See T. R. Glover, *Studies in Virgil* (London, 1904), pp. 99–104.

41. Virgil, *Aeneid*, 1.1–6. All references to Virgil are to the translation of H. R. Fairclough (London, 1937). For particulars about Virgil's treatment of the Aeneas myth and his modifications of popular tradition, see Glover, *Studies in Virgil*, pp. 121–23, and G. K. Galinsky, *Aeneas, Sicily and Rome* (Princeton, N.J., 1969), particularly 161–62; for a useful summary of the opinions on the historical, topographical, and archeological controversies, see Russell Meiggs, *Roman Ostia* (Oxford, 1960), pp. 483–87.

42. See Galinsky, *Aeneas, Sicily and Rome*, p. 162, for further historical details about Aeneas's role in the founding of Rome.

43. Cited, Glover, *Studies in Virgil*, p. 122; see Meiggs, *Roman Ostia*, p. 485, for particulars about the Tiber, its habits and its harbor: Ostia was a notoriously unhealthy spot, whatever Virgil implies to the contrary.

44. See 8.500–600, and 10.163–214, for Aeneas's recruitment of allies; there is a similar, complementary description of Turnus's troups at 7.615–815.

45. Galinsky, *Aeneas, Sicily and Rome*, p. 162, in his discussion of the *Cista Pasinati*, makes a similar point about the historical association between Tiber, Aeneas, and Rome.

46. C. W. Mendell, "Lucan's Rivers," *Yale Classical Studies* 8 (1942), 3–22. Passages from Lucan are from the edition and translation of J. D. Duff (London, 1928). The Latin text of these passages is unusually effective in evoking the

primeval strength of the landscape as a complement to the heroic conflict of Pompey and Caesar—as we can see from the following selection:

> Interea trepido descendens agmine Magnus
> Moenia Dardanii tenuit Campana coloni.
> Haec placuit belli sedes, hinc summa moventem
> Hostis in occursum sparsas extendere partes,
> Umbrosis mediam qua collibus Appenninus
> Erigit Italiam, nulloque a vertice tellus
> Altius intumuit propiusque accessit Olympo.
> Mons inter geminas medius se porrigit undas
> Inferni superique maris, collesque coercent
> Hinc Tyrrhena vado frangentes aequora Pisae,
> Illinc Dalmaticis obnoxia fluctibus Ancon.
> Fontibus hic vastis inmensos concipit amnes
> Fluminaque in gemini spargit divortia ponti. (2.392–404)

47. It is interesting that Shakespeare attributes a similar corruptive, emasculating influence to the Nile region in *Antony and Cleopatra*, but it is Antony's *Roman* concept of manhood that is rendered effeminate, while his virile love of life is enriched in Egypt.

48. Semple, *Influences*, p. 367; the river gained even closer association with Roman law through its association with Janus and his relation to bridges and aqueducts: see Joan Holland, *Janus and the Bridge* (Rome, 1952).

49. To make use of Acheloüs at all in this episode, Ovid had to send Theseus in the wrong direction: to go from Calydonia to Athens one would travel east; Ovid sends Theseus out of his way, west to the river. Unless otherwise stated, passages from Ovid are from the edition of F. J. Miller (London, 1916).

50. The contrast between Aristaeus and Orpheus emerges when we learn of the beekeeper's responsibility for Eurydice's death, and it emphasizes the need for the husbandman to manage his destiny actively and to reject the debilitating passion that brings Orpheus to his death. This treatment of the Orpheus myth is original to Virgil: for a discussion of these parallel figures, see W. S. Anderson's "The Orpheus of Virgil and Ovid: *flebile nescio quid*," in *Orpheus: The Metamorphoses of a Myth*, ed. John Warden (Toronto, 1982), pp. 25–50.

51. See Friedrick Klingner, *Virgil: Bucolica, Georgica, Aeneas* (Zurich, 1967), pp. 326–66, especially 354–66, for this historical background of Virgil's treatment of the Orpheus myth.

52. For an allegorical reading of the cave motif dating from the third century A. D., see Porphyry, *On the Cave of the Nymphs in the Thirteenth Book of the Odyssey*, trans. T. Taylor (London, 1917).

53. 1.509–14: the edition and translation used here is that of J. G. Frazer, 5 vols. (London, 1929).

54. See Frazer's Commentary, 3: 110–12, for Ovid's modification of the sacred rituals of the feast. The name of the river, "Numicius," means "divine power"; see A. G. McKay, *Vergil's Italy* (New York, 1970) p. 157.

55. Statius, *The Villa of Marsilius Vopiscus at Tibur*, 11. 1–6, from J. H. Mosley's translation of Statius's *Works* (London, 1928).

56. Lines 101–20, from Sidonius, *Poems and Letters*, trans. W. B. Anderson (Cambridge, Mass., 1936).

57. Sidonius, *In Honour of . . . Anthemius, Consul for the Second Time*, 11. 220–29 and 331–44.

58. From Claudian's *Panegyric on the Consulship of Fl. Manlius Theodorus*, trans. M. Platnauer (London, 1922).

[CHAPTER II]

1. Seneca, *Naturales Quaestiones*, trans. T. H. Corcoran (London, 1971), p. 207. Seneca was born on the eve of the Christian era and at the height of the age of Augustus, and writing after relinquishing his power to Nero. He was a contemporary of Philo Judaeus, Tacitus, and Pliny, in each of whom we can perceive a capaciousness in their perspective on the physical world and a sophisticated exegetical approach to questions of natural philosophy and geography that reflects the cosmopolitan myth of empire that nurtured them and that, in fact, helped to make them principal sources and models for the scholastic, allegorical, and exegetical tradition that flourished after the collapse of Rome, in the work of Macrobius, Boethius, and Capella, for example. Seneca's strong interest in natural philosophy, with his balance of science and sententious, even allegorical, rhetorical modes, is an important stage in intellectual and methodological developments prior to the Christian encyclopedists. My objective here, modest enough, is to suggest how Seneca's natural history reflects this place in history, as one whose intellectual perspective is the natural offspring of the Augustan ideal and also clearly akin to that of the moderns, as Virgil, for example, was not. In these authors we begin to see a world view which, though drawn largely from libraries, is as wide as their literary learning, and its scope is greater than anything before it, comparable only to the early medieval writers'. At one point or another these authors give particular attention to developing the river motif in a way that exemplifies their art and thought.

2. Ibid., pp. 275 and 229.

3. True of the scholarly writers of the first century A. D., who were compiling the wealth of knowledge from the empire, it becomes even more the case in the next three centuries, when compilation turns into exegesis. Particularly in the fifth and sixth centuries the scholastic and encyclopedic authors thought of themselves as preserving the knowledge of the ancients, even as they submitted it to distorting, often Neoplatonic syncretic systems. Geographical knowledge occupied an important place in their studies, and in authors such as Macrobius and Capella we find not only epitomies of ancient geographical and cosmographical learning—from Plato and Aristotle, as well as Seneca—but also the *corpus* of their own early medieval, Neoplatonic, and allegorical interpretation. Modern geographers and historians of the period stress the importance of these authors for the consolidation and preservation of geographical learning: see particularly, William Harris Stahl, *Roman Science; Origins, Development and Influence to the Later Middle Ages* (Madison, Wisc., 1962) and Idem., "Astronomy and Geography in Macrobius," *Trans. Amer. Philol. Assoc.* 73 (1942), 232–58; and George H. Kimble, *Geography in the Middle Ages* (London, 1938). A work such as Macrobius's *Commentary* (2.16.22–24), for example, presents an interesting mélange of scientific geography, including a discussion of the rivers, which adapts Plato and other Greek and Latin authors, and concluding with a rhapsodic digressive analogy between the soul, human learning, and the rivers of geography. The passage (quoted as an epigraph to this chapter), like Seneca's writing, conveys a clear idea of how close were the world of the imagination or intellect and that of geography for these authors, and how unlike their ancient sources their own myths of geography were.

4. Joachim of Fiore, *Figurae*, ed. M. Reeves and Beatrice Hirsch-Reich (Oxford, 1972), pp. 130–31.

5. Anne Ross, *Pagan Celtic Britain: Studies in Iconogrophy and Tradition* (London, 1967), p. 20.

6. For particulars about Celtic river cults, see ibid., pp. 104 and 218; J. A.

MacCulloch, *Medieval Faith and Fable* (London, 1932), p. 27; Joan P. Alcock, "Celtic Water Cults in Roman Britain," *Archeological Journal*, 122 (1965), 1–12. Interestingly, just as the waters of the Nile were transported throughout Europe with the cult of Isis, so too the sacred waters of the Jordan were disseminated with the spread of Christianity.

7. For changes in the European geography at this time, see C. T. Smith's chapter on the classical world in *An Historical Geography of Western Europe before 1800* (London, 1976), pp. 57–114, particularly p. 86.

8. *The Geography of Strabo*, 8 vols., trans. H. L. Jones (London, 1917–1926), 4:1–2.

9. Ausonius, *The Moselle*, 11.374–80; the translation and edition used here and throughout is that of Hugh G. Evelyn White (London, 1919). A contemporary of Augustine and Orosius (who wrote a "history against the pagans"), Ausonius is tactfully silent on religious matters. Yet, his perspective on Rome, that is, from an intellectual and geographical distance just bordering on independence, is also the product of his age.

10. It is important to recognize the amount of chronological and intellectual overlap between the pagan literature of late antiquity and the early exegetical and Christian writings. Philo's commentaries, written before A.D. 50, attempt to reconcile Alexandrian Judaism with ancient learning, and they had immense influence on the Church Fathers. Like him, the patristics were writing in a scholastic tradition established well before Christianity and based on syncretistic methods. There were, of course, radically different opinions among the exegetes about the relation between Christian and pagan learning, some, such as Jerome, being more tolerant than others. Ambrose, for example, being less tolerant but no less indebted, tried to prove that the wisdom of the ancients was based on their reading of Scripture. The questions dividing them were still controversial for Erasmus and Colet in the Reformation, and authors' relative positions in the controversy are still at issue. For our purposes, though, they all made the distinction between ancient and modern and used similar exegetical and rhetorical techniques to defend their positions, and they each reflect a similar intellectualized view of the world. See, for example, E. R. Curtius's summary of the debate, in *European Literature and the Latin Middle Ages*, trans. Willard R. Trask (New York, 1953), pp. 36–39 especially p. 39.

11. Cited (appropriately enough) in Sir Walter Ralegh's *History of the World* (London, 1677) p. 22; Ralegh's own work represents the resurgence of this debate over allegory and rhetoric in the Renaissance. Epiphanius too was a contemporary of Ausonius, Augustine, and Orosius. More extreme than the last two in his dislike of pagan, Greek learning, he attacked allegorical methods which seemed to read meanings into Scripture and history and stressed their "literal" truth. For the modern reader, his exegesis also qualifies as allegorical. As Victor Harris summarizes the allegorical and exegetical debates, the "issue was never really whether an allegorical or a literal reading could be better justified, but rather what precisely was meant by a literal interpretation" ("Allegory to Analogy in the Interpretation of Scriptures," *Philological Quarterly* 45 [1966], 2). His point is well taken, for each of these authors imposes religious and cultural myths on what they perceive to be an historical landscape.

12. Philo Judaeus, *The Allegorical Intepretation*, in *Works*, 10 vols., trans. F. H. Colson and G. H. Whitaker (London, 1929), 1: 163–65. It is interesting that in the King James version of the Bible, the word "spring," in Genesis 2:6, is translated as "mist"—the translators were not intent upon retaining this allegorical geography.

13. Saint Ambrose, *De Paradiso*, in *Corpus Scriptorum Ecclesiasticorum Latinorum*, vol. 32, *Sancti Ambrosii Opera*, ed. C. Schenkl (Vindobonens, 1897; reprinted

New York and London, 1962), pt. 1, 273. Ambrose offers but one of the many possible examples of this method of imposing cultural myths on the landscape of biblical history. One other noteworthy example, the very title of which suggests the full range of this response to landscape in terms of a Christian ethos, is Cosmas Indicopleustes, *Christian Topography* (mid-sixth century). For discussion of Ambrose's allegorical methods, see A. Paredi, *Saint Ambrose, His Life and Times*, trans. M. Joseph Costelloe (Notre Dame, Ind., 1964), pp. 260–64.

14. Ambrose, *De Paradiso*, pp. 272–76.

15. Ibid., pp. 52ff. Augustine also interprets this landscape as one figuring unity and peace with God: *De Civitate Dei*, 20.21. His religious myth of the world's unity will be secularized by Spenser.

16. Curtius, *European Literature*, p. 39.

17. Ibid., pp. 452–57, speaks about Isidore's relation to early Christian poetics and the "system of correspondence" which coordinates history and knowledge; throughout his section on Early Christian and Medieval Literary Studies (pp. 446–67), one cannot help but be impressed by the extent and efficacy of the Church's efforts to assimilate pagan antiquity. Kimble, *Geography in the Middle Ages*, also emphasizes the dependence of these figures upon the ancients for their geographical lore. Indeed, while the Church Fathers might officially deprecate pagan authorities, or at the very least qualify their credibility, they realized that the *corpus* of learning went beyond the Church and could not be framed by its tenets. Even those most resistant to the ancients had to resort to them for the substance and methods informing their perception of the world, so that at the least they must acknowledge these origins of their learning, if only to repudiate them. For example, Orosius's *Historia adverso Paganos*, the first Christian history of the world, written as a supplement to Augustine's *De Civitate Dei*, uses pagan *scientia* to denounce the pagans; for many centuries this work was used as a compendium of ancient learning.

18. See Kimble, *Geography in the Middle Ages*, passim, for fuller discussion of the influence of these authors on medieval geography.

19. Dionysius the Areopagite, *On Divine Names*, in *Works*, trans., The Rev. John Parker (London, 1897), p. 125. Seneca's violently creative torrent is described very similarly, in terms of a simple, self-sufficient cycle which reflects universal order.

20. Ambrose, *De Paradiso*, p. 66.

21. Yi-fu Tuan, *The Hydrologic Cycle and the Wisdom of God* (Toronto, 1968), traces the evolution of our understanding of the hydrologic cycle from antiquity through the nineteenth century, and it is remarkable how little advancement was made on the basic cycle described in Ecclesiastes.

22. Sermon 13, from *The Works of Bernard of Clairvaux, Vol. 2: On the Song of Songs I*, trans. Kilian Walsh (Spencer, Mass., 1971) p. 87. See also Bernard's use of the *topos* in Sermons 33 and 51.

23. Catherine of Siena, *The Orcherd of Syon*, ed. Phyllis Hodgson and Gabriel M. Liegey, *Early English Text Society* no. 258 (London, 1966), p. 61. All references to Catherine's work are to this edition.

24. Ibid., pp. 62, 68.

25. Ibid., pp. 72, 80.

26. Joan Holland, *Janus and the Bridge*, pp. 24–26.

27. Ibid., pp. 61–62, 69.

28. The title is an ancient one whose meaning—"bridge maker"—identifies the primitive *rex sacrorum* with some of the symbolic significance of fording water and the *via sacra*. For pagan and Christian the priest was the keeper of holy law and wisdom. See Georges Dumezil, *Archaic Roman Religion*, trans. Philip Krapp (Chicago, 1966), pp. 581–88.

29. Marcia Eliade, *The Myth of the Eternal Return*, trans. Willard R. Trask, Bollingen Ser. 46 (New York, 1954), pp. 6, 34.

30. Catherine of Siena, *The Orcherd of Syon*, p. 124. It was a medieval common-place that the celestial order was recapitulated in a natural and, a second time, in an infernal form: Eliade discusses the mythic pattern represented by such analogies in *The Myth of Eternal Return*.

Catherine's polemic against nature is just one aspect of the debate about nature and learning that I only broadly outline here. For fuller survey of issues and authors in this debate, see Curtius, *European Literature*, pp. 108–22; Kimble, *Geography in the Middle Ages*, discusses the relation of this controversial literature for the preservation of geographical knowledge.

31. J. K. Hyde, "Medieval Descriptions of Cities," *John Rylands Library Bulletin 48* (1965), 309–34, discusses the tradition and generic characteristics of the *encomium urbis*. The two basic components of the form are the river and the city's fortifications, and together they define the thematic juxtaposition of nature and art. Hyde overemphasizes the importance of military fortifications in this form: even in the earliest examples, authors dwell on other natural and architectural beauties, or praise aspects of the city's religious or commercial life.

32. Ibid.

33. William Fitz-Stephen, *A Description of the Most Noble City of London* [trans. R. Gough?], (London, 1772), p. 26. The description of one's native city was a standard classroom exercise which developed one's style as well as one's civic spirit. Another particularly good British example from the twelfth century is the description of Durham in Laurence of Durham's *Dialogi Laurentii*. The city descriptions of Alexander Neckham (d. 1217) in *De Laudibus Divinae Sapientiae* were also popular in the Renaissance and were quoted frequently by William Camden in his *Britannia*. For extensive European examples, see Hyde, "Medieval Descriptions of Cities," and Siegfried Bauk's dissertation, *De Laudibus Italiae* (Konigsberg, 1919).

34. Gildas, *The Works of Gildas*, in *Six Old English Chronicles*, ed. J. A. Giles (New York, 1848), pp. 300, 306: Gildas's historical description of Britain was immensely influential in the Middle Ages and the Renaissance.

35. Geoffrey of Monmouth, *History of the Kings of Britain*, trans. Lewis Thorpe, (Harmondsworth, Middlesex, 1966), pp. 73 and 53. Geoffrey plagiarizes Gildas's description of the British rivers when describing the favorable setting for the events surrounding the founding of New Troy.

36. Ibid., p. 177.

37. The passages are from Richard C. Hoare's edition and translation of the author's works (London, 1806), pp. 243 and 5. Giraldus's introductory remarks to his works are interesting for what they tell us of his sense of literary form. His *Description of Wales* has Virgilian qualities, but is not epic: in the scholastic mode, it is an exercise in descriptive composition. The *Itinerary Through Wales* is also Virgilian, but it is not scholastic in the way that the *Description* is; significantly, it is here that he most frequently and vigorously reacts against Geoffrey's influence; *The Topography of Ireland*, he suggests, is distinctly Ovidian in its epic qualities. In each case, classical models define his approach to his national, historical and topographical material.

[CHAPTER III]

1. While much is made in discussions of landscape poetry about "topothesical" description, it should be observed that both real and imaginary landscapes were

subject to the same formal and rhetorical guidelines. Whether a landscape is real or imagined is not the important consideration, since one might be used to serve the other. Both were aspects of rhetoric, tools used to advance description and invention. See, for example, Richard Sherry, *A Treatise of the Figures of Grammer and Rhetorik* ([London], 1555), p. 15, for definition of the terms. It was assumed that the Renaissance poet would combine elements of both in his description: the question was, what did he create, what does he show us as a result of this chemistry? For an understanding of topographical literature, then, we must not look for a shift from one kind of description to another, but for the changing emphasis in the treatment of the two.

2. The best and most important example of this is William Camden's *Britannia*, published in seven Latin editions between 1586 and 1604 and translated by Philemon Holland in 1610. Camden's objective is a historical landscape; he collects the oldest information, usually Roman, about Britain in order to try to restore England to its British past. But many other examples might be offered: for Stowe, Speed, and Harrison, to describe a setting, to a large extent, involves its re-creation through historical accounts.

3. For a more detailed examination of this aspect of the river motif, see W. H. Herendeen, "The Rhetoric of Rivers: The River and the Pursuit of Knowledge," *Studies in Philology*, 78 (1981), 107–27. For Browne's impatience over self-perpetuating misconceptions concerning the Nile, see the chapter on the Nile in *Pseudodoxia Epidemica* in *Works*, 4 vols., ed. Sir Geoffrey Keynes (London, 1928), 2: 447–50.

4. Ibid., 3:319; as the commonplace books (from which this passage is taken) reveal, Browne read ancient and medieval authors very carefully and with particular interest in historical geography.

5. Giovanni Botero, *The Cause of the Greatnesse of Cities*, trans. T[homas] H[awkins], (London, 1635), pp. 38–39 and 41.

6. Abraham Ortelius, *The Theatre of the World*, trans. John Norton (London, 1606), p. xxxiii.

7. Lambert Daneau, *The Wonderfull Woorkmanship of the World*, trans. T[homas] T[wyne], (London, 1578), p. 21.

8. William Harrison, *The Description of Britain*, comprising the first two books of Holinshed's *Chronicles* ([London, 1586], London, 1807), 1:79; I have used the 1807 edition throughout.

9. William Camden, *The Britannia*, 4 vols. trans. R. Gough (London, 1806), 1:39. Unless otherwise indicated, references are to this edition of the *Britannia*. This passage shows quite nicely how, in the Renaissance, the material world is regarded as being protean in much the same way that time itself is.

10. See, for example, Semple, *Influences*, p. 347.

11. Throughout his Preface, Cuningham discusses the importance of geography and its influence on, and relationship to the other disciplines.

12. See, for example, Joseph Hall's verses "To Camden" in his *Virgidemiarum* ([London, 1603]).

13. William Lambard, *Perambulation of Kent* (London, 1806), pp. 195–97.

14. Humphrey Lhuyd, *The Breviary of Britain*, trans. Thomas Twyne (London, 1573), p. 24. It is arguable that rivers so named had proper names as well, but significantly these have been dropped and the generic name alone remains. Usually rivers which are simply named "the river" are of some considerable importance, the Nile being the most notable example. Of course there are many other names (or parts of names) in all languages which designate water or the river, such as Bourne, Beck, Esk, Ouse, and Wye. Eilert Ekwall's *English River-Names* (Oxford, 1928) is the definitive study of this subject (see particularly pp. 1i–1ii).

15. See Thomas Westcote's *View of Devonshire*, ed. George Olwer and Pitman

Jones (Exeter, 1845), p. 348, and John Selden's commentary to Song One of Drayton's *Poly-Olbion* (London, 1613), for Renaissance recognition of the river's role as *genius loci* in religion, verse, prose, and fiction of all ages; it is important to realize that authors use this ancient device quite literally and consciously when they treat their local rivers in literature.

16. Ortelius, *The Theatre of the World*, p. xxxi.

17. Lambard, *Perambulation of Kent*, p. 232; Camden, *Britannia*, 1:197.

18. See note 13 above; Selden, Camden, and Robert Cotton, early enthusiasts in antiquarian matters, were interested in the archeological evidence for Isis worship in Britain.

19. Richard Linch, *The Fountaine of Ancient Fiction* (London, 1599), p. iv.

20. See, for example, P. Mexia's *The Forreste*, trans. Thomas Fortescue (London, 1571), fols. 78–80, or Lambert Daneau's *Geographiae Poeticae, id est, universe terrae descriptionis* ([Geneva], 1580).

21. Westcote, *View of Devonshire*, pp. 247–48.

22. As Frances Yates says (*The Valois Tapestries*, London, 1959, p. 53): "This plot of the water-creatures doing obeisance to the monarchy was to be utilized again and again"—particularly on the artificial waters of Fontainebleau and on the river Ladour at Bayonne. The setting and spectacle, following designs by such artists as Caron, incorporated all the arts: there was music, performed by Arion, Triton, and the nymphs, and accompanied by Ronsard's verses (sung by the nymphs) and water ballet, as well as a thorough metamorphosis of the landscape and interior design. The events were celebrated in the tapestries of Lucas de Heere. This bringing together of all the gods of the world's waters, particularly those of the seas and rivers, was obviously meant to support the dominant political theme of unity and the reconciliation of the Protestant and Catholic factions. As we will see in the following section, unity or concord is a principal theme conveyed by the river in the Renaissance. For a full account of these fêtes, see Yates, *The Valois Tapestries*, pp. 51–72, and for the relation of Pontus de Tyard's essay to the events and subsequent tapestries, see Yates, *The French Academies* (London, 1947), pp. 131–51. Perhaps it should also be emphasized here how close the work of the topographers, such as Braun, Hogenberg, and Saxton, was to this courtly trend of mythologizing the landscape of Europe according to a rather fanciful sense of classical myth and modern geography. Their maps and perspectives, further illustrated with examples of native costume, mythical figures, and resplendent architecture, had their influence on the painting, entertainments and other arts of the day (see *The Valois Tapestries*, pp. 13–16), and were also reproduced in topographical tapestries; there is, for example, a series of tapestries of English countries, based on Saxton's maps, now in the Victoria and Albert Museum. And we might also point to the frequent appearance of the river theme in the architectural and monumental sculpture of the period, the most obvious example being Bernini's *Fountain of Rivers* in Rome.

23. See Elizabeth's welcome to Norwich in 1578, in which the river motif suggests the approbation of the *genius loci* (quoted above, epigraph to Part 1); or George Peele's Lord Mayor's pageant for Wolstan Dixi in 1585. Elizabeth's progress to Kenilworth in 1575 was greeted by several local aquatic *genii* representing native British lore and suggesting a determination to animate the landscape with indigenous legends and to get away from predominantly classical motifs, such as those most common on the Continent. One has only to look through John Nichol's *The Progresses and . . . Processions of Queen Elizabeth* (London, 1828), to get an idea of the popularity of the river motif in such spectacles.

24. Henry Reynolds, *Mythomystes* (London, [?1632]), pp. 57 and 67.

25. The river is a common vehicle for the Empedoclean themes of the Neopla-

tonists, who found it adaptable to their cosmic myth of love, concord, and unity, although their philosophical allegory removes it from the landscape: Spenser embodies their myths in the material world. Their interest in marrying platonic philosophy with Christianity illustrates the continuity of the motif. See, for example, Pico della Mirandola's *Heptaplus*, third exposition, his *Of Being and Unity*, Marsilio Ficino's commentaries on Plato, or Giordano Bruno's *Expulsion of the Triumphant Beast*, where these shared ideas about unity and concord are developed, and the occasional use of the river motif betrays its evolution from antiquity and the allegorists, to their peculiarly Renaissance cosmology.

26. Walter Ralegh, *The History of the World*, in *Works*, 8 vols. (Oxford, 1829), 2: 61; citations from Ralegh's *History* are from this edition; the emphasis here is mine.

27. Ibid., p. 66.

28. Ibid., p. 62.

29. Ibid., p. 127.

30. Ibid.

31. Ibid., p. 202.

32. Ibid., p. 179.

33. Ibid., p. 208.

34. Ibid., pp. 208–9, 258.

35. See Smith, *Historical Geography of Western Europe*, pp. 331–38 (specifically p. 332), for discussion of the changing human landscape of the late Middle Ages and the Renaissance.

36. *Gesta Grayorum*, p. vi.

37. Cited Smith, *Historical Geography of Western Europe*, p. 369. Antwerp is a good example of a city whose growth reflects the changes in commercial routes and particularly the improvement of the waterways; its prosperity was closely related to the increased traffic on the Sheldt, the Rhine, and the North Sea. It relied completely on the freedom of navigation along these routes, and when this was impeded in the last quarter of the sixteenth century, its importance diminished rapidly. The city illustrates what Renaissance political scientists recognized as the inherent limitations of any center relying solely on trade.

38. For the importance of the coasting trade in England and for further particulars about the principal cities and commodities it served, see T. S. Willan, *The Inland Trade: Studies in English Internal Trade in the Sixteenth and Seventeenth Centuries* (Manchester, 1976), pp. 15–49. Although there was much interest in developing the rivers, conflicting objectives of various groups—landowners, mill owners, and shippers—made the implementation of change nearly impossible. The body in charge of the rivers was the Commission of Sewers, but their authority extended principally to matters of drainage rather than navigation, and ultimately they had no control over the use of the river banks; for this, an Act of Parliament was necessary. Alan R. H. Baker, "Changes in the Later Middle Ages," in *A New Historical Geography of England*, ed. H. C. Darby (Cambridge, 1973), pp. 237–47, discusses the relatively unchanged state of internal trade in England between 1300 and 1600. For particulars about Parliamentary activity concerning the rivers, see F. V. Emery, "England *circa* 1600," in Darby, *A New Historical Geography*, pp. 287–93, and T. S. Willan, *River Navigation in England, 1600–1750* (London, 1936), passim.

River improvement in Europe was further advanced, most obviously in the Low Countries, but Italy had developed systems of canals and locks in the fifteenth century, and in sixteenth-century France, under Henry IV, an intricate canal system linking the Loire, the Seine, the Meuse, the Saône, the Rhône, the Garonne, and the Mediterranean was fully planned, and was largely implemented by his successor. The scheme reflects the extent to which river and sea were regarded as one complex and inseparable water system.

For West Country poets referring to the Exeter Ship Canal, see Thomas Kidley, "Kidley's Hawkins," B.M. MS Sloane 2024, and Charles Fitz-Geoffrey, *Sir Francis Drake. His honorable Lifes commendation* (Oxford, 1596).

39. The best known literary treatment of the river as mediator of hill and vale and as a figure of moderation is John Denham's *Cooper's Hill*.

40. G.W., *Newes out of Cheshire of the Newfound Well* (London, 1600), sig. C^r.

41. See Semple, *Influences*, pp. 351 and 356–58, for discussion of the river's unifying effect in geography; a perverse application of this is in Napoleon's annexation of Belgium and Holland on the grounds (literally) that they had been created by the alluvium of French rivers.

42. Gilles Corrozet and Claude Champier, *Le Cathologue des villes*, fols. 50–50^v.

43. Robert Johnson, *The Travellers Breviat, or an historical description of the most famous kingdoms in the World* ([London], 1601), p. 7. Throughout this work Johnson borrows extensively from the Italian and French historians and topographers, particularly Botero, whose work was well known and often translated (and modified) in England during the late sixteenth and seventeenth centuries.

44. Giovanni Botero, *The Cause of the Greatnesse of Cities*, trans. T[homas] H[awkins], (London, 1635), p. 21.

45. Ibid., p. 24

46. The importance of this wordly view of the city needs to be emphasized; it is reflected visually in the monumental work of Georg Braun and Franz Hogenberg, *Civitates Orbis Terrarum* (Antwerp, 1572–1618), and by the doleful words of Drummond of Hawthornden in *A Cypresse Grove*: "By Death wee are exiled from this faire Citie of the World."

47. See Botero, *Cause*, pp. 27, 38, 48–50.

48. Giovanni Botero, *Relation of the Most Famous Kingdomes . . . throwout the World* [trans. Robert Johnson], (London, 1630), p. 41.

49. *Cause*, pp. 32–33. The inseparability of the seas and the rivers, and Botero's general fascination with the rivers find further expression in a tract which is bound with the present work, but evidently meant for separate publication: *Observations Concerning the Sea* (also translated and dated, London, 1635). This is essentially a reworking of Platonic and Aristotelian hydrology in terms of his pious but secular humanism.

50. Giovanni Botero, *Relation of the Most Famous Kingdomes*, p. 125.

51. Philip Sidney, *A woorke concerning the trewnesse of the Christian religion* (London, 1587), in *Works*, 4 vols., ed. Albert Feuillerat (Cambridge, 1963), 3:276.

52. René de Lucinge, *The Beginning, Continuance, and Decay of Estates*, trans. I. F[inet], (London, 1606), p. 119.

53. Pierre de la Primaudaye, *The French Academie*, trans. T.B., (London, 1586), Epistle Dedicatorie.

54. Pierre de la Primaudaye, *The Third Volume of the French Academie*, trans. R. Dolman (London, 1601), pp. 269, 265, 263. Throughout this third volume, Primaudaye is concerned to explore the social, natural, and geographical manifestations of concord and harmony, and his views are redolent of those of Spenser and the Neoplatonists.

55. Francis Bacon, *Advancement of Learning*, in *Essays Civil and Moral* (London, 1910), p. 156.

56. For a typical example of how clearly the individual's inner being was regarded as a reflection of the external world and how one's psyche identified with the political topography of the nation, see Sidney's verses, *The 7 Wonders of England*.

57. The Hellenizing of the European landscape and literary tradition is one of the most basic impulses in the Renaissance. The psychological identification between the modern poet and his classical counterpart seems to have been carried furthest by the French. Some of the different positions on the relation between vernacular poetry and the classical tradition can be seen, for example, in Joachim du Bellay's *La Deffence et illustration de la langue Françoyse* (Paris, 1549) and Pierre Ronsard's . . . *L'Art Poetique françoise* (Paris, 1565). Much has been written about this, and the Pléiade poets' interest in Hellenic antiquity, and fuller treatment of the subject can be found in Elizabeth Armstrong, *Ronsard and the Age of Gold* (New York, 1966), and Isidore Silver, *Ronsard and the Hellenic Renaissance in France: Ronsard and the Greek Epic* (St. Louis, Mo., 1961), for examination of the full extent of their determination to recreate the context of the ancient world.

58. Richard Brathwait, *The Schollers Medley; or an Intermixt discourse upon historicall and poeticall relations* (London, 1614), p. 68. Brathwait's critical concerns here are quite interesting. He is discussing the propriety of mixing history and fiction, and how to combine them in proper proportion. His argument might be compared with Sidney's, which separates the historian and the true poet, who absorbs history into his higher sphere. Brathwait also stresses the importance of creating a credible landscape in these poetical histories; his comments are a good illustration of the Renaissance writer's awareness of how much of his descriptive topography is the product of a shaping imagination.

59. *EKaTomTTAOIA, or Passionate Centurie of Love* ([London, 1582]), p. 12.

60. The motif of the river crossing as an image of cultural identification or initiation appears frequently in the Italian Renaissance. Olga Rorzi Pugliese, in "Passage to Humanism: A Renaissance Topos," *NEMLA Italian Studies* 5 (1981), 15–23, examines how Petrarch, Bruni, and Machiavelli use the *topos* as a way of defining their humanistic ideals.

61. It is striking how frequently Renaissance poets strive to identify themselves with a landscape and how the landscape is given a "political" as well as a "personal" significance by them. Fletcher's Cam (or Cham) is the same river as Milton's "Grant"; Cambridge's river was known by both names.

62. The fashion for literary posturing and badinage was an important part of the poet's persona, and it was served by the shorthand reference to the river. Role-playing was not just a matter of pretension, but one aspect of Renaissance poetics, a means by which important themes could be explored, as we see in the work of Petrarch, Ronsard, Spenser, and Milton, for example. The subject enters Pugliese's comments on the Italian humanists in "Passage to Humanism", and Armstrong's discussion of the Pléiade poets in *Ronsard and the Age of Gold*, for example.

63. Jacopo Sannazaro, *Arcadia*, trans. R. Nash (Detroit, Mich., 1966), p. 112. Page references, hereafter embodied in the text, are to this edition.

64. Sannazaro's influence on the English pastoral has often been referred to, and it is most conspicuous in the work of Sidney and William Browne. As we will see, one of the most often emulated features of his pastoral world is the cave of the river nymph. It has not been sufficiently stressed, but this influence extends to the development of a psychological landscape in which we move readily between material and psychic dimensions. Sannazaro had an especially strong impact on the *Old Arcadia*, as A. C. Hamilton points out in *Sir Philip Sidney: A Study of his Life and Works* (Cambridge, England, 1977), pp. 42–44. Note that as the national landscape and its rivers became increasingly absorbed into poetic myth, the generally vague, metaphoric pastoral world of Sidney becomes distinctly native in Browne's *Britannia's Pastorals*. For Continental influences on Browne (including

Sannazaro), see Joan Grundy, "William Browne and the Italian Pastoral," *Review of English Studies*, new series, 4 (1953), 305–16.

65. Some of these imperfectly assimilated Continental influences on the English pastoral are evident in such works as Thomas Watson's *Amyntas* (1585), and most of Drayton's early poetry; John Dickenson's *Arisbas, Euphues amidst his Slumbers* (1590), and Abraham Fraunce's *The Countesse of Pembroke's Yvychurch* (1592).

66. William Cuningham, *The Cosmographical Glasse* (London, 1559), fol. 7. Cuningham's definition is the standard for the Renaissance, and it was paraphrased frequently by numerous authors.

67. Lambard, *A Perambulation of Kent*, p. 474. An interesting example in verse of this objective of describing Europe in terms of its geographical and political divisions is Richard Zouch's *The Dove, or Passages of Cosmography* (London, 1613); Zouch's method of soaring over the landscape and surveying it through the eyes of an aerial muse is similar to Drayton's and William Browne's.

68. Westcote's *The View of Devonshire* was written in 1630, although it was not published until 1845. It is part of the sudden outpouring of regionalistic literature, particularly in the West Country, that occurred during the second and third decades of the century. Other West Country topographical writers—all of whom were known to each other—are Tristram Risdon, Nathaniel Carpenter, William Browne, and (from the previous generation) Richard Carew. Page references to Westcote will be absorbed into the text.

69. In many other authors in prose and verse, this link between the descriptive form of their work and the mainsprings of language is identified with the river. For William Lambard, to name only one, the name of the Medway seemed to describe its course through the center of Kent, and in structuring his *Perambulation of Kent* with the river, he felt that he achieved a narrative form that mirrored nature's.

[CHAPTER IV]

1. A recent and very characteristic view of English topographical literature is James Turner's *The Politics of Landscape: Rural Scenery and Society in English Poetry, 1630–1660* (Cambridge, Mass., 1979). Here, as in so much of the critical tradition ably initiated by Robert Aubin in his study, "Materials for study of the Influence of *Cooper's Hill*," *English Literary History* 1 (1934), 197–204, the genre in England is concentrated in the second quarter of the century. For an assessment of Turner's approach to the genre, see W. H. Herendeen, "Rick Burning in Renaissance Studies," *Univ. Toronto Quarterly* 51 (Winter 1981–1982), 210–16.

2. Renaissance scholars' preoccupation with the "Tudor myth" has not proved to be a very fruitful approach to the period, partly because it is taken as an end in itself, and not recognized as being but one aspect of the myth-making process indulged in by authors of the period.

3. *Tudor Treatises*, ed. A. G. Dickens, *Yorkshire Archeological Society Record Series* 125 (1959), 38. For a fuller view of the response to the Dissolution, see *Three Chapters of Letters Relating to the Suppression of Monasteries*, ed. Thomas Wright, *Camden Society* 26 (London, 1843).

4. Margaret Aston's article, "English Ruins and English History: the Dissolution and the Sense of the Past," *Journal of the Warburg and Courtauld Institutes* 36 (1973), 231–55, provides useful and more detailed examination of these events and the response to them, and a rather different analysis of their impact on historical activity. She also stresses their influence on the graphic arts of the eighteenth

century, and I want to suggest here their more immediate effect on the literary imagination.

5. Ibid., p. 231.

6. *The New Year's Gift*, in *The Itinerary of John Leland*, 9 vols. ed. T. Hearne, 3d ed. (Oxford, 1770), 1:xxii. References to the *Genethliacon* (1543) and the *Cygnea Cantio* (1545) are to their appearance in volume 9 of this edition of *The Itinerary*; line references will be contained in the text.

7. Leland is frequently spoken of as the "King's Antiquary," but it is not known whether this was in any respect an official title. Leland's importance at the threshold of the English Renaissance has not been adequately studied. Leicester Bradner's discussion of his work in *Musae Anglicanae* (New York, 1940), pp. 25–32, continues to be the best published assessment. For discussion of his literary influence, see W. H. Herendeen, "Spenserian Specifics: Spenser's Appropriation of a Renaissance *Topos*," *Medievalia et Humanistica*, new series, 10 (1981), 159–62. His importance as a Reformation author is addressed by James Carley's "Four Poems in Praise of Erasmus by John Leland," in *Erasmus in England* 11 (1981–1982), 26–27.

8. Janus Vitalis's epigram, "*Qui Romam in mediam quaeris*," was immensely popular throughout Europe, and is representative of the use of the tower and the river as a *topos* for the ruins of time. The English used the motif and his verses to point to the vanities of Catholic Rome. I have used William Browne's translation (in G. Goodwin's edition of his *Works*, 2 vols. [London, 1893], 2:301) to illustrate its enduring popularity, although I might have cited Spenser's or du Bellay's versions.

9. Camden, *Britannia*, tr. Philemon Holland (London, 1610), 1: Kent.

10. See, for example, Thomas Churchyard, *The Worthines of Wales* (London, 1587), p. 82; further page references will be contained in the text.

11. Camden, *Britannia*, 4 vols., trans. and ed. R. Gough (London, 1806), 1:379. See 1:clxxv, for Camden's important explanation of the organizing principles of the *Britannia*, and his objectives in combining regional, political (and demographic), and linguistic divisions of the country. While I use the Gough edition in discussing the prose and the verse, a convenient edition of the verse alone has recently been published by George Burke Johnston: "Poems by William Camden, with Notes and Translations from the Latin," *Studies in Philology* 72 (1975). This is particularly useful, not only because it contains Camden's Latin verse, Holland's translation, and Basil Kennet's translation of the *De Connubio* for the Gibson editions, but also because Johnston has tried to reconstruct the fragments of the *De Connubio* in their "proper" geographical order, and this makes his edition especially helpful for following my commentary.

12. See also Camden, *Britannia*, 2:3, 37, 47, for additional examples of Camden's use of the rivers to organize the landscape and the narrative. Camden repeatedly calls attention to these structuring devices and to the presence of multiple political and historical influences dividing the country, so that we are often reminded of his use of the geography as a underlying unifying principle.

The implications of how Renaissance authors use historical materials, and particularly how they put historical data into different combinations in order to test our knowledge of history, become more suggestive the more we look at Shakespeare's plays. Camden's method of looking at historical periods from several points of view is very similar to Shakespeare's.

13. For a general discussion of the convention of the river marriage, see J. B. Oruch, "Spenser, Camden, and the Poetic Marriages of Rivers," *Studies in Philology* 69 (1967), 606–20, and Herendeen, "Spenserian Specifics," pp. 159–66.

14. Joan Evans's *A History of the Society of Antiquaries* (Oxford, 1955), particularly pp. 9–11, and Linda Van Norden's "The Elizabethan Society of Antiquaries," unpubl. diss. (University of California at Los Angeles, 1946), are still the fullest historical studies of the society. Much work remains to be done on the manuscript materials relating to the work of the society.

15. The objectives of the society are put forth in their petition to Elizabeth just before her death; two drafts survive in the British Library, Cotton manuscripts: Faustina E.v.12, and Titus B.V.67. We get a sense of the scholarly interests of the society from the papers that were presented at their gatherings, many of which were discovered by Thomas Hearne and (at a later date) Thomas Ayloffe. These were published as *A Collection of Curious Discourses*, 2 vols., ed. T. Ayloffe (London, 1771).

16. *Curious Discourses*, 1:216, 276, and also Linda Van Norden, "Peiresc and the English Scholars," *Huntington Library Quarterly* 12 (1949), 370.

17. Evans, *History of the Society of Antiquaries*, p. 11.

18. *Curious Discourses*, 2:326. Of course authors had "mythologized" history for centuries, and Leland was among them. But it is one thing to assert the legitimacy of Arthurian legend, which authors had already been debating for three hundred years, and it is quite another to confine one's work to British materials. The one has to do with historical polemics, the other with the epistemology of history.

19. For a full account of the dating of the society's activities, see Linda Van Norden, "Sir Henry Spelman on the Chronology of the Elizabeth College of Antiquaries," *Huntington Library Quarterly* 13 (1949–1950), 138.

20. See B. M. MS. Faustina E.v.12.

21. *The Life and Minor Works of George Peele*, ed. D. H. Horne (New Haven, Conn., 1953), p. 210.

22. In *The Works of Thomas Campion*, ed. and trans. W. R. Davis (New York, 1967), p. 363.

23. Kidley's "Hawkins" was written while he was at Exeter College, Oxford; it is now B. M. MS. Sloane, 2024.

24. This expression of his debt to Sidney is made in the dedication of *The Ruines of Time* to the Countess of Pembroke. There are, of course, numerous other instances of Spenser capitalizing on the Sidney connection, both before and after Sir Philip's death.

25. See Herendeen, "Spenserian Specifics," for a more detailed account of the development of Spenser's reputation as a river poet.

26. Bod. MS. Rawl. Poet. 85, fol. 94^v. Throughout the poem, Colyn is the shepherd Perin and Thenot speak about when preparing their song. It seems certainly an oversight when in finally offering their song, Perin uses the name Cuddy: "Butt if yee lyste to heere a sorye fytt/That Cuddy could in dollful verse endyte" (94^v). It is clear from the context, as well as from what follows, that Colyn is meant: the song is, indeed, one of Colin Clout's. Later in the poem Cuddy's name is mentioned in a different context, and the allusion is all the more suggestive here since he resembles Spenser's Cuddy, just as the elegist's Thenot resembles Spenser's figure of that name.

27. Ibid., fol. 95.

28. Ibid., fol. 96^v.

29. Bryskett's verses were registered in 1587; evidently Spenser held up the publication of the volume until 1596. I use J. H. Pafford's edition of Bryskett's *Works* (1972). The poems are usually published (rather confusingly) with Spenser's works and are to be found in both the De Selincourt and Variorum editions. Line references will be included in the text.

30. Charles Fitz-Geoffrey, *Sir Francis Drake. His Honorable Lifes Commendation* (Oxford, 1596), sig. B7ᵛ.

31. Ibid., sigs. C6–C6ᵛ.

32. We see Spenser's understanding of the word "poet" as "maker" in *April* 1, 1.19; Sidney discusses this meaning in *Defense*, p. 7. It is also echoed in the word "fashion," as Spenser uses it in the letter to Ralegh.

33. Throughout my discussion I use the Variorum Edition of *The Works of Edmund Spenser*, 11 vols., ed. Edwin Greenlaw et al. (Baltimore, Md., 1932–1957).

34. See Herendeen, "Spenserian Specifics," pp. 166–79.

35. Allegorical readings tend to emphasize reader strategy at the expense of the public themes that always lie behind the allegory. Michael O'Connell, *Mirror and Veil: The Historical Dimension of Spenser's "Faerie Queene"* (Chapel Hill, N.C., 1977) is one recent study which puts the allegory within this larger context. It is interesting that the river episodes in Spenser's verse have generally been treated rather hastily by his critics. I suspect that this is partly because they do not submit to allegorical reading as other characters or episodes do—because they are better described as *topoi* than *figurae*.

36. Several critics have remarked on the ambiguity of the figure of Verulam, and from different points of view. See Millar MacLure's perceptive remarks in "Spenser and the ruins of time," in *A Theatre for Spenserians*, ed. J. M. Kennedy and J. A. Reither (Toronto, 1973), pp. 7–8. This ambiguity goes to the heart of the Renaissance image of the river, its cities and towers; see also D. C. Allen, *Image and Meaning* (Baltimore, Md., 1960), pp. 62–66, and Carl J. Rasmussen, "How weak be the Passions of Woefulness: Spenser's *Ruines of Time*," in *Spenser Studies* 2 (1981), 159–83.

37. The lines on Camden have been recognized as central to Spenser's poem; see, for example, Rosemund Tuve's "Spenserus," in *Essays by Rosemund Tuve: Spenser, Herbert and Milton*, ed. Thomas P. Roche, Jr. (Princeton, N. J., 1970), pp. 148–50.

38. They also demonstrate what R. Gottfried calls "myths of locality," in "Spenser and the Italian Myth of Locality," *Studies in Philology* 34 (1937), 107–25. Many of the works identified by Gottfried are concerned with local river myths and provide an important body of Continental literature which, like Spenser's rivers, reflects this interest in mythologizing the landscape. As etiological myths these bring together themes of social order and national origins and are, therefore, well suited for a cultural mythology.

39. William Blissett, "Spenser's Mutabilitie," in *Essays in English Literature from the Renaissance to the Victorian Age*, ed. Millar MacLure and F. W. Watt (Toronto, 1964), p. 261.

40. Isable MacCaffrey, *Spenser's Allegory: The Anatomy of Imagination* (Princeton, N. J., 1976), p. 6.

41. MacCaffrey, ibid., stresses the fact that this aspect of allegory is central to Renaissance concepts of the imagination and the process of invention and discovery. She also helpfully identifies this as part of Christian poetics—the function of poetry in a fallen world where understanding and the redemption of nature must advance circuitously (p. 47). Her approach to Spenserian allegory provides a helpful theoretical context for my treatment of the river episodes.

42. Alastair Fowler's "The River Guyon," *Modern Language Notes* 75 (1960), 289–92, makes the initial identification between Guyon, temperance, and the river of Paradise. Spenser's use of the scriptural river and its exegetical interpretation for characterization suggests how biblical and medieval aspects of the motif are adapted by the Renaissance poet.

43. A. C. Hamilton, *The Structure of Allegory in the "Faerie Queene"* (Oxford, 1961), pp. 159ff, speaks of Book 4 as the contest between love and discord. Most critics recognize the inadequacy or anomalousness of the book's nominal virtue, and address the problem in terms of the fundamental Spenserian theme, the relation between love, friendship, and concord. Thomas P. Roche, Jr., for example, in *The Kindly Flame: A Study of the Third and Fourth Books of Spenser's "Faerie Queene"* (Princeton, N. J., 1964), pp. 202ff, de-emphasizes the importance of friendship in favor of the broader theme of *concordia discors*.

44. See, for example, G. Hough's discussion of the relation between Venus and Concord, in *A Preface to "The Faerie Queene"* (London, 1962), p. 188. Harry Berger relates the episode in Venus's Temple to the river pageant, and discusses them in terms of Spenser's Empedoclean themes in "Two Spenserian Retrospects," *Texas Studies in Literature and Language* 10 (1968–1969), 6–22.

45. For a study of the importance of memory in the Renaissance, and the range of experience that is summoned through the arts of memory, see Frances A. Yates, *The Art of Memory* (London, 1966).

[CHAPTER V]

1. E[dward], W[ilkinson], *His Thameseidos* (London, 1600), Book 3. The work, though occasionally referred to in connection with Camden's and Leland's river poems, has been otherwise virtually ignored by critics. Approached best in terms of the author's national fiction and his Spenserianism, it suggests much about the amount of work that remains to be done on the subject of Spenser's imitators.

2. Ibid., Book 2.

3. The history and range of the form can be surveyed in O. B. Hardison's *The Enduring Monument: A Study of the Idea of Praise in Renaissance Literary Theory and Practice* (Chapel Hill, N. C., 1962) and Theodore C. Burgess's *Epideictic Literature* (Chicago, 1962). For more specific discussion of ways in which it involves the poetic persona, see W. H. Herendeen, "'Like a Circle Bounded in Itself': Jonson, Camden, and the Strategies of Praise," *Journal of Medieval and Renaissance Studies* 2 (1981), 139–67.

4. Ruth Wallerstein's "The Laureate Hearse," in *Studies in Seventeenth Century Poetic* (Madison, Wisc., 1950), pp. 11–148, examines the elegiac mode, and its search for understanding, in relation to seventeenth-century poetics; she also speaks generally (pp. 59–67) of the Spenserian qualities of many of the elegies on Henry. Although her concerns are quite different from my own, her discussion reinforces my examination of the national self-consciousness of the form.

5. [Richard Niccols], "A true Subject's Sorow, for the loss of his late Soveraigne," in *Expicedium. A Funeral Oration* (London, 1603), sig. B2. John Lane's poem is *An Elegy upon the Death of . . . Elizabeth* (London, 1603).

6. This is contained in the collection of elegies, *Sorrowes Joy, or a Lamentation for the Late deceased Soveraigne* (Cambridge, 1603).

7. See E. C. Wilson, *Prince Henry and English Literature* (Ithaca, N. Y., 1946) for Prince Henry's popularity and the hopes that were fixed on him. Although Wilson is not concerned to identify such a generic pattern, the materials he identifies and discusses here and in his similar study, *England's Eliza* (London, 1938), have generic similarities which go beyond the elegiac mode, and develop common national images, so that the elegies on Henry further define their sorrow by recalling the national sentiments expressed at Elizabeth's death.

8. Robert Allyne, *Funerall Elegies*, "Elegy Three."

9. Brooke's poem, "A Funerall Elegie on the Prince" and Browne's "An Elegie on the Never Inough Bewailed Death of . . . Henry, Prince of Wales," both of which use the river motif, were published together in *Two Elegies* (London, 1613).

10. Lines 113–20. I use L. E. Kastner's edition of the *Poetical Works of William Drummond* (Manchester, 1913); further references to Drummond's work will be contained parenthetically in the text.

11. Augustine Taylor, *An Epithalamion* (London, 1613).

12. Stanza 22. I use A. Davenport's edition of *The Collected Works of Joseph Hall* (Liverpool, 1949).

13. Stanza 61. It seems very likely that in developing his themes here, Hall had both Camden and Spenser in mind; he tends to link their names with Sidney as we see in his verses on Camden.

14. Patrick Hannay, *Two Elegies on the Death of Queene Anne* (London, 1619), "The Second Elegy."

15. In *Works*, 11 vols. ed. C. H. Herford and Percy and Evelyn Simpson (Oxford, 1925–1950), 7:86–87.

16. The phrase appears among Daniel's prefatory remarks to *Tethy's Festival*.

17. Printed in *Original Letters of Eminent Literary Men*, ed. Henry Ellis, Camden Society 23 (London, 1843), 98. Lawrence Stone, *The Crisis of the Aristocracy, 1558–1641* (Oxford, 1965), pp. 392–98, discusses and documents the move from London during this period. As I have emphasized, this polarity between London life and country life must not be oversimplified, but the changing focus away from London is quite clear. We get some sense of how this affects literary sensibilities over the years from the ideas and forms discussed by Earl Miner in *The Cavalier Mode from Jonson to Cotton* (Princeton, N. J., 1971).

18. Cited in Evans, *History of the Society of Antiquaries*, p. 13.

19. Joan Grundy, *The Spenserian Poets* (London, 1969), pp. 1–8.

20. I use F. S. Boas's edition of *The Poetical Works of Giles and Phineas Fletcher*, 2 vols. (Cambridge, 1909).

21. "To my ever honoured Cousin, W. R. Esquire," in *Works*, 2:229. All of Fletcher's verse has this autobiographical quality, so that his larger themes of poetry and the place of the poet in the nation are developed in terms of a very personal pastoral myth—one, however, in which the poet resists his pastoral life, as critics tend not to notice.

22. In both episodes the poets are commenting on the poet's relation to society and slightly more detailed comparison will further demonstrate the very different contexts and implications in the two works. Colin's retreat on Arlo Hill is a sacred *locus amoenus* whose delights—the graces—are not vouchsafed the courtly Calidore, who, tainted by the Blatant Beast, indiscreetly intrudes on Colin's orgy of music. The poetic ideal here is vulnerable to the court's intrusion, but unlike Fletcher's shepherd, when Colin breaks his pipes he suffers no despair, does not lament the inadequacy of his music, and does not express any dissatisfaction with the ability of the world (reflected here in the landscape of Arlo Hill) to sustain his art. Furthermore, the beneficial influence of the vision he stole works soothingly on Calidore, whose civility (st. 29) is kindled by the graceful setting and company. The mythic landscape of the poet, then, influences the social world and is appreciated by it. As in *Colin Clout comes home againe*, Colin makes his landscape his choice (to paraphrase Marvell), and while the court does not foster poetry to the extent that it should, it is clearly susceptible to the influence of grace through poetry. Significantly, there is a healthy intercourse between court and country which is absent from Fletcher's world.

23. "To . . . W. R. Esquire."

24. Phineas Fletcher, "To E. C. in *Cambridge*, my Sonne by *the University*," in *Works*, 2:231.

25. The rivers, national and local, pervade Drayton's verse. His early work in particular uses the Anker and its associations with Lucy, Countess of Bedford, and his happy, formative years at Polesworth. But even here, one is always aware of the poet's greater aspirations, and that this is but a smaller tributary to a larger water.

26. See, for example, Michael Drayton, *Amoures*, Sonnet 24, in *Ideas Mirrour* (1594). In discussing Drayton's verse, and *Poly-Olbion* in particular, I use J. William Hebel's edition of *The Works of Michael Drayton*, 5 vols. (Oxford, 1931–1941).

27. See notes 28 and 30, below; Drayton criticism seems to be at an impasse and has not gone much beyond these important studies. Alice d'Haussy's *Poly-Olbion, ou L'Angleterre vue par un Elizabethain* (Paris, 1972), however, does begin to make specific advances on the study of Drayton's historical landscapes.

28. Grundy, *Spenserian Poets*, p. 130.

29. E. G. R. Taylor, *Late Tudor and Early Stuart Geography, 1583–1650* (London, 1934), p. 51. The maps, engraved by Hole, are based on Saxton's originals.

30. William H. Moore's "Sources of Drayton's *Poly-Olbion*," *Studies in Philology* (1968), 785–87, and Robert R. Cawley, "Drayton's use of Welsh History," *Studies in Philology* 65 (1925), 234–55, are characteristic of the consistently historical approach to *Poly-Olbion*. Of course, this emphasis on Drayton's historical interests is quite legitimate. Nevertheless, the poem has persistently eluded critical analysis. Drayton's concern is not with history for its own sake, and only very recently (see above, note 27) have critics begun to ask why Drayton blends history and geography in this way, and to look carefully at the poet's techniques for more than just a general statement about his nostalgic regard for the glories of the British past.

31. By far the best study of *Poly-Olbion* to date, one which examines Drayton's debt to Camden and uses the historical materials to advance a critical reading of the poem, is Alice d'Haussy's. Haussy makes important comparisons of structural patterns in the *Britannia* and *Poly-Olbion*; her conclusions about Drayton's use of history are very different from my own, and her work is an important contribution to our understanding of Drayton's poetic.

32. The opposition here is set in balance by Wrekin, who, from his height, can see into both Cambria and England. It should be added that by the end of his long harangue, he has become a comic figure. His and Arden's set speeches unite the opposing rivers in a unanimous cry for relief from their historical erudition. Drayton often uses humor as a mediator in these historical disputes.

33. That is, in the conflict between lyric and pastoral modes reflected in the conflict between Apollo and Marsyas. Drayton's adaptation of the original significance of this classical *topos* suggests how fully he understood the river motif. This specific treatment of the myth is uncommon in the Renaissance, although it is implicit in the pastoral dialogues.

34. For a survey of the reception of *Poly-Olbion*, see G. Tillotson, "Contemporary Praise of *Poly-Olbion*," *Review of English Studies* 16 (1940), 181–83.

35. See Browne's commendatory poem to *Poly-Olbion*, Part 2. Browne was not the only one to regard Drayton in this light; Abraham Holland, a friend of both poets, speaks of Drayton as "my honest father" (Bod. MS. Ashmol. 36).

36. Grundy, *Spenserian Poets*, p. 148. In the following discussion, I use G. Goodwin's edition of *Britannia's Pastorals*, in *The Poems of William Browne* (London, [1893]).

37. As Joan Grundy says (ibid., p. 148): "from there on [2.1.817], the poem has,

geographically speaking, a direction." This sudden realization of how to use his rivers, though, is not necessarily inspired by Drayton; as Grundy suggests (p. 131), this method of using the rivers to plot the course of his narrative is fundamentally that of topographical and chorographical description generally.

38. Such complaints intensify in succeeding books (see also 3.1. 11–17), so that it becomes clear that his Spenserian and Draytonian treatment of the personified landscape becomes less and less suitable for him. His pleasure is in a landscape free of historic narrative, so that in these later songs, the disparity between mankind and nature becomes more marked.

39. This three-volume manuscript, B. M. MSS. Add. 14824, 5, 6, was begun before 1600 and was still being written at the time of Princess Elizabeth's marriage. For a summary of its contents, see J. H. H. Lyon's *A Study of "The Newe Metamorphosis"* (New York, 1919).

40. B. M. MS. Sloane 2024. The poem dates from 1624, although it bears the mark of a later date as well, for the poet returned to the manuscript twelve years later, in 1636, to revise it, though for what reason he does not state.

41. Bodleian MS. Rawl. Poet. 28.

42. The evolution we are identifying here merges at this point with the social ideal of conviviality, a personal friendship, and camaraderie which Miner identifies in *The Cavalier Mode*.

43. *Poly-Olbion*, p. 391. This rather fine display of "vaporing" marks the increased bitterness characteristic of the "Stuart" half of the poem.

44. Bod. MS. Tanner 94; Ethel M. Portal, "The Academ Roial of King James I," *Proceedings of the British Academy* 7 (1915–1916), 196. In 1621 Bolton addressed the general public concerning his desire to revitalize the original society; thereafter followed numerous addresses and petitions setting forth his intentions. See particularly Bod. MSS. Harl. 6103 & 6143, for Bolton's heroic conception of his enterprise.

45. Now Bod. MS. Harl. 6103; see Portal, p. 192.

46. Evans, *History of the Society of Antiquaries*, p. 16. Although, as Evans points out, Bolton's plan helped to crystallize the conception of the academy in England, and although, in its idealized form, it resembled the Italian societies and even Bacon's National Academy, its objectives were very different from theirs.

47. Portal, "The Academ Roial," p. 197.

48. See the biography of Lloyd in the *Dictionary of National Biography* for his hand in securing Spenser's burial. For Lane's connection with the elder Milton, see *The Life Records of John Milton*, 5 vols., ed. J. M. French (New Brunswick, N. J., 1949–58),1:37–40.

49. Earl Wasserman, in *The Subtler Language* (Baltimore, Md., 1959), pp. 48–49, speaks of the "transforming act" that distinguishes the topographical literature of the mid-seventeenth century. What I have been attempting to demonstrate is that this act of transformation which shapes the landscape while describing it, is also at work in the earlier years of the Renaissance, and is, in fact, fundamental to the response to landscape in European literature.

50. See, for example, Milton's *First Elegy* to Charles Diodati, *Damon's Epitaph*, *To Manso*, and the epistles to Milton from Charles Dati and Antonio Francini, all examples of literary role-playing redolent of the Italian humanists.

51. The poem was first published in 1651; I use L. C. Martin's edition of Vaughan's *Works* (Oxford, 1914).

52. I use the text in *The Poetical Works of Sir John Denham*, ed. Theodore Banks, 2d ed. (New Haven, Conn., 1966); the emphasis here is my own.

53. In this respect, the image is disembodied and ambivalent; it seems to be identified with Charles, and yet, as an image of moderation, it also extends to the

parliamentary forces of reform. It gains still further abstraction (and political neutrality) from its association with the poet's style.

54. Rosalie Colie's *"My Echoing Song": Andrew Marvell's Poetry of Criticism* (Princeton, N. J., 1970) is a study of how Marvell's poetry relates to and confounds traditional genres.

55. All passages are from George deF. Lord's edition of Marvell's *Complete Poetry* (New York, 1968).

56. See Colie's discussion of Marvell's use of visual traditions and optical effects to create ambiguity in the poem (*"My Echoing Song,"* pp. 201–11).

57. Stressing the poet's wit and playfulness, Ann E. Berthoff, in *The Resolved Soul: A study of Marvell's Major Poems* (Princeton, N.J., 1970) pp. 184–185, speaks of the solitude and sensuousness of this episode; it is here that, temporarily, the ideal of the *beatus ille* seems to be exuberantly realized, although the speaker is (literally) brought up by the approach of Maria.

58. Maria gives meaning and order to Nunappleton, the speaker, and nature; from her they gain a higher degree of self-knowledge: "See how loose Nature, in respect/To her, itself doth recollect." Heavenly, graceful, she is the ideal that strives for realization in nature, and in this she functions in the poem as an antetype; Colie (*"My Echoing Song,"* p. 269) speaks of her as "hieratic," and Berthoff (*The Resolved Soul*, p. 188) describes her as the "genius of the place from whom nature itself learns, by whom nature is given direction and purpose."

59. William Wordsworth, *The Prelude* (1850), ed. Carlos Baker (New York, 1948), 1. lines 269–86. The following lines from Joyce's *Finnegans Wake* (New York, 1939), are from the opening and closing passages of the work, and suggest both the cultural and personal dimension of the legendary figure of Anna Livia Plurabelle or the Liffey. According to Joyce, *Finnegans Wake* contained all the world's rivers.

Index